Developing Skills for Instructional Supervision

Developing Skills for Instructional Supervision

Edited by James M. Cooper

University of Houston–University Park

Longman

New York and London

Developing Skills for Instructional Supervision

Longman Inc., 1560 Broadway, New York, N.Y. 10036
Associated companies, branches, and representatives throughout the world.

Developmental Editor: Lane Akers
Editorial Supervisor: Thomas Bacher
Interior Designer: Thomas Bacher
Production/Manufacturing: Ferne Y. Kawahara
Composition: The Saybrook Press, Inc.
Printing and Binding: Interstate Book Manufacturers, Inc.

Library of Congress Cataloging in Publication Data
Main entry under title:

Developing skills for instructional supervision.

Bibliography: p.
Includes index.
1. School supervision—United States. 2. Teaching—Evaluation. I. Cooper, James Michael, 1939–
LB2805.D47 1984 371.1′44 83-26814
ISBN 0-582-29019-8

Manufactured in the United States of America
Printing: 9 8 7 6 5 4 3 2 1 Year: 92 91 90 89 88 87 86 85 84

CONTENTS

PREFACE

There are scores of books on the market today that treat the topic of instructional supervision. Most of these books are written from an educational administration viewpoint, primarily concerned with leadership, change, management, decision making, and problem solving. More recently, several books have been written on that part of instructional supervision called *clinical supervision* and focus more directly on observational and human relations skills. Most of the books on instructional supervision are designed to help the reader develop an understanding of theory as it affects instructional supervisor, with only a minor emphasis on the development of the skills necessary to function as an effective supervisor. Understanding theory is important for supervisors, but so is being able to demonstrate those supervisory skills that are necessary to work effectively with teachers. Most supervisory books do identify the skills or tasks that supervisors perform, but are not performance oriented to help the beginning supervisor acquire these skills.

This book is based on the premise that one reason instructional supervisors have been perceived as ineffective is that they have not been sufficiently trained in key skill areas required of supervisors. Lacking these skills, many supervisors have by and large failed. Certainly, organizational factors, unrealistic supervisory loads, and inherent conflicts in the supervisor's role have contributed their share to supervision's ineffectiveness. While these problems are largely beyond the power of this book to address or solve, the skill level of supervisors is something that can be enhanced and it is this target area that the book addresses. Important supervisory skills have been identified and form the basis for each chapter. Each chapter contains objectives for the reader, explanatory materials, practice exercises, mastery tests, and answer keys that are geared toward each supervisory skill area. The book is designed to be self-instructional.

It is the authors' belief that after having completed this book, the instructional supervisor will have the increased ability to function effectively in the day-to-day tasks required of supervisors.

James M. Cooper

CONTRIBUTORS

James M. Cooper is professor of curriculum and instruction at the University of Houston–University Park. He received his Ph.D. in education from Stanford University. He is co-author, with Kevin Ryan, of *Those Who Can, Teach,* a first-experience book for prospective teachers, and *Kaleidoscope: Readings in Education.* He is also the editor of *Classroom Teaching Skills,* a textbook designed to help teachers integrate theory with practice in developing teaching skills. He has written books and articles in the areas of supervision of teachers, microteaching, competency-based teacher education, and teacher education program evaluation. His articles have appeared in such journals as *Phi Delta Kappan, Journal of Teacher Education, Educational Leadership Elementary School Journal, Elementary English,* and the *Journal of Research and Development in Education.* He is the author of "Supervision of Teachers," an article appearing in the *Encyclopedia of Educational Research* (5th ed.). His research efforts have recently focused on the effects of peer clinical supervision as implemented by certified teachers. He was director of one of the USOE Model Elementary Teacher Education Programs at the University of Massachusetts and later was associate dean for graduate studies in the College of Education at the University of Houston.

J. Bruce Burke is professor of teacher education at Michigan State University. He received his Ph.D. from Syracuse University, where he was a Woodrow Wilson fellow. He is the author of *The Individual and the School,* a workbook for prospective teachers. He also is the author of several chapters in educational books, including "Communicating with Students" in Donald Orlosky's *Introduction to Education* and "Competency-Based Curricula Design" in W. R. Houston's *Competency-Based Teacher Education.* He has written articles and research reports in the areas of interpersonal communication skills, affective education, humanities education, and student perceptions of disruptive school behavior. His work has appeared in *Educational Technology* and *Counselor Education and Supervision.* With Norm Kagan, he directed two National Institute for Mental Health projects: "Studies in Human Interaction in Schools" and "Using Physiological Recall to Develop Interpersonal Sensitivity in Medical Students." He developed, with Judith Lanier, twelve educational films on concepts in education psychology. He was one of the founders of the National Association for Humanities Education and a former director of the Humanities Teaching Institute at Michigan State University. His current research focuses on community/collaborative models for teacher preparation programs.

Gerald R. Firth is acting dean of the College of Education and professor of curriculum and supervision of the University of Georgia at Athens. He earned his B.S. from the State University of New York at Albany; his M.A. and Ed.D. from the Teachers College of Columbia University. He is co-author of *Instructional Supervision: A Behavior System* and *The Curricular Continuum in Perspective.* He has written chapters in yearbooks of the Association for Supervision and Curriculum Development and other texts, as well as publishing widely in professional journals including *Educational Leadership*, *Educational Forum*, *Phi Delta Kappan*, *Journal of Experimental Education*, and *American School Board Journal.* He is a representative to the State Advisory Council on Instructional Services and the Executive Committee of the Academic Council on Teacher Education. In addition to experience as superintendent of a large metropolitan school district, he has been a faculty member and administrator for the State University College at New Paltz, State University College at Oneonta, State University of New York at Buffalo, University of Minnesota, University of Alabama, and the University of Georgia. He also has served as director of a Ford Foundation project on small schools and of a campus laboratory school. His activities in international education have been centered in Mexico, Colombia, Ecuador, Venezuela, Panama, and the Dominican Republic.

Larry W. Hughes is professor of educational leadership and cultural studies at the University of Houston–University Park. A native of Toledo, Ohio, he has held teaching and administrative positions in Texas, Tennessee, Ohio, and Michigan. His Ph.D. was received from Ohio State University. He has been a teacher, principal, supervisor, and superintendent and has also held such university posts as department head and associate dean of academic affairs.

He is the author or co-author of five books including the recently revised *The Elementary Principal's Handbook: Guide to Effective Action* (1984). Among his other books is *Desegregating America's Schools* published by Longman Inc. (1980). He is author of over fifty articles in such professional periodicals as *Phi Delta Kappan*, *Educational Administration Quarterly*, *Educational Leadership*, *Journal of Teacher Education*, *Planning and Changing*, and *The American School Board Journal* among others. He also has several chapters in edited works and numerous monographs to his credit. He is a writer and producer of training films and assessment center simulation materials.

Other than time management, his research and development efforts include organizational management, assessment center technology, and desegregation. He is a frequent consultant to such federal agencies as Department of Defense, Department of Justice and the United States General Accounting Office and to private sector organizations, as well as school systems. His work in these agencies and his management seminars reflect his research and development interests.

Robert F. McNergney is an associate professor of education at the University of Virginia. He received his Ph.D. in education from Syracuse University. He is co-author, with Carol Carrier, of *Teacher Development*, a book on evaluating teachers for purposes of helping them improve their instructional performances and encouraging their personal growth. He has written articles and essays on supervision, teacher centers, individual differences, training, and evaluation. His writing has appeared in such publications as the *Journal of Teacher Education*, *Theory into Practice*, *Improving Human Performance Quarterly*, and *The Washington Post*. He has served as director of competency-based teacher education at the State University of New York, Potsdam, coordinator of elementary field experiences at the University of Minnesota, and director of teacher education at the University of Virginia.

Donald M. Medley is distinguished professor of educational research at the University of Virginia and was formerly professor of education in the Division of Teacher Education of the City University of New York and a senior research psychologist and head of the Teacher Behavior Research Group at Educational Testing Service, Princeton, New Jersey. He earned the M.A. and Ph.D. degrees at the University of Minnesota. Professor Medley is the author of chapters in the first *Handbook of Research on Teaching* (with H.E. Mitzel), the fifth *Encyclopedia of Educational Research*, and the *International Encyclopedia of Education*, and *Measurement-Based Evaluation of Teacher Performance* (with H. Coker and R. Soar), published by Longman Inc. (1984), as well as of more than fifty monographs and articles in journals including the *American Educational Research Journal*, *Contemporary Psychology*, the *Elementary School Journal*, *Educational Psychology*, and *Journal of Applied Psychology*. His research interests center on the behavior of teachers, the nature of teacher effectiveness, and teacher evaluation.

John W. Newfield is associate professor of curriculum and supervision at the University of Georgia. He began his experience in education with jobs as a junior high school and high school mathematics teacher in New Mexico. He received his Ed.D. from the University of New Mexico. Prior to coming to the University of Georgia he taught at the University of New Orleans. He has written articles in the areas of curriculum development and implementation. His current research interests are in these areas, in the study of curriculum integration, and the development, structure, and use of curriculum guides.

Joyce Putnam is an associate professor of teacher education and staff development at Michigan State University, East Lansing, Michigan, where she received her Ph.D. in teacher education, curriculum and evaluation. She coauthored with Jere Brophy "Classroom Management in the Elementary Grades" in the *The Seventy-Eighth Yearbook of the National Society for the Study of Education* . Among her publications are articles entitled "Yes, Virginia Teachers Do Make Decisions," "Professional Development through Inservice that Works," and "Classroom Management and Organization for a Learning Community Classroom." Her work is also cited in "School-Focused Inservice: Descriptions and Discussions." Dr. Putnam is the conceptual and procedural coordinator for the newly developed field-based multiple perspectives teacher preparation program. She has been the director of a five year federally funded staff development project at Michigan State University. Her research has been in the areas of staff development, teacher planning, teacher decision making, and classroom management and organization. Currently her research focuses on the decisions made by a teacher educator while modeling the teaching of reading in an elementary school classroom. Dr. Putnam also is involved in a study designed to identify the decisions teacher educators make and the database they use for their decisions.

Richard W. Saxe is professor and chairman of administration and supervision at the University of Toledo. His Ph.D. was earned at the University of Chicago. His most recent books are *School and Community Relations in Transition* (1984) and *Educational Administration Today: An Introduction* (1980). Articles by Professor Saxe have appeared in educational journals including the *Phi Delta Kappan*, *Journal of Teacher Education*, *National Elementary School Principal*, *Bulletin of the National Association of Secondary School Principals*, *Elementary School Journal*, and *Education and Urban Society*. His most recent research has been in the area of planning and policy formation. He was associate director of one of the USOE Model Elementary Teacher Education Programs and later associate dean for research and development in the College of Education and Allied Professions at the University of Toledo.

INTRODUCTION AND OVERVIEW

1

James M. Cooper

Supervision is a term used to describe a wide variety of behaviors carried out by a diverse group of people within the context of specific school systems. "Instructional supervision" is defined by Alfonso, Firth, and Neville (1981) as "behavior officially designated by the organization that directly affects teacher behavior in such a way as to facilitate pupil learning and achieve the goals of the organization" (p. 43). A more comprehensive definition of teacher supervision can be found in the *Dictionary of Education* (Good, 1973): "all efforts of designated school officials directed toward providing leadership to teachers in the improvement of instruction; . . . the stimulation of professional growth and development of teachers; the selection and revision of educational objectives, materials of instruction, and methods of teaching; and the evaluation of instruction" (p. 574).

Although most contemporary writers agree that the primary purpose of supervision is to improve instruction, Mosher and Purpel (1972), Harris (1978), and Blumberg (1978) all indicate that a review of the literature reveals virtually no research suggesting that supervision of teaching makes an appreciable difference in the way teachers conduct their classes. The role expectations for supervisors are ambiguous and often conflicting, for example, helper versus evaluator, administrator versus consultant. Significant research on supervision is scarce, and theory is underdeveloped. The ratio of teachers to supervisor is usually so disproportionate as to make meaningful interaction an unrealistic expectation. Supervisors often lack appropriate status and leverage within the organizational system. Training and certification programs for supervisors stress administrative competence rather than emphasize diagnostic skills for analysis of teaching. The lack of clear-cut evidence on what constitutes effective teaching behavior undermines the supervisor's position as an expert on teaching competence. All of these reasons, and others, combine to make the current supervisor's role in the school organization a rather weak one.

In spite of this situation, a review of the research on teacher supervision reveals that although teachers see little benefit in supervision as it is currently practiced, they still see a need for supervision (Cooper, 1982). Teachers want supervisors to be supportive, to be unobtrusive during classroom visitations, and to treat teachers as professionals by sharing in decision-making processes (Carman, 1970). Many of the aspects that teachers want to see in teacher-supervisor relationships are embodied in the type of supervision known as "clinical supervision."

Developed at Harvard University by Morris Cogan, Robert Goldhammer, and Robert Anderson, this form of supervision has generated considerable interest in recent years. Clinical supervision can be defined as "that phase of instructional supervision which draws its data from first-hand observation of actual teaching events, and involves face-to-face (and other associated) interaction between the supervisor and teacher in the analysis of teaching behaviors and activities for instructional improvement."[1] Clinical supervision is based on the proposition that the relationship between supervisor and teacher is mutual, and that the two work together as colleagues rather than in a supervisor-subordinate relationship. Phases or cycles of the clinical supervision model include establishing the supervisor-teacher relationship, agreeing on the focus of the observations, observing and collecting descriptive data, analyzing the data, discussing the data's meaning and implications for the teacher's behavior, and planning for long-term teacher development and future observations. To make this model of supervision work, supervisors must be willing to spend considerable time working with individual teachers on classroom problems or issues that the teachers themselves have identified and about which they want more information. In doing so, the supervisor must have planning, data-collecting, analysis, and human relations skills. Although the basic tenets of clinical supervision appeal to many educators, there is little evidence to indicate that it is being widely used. Concerns over adequate training for supervisors, time demands on both teachers and supervisors, and whether or not the ideal of colleagueship is attainable in current supervisor-teacher relationships have thus far impeded the widespread implementation of clinical supervision (Sullivan, 1980).

SUPERVISORY ASSUMPTIONS

Although this book on supervisory skills is not based solely on the clinical supervision model, there are some assumptions on which the book is founded that are common to this model. A review of some of these assumptions will assist you in understanding the book better.

Assumption 1: Instructional improvement is not a superficial process; hence, it requires considerable time and effort.

Helping teachers change their teaching behavior is not a process accomplished quickly or easily. One of the major problems with past supervisory effort has been its one-shot, quick-fix approach. In its worst form, the supervisor shows up unannounced halfway through class, hurriedly scribbles a series of highly subjective notes on a legal pad, and leaves for another "observation" five minutes before the class ends. There is little or no follow-up, and the supervisor has little or no notion of what the teacher was attempting to accomplish, how the lesson is related to what was done the day before, or what is planned for the following day. David Berliner (Brandt, 1982) and Joyce and Showers (1982) argue that if we really want to see teachers change their teaching behaviors, someone needs to "coach" them as they try out new teaching practices in their own classrooms. Unless someone spends the time doing this coaching, they state, in-service efforts aimed toward changing teaching behavior are by and large doomed to fail. One reason there is no research suggesting that supervision makes a difference in how teachers conduct their classes is that the time and effort required of supervisors to insure that this change occurs has been lacking. Unless the time and effort are forthcoming we should not expect to see many beneficial results from supervision.

Assumption 2: When dealing with adult professionals, no one changes another person's behavior.

Each person has the power to change his or her own behavior, and usually makes significant changes only when convinced that such changes are in the individual's self-interest. Sometimes teachers may change their behavior in response to an external threat, such as administrative evaluation, but such changes are usually transitory rather than enduring and are often exhibited only when the source of the threat is present. Esteem, both self-esteem and respect from others, is a more compelling motive for change. People receive satisfaction from being competent at their jobs. If they are convinced that there is a discrepancy between what they want to occur in their classrooms and what actually happens, a dilemma is created that needs resolution. Teachers are more likely to change their teaching behavior in response to this dilemma than in response to an administrative dictum, and the ensuing change is more likely to be a lasting one. Supervisors, therefore, will be more effective in helping teachers improve instruction if they focus on areas of teacher interest or concern, rather than imposing their own wills on the teacher. Greater trust and communication are also likely to result from this approach. Promoting efforts toward personal professional growth for teachers is psychologically healthier and more enduring than pretending that external threats can make teachers more effective.

We have lived with a history of educational systems depending heavily on external sources of initiation of action. "If the curriculum is going to change, the action must begin with the central offices." Yet, all that has been learned about how human motivation for change works suggests that internal ownership of the initiatory action is necessary to assure success. The missing ingredient in teacher motivation for growth is commitment, yet commitment cannot be demanded; it grows from the inside out. The conviction grows from participation that what is evolving is both personally and professionally worthwhile. Motivation grows as individuals and groups see progress toward desirable goals. And in the end the commitment emerges that we are responsible for the quality of professional lives we live.

Assumption 3: Goal-directed behavior is more effective in achieving instructional improvement than behavior that is not focused on specific outcomes.

Although this statement may appear obvious, in practice it is often ignored. Vague or general admonitions to improve can be extremely frustrating. A statement such as, "I need to improve my classroom discipline," may identify a topic or area of concern, but it offers no help at all to the teacher in terms of what the specific problem is or what he or she should do about it. Supervisors need to help teachers identify their concerns in specific, behavioral language and set objectives for themselves and their students in the same kind of language. Changes in teaching behavior are much more easily achieved and evaluated if outcomes are stated as specifically as possible. Supervisors will also find it much easier to collect relevant observational data if a high level of specificity is achieved.

Assumption 4: Objective recording and descriptive reporting of teaching data are more useful for instructional improvement than subjective, evaluative statements.

Separating information or facts from an interpretation of their value or significance is an important skill for supervisors. Supervisors who frequently make judgments about classroom occurrences often have trouble establishing a trusting working relationship with teachers. Individuals do not like to feel that others are constantly judging them or their actions. In addition, supervisory judgments are not as useful to teachers in helping them change their behavior as are data that are more descriptive in nature. Descriptive data give the teacher and supervisor an idea of what happened in the lesson, allowing them to make value judgments at a later time. If the supervisor reports only his or her judgments to the teacher and not the descriptive data, the teacher never gets to analyze the data and form his or her own opinions. In the absence of descriptive information, disagreements between the supervisor and teacher are more likely to occur.

Assumption 5: Teaching, as an intellectual and social act, is amenable to intellectual analysis.

Teaching behavior, like most human behavior, tends to be patterned rather than random. The organization of the school, the tasks demanded of teachers, and the teachers' own habits all contribute to make many aspects of teaching behavior repeat in recurring and characteristic patterns. As such, these patterns of behavior can be studied by supervisors and teachers in attempts to determine the effects of these patterns on student learning. As we develop our analysis skills and form conceptual frameworks to guide us, our understanding of teaching processes continue to grow.

Assumption 6: Supervisors demonstrate leadership most effectively as a participant in the process of educational growth.

The supervisor as a participant says, "I have a stake in the problems, processes, and outcomes of collaborative actions." This is in contrast to supervisors who see themselves as experts who have a collection of ready-made solutions to a finite list of problems or in contrast to those supervisors who see themselves as the provider of resources, as in "Tell me what you want and need and I'll go and get them for you." Both orientations have a technical view of the job of supervisor. What is presented in this book is a view of the supervisor who sees himself or herself as committed to the process of problem identification and to the outcomes of the total system.

WHAT'S NEEDED?

Improving the quality of instructional supervision in the school systems of our country is an extremely difficult task. Supervisors' ambiguous roles, conflicting functions, and excessive demands have resulted in an ineffective form of supervision in many American schools. One reason for this state of affairs is that too many of our instructional supervisors lack the knowledge and skills necessary to function effectively. It is toward that remedy that this book was written. Hopefully, this book can help supervisors to acquire knowledge and skills to help teachers improve instruction.

Lack of knowledge and skills on the part of individual supervisors is only one of the problems plaguing supervision. As long as the current organizational structures, roles, and expectations exist, significant improvement of instructional supervision within school districts will be retarded. New forms of supervision in which teachers assume more responsibility and a more active role are needed. Supervisory behavior must allow for more self-direction by teachers. When there are sufficient numbers of trained instructional supervisors to work with teachers and peer-supervision programs have been implemented to help relieve the burdensome load of supervisors, then more positive effects of instructional supervision can be expected.

THIS BOOK'S DESIGN

Writing a book on instructional supervision is a difficult proposition. Unlike counselors, principals, or librarians, whose jobs are fairly specifically defined, supervisors perform a myriad of different functions depending on the role expectations expressed by individual school districts. Furthermore, because the functions of supervision are performed by so many varied personnel, differing from school system to school system, the role of supervisor is clouded with ambiguity. Although there is agreement about the general goal of supervision, that is, improvement of instruction, there is no consensus as to the methods by which this goal can be achieved, or even who should have which responsibilities for its achievement. Goldhammer, Anderson, and Krajewski believe that "this confusion arises because seldom is there a person or agency within the school system solely responsible for providing instructional supervision; neither is there a single client constituency—a group or activity which is the beneficiary of such supervision. Rather, instructional supervision responsibilities are assigned to whichever person/agency is best able to absorb them without much disturbance of the ongoing operation."[2] Given the ambiguity and confusion that exist regarding supervisory personnel and their responsibilities, the task of conceptualizing and writing this book was indeed a challenging one.

The starting point was to review the literature on instructional supervision to determine what, if any, agreement existed regarding the tasks and functions that supervisors were expected to perform. Surprisingly, there is considerable consensus regarding this matter. According to Harris (1975), the real core of a program of supervisory services is usually found in five task areas: evaluation, curriculum development, in-service education, materials development, and staffing. Sergiovanni and Starratt (1979) concur with Harris's first three tasks, but add a fourth, improvement of teaching.

Christiansen and Turner (1977) surveyed a sample of superintendents, supervisors, and professors of supervision to determine their perceptions regarding appropriate tasks for an instructional supervisor. Seventy percent or more of the sample considered the following tasks to be appropriate:

- Develop standards of teaching effectiveness
- Conduct staff meetings
- Conduct in-service programs
- Observe teaching
- Work with community groups
- Evaluate programs
- Determine educational goals

Lists of supervision tasks developed by other experts in the field of supervision are remarkably similar to those already presented.

In order to carry out successfully the major task areas identified by Harris, Sergiovanni and Starratt, and Christiansen and Turner, there are key skills and competencies that supervisors need to demonstrate. Each chapter in the book focuses on one of these supervisory skills. Within each chapter a cognitive map includes the purpose of the skill, its various elements and their sequencing, and the nature of the final performance. Most of the chapters consist of self-contained materials that require practice and provide you with feedback on your efforts. It will be necessary, however, to practice far more than is possible in this book if you want to develop a high level of competence in supervisory skills.

Format of Each Chapter

Each chapter is written with a common format that contains (1) a set of objectives, (2) learning materials and activities, and (3) mastery tests.

1. Objectives: The objectives, stated in terms of learner outcomes, specify the competency or competencies you will be expected to demonstrate. Wherever it is appropriate, the objectives will be arranged in a learning hierarchy, leading you from relatively simple objectives to more complex ones.

2. Learning materials and activities: Each objective has an accompanying set of reading materials written specifically for that objective. In addition, some of the authors have provided back-up activities for those who want additional work on a particular objective. The nature of the reading materials and activities varies depending on the specific objective for which it was constructed.

3. Mastery tests: Each chapter contains mastery tests with answer keys to enable you to assess whether or not you have achieved the objectives. These mastery tests assess your learning after you have completed the reading and back-up activities related to each objective. This technique allows you to discover immediately after completing each section whether or not you have met the objective satisfactorily.

This format (objectives, learning activities, and mastery tests) is a very efficient design because all the materials are geared to help the reader achieve the stated objectives. Extraneous and inconsequential materials are eliminated, allowing students to make best use of their time. If used properly, the format increases the probability that you will be able to acquire a beginning level of competency in these basic supervisory skills.

Description of the Skills

The book is divided into three major sections: managerial skills, technical skills, and human relations skills. Within these three sections there are nine supervisory skills, ordered as follows:

Managerial Skills
- CHAPTER 2 *Planning and Goal Setting*
- CHAPTER 3 *Organizing and Managing Time*

Technical Skills
- CHAPTER 4 *Observation*
- CHAPTER 5 *Analysis*
- CHAPTER 6 *Evaluating Teachers*
- CHAPTER 7 *Evaluating Programs*
- CHAPTER 8 *Curriculum Development and Selection*

Human Relations Skills
- CHAPTER 9 *Interpersonal Communication*
- CHAPTER 10 *Leadership and Motivation*

Managerial skills are those required for making arrangements and setting conditions for promoting the attainment of goals, and relating supervisory work to other parts of the organization. The managerial skills of goal setting, planning, organizing, and managing time are ones that the supervisor needs not only to support the school district as a whole, but also to perform tasks such as conducting in-service programs, running meetings, and determining educational goals.

Technical skills are those related to specialized aspects of the instructional supervisor's role requiring pertinent knowledge and frames of reference necessary to perform specific roles. The supervisor's roles as classroom observer, teacher evaluator, program evaluator, and curriculum developer and/or selector require specialized technical skills that are generally not applicable to other supervisory roles and functions. Nevertheless, these technical skills are extremely important to carry out those particular roles effectively.

Human relations skills serve as a foundation on which the managerial and technical skills are based. The human relations skills of interpersonal communication, motivation, and leadership are vital for instructional supervisors. Elements of these skills include providing warmth and friendliness; resolving conflict and relieving tension; providing personal help and encouragement; showing understanding and tolerance of different points of view; and showing fairness and impartiality.

Planning and Goal Setting Richard W. Saxe examines the types of planning and goal setting typically expected of instructional supervisors. Supervisory planning operates within the context of existing policies on curriculum, personnel, and school board statements on goals. As such, supervisors are constrained and limited to goal setting and planning that fit within overarching policies and plans established within the school district. In spite of these limitations, the supervisor has considerable need for specific skills and techniques that can help in developing and carrying out goals and plans. The specific skills treated by the chapter include conducting needs assessments, applying brainstorming processes, applying force field analysis techniques, and applying Gantt and PERT charts to solve supervisory problems.

Organizing and Managing Time One of the most frequently heard supervisory laments is, "There just isn't enough time to get everything done." Although this complaint is not unique to supervisors, there is no doubt that supervisory loads and assignments are notoriously burdensome. Supervisors usually have more teachers assigned to their supervision than they can possibly cope with effectively. They are often assigned ad hoc jobs that consume time needed for their regularly assigned duties. Although organization and time management skills are important for many professionals, they are especially important for supervisors.

In this chapter, Larry W. Hughes helps the reader to develop the skill of getting and keeping control of time. Among the specific techniques he shares with the reader are how to make better use of discretionary time, developing skills in delegation, how to conduct more effective conferences, committees, and meetings, and how to avoid interruptions.

Observation If there is any one activity most commonly associated with supervision, it is probably observation of teaching. Effective supervisors need to be effective observers of classroom interaction. James M. Cooper identifies potential problems related to classroom observation, helps the reader to develop behavioral indicators for given areas of teacher interest or concern, and discusses a variety of techniques, including their strengths and weaknesses, for collecting observational data. The chapter presents a number of different observation instruments that supervisors can use. The culminating objective of the chapter is to have the reader develop appropriate observational instruments based on specified areas of teacher interest or concern.

Analysis Observation and analysis are closely related; observation flows into analysis naturally and easily in the supervision process. Using most of the techniques and instruments introduced in the observation chapter, James M. Cooper helps the reader to develop the skills of displaying and interpreting observational data. Criteria for analyzing data are presented and the reader is given simulated data for a number of different observation instruments to analyze and interpret. The effect of teaching patterns on student learning is also discussed, and the reader is given the opportunity to identify teaching patterns from transcripts of lessons.

Evaluating Teachers A great dilemma for persons charged with supervisory responsibilities is how to balance their conflicting roles as evaluators and helpers. Supervisors are expected to develop open, trusting, and supportive interpersonal climates with teachers, while they are also expected to make judgments regarding teachers' effectiveness and fitness to remain in the school district. Robert F. McNergney and Donald M. Medley explore this dilemma and ways of overcoming the problem. They also present some research findings on effective teaching and examine a model of teacher decision making that can assist the supervisor in performing the evaluation function.

Evaluating Programs Donald M. Medley and Robert F. McNergney explore another important evaluation function of supervisors in this chapter—that of program evaluation. As developers of in-service programs and workshops, as well as curriculum developers, supervisors are often required to judge the effectiveness of programs or curriculum materials. The authors describe several models for evaluating programs, including objective-based, discrepancy, and goal-free approaches. The authors also explore different procedures and skills required to evaluate program inputs, processes, and outcomes.

Curriculum Development and Selection Curriculum development, as you may recall, was one of Ben Harris's five general tasks of supervision. Gerald R.

Firth and John W. Newfield recognize that curriculum is often influenced as much by selection decisions as by local curriculum development; therefore, they orient their chapter to help the supervisor develop competencies related to both development and selection of curriculum. Four specific tasks around which they organize their chapter are:

1. Identifying curricular issues in educational settings
2. Establishing an approach to guide curriculum development
3. Selecting instructional materials
4. Managing the curriculum development and selection processes

Interpersonal Communication In this chapter, J. Bruce Burke presents information about what makes for effective communication between supervisors and teachers. Drawing on theoretical and empirical knowledge, specific interpersonal leadership skills are described, including those related to attending, responding, and facilitating behaviors. Effective interpersonal communication is not, however, simply a matter of skill development. Professor Burke emphasizes that attitudes and values also influence the effectiveness of a communication. The chapter provides the reader with numerous practice situations to develop appropriate ways of responding to teachers' statements that will help create positive communication.

Leadership and Motivation Instructional supervisors are usually expected to assume leadership responsibilities so that schools can better achieve their goals. Without successful leadership behavior, instructional supervisors cannot perform effectively. Supervisors must possess knowledge about motivational factors in an organizational climate and skills to encourage and inspire teachers in their pursuit of instructional improvement. In this chapter, Joyce Putnam presents a model for cooperative professional development that was tested during 10 years of Teacher Corps–sponsored projects. The model helps the supervisor to work with individuals and groups of teacher and other educational personnel to identify problems, resolve conflicts, and share authority and responsibility. Professors Burke and Putnam collaborated on the design and research for both Chapters 9 and 10. They retain, however, individual responsibility for the initiation and execution of their separate chapters.

NOTES

1. R. Goldhammer, R.H. Anderson, and R.J. Krajewski, *Clinical Supervision: Special Methods for the Supervision of Teachers*, 2d ed. (New York: Holt, Rinehart and Winston, 1980), pp. 19–20.
2. Ibid., p. 18.

REFERENCES

Alfonso, R.J., G.R. Firth, and R.F. Neville. *Instructional Supervision: A Behavior System*, 2d ed. Boston: Allyn and Bacon, 1981.

Blumberg, A. "Supervision: An Organizational Category in Search of Itself." In *Instructional Supervision: Research and Theory*. National Conference Papers, National Invitational Conference on Instructional Supervision: Research and Theory, Kent State University, Kent, Ohio, 1978.

Brandt, R. "On Improving Teacher Effectiveness: A Conversation with David Berliner." *Educational Leadership*, vol. 40 (October 1982):12–15.

Carman, B.D. *Roles and Responsibilities in General Supervision of Instruction: A Synthesis of Research Findings, 1955–1969*. Ph.D. diss. Florida State University, 1970.

Christiansen, M., and H. Turner. "The Roles and Preparation of Instructional Supervisors." In *Certificating the Curriculum Leader and the Instructional Supervisor*, edited by Allan W. Sturges. Unpublished report from the ASCD Working Group on the Role, Preparation, and Certification of Curriculum Leader and Supervisor, 1977.

Cooper, J.M. "Supervision of Teachers." In *Encyclopedia of Educational Research*, 5th ed., edited by Harold E. Mitzel. New York: Free Press, 1982, 1824–1834.

Goldhammer, R., R.H. Anderson, and R.J. Krajewski. *Clinical Supervision: Special Methods for the Supervision of Teachers*, 2d ed. New York: Holt, Rinehart and Winston, 1980.
Good, C.V. *Dictionary of Education*, 3d ed. New York: McGraw-Hill, 1973.
Harris, B.M. *Supervisory Behavior in Education*, 2d ed. Englewood Cliffs, N.J.: Prentice-Hall, 1975.
Harris, B.M. "Interfacing Personnel Development, Curriculum and Evaluation." In *Instructional Supervision: Research and Theory*. National Conference Papers, National Invitational Conference on Instructional Supervision, Kent State University, Kent, Ohio, 1978.
Joyce, B., and B. Showers. "The Coaching of Teaching." *Educational Leadership* 40 (October 1982): 4–8, 10.
Mosher, R.L., and D.E. Purpel. *Supervision: The Reluctant Profession*. Boston: Houghton Mifflin, 1972.
Sergiovanni, T.J., and R.J. Starratt. *Supervision: Human Perspectives*, 2d ed. New York: McGraw-Hill, 1979.
Sullivan, C.G. *Clinical Supervision: A State of the Art Review.* Washington, D. C.: Association for Supervision and Curriculum Development, 1980.

PLANNING AND GOAL SETTING

2

Richard W. Saxe

OBJECTIVE 1 To describe the hierarchy of purposes, goals, and objectives of supervision
OBJECTIVE 2 To discriminate between strategic and operational planning
OBJECTIVE 3 To describe and apply procedures of needs assessment to issues in supervision
OBJECTIVE 4 To describe and apply the process of brainstorming to issues in supervision
OBJECTIVE 5 To describe and apply the force field technique of problem analysis to issues in supervision
OBJECTIVE 6 To describe and apply appropriate criteria for assessing the merits of alternative supervisory practices
OBJECTIVE 7 To describe and apply a procedure for task management
OBJECTIVE 8 To describe and apply a Gantt Chart to a problem in supervision
OBJECTIVE 9 To describe and apply a PERT Chart to a problem in supervision

INTRODUCTION

It is difficult to discuss planning for supervision because the issue is part of the more comprehensive task of planning how best to educate students in school districts and schools. This context of planning, if we approach planning for an existing, functioning system rather than for some hypothetical, boundary free, yet-to-be-created system, immediately suggests both constraints and resources. It is our challenge in these pages to deal with the skills involved in planning for the more mundane, real world of education rather than enjoying the heady freedom of planning for the ideal. A representative general systemwide goal is supplied below. It is almost certainly compatible with the most general goals of districts anywhere.

> PROTOTYPE
> Mission of an Entire School District
>
> The schools of this district operated by the board of education in the public interest shall determine the educational ideals, goals, and values of the community, develop policies to accomplish these ideals, goals, and values, and ensure that the policies are implemented by the superintendent and the employees of the school district.

Further guidance for supervisors will be provided by policies on curriculum, community relations, and personnel. These, too, at least in general policy statements of boards of education, are so similar that we need not recreate them here.

What we do need to determine is the explicit or implied goal of *supervision* according to a typical (or an actual) board of education. In Chapter 1 we reviewed the purpose of supervision. Some guidance might also be found in job descriptions. Tradition is not a good guide because in too many cases not even veteran educators were present at the time supervisory practices were initiated and the original purposes can only be inferred.

To determine the purpose of supervision in the same general terms as the purpose of the educational system is easy: it is *the improvement of instruction. Everyone says so.* This writer said so himself at the oral examination for his first principalship. I might have been quoting any of the writers of that time, possibly Kimball Wiles, A. S. Barr, Chester McNerney or Briggs and Justman.[1] The benevolent inquisitor on the Board of Examiners smiled tolerantly acknowledging the inevitable, expected response to his equally predictable question and then suggested that I, the candidate for a principalship, might add a bit more to my answer.

Arriving at a general conceptualization of the purpose of supervision is more than ritual behavior. It is possible, even at this general level, to suggest important guidelines that would affect how and with whom one works to improve instruction. Chances are that my long-forgotten answer to the query mentioned something about working with teachers so that they could be more effective with their students. Another possible answer at that time might have stressed a more directive role, something like making sure that all teachers followed appropriate practices in carrying out the policies of the board of education. Still another candidate might have said something to the effect that he or she would improve instruction by sharing expertise and new ideas with the faculty so that they in turn could use the new practices and ideas to become more effective in their own teaching.

Those were among many possible answers then. Today (30 years later) the general purpose of supervision remains an easy question without a definitive answer. As you consider the question remember that the purpose of supervision must, of course, relate to the purpose of the school district. Perhaps it should also reveal whether or not you subscribe to the dual mission of assisting with the accomplishment of district goals at the same time as supporting the personal and career aspirations of teachers.

The attitudinal meaning can be inferred from the mission statement of supervision but usually the associated functions can be carried out in any number of ways. That is, one supervisor could plan with teachers to improve instruction in a nonthreatening, collegial, supportive manner; another in a bureaucratic–minimum standards fashion; a third in a paternalistic, authoritative manner; and so on. It is up to my colleague in Chapter 9 to reveal the nuances of meaning attached to the way one employs the skills of supervision. So, we turn to the development of planning skills for democrats, autocrats, bureaucrats, and supercrats of any orientation.

OBJECTIVE 1 TO DESCRIBE THE HIERARCHY OF PURPOSES, GOALS, AND OBJECTIVES OF SUPERVISION

Our introductory comments have already moved the discussion from the most general level of planning, purpose, or mission, and brought us to a consideration of goals. Goals are drawn from the mission of the institution but reveal more of the ways that the mission is to be accomplished. Goal statements are broad and general declarations of what it is that the institution will do to accomplish its mission. Goals are not drawn solely from the mission statement since, as we shall maintain in another section of this chapter, the needs of those to be served by the institution—our educational clients—must be served and those needs are not static over time. And, particularly in regard to educational supervision, the capability of the institution is a crucial, though oft-ignored consideration. Often I and perhaps some of my colleagues have delineated and advocated splendid supervisory models that were patently impossible to implement given the personnel and resources of educational systems then in place. In fairness to those who advocated the impossible, it should be noted that the models, if implemented, would have made for better educational environments and almost certainly would have resulted in improvements in instruction. The trouble was, and is, that the limited resources available would not, could not, be assigned to supervision.

At the level of goals, we can easily see the capability influence if we speculate about the effects of complying with the desires of the army of special interest groups presently in the field. There is not time enough, there are not resources of any kind in sufficient quantity, to meet all of the demands, no matter how well-intentioned they may be. Put simply, schools can't do any more (that is, accept other goals) unless they get more resources. It is probably not necessary to remind readers of this book that schools are almost certainly overextended as it is. The sad lesson of this condition (capability as a factor in goal setting) for supervision is that the demands for improved performance will remain undiminished, will even increase, while the resources available for supervision will, at best, remain constant, possibly decrease. We cannot ignore the realities of the institutional context of our would-be clinical supervisors.

To recapitulate, goals are derived from the mission statement, must relate to the needs of clients, and must be appropriate to the capability of the educational institution. It is time to structure some goals for supervision. Certainly a goal for learners in any school system is to become competent in the basic skills. A related goal for supervision then, can be: To arrange for the necessary conditions and resources to enable teachers to effectively instruct students in the basic skills. Or, perhaps: To provide the appropriate in-service education to promote the effective teaching of basic skills. Or: To support effective teachers and assist those ineffective or somewhat effective teachers to improve their teaching skills.

Note that all of these goal statements are quite general. The next level of specificity could be subgoals but, since these, too, are at a general level (that is, subgoals for basic skills would mention reading and mathematics), we move directly to objectives. Objectives are specific, some would insist measurable, statements of what the educational institution intends should be accomplished by a given time.

A baker's dozen of representative objectives for supervisors follows:

1. Supervisors will observe and assess each new teacher in the district at least five times annually.

2. Supervisors will design and administer a survey to determine the most common problems in the use of (a new instructional material, textbook, curriculum guide, whatever).

3. Supervisors will organize and initiate an in-service program to eliminate the problems associated with the new instructional materials, etc.

4. Supervisors will assist district building administrators in attempting to improve the skills of tenured teachers rated unsatisfactory.

5. Supervisors will plan and arrange the demonstration of exemplary instructional practices with a new or revised curriculum objective.

6. Supervisors will assemble an exhibit of new social studies teaching materials and arrange a critique of their utility for district purposes.

7. Supervisors will conduct a meeting with teachers in selected schools to demonstrate and review the district teacher evaluation materials and procedures.

8. Supervisors will facilitate the interschool visiting of teachers of the same subject, same level.

9. Supervisors will identify outstanding teachers and recommend them for service on districtwide committees.

10. Supervisors will assist building administrators in determining appropriate applications of current and pending legal and regulatory provisions and prohibitions.

11. Supervisors will participate in the appropriate professional organizations and represent their district to the organizations and the organizations to the district.

12. Supervisors will publish their general schedule but will make provision for special, prompt attention in case of urgent, unexpected problems.

13. Supervisors will maintain and have published annotated lists of teaching aids in their area of specialization.

The objectives listed all specify something that the supervisor is to do. In all cases it should be possible to demonstrate empirically that the objective has been met. Some objectives will be prepared for the supervisor by others, some will be jointly structured, and others the supervisor will identify for himself or herself. Of course, they must be in harmony with the mission and the goals of the school system.

Mastery Test

OBJECTIVE 1 TO DESCRIBE THE HIERARCHY OF PURPOSES, GOALS, AND OBJECTIVES OF SUPERVISION

1. Place the following terms in order of specificity—that is, list the most general first, the most specific last.

   Goal

   Objective

   Mission/Purpose

2. Prepare a statement for supervision in each of the following categories.

   a. Objective

   b. Goal

   c. Mission/Purpose

Answer Key

Mastery Test, Objective 1

1. Mission/Purpose

   Goal

   Objective

2. a. The mission or purpose statement should refer to the basic reason for the supervision in the district. It should tell supervisors in most general terms the reasons for the existence of supervision.

   b. The goal statement should be general but should signal a major emphasis of the supervisory program.

   c. The statement for the objective should be specific and should refer to observable-behavior or measurable results.

If you are not certain of the appropriateness of your responses you should reread the sections describing purposes, goals, and objectives, especially the examples.

OBJECTIVE 2 TO DISCRIMINATE BETWEEN STRATEGIC AND OPERATIONAL PLANNING

Education has recently been plagued by problems associated with participative decision making. The current arguments swirl around freedom of choice of schools and are encompassed in positions for or against issues such as tuition tax credits or educational vouchers. The participants in this case are parents (on behalf of their children) and the political action is being waged at the highest levels of national government—the Congress and the incumbent administration. This is, at present, clearly a strategic issue having to do with contending basic value positions. The issues are raised outside the educational system and relate to the perceived needs of students, changed objectives for the educational system, and a reallocation of resources. In this case there is no direct role for individual educators, parents, or students. Organizations and representatives will be the participants in the strategic decision: To be or not to be: tuition tax credits.

When the strategic decision is secure (deciding not to change is, of course, every bit as much a decision as accepting a new educational strategy) it will be time for operational planning. Then, parents and educators at different levels will find appropriate roles as participants in planning how to accomplish the new or unchanged educational strategy. At this time the participants will be dealing with issues internal to the educational system(s) concerned. Now, their participation is not only appropriate, it is necessary.

We have no intention of entering the strategic planning arena concerning tuition tax credits and related issues. It serves only as an easy example, familiar to all readers, to distinguish between strategic and operational planning. To exploit this advantage further, consider how this same issue deals with another perennial educational planning dilemma: top down versus grassroots or bottom-up planning. Those who write about educational change have often found the causes of failure in the lack of participation in planning by teachers who usually are directly involved in the implementation of the contemplated change. Moreover, those of us who are students of educational administration must be familiar with a spate of hortatory rhetoric urging democratic administration. Democratic administration usually mandated participation in planning by all those who would be affected by an action. The example of tuition tax credits clearly demonstrates that top-down planning is most appropriate for strategic planning. It would be impossible to administer and coordinate a variety of different policies that could result from different districts (or even different states in this case) doing their own strategic planning. And, conversely, it would be chaotic for the strategic plan makers to attempt to resolve the specific issues of choices of schools, reallocation of services, and reorganization of schools at the top level. So—not all planning need be grass roots and everyone concerned need not participate in all planning. Strategic planning considers what is to be done and is top-down planning. Operational planning considers how to do it and requires the participation of doer's in the planning.

We need now to see how these concepts of planning may apply to supervision. A potential strategic issue is the requirement that students take and pass tests on minimum competencies at different grade levels. Such a decision could be made by a state legislature or a board of education. The allocation of supervisory support could be made by these same bodies or by a superintendent and the central administration of a school district. This we would think of as strategic planning.

At building levels and within an area or county office of instructional services others would need to consider and devise ways to carry out the newly required function. Decisions about teacher in-service education, details of test preparation and administration, and the like become the focus of operational planning for those who will supervise the competency identification, teaching, and testing.

Mastery Test

OBJECTIVE 2 TO DISCRIMINATE BETWEEN STRATEGIC AND OPERATIONAL PLANNING

1. A list of supervisory planning activities follows. Indicate whether it is more representative of strategic or operational planning.

    a. Require all teachers to demonstrate certain competencies in order to receive tenure.

b. Determine allocation of supervisory services in a school district.
c. Schedule a series of workshops for teachers in a school district.
d. Adopt a SEAP (State Educational Assessment Program) for your state.
e. Adopt Mortimer Adler's PAIDEA concept as a curriculum guide for your district.
f. Assign students to alternative learning centers.
g. Stipulate units for graduation from district high schools.
h. Assign planning time to teachers.
i. Require six semester or nine quarter hours of university credit for district teachers for promotion on salary schedule.
j. Add or remove supervisory support for a district.

2. Here is a list of position titles of persons who may be involved in planning for education. Indicate whether persons in that position are more likely to be involved in strategic or operational planning.

Assistant Superintendent	Parent
Board Member	Subject Supervisor
Congressman	Superintendent
Department Chairman	Teacher
Legislator	Student
Principal	

3. Two generally accepted notions about the way planning is supposed to be in education are that all who will be involved in an activity should participate in its planning and that the best planning is from the bottom up. Comment on the validity of the notions from the concept of strategic and operational planning.

Answer Key

Mastery Test, Objective 2

1. a, d, e, and g are probably strategic; b, c, f, h, i and j are examples of operational planning.
2. Assistant superintendent, board member, congressman, legislator, and superintendent are likely to be at strategic planning level; the others at operational levels.
3. The general notions about planning refer more to operational planning than strategic planning. Strategic planning must precede operational planning. To attempt a bottom-up approach beyond the operational level would lead to frustration and apathy for planners at lower levels when their plans were ignored or drastically altered to conform to strategic plans.

OBJECTIVE 3 TO DESCRIBE AND APPLY PROCEDURES OF NEEDS ASSESSMENT TO ISSUES IN SUPERVISION

As we noted in our discussion of goals and objectives, one important influence on the goals of education—and thus an influence on the goals of supervision—is our clients. So, we must as supervisors have some skills in ways of finding out what our clients want of their schools and how they perceive our current efforts. This seems a simple enough matter: Why don't we just ask them? We shall do so, but it may not be so simple a matter as it seems.

Before we can even begin our planning of how to survey our clients, we need to identify them. The most obvious groups that come to mind are students, their parents, and their organizations. However, in a way, the entire community has a valid claim to consideration in planning. In my home town when the schools had closed for lack of funds and were again approaching closure, client groups surfaced everywhere. We learned that real estate brokers were interested in schools, as were bankers, clergy of all faiths, and this time even the usually invisible power brokers came into the open on behalf of schools.

Others with a strong claim for consideration in educational planning are readers of this text and their colleagues—educators and staff personnel of all kinds who deliver or support the delivery of the educational service.[2] Organizations representing these service delivery groups also have an interest in our planning on behalf of their local members and indirectly on behalf of their members everywhere. There is no need to remind supervisors of the propriety of assessing the needs of this group; teachers are often the primary reference group for supervisors since the supervisor cannot hope to interact personally and directly with students to improve instruction.

There is at least one other class of clients, one other category of reference groups: the board of education and others who make laws and policies for schools. There are also associations representing some of these groups.

Thus, depending upon the issue, there are at least the three categories of clients that have some claim on planning for education:

- Students and parents (and their organizations)
- Educators and staff (and their organizations)
- Policy makers (and their organizations)

We are all aware of interest groups that may make strong demands on the educational system depending on the issue.[3] The three categories listed make no provision for other governmental agencies that relate to the educational enterprise, nor for business and industrial interests. These and other groups with a stake in education may be important sources of information depending on the issue involved.

The next consideration is how to approach the group or groups to be surveyed. Our society is accustomed to polls, so one would think it easy to ask for information in this manner. Wrong! Gallup and Harris are uninvolved, objective collectors and disseminators of information about anything or everything. Not so for educators. Even as we collect data we may be perceived as attempting to influence respondents. When we ask groups, in effect, what do you want from us, there is a natural expectancy created that what the clients say they want will, in due course, be forthcoming. Since all groups will not agree, and all individuals in even one group will not agree, this is an unfortunate impression. The uses to which the information will be put need to be clearly understood in advance. This puts an obligation on educators as pollsters. One use of surveys has been to lay the ground work for a subsequent request for resources. As with many political actions, this practice will not be challenged so long as it works. The trouble is that groups have been influenced so often by this 1–2, survey-levy approach that it gives off an odor of manipulation, and who wants to be manipulated? Moreover, do nice folk like educators engage in manipulation? So we need to be open about the reasons for asking for information—from any group.

Another, more easily resolved issue, is to be sure that enough of the right groups are queried and respond to our request for information. The research or institutional data processing guru in your district can advise as to sample selection and necessary sample size. If you are drawing your own sample, remember to randomize it in some way if you need to act on the results—taking every fifth or tenth name on a personnel list may sometimes be enough. More often supervisors will not be dealing with samples but the entire population of teachers of a subject or at a common grade level.

An issue that is only indirectly related to our concern with the skill of needs assessment is whether we are obliged to attempt to meet client perceived needs or whether there are other criteria that should carry more weight in planning. That is, what if our clients "need" a frivolous curriculum change or activity. What if our population of teachers "needs" to have a veto over the admission of students into their classes, or if the public "needs" to teach scientific creationism, or students "need" access to Pac Man? Questions such as these will not arise if we are careful in the construction of our survey and clear in our purposes because they are questions of value not fact.

There are many sources of help in assessing the needs of any of the educational reference groups. There are commercial packages complete with manuals and data-processing programs if it is a large-scale operation. One very popular package will permit comparison of the needs of your clients with others throughout the nation. The results will doubtless tell you that your clients are concerned about discipline and want the schools to emphasize reading and mathematics. But, you already knew that! We have identified and described these approaches to needs assessment elsewhere and do not believe this discussion is relevant to the skills of supervisors.[4] Such broad-gauge public surveys are generally designed to sample public opinion. In these pages we are moving toward a more parochial view—that of administrators, teachers, staff, and students. Our particular focus is on teachers, the primary reference group for supervisors in education. Supervisors, in their roles as administrators or as members of a management team, may be involved in community surveys but that is not their usual role.

Let's begin our consideration of the skill of needs assessment in a simple supervisor–individual teacher relationship. We may assume that our purpose is to help the individual teacher determine his or her personal professional objectives. Here we rule out, for the time, personal objectives for a good life (happy marriage, salary increase) even though these concerns may be related to professional objectives.

One way to begin would be to ask a series of general, but leading questions. In this way a supervisor might ask questions such as:

- What aspect of teaching seems to be the most difficult for you?
- What concerns you most about your teaching assignment this term?
- What kind of problems do you expect to meet in your current assignment?
- What kind of help do you think would be most valuable at this time?

The answers to these questions given during either an informal or formally scheduled interview would begin to move the supervisor toward identifying the perceived needs of a particular teacher. Almost certainly such needs would be congruent with the district/school mission and the related objectives. Note, however, that we are attempting to arrive at the needs in a personal manner. This is sometimes called an inductive approach. An alternative procedure would be to follow a kind of management by objectives approach (MBO) and stipulate needs for the teacher by a process of logical deduction. An example of the deductive approach follows.

School district objective: Provide an education that will result in all graduates possessing the skills of computation necessary in present day adult life.

Local school objective: Provide needed resources and experiences so that 80 percent of sixth-grade students pass the sixth-grade mandatory State Educational Assessment Program Test in mathematics in their first attempt.

One teacher's objective: Arrange and administer instruction and practice opportunities for all students so that they can successfully demonstrate competence on at least two out of three questions dealing with the following type problems:

$1/6 \times 1/4 = \square$ $\quad \begin{array}{r} 783 \\ \underline{-97} \end{array}$ etc.

Using the MBO–deductive approach the supervisor can infer needs and objectives for teachers and for the supervisor as well. In a way, if the real world of schools were to be so tightly, logically constructed as the MBO approach itself, all of the supervisor's activities could be spun off of the same set of objectives. For example, in-service activities should be designed to enable teachers to meet their MBO-derived objectives, and staff development programs should build in increasing expertise in the areas given priority in the published MBO materials. There may sometimes be this perfect fit between the MBO mandates and individual needs, but usually, it doesn't happen. For one thing, tight focus on the substantive elements of an MBO plan generally precludes the necessary attention to other skills in the interpersonal domain. At any rate, there is no dilemma here of meeting prescribed district needs turned to objectives OR teacher needs turned to objectives—they are parts of a larger whole related in somewhat the same way as were strategic and operational planning in our previous discussion. And, psychologically, supervisors are in a more influential position if they can plan with teachers to help accomplish the teacher's objectives, which will most certainly contribute to the accomplishment of the district objectives.

To return to our example of a supervisor working with an individual teacher, another way of gathering information about that teacher's needs might be to ask the teacher to list several objectives, several things he or she might think need attention. Some remarks to elicit this kind of response are:

- List several things you would especially like to work on this term
- Write down some things about the school (or the department or class or whatever) that you think should be improved

This information is, of course, important for working with the one teacher concerned, but it can also be used by the supervisor to identify common needs distributed among several teachers.

The list of needs secured in this way can be assembled for a group of teachers and distributed for rating (very important, important, not very important, unimportant) or ranking (1 for most important, 2 for next most important and so on). The supervisor need not promise to work on the most important need first. Sometimes, it is a good tactic to tackle a simpler task first and build on the attendant feelings of success. An alternative way of generating a list of potential needs would be for the supervisor to devise the list based on his or her awareness of individual teacher abilities and district priorities. Figure 2.1 is a sample form using this approach.

The supervisor should compute an average rank for each item on the SOTS form. This information may be helpful in planning to work with a small group whose members have a common concern. It is also important that the supervisor take note of and respond somehow to the objective ranked most important by each teacher even though the group may not share this priority.

There are any number of ways of generating lists and securing reactions to the objectives listed. We provide another example to suggest the variety of approaches and to demonstrate the possible influence of a different tone. This form (see Figure 2.2) places the emphasis on something that the supervisor should do. It also discriminates more precisely between objectives perceived as highly important and those of much lesser importance (for the group).

Directions: Here are some things mentioned by yourself and other teachers that might deserve special attention this term. Please look over the entire list and then rank them in order of *how interested you are personally* in working on each objective. Enter "1" in the space next to the objective you are most interested in working on and so on, enter "10" next to that item you are least interested in working on.

OBJECTIVE	RANK
Communicating with parents	______
Getting and using an inventory of community resources	______
Getting some kind of student feedback on my teaching methods	______
Improving student achievement in reading in measurable ways	______
Improving the way I handle classroom disturbances	______
Learning how to evaluate my own teaching more objectively	______
Learning to teach and plan with other teachers (and aides) more effectively	______
Making the curriculum and my lessons more meaningful for students	______
Trying something new	______
Trying to individualize my teaching	______

Teacher's name __________________

FIGURE 2.1 Some objectives to stress (SOTS).

Analysis of the SOPS data will suggest high-priority areas for teachers. The items on the list can be secured by interviews or open-ended written questions, or inferred from the supervisor's observation.

Other open-ended problems designed to be responsive to teacher concerns are easily formulated. Consider some samples:

- The kind of help I could *really* use now is . . .
- What bugs me most about (the school, the supervisor, teaching, whatever) is . . .

Our emphasis on needs assessment has been on the perceptions of teachers as the primary reference group of supervisors. We have previously identified other groups with some right to identify needs and prescribe objectives. Among these were citizens, students, administrators, and policy makers. Some supervisors serving teachers in many schools may gather all of their data about the needs of teachers in these schools from the administrators in charge of the schools. Although this is a more efficient use of time, it may yield quite a different set of priorities. We cannot justify collecting comparative data merely to satisfy our intellectual curiosity, but we can defend collecting the same data from administrators through a minor change in the wording of the questions. The responses of the administrators could be analyzed separately or merged with the data for teachers. It will come as no surprise to supervisors to have empirical support for the prediction that administrators will perceive different needs for the schools and their teachers than will the teachers.

The same phenomenon of different perceptions would occur for the other reference groups. The interesting question when such groups differ widely is to determine which groups have the better perception of the particular objective concerned.

Directions: A list of suggested activities for our in-service work this term follows. The list was assembled from faculty suggestions and contains suggested ways that (the supervisor) should work with teachers this term. To complete the form:

1. Assume that you have a total of 30 counters (enter Xs or ✓s) to stand for how important each of the several items is to you.
2. Use *all* of your 30 counters. The more counters you put next to a topic, the more important it is in your opinion.
3. Give at least one topic five counters.
4. If you agree that a topic is worthy of any attention at all you should show this by giving it at least one counter.

	1	2	3	4	5
Assist teachers to develop interpersonal skills					
Assist teachers to gather and use data about school, classroom, and community environments					
Assist teachers to translate knowledge of educational research into instructional practices					
Assist teachers to understand and use techniques and instruments designed to diagnose students' academic and social needs					
Assist teachers to develop instructional goals and objectives					
Assist teachers to design, develop, and maintain environments that facilitate learning					
Assist teachers to understand and use effective techniques of classroom management					
Assist teachers to evaluate instructional effectiveness by collecting, analyzing, and interpreting data on teacher and student behavior					
Plan and conduct individual conferences with teachers					
Demonstrate effective planning, organizing and managing skills					
Assist teachers to design and implement personalized learning plans					
Assist teachers to develop or adapt instructional programs and materials					

FIGURE 2.2 Supervisor's objectives priority sheet (SOPS).

Mastery Test

OBJECTIVE 3 TO DESCRIBE AND APPLY PROCEDURES OF NEEDS ASSESSMENT TO ISSUES IN SUPERVISION

1. Identify three major categories of individuals or groups that have a claim to participate in determining the needs of education.

2. Make your own Some Objectives to Stress form listing at least five things together with the directions you would give to teachers on how to rate or rank the items.
3. Distinguish between inductive and deductive approaches to needs assessment.

Answer Key

Mastery Test, Objective 3

1. The three major categories are:
   a. Students, parents, and their organizations
   b. Educators, staff, and their organizations
   c. Policymakers and their organizations
2. The form should be clear and the directions should be simple. Items should be listed in random or alphabetical order so as not to suggest the supervisor's opinion about the relative importance of the items.
3. The inductive approach begins with individuals from whom the supervisor infers needs. The deductive approach begins with goals from which the supervisor logically derives teacher needs.

OBJECTIVE 4 TO DESCRIBE AND APPLY THE PROCESS OF BRAINSTORMING TO ISSUES IN SUPERVISION

Even when the needs have been assessed, the objectives inferred, deduced, or induced, the task of planning is far from complete. A tentative solution to meet the objective, to solve the problem, needs to be devised and implemented. We emphasize *tentative* because there are many ways to accomplish any objective and at several points in the process of solving the problem or meeting the objective we may revise our tentative solution or adopt a completely different, superior solution.

To begin considering solutions to the problem presented in meeting an objective we shall describe a creative activity known as *brainstorming*. Brainstorming is a technique sometimes used to identify problems or to stimulate a quantity of possible (sometimes impossible) solutions to a problem. This is a group technique based on the assumption that most groups, certainly most groups of educators, have all kinds of ideas that are seldom considered about problems and their solutions. Through brainstorming we attempt to draw out as many of these ideas as quickly as possible. The rapidity of idea generation is intended to stimulate the flow of ideas and discourage the early adoption of the first attractive solution offered.

PROCEDURE

The supervisor should be sure that the purpose of the activity is clear. If it is to solve a problem, the problem should be as specific as possible, and clearly stated. The goal for improvement should also be explicit.

It is difficult to work with more than about 10 persons, so it may be necessary to arrange two or more groups to accommodate larger numbers, say a faculty of 20 teachers. It is then possible to combine and compare the ideas from all groups.

Some advance attention to detail is important. There must be some way of recording the ideas as they are generated. One person could agree to serve as a recorder, but if ideas come quickly—as we hope they will—more than one recorder may be needed. Large sheets of newsprint on easels are often used. Working in schools, I have found the ubiquitous chalk board quite adequate. I take a position on one side of the board and a teacher stands at the other side. Then, as the ideas come thick and fast we alternately record them. The problem with this is that we have no enduring record until someone copies the ideas from the board.

Participants in a brainstorming session should be informed of a few essential rules. When these are violated the supervisor needs to informally but quickly remind participants of these rules. The usual ground rules are:

1. *No criticism.* There is no such thing as a bad idea at this stage. It is not fair to throw cold water on an idea by telling why it won't work or that it was previously tried unsuccessfully. For once, it is appropriate and may be quite helpful to be silly and suggest "far out" solutions.
2. *Go for quantity.* The more ideas generated, the better the chance the process will result in some useful ideas.
3. *Build on the ideas of others.* It needs to be clear that there is no "ownership" of ideas at this stage. It is quite appropriate to build on someone else's idea (the jargon for this is to "piggy-back") or combine it with one of your own. You need not favor a solution to offer it; the purpose is just to get the ideas out so that they may stimulate others.

Mark Twain may have been brainstorming a solution when he came up with a way to end the submarine menace in World War I. His strategy: boil the water in the oceans. When people asked just how this should be accomplished, Twain is reported to have replied that it was his job to think of a solution and someone else's job to carry it out. Even though those solving our educational problem may have to carry out the solutions themselves, it helps if they can take Mark Twain's attitude during the time they are thinking of all the possible solutions—practical as well as silly.

The attitude of the supervisor during brainstorming is important. It is necessary to be enthusiastic and nonjudgmental. If teachers can tell by the supervisor's nonverbal response that he or she thinks some ideas are ridiculous, it would tend to discourage creative thinking. When, if, the flow of ideas slackens, the supervisor should throw out a wild idea or two to stimulate others.

A listing of ideas elicited by an actual brainstorming session will illustrate the way the ground rules affect results. The group was six county supervisors with responsibilities for serving teachers in five local districts. Each supervisor had a territory that included five or six schools and over 100 teachers. The problem was that the supervisors did not have time to relate to teachers in any but the most cursory fashion. The goal for brainstorming was to find ways to make better use of their time. The first suggestions that followed were:

- Work in just one school for a month at a time
- Rotate districts and serve a different district every year
- Add 20 more supervisors
- Quit traveling, make teachers come to us
- Specialize more
- Work only with nontenured teachers
- Work only with volunteers, with teachers who request our help
- Hire two more secretaries for record keeping and paper work
- Give each school a bank of money for supervisory support and let them bid for services

- Work a six-day week (for extra pay) and hold open house for teachers on Saturday
- Stop supervising in schools and offer workshops and in-service work for credit
- Add 10 interns half time from outstanding teachers
- All of us go to the same school at once and work with the entire faculty
- Stop trouble shooting and ask the superintendent to assign that to another office

Enough of the suggestions have been listed to show how the process works. Adding 20 supervisors would be considered a silly suggestion but it raises the issue of seeking additional personnel and may have stimulated other ideas in the same vein. Stopping on-site supervision is a radical departure that might never have been considered without the liberating ground rules of brainstorming. All in all, we can see that these six professional supervisors are acutely aware of the inadequacy of their program and have creative alternatives that potentially would enable them to be more influential.

Ideas such as those provided in the example need to be preserved for review and further analysis. That process is best delayed until we present that skill in a separate objective.

Mastery Test

OBJECTIVE 4 TO DESCRIBE AND APPLY THE PROCESS OF BRAINSTORMING TO ISSUES IN SUPERVISION

1. List the ground rules for brainstorming.
2. What, if anything, should the supervisor do during a brainstorming session if one teacher continually criticizes the contributions of other teachers?
3. List a problem as you would present it to a group of teachers for a brainstorming session.

Answer Key

Mastery Test, Objective 4

1. The rules are:
   No criticism
   Go for quantity
   Build on the ideas of others
2. Since the atmosphere must be informal for brainstorming it is essential that the supervisor avoid an authoritarian stance in enforcing the first rule of brainstorming—no criticism. However, it is also necessary that the criticism be stopped before it throws cold water on the creative fires of others. The supervisor might admonish in a light vein something like:
   Not fair (name of teacher)!
   You know the rules (name of teacher)!
   Think up or shut up!
3. Your problem statement should be specific and easily understood. The goal for improvement should be explicit. Finally the topic should be one familiar to all of the persons likely to participate in your brainstorming session.

OBJECTIVE 5 TO DESCRIBE AND APPLY THE FORCE FIELD TECHNIQUE OF PROBLEM ANALYSIS TO ISSUES IN SUPERVISION

The force field is a well-known problem-analysis technique.[5] The logic of this approach assumes that we may view any situation as in balance—in equilibrium—as a result of the effect of opposing forces. For supervisors, this means that any plan for in-service work or staff development will be affected by a number of influences—forces in the particular force field. To use the force field as a planning tool we begin by identifying these forces.

The first task is to identify present conditions in regard to the issue concerned. This is the position in equilibrium or the status quo. The force field will be used to enter data responsible for that equilibrium in anticipation of making changes that will move us away from status quo toward an improved condition— the goal for improvement.

These two conditions, status quo and the goal for improvement, are conventionally set down on different sides of a diagram representing the situation. Before introducing the other conventions of force fields, it may help if we use a hypothetical supervisory problem. For this purpose assume that the present condition is that: Teachers resist and resent supervisory observation, do not request observations and, if observed, appear to select nonrevealing teaching activities. Assume that the goal for improvement is that: Teachers appreciate the value of supervisory observation and cooperate fully in the process.

The supervisor working with the planning group, which in this case could be teachers or other supervisors, attempts to identify as many as possible facilitating, driving, or enabling forces—those forces that tend to cause movement toward our goal. Some of these probably would be:

- Supervisors are aware of the need for change.
- Some teachers already accept observation.
- The superintendent and board have acknowledged a desire to respond to external pressures for accountability.
- There is evidence of widespread concern that graduates of the district schools are deficient in certain areas.
- The state Department of Education has allocated funds specifically to support supervisory activities.

The planning group would next attempt to list as many possible opposing, restraining, or hindering forces—those forces that tend to resist movement toward the goal for improvement. Some of these probably would be:

- The tradition of supervisory observation in the district has created a negative impression among teachers in general.
- Several teachers openly oppose observation.
- Some supervisors are reluctant to engage in a regular program of supervision for fear of alienating teachers.
- Some supervisors lack skills in conferencing and observing.
- Observations and conferences are time consuming.
- Veteran teachers have come to see themselves as no longer needing observation.
- Nontenured teachers fear for their jobs.
- Schools are dispersed over a considerable distance.

In compiling your list of facilitating and opposing forces, it is helpful to consider different categories of forces such as psychological, political, sociological, institutional, and historical. A common way of categorizing forces is to identify all possible facilitating and/or opposing forces in yourself, groups, other individuals, and society.

Examples of these in our force field would be:

YOURSELF: I feel uncomfortable observing veteran teachers.
GROUPS: The board of education advocates accountability.
OTHER INDIVIDUALS: Some teachers accept supervision.
SOCIETY: There is widespread concern about the competence of graduates.

The purpose of this approach is to identify all facilitating and opposing forces.

We are now ready to examine the force field (Figure 2.3). The line down the center of the page represents the way things are. The dotted line on the right represents our goal for improvement.

The force field as it now stands provides a display of forces and persons for and against our goal of cooperation in supervisory observations. However, it should be apparent that a simple numerical analysis of forces for and against will not be very helpful in planning future activities. To add to the utility of the force field we can next rank the forces according to their importance in helping or hindering movement toward the goal. Some consultants suggest ranking only the restraining forces because they will base their planning on overcoming these forces. However, it seems likely that all forces should be ranked in the event that our planning might seek to strengthen important facilitating forces. Using this approach, all forces whether for or against our goal will be ranked beginning with number one for the most important force regardless of its direction and so on until all forces on both sides have been ranked.

There are other determinations that we can make about the forces that will enable us to make a more valid analysis. We could consider and rate each force according to how difficult our planning group believes it will be to change the

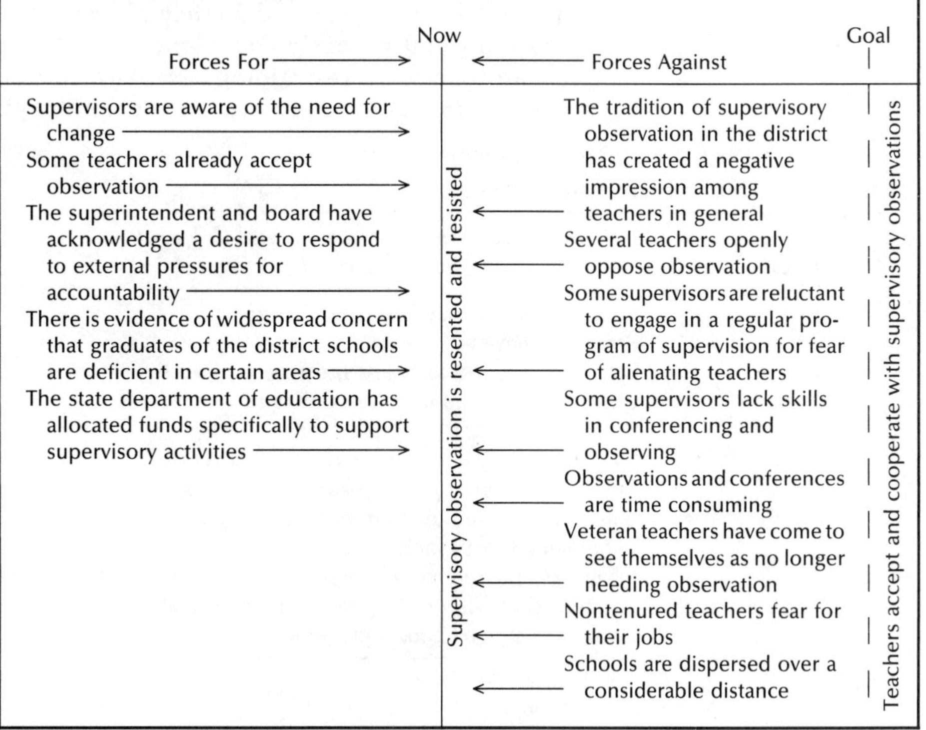

FIGURE 2.3 Sample force field.

force. Thus, we could use a number code (1 = easy to change; 2 = moderately difficult to change; 3 = very difficult to change), or a letter code (H = hard; M = medium; E = easy), or insert three columns wherein we could check the difficulty of changing the force. Probably we would invent a symbol to represent the forces that the planners believe to be impossible to change.

Another important assessment of the forces is to indicate our certainty as to whether each entry is really a force and whether it is properly assigned to the For or Against side of the diagram. The planners are now concerned with how sure they are, how clear it is that their identification of the force is based on objective data. Again, we could enter this decision as a number, or a letter, or a check in a column.

Readers will already be thinking about ways to use these rankings and ratings in their planning, but before we discuss that let's take another look at the force field data, this time in one long list. The list could be prepared with For forces first in the order they were identified, followed by Against forces, in rank or alphabetical order, or in whatever order best serves your purposes (see Table 2.1).

The sample force field and the force field analysis forms support planning and subsequent strategy. First we should examine the interaction of the ranking and ratings. If there are any forces that are ranked high in importance but not clear, we should gather more data to permit a more accurate diagnosis of the situation. In our example, the force *some supervisors fear alienating teachers* is ranked number 3 in importance but we are not clear about it. Similarly the force *some supervisors lack skills* is second in importance even though we are only partly clear about it. Both of these are examples of the need for more information.

After analyzing the force field the supervisor and the planning group would plan their strategy to move toward the goal. There are four approaches suggested by force fields. We can attempt to *strengthen a force, weaken a force, add a new force, or eliminate a force.* In our example we have no forces that are easy to change, but if there were any, that could be a place to start and enjoy some success, and possibly begin to move toward the goal. If we look at the three most important forces, we note that they all concern supervisors. These could be addressed simultaneously and might be the best way to begin this particular problem because the restraining forces now outweigh the enabling forces. After strengthening these three forces we could attempt to weaken some restraining

TABLE 2.1 Force Field Analysis

Rank Order of Importance	*Goal: Teacher's Will Accept and Cooperate with Supervisory Observation*	*Ease of* Change*	*Clarity**
1	Supervisors aware of need to change	M	C
6	Some teachers accept supervision	M	PC
4	Superintendent and board favor accountability	H	C
9	Concern that graduates are deficient	H	NC
5	State department provided funds	H	C
10	Negative tradition of supervisor's observation	H	C
7	Several teachers oppose observation	M	PC
3	Some supervisors fear alienating teachers	H	NC
2	Some supervisors lack skills	M	PC
11	Observations and conferences are time consuming	H	C
8	Attitude that veteran teachers don't need observation	H	NC
12	Schools dispersed geographically	H	C

**Code* Change: E = easy to change
M = medium difficulty
H = hard to change
Clarity: C = clear
PC = partly clear
NC = not clear

forces. Of course, we have no way of knowing for the hypothetical case what forces could be added, but this possibility should not be overlooked. As for eliminating forces on the restraining side, the only possibility appears to be the geographical dispersion of schools. A plan for supervisor assignment to one school for an extended time or similar options could, in effect, remove this negative force. This is not to say it should be done, that would await the formulation of a preferred solution to the problem.

Force fields are a useful tool in conceptualizing a problem situation. They are often followed by a brainstorming session when planners deal with each force in turn, seeking ways to strengthen supporting forces and weaken opposing forces.

Mastery Test

OBJECTIVE 5 TO DESCRIBE AND APPLY THE FORCE FIELD TECHNIQUE OF PROBLEM ANALYSIS TO ISSUES IN SUPERVISION

1. Draw the format for a force field entering the appropriate headings.
2. List at least three categories of forces that may be helpful in thinking about facilitating and opposing forces.
3. In what ways should forces be ranked and rated to help with analysis and planning?
4. What general tactics are possible in terms of a force field to move from present conditions to the goal?

Answer Key

Mastery Test, Objective 5

1. The drawing should include these elements properly labelled.

Now

Goal

Forces for →

← Forces against

Way things are

Way things should be

2. Three of the following four categories of forces should appear in this answer:

Forces within yourself

Forces within groups

Forces within other individuals

Forces within society

3. Forces may be ranked in order of their importance in regard to reaching the goal. They may be rated for ease of change and according to how certain you are that they exist as you describe them.
4. To move toward the goal we may:

   Add a force

   Eliminate a force

   Strengthen a force

   Weaken a force

OBJECTIVE 6 TO DESCRIBE AND APPLY APPROPRIATE CRITERIA FOR ASSESSING THE MERITS OF ALTERNATIVE SUPERVISORY PRACTICES

Multiple potential solutions to problems in supervision can be, as we have seen, generated by brainstorming, force field analysis, or by other responses to the needs of schools and their clients. We now need to consider a way of selecting the most appropriate solution from those suggested.

The supervisor will rarely be in a situation where he or she has complete latitude to implement an ideal solution regardless of cost or other factors. Educators are usually in the position of selecting a plan that is the best approximation of the ideal solution that can be supported economically and politically. Although educators have an opportunity and an obligation to exercise their expert professional judgment, that judgment must be tempered by the limitations of the situation and the need to strike a balance between often vague, sometimes conflicting, goals and objectives of the several reference groups.[6]

One way of narrowing down the potential solutions and identifying the one most likely to succeed is to set down the important criteria by which the solution is to be judged and, then, to rate each of the potential solutions on these criteria. Summing the scores on these criteria should enable us to focus on the best possible compromise between the ideal and the practical.

The specific criteria to be satisfied will vary depending upon the issue and the participants. A common approach in business is to do a cost analysis of each option.[7] Cost must concern supervisors as well and we shall call this criterion *efficiency*, by which we mean how much the plan costs compared to the benefits, as well as the actual cost in resources. Another criterion is certain to be *feasibility*. By feasibility we mean not only Can we do it? but also Is it appropriate for us to do it? In a semisacred area such as education, every solution that might work is not necessarily feasible, in that it is not "right" for educators to act in certain ways. Finally, any set of criteria will include *effectiveness*. Effectiveness refers to whether the plan will solve the problem, accomplish our objective, get the job done. Although we shall not apply it as a criterion in our example, it is a good idea to consider the *side effects* of each plan, for almost any plan will have bad as well as good side effects for one or another of our client groups.

One of our implicit objectives in this chapter is to introduce several typical issues in supervision. For this reason, we will apply the procedure for selecting a course of action to a new problem rather than continuing to see one issue through from planning to implementation. The objective actually addressed by the faculty of a K–6 grade school with 22 teachers was how to accomplish analysis of their own teaching behaviors in a nonthreatening way. The solutions offered by a brainstorming session included:

1. Each teacher should pick a trusted colleague to observe teaching while a substitute or the administrator takes over the peer observer's class.

2. Noneducator observers should be recruited from the community.
3. Professors from nearby universities should observe and counsel the teachers.
4. Staff administrators from the central office should make monthly observations.
5. Lessons should be audiotaped by teachers and analyzed anonymously using Flander's Interaction Analysis or some other system.
6. A district teacher or teachers should be placed on a year's special duty to do nothing but work with teachers by analyzing their teaching behavior.
7. The teachers' association should assign a specialist to be paid half by the association, half by the district.
8. Principals of adjacent schools should be paired and each principal should observe teachers in the other's school.
9. Teachers should videotape lessons, receive instruction in analysis systems, and meet, if they wish, with their colleagues to plan improvements. Tapes will be under control of each teacher at all times.

We have given each plan a short title listed along the rows or the left side of the Forecasting Results of Alternate Plans (FRAP) form (see Table 2.2). Across the columns we have entered the chosen criteria. The planners (faculty in this instance) rated each plan on each criterion from 1 (low) to 5 (high). The final column yields the total score for each plan. Whether the scores are group consensus or the totals of scores of all planners is a matter for the supervisor's judgment.

The results of this activity show that, of the plans listed on the FRAP form,[8] the most promising alternative is for the teachers to videotape their own lessons. This is, in fact, the solution implemented in the school concerned. Two video tape recorders (VTRs) were set up before school by sixth-grade volunteers trained by the principal. The volunteers returned during recess or lunch to take down the VTRs. One VTR was directed at the class, the other at the teacher. The interaction of teacher behavior and student response could be observed by a simple split-screen technique. Teachers eventually shared their tapes with their colleagues in several evening sessions which they arranged to discuss teaching techniques. We are not concerned here with the merits of the solution, but with the process by which the alternatives were evaluated. The FRAP activity is an aid to decision making. The several ways of arriving at decisions or arranging decision-making groups will be discussed by colleagues in other chapters.

TABLE 2.2 Forecasting Results of Alternate Plans Non-threatening Observation

Alternate Plans	*Efficiency*	*Feasibility*	*Effectiveness*	*Total*
1. Trusted colleague	5	4	2	11
2. Noneducator observer	3	2	1	6
3. Professors	1	3	4	8
4. Staff administrators	3	3	2	11
5. Audio tapes	5	5	2	12
6. Special duty teacher	4	3	2	9
7. Association specialist	4	4	2	10
8. Principals	3	3	2	8
9. Video tapes	5	5	4	14

Mastery Test

OBJECTIVE 6 TO DESCRIBE AND APPLY APPROPRIATE CRITERIA FOR ASSESSING THE MERITS OF ALTERNATIVE SUPERVISORY PRACTICES

1. Comment on this assertion: "The competent supervisor will in all instances identify the ideal solution to a problem and resist attempts at compromise."
2. Name three criteria likely to be used to assess the merits of alternative plans.
3. Based on your experience, identify other criteria that may be important in assessing the merits of plans in education.

Answer Key

Mastery Test, Objective 6

1. Your answer should acknowledge the need to consider the context of the issue concerned. The values and expectations of other reference groups must be considered as well as the multiple claims on limited resources. Supervision will seek the best decision possible to implement. This may not always be the best possible decision.
2. Efficiency
   Feasibility
   Effectiveness
3. Answers will vary. Side effects should be considered. Perhaps headings on adequacy of facilities, time required, personnel needs, and the like would help in some situations.

OBJECTIVE 7 TO DESCRIBE AND APPLY A PROCEDURE FOR TASK MANAGEMENT

We are ready now to consider the use of planning tools as aids to the implementation of our plans. We shall, again, change the issue to which we apply the tool of task management. The issue this time is another "old chestnut" for supervisors: planning time.

The present arrangement in the school concerned permits teachers in a given department, team, or grade level to meet from 8:00 A.M. to 8:30 A.M. three days a week to plan future lessons and arrange details of on-going activities. The teachers and you, the supervisor, are not satisfied with this and have determined to find, somehow, more planning time. You have made a force field and brainstormed ways of solving the problem of getting more planning time. The planning group, consisting of the teachers and the supervisor, has prepared a list of things that must be done. The list includes:

- Make an analysis of how you spend your present planning time from 8:00 A.M. to 8:30 A.M. three times a week
- Visit other teams/departments in your own school and other schools to see how they arrange planning time
- Check the professional literature in libraries and ERIC to see if good ideas are reported there
- Take the problem to the school coordinating council (instructional improvement committee, curriculum council, cabinet, or similar body) and ask for data and suggestions

- Meet with special teaching and support staff to discuss their needs to plan with you
- Collect data about the cost of alternative ways of getting more planning time that came out of your brainstorming (for instance, monthly retreat, no students for one-half day a week, hire substitutes one day a month, one evening meeting each week, etc.)
- Meet with building and/or district administrators to explore resources and constraints
- Meet with parents (or perhaps the building parent advisory council) to explore attitudes about issues concerning student nonattendance for a half day
- Prepare a trial version of your new planning schedule
- Submit the schedule to building administration and coordinating committee for reaction and approval
- Decide how to evaluate the success of the new procedure(s)
- Inform all faculty, staff, students, and parents of new planning procedure(s)
- Do it
- Evaluate it
- Accept, revise, or reject it

One way of organizing people and time to accomplish this list of activities is a simple assignment sheet. On this form you would list all of the activities needed to accomplish your objectives adding columns for the starting and ending dates and stating the name(s) of the person(s) responsible for each activity. Figure 2.4 (p. 34) shows one version of a form for doing this.

Sometimes additional columns are added to the assignment sheet for items such as resources required (possibly in hours) or to remind those responsible of the reason for the activity in a column headed Purpose or Why. The completed assignment sheet provides an improved perspective on the overall task, in this case improving planning time and procedures.

Mastery Test

OBJECTIVE 7 TO DESCRIBE AND APPLY A PROCEDURE FOR TASK MANAGEMENT

1. What elements should be included in a simple task assignment form?
2. Draw a partial task assignment form and enter two or three activities necessary to accomplish some objective of your own choosing.

Answer Key

Mastery Test, Objective 7

1. The minimum essentials of an assignment form are the tasks, a time, and the name of the person or persons responsible for the task.
2. Answers will vary. The activities should be listed in chronological order, and the elements of task, time, and person should be present.

Task Statement: To discover and implement improved planning procedures
Starting Date ____________ Completion Date (est.) ____________

Activity	*Start*	*Done*	*Responsible*
1. Analyze use of present planning time			
2. Visit other departments/grade levels			
3. Visit other schools			
4. Check professional literature			
5. Make ERIC search			
6. Inform and consult school council			
7. Meet with special teachers			
8. Meet with support staff			
9. Determine costs of alternatives			
10. Meet with administrators			
11. Meet with parent advisory committee			
12. Draft new planning schedule			
13. Get administrative and building council approval			
14. Inform faculty, students, parents			
15. Design evaluation procedures			
16. Implement new procedures			
17. Evaluate new procedures			
18. Accept, reject, or revise new procedures			

FIGURE 2.4 Sample assignment sheet—incomplete.

OBJECTIVE 8 TO DESCRIBE AND APPLY A GANTT CHART TO A PROBLEM IN SUPERVISION

A Gantt chart is another aid to planning that could be used in connection with or instead of the assignment sheet. It is an improvement in that it shows how some activities may overlap. Planners can see immediately not only what activities need to be accomplished first but also what activities can be worked on at the same time. To show the relationships among Gantt, assignment sheets, and PERT charts (our next objective) we must stay with the same issue, devising a new procedure for teachers' planning.

The Gantt chart, developed by Henry Gantt during World War I, is still a useful tool to identify all of the processes needed to accomplish our task.[9] To prepare a Gantt chart for our planning problem, list again the activities identified on the assignment sheet. Next to these enter the units of time most appropriate for the problem. We shall use weeks for the example. Then to complete the chart you start an arrow in the space beneath the week in which an activity may begin. The arrow is continued to the place underneath the week in which the activity is scheduled to be completed. Inspection of the sample Gantt chart in Figure 2.5 shows the procedure.

Note that the entire task is scheduled to be accomplished in just 15 weeks and consists of 18 different activities. Such a chart should be helpful to the supervisor and the planning team as well as to all of the other individuals and groups that will ultimately be affected by the changes in planning procedures. Moreover, the discipline and attention to detail required in projecting the activities, time requirements, and relationships should result in fewer errors and delays. For some one-shot, nonroutine activities, the Gantt chart may be adequate. However, the chart does not give supervisors the definite sequencing requirements they may need for some projects.

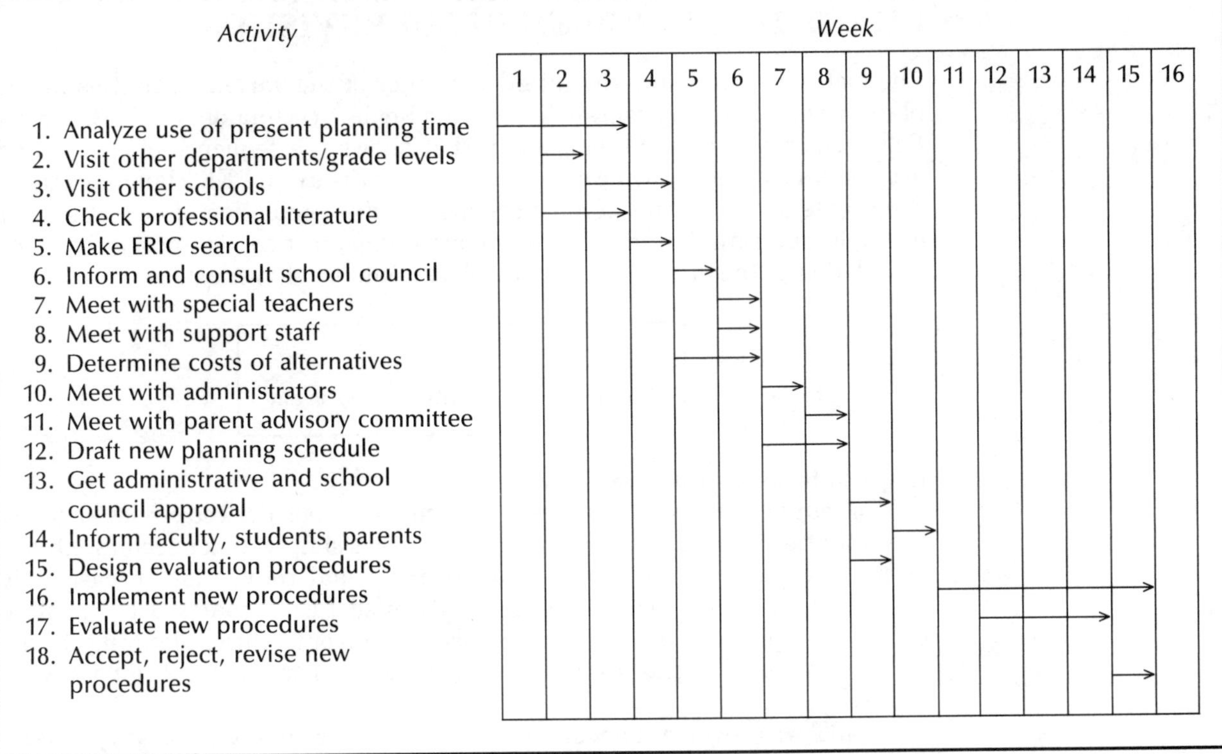

FIGURE 2.5 Sample Gantt chart for improving planning procedures.

Mastery Test

OBJECTIVE 8 TO DESCRIBE AND APPLY A GANTT CHART TO A PROBLEM IN SUPERVISION

1. What is the major advantage of a Gantt chart over an assignment sheet?
2. Prepare a Gantt chart for the following activities. Assume they do not overlap.

Conduct needs assessment	2 weeks
Analyze data	1 week
Prepare report	1 week
Present findings to educators and citizens	1 week

Answer Key

Mastery Test, Objective 8

1. The Gantt chart shows how activities may overlap.
2.

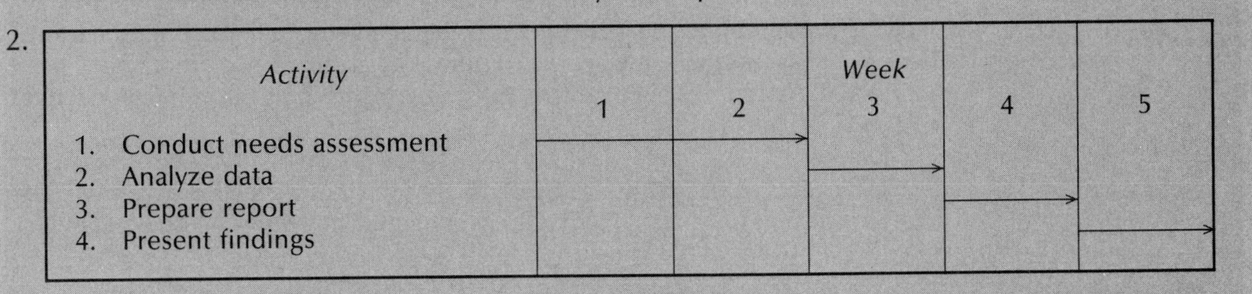

OBJECTIVE 9 TO DESCRIBE AND APPLY A PERT CHART TO A PROBLEM IN SUPERVISION

The tool that best shows the interdependency of the various activities in the planning problem is a Program Evaluation Review Technique (PERT) Chart. A PERT chart is a diagram or pattern that shows the sequence of events and activities as well as the time between events. In the usual PERT language there are events and activities. Events are merely the completion of activities. For example our actual study of present planning practices is an activity. The completion of the study is an event. That would be shown as:

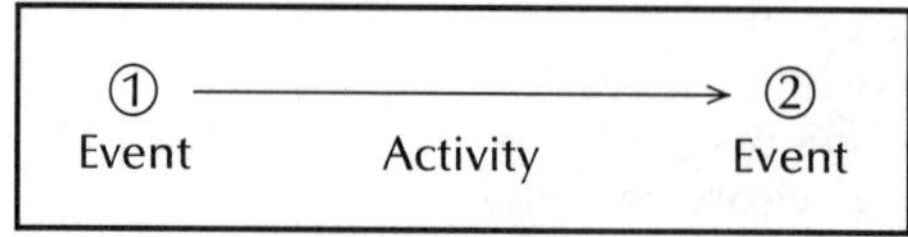

It would be described as activity 1–2.

For our present purposes, it will be simpler to consider the circles as being the activities from start to finish and the arrows simply as connectors. This is often done, but readers should know of the usual convention in case they encounter the more common usage in detailed PERT charts used in more complicated projects such as federal project reports or facilities planning charts. What we present in this section is an adaptation of the usual PERT network process.

PERT was developed about 1957 to control the complex U. S. Navy Polaris Project, by Lockheed; Booze, Allen, and Hamilton; and the U. S. Navy Special Projects Office.[10] In this project it was necessary to manage the activities of 3,000 separate contracting units. PERT has since been used in the space program and even today may be required as part of a request for state or federal education grants.

It was in regard to a United States Office of Education Request for Proposals that I first encountered PERT. Since the concept was somewhat new, I agreed to seek the advice of Professor Desmond Cook, then at Ohio State University, an acknowledged expert in regard to this planning tool. Professor Cook asked me to identify all of the essential activities in our proposed project and then to tell him which came first and so on. By experimenting with several diagrams and moving the events about as I discussed the project plan, he prepared the chart. The point of this anecdote is that to structure the appropriate PERT chart required two kinds of expertise—that of the planner, in this case Dr. Cook, and that of the specialist, in this case someone familiar with teacher education.[11] Hopefully, supervisors will be able to represent both of these areas of competence in planning projects less monumental than the Polaris submarine or the Saturn space project.

Before attempting to construct the PERT chart for our planning project we will establish the sequencing relations, drawing our information from the completed Gantt chart. The new information featured here is found in the column headed Immediate Predecessor (see Figure 2.6). This will be most helpful when we make the PERT chart.

Examination of the completed PERT chart (see Figure 2.7) shows how some activities may be carried on at the same time. These are termed *parallel activities* and there are several examples beginning with numbers 1, 2, and 4, reviewing present planning, visiting other departments, and checking the literature. We also see that some activities cannot be started until others have been completed. Activity 12, for example, must follow activity 9 but is independent of activities 10 and 11.

Events of special importance are sometimes drawn in a rectangle instead of a circle. In this chart activities 10 and 16 are considered such important events. They are termed *milestones* in PERT terminology. The symbols Ⓢ and Ⓣ stand for

Activity	Weeks Required	Immediate Predecessor
1. Analyze use of present planning time	3	—
2. Visit other departments/grade levels	1	—
3. Visit other schools	2	2
4. Check professional literature	2	—
5. Make ERIC search	1	4
6. Inform and consult school council	1	1, 3, 5
7. Meet with special teachers	1	6
8. Meet with support staff	1	6
9. Determine costs of alternatives	2	5
10. Meet with administrators	1	7, 8, 9
11. Meet with parent advisory committee	1	10
12. Draft new planning schedule	2	9
13. Get administrative and school council approval	1	12
14. Inform faculty, students, parents	1	13
15. Design evaluation procedures	1	12
16. Implement new procedures	4	14, 15
17. Evaluate new procedures	1	16
18. Accept, reject, or revise new procedures	1	17

FIGURE 2.6 Sequencing relationships for planning procedures project.

start and *terminate*. Sometimes the network is drawn over a time line similar to the way our Gantt chart was set up. More often the time(s)[12] is shown in a small figure inserted along the arrow as we have done in the PERT Planning Network (see Figure 2.7). As you can see, the length of the arrows is not proportional to the time needed for the related event.

The insertion of the times required by each activity enables us to use the PERT chart to calculate *Critical Path* and *Slack Time*. Critical path is that path through the network that requires the longest completion time. Obviously, any delay on this path can result in a delay in the entire project. Designers of PERT networks set their goal of finishing on schedule, and work back to the start from the completion date. To determine the critical path through a network, identify the possible paths from S to T and add up the time required to complete each path. We will abandon our PERT chart for the planning problem to illustrate this concept because it is not a good example of either critical path or slack time. (There are eight paths and all but one require 15 weeks, hence all are critical. Only along path S–4–5–9–12–15–16–17–18–T do we get one week of slack for each event from 4 to 15.)

In the sample PERT network shown in Figure 2.8 there are six activities and only two paths. Path A is S, 1–2–4–6–T. Path B is S–1–3–5–6–T. Path A requires 8 weeks and Path B, the longest or critical path, requires 16 weeks.

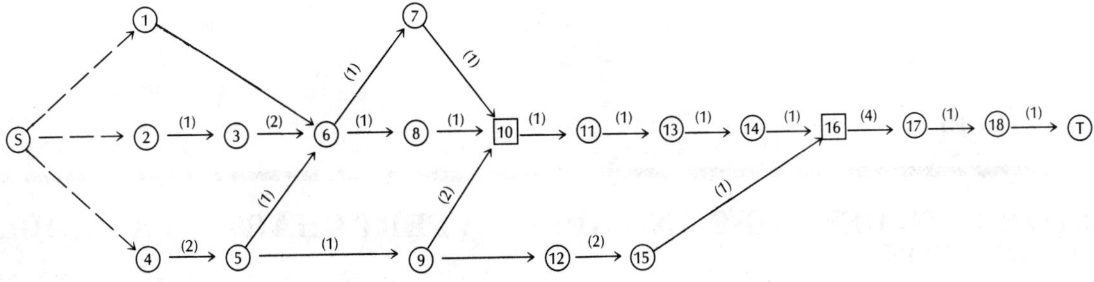

FIGURE 2.7 Pert network for improved planning procedures.

Slack time is the difference between the latest time an activity can be completed and not delay the project (TL) and the earliest time it can be completed (TE). Obviously all of the events on the critical path have no slack time. To find TL for an event, start at the completion time for the entire network and work back. Thus, in Figure 2.8, TL for event 4 is 11 weeks (16 weeks for the end of project less 1 week for event 6 and 4 weeks required for event 4 itself). TE is found by beginning at the start and adding the times required for each event. Thus, TE for event 4 is 3 weeks (2 weeks for event 1 and 1 week for event 2). Slack time for event 4 is then:

$$\begin{aligned} \text{Slack} &= \text{TL} - \text{TE} \\ &= 11 - 3 = 8 \text{ weeks.} \end{aligned}$$

Slack time is important in complex projects because it permits the transfer of personnel and equipment from one activity to another if necessary to remain on schedule. For supervisors it will be a sometimes necessary cushion of extra time available to compensate for the unexpected crisis that takes his or her efforts away from the project. It also reminds us that if we must attempt to shorten the project, it does no good to cut down on time for events not on the critical path. To gain time planners may resequence activities and thus create a new critical path, apply additional resources, or use different procedures that require less time in events along the critical path.

Review

It is likely that supervisors will find the adaptation of PERT charting used in the planning example adequate for most projects. PERT is merely another way of scheduling activities leading to our goal and of monitoring progress toward that goal. To prepare the network it was first necessary for us to identify all of the activities necessary to accomplish the task. These were then arranged in sequence and a diagram was prepared showing the interdependence of these activities. Times for each activity were estimated and entered along the arrows of the diagram. For most PERT charts there are multiple paths from the start to the terminus. The path requiring the longest time is called the critical path. The concept of slack time is defined as the difference between the latest time an event can be completed and not delay the project and the earliest time it can possibly be completed.

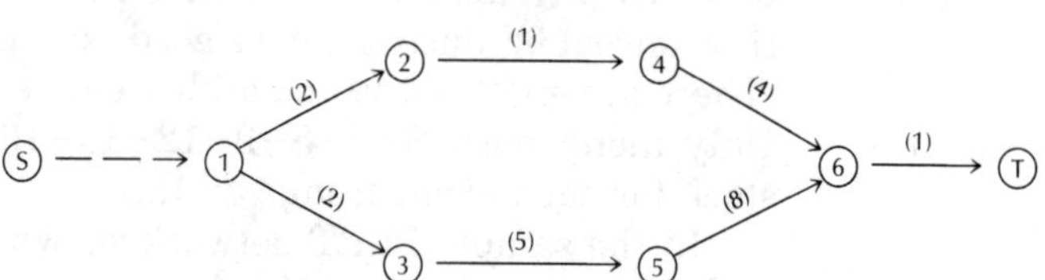

FIGURE 2.8 Sample Pert chart to illustrate critical path and slack time.

Mastery Test

OBJECTIVE 9 TO DESCRIBE AND APPLY A PERT CHART TO A PROBLEM IN SUPERVISION

1. In what way is a PERT chart an improvement over a Gantt chart as an aid to planning?

2. Here is part of a PERT chart.

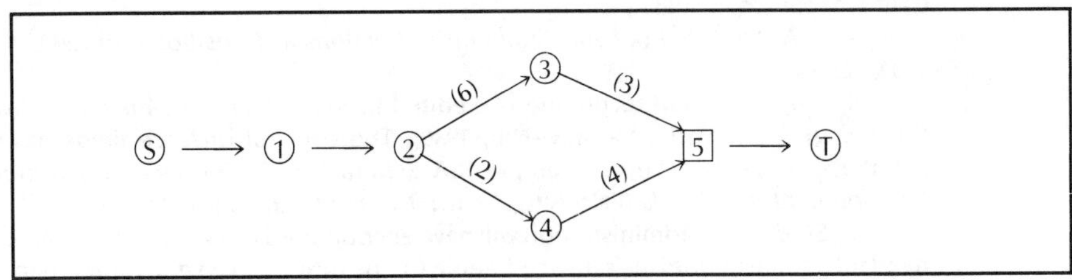

Indicate in the space provided which of the following statements are true?

Events 2 and 3 must both be completed before event 5. ________

Events 3 and 4 can be accomplished concurrently. ________

Event 2 must be completed before event 4. ________

3. Identify the critical path for the network above by listing the symbols and event numbers on the critical path.
4. How much time is required for the project if the time units represent days?
5. How much slack time is available for event 4?

Answer Key

Mastery Test, Objective 9

1. The PERT chart shows the interdependency relationships of activities better than a Gantt chart.
2. All of the statements are true.
3. S–1–2–3–5–T.
4. Twelve days.
5. Three days. (The entire project takes 12 less 1 day for event 5 less 4 days for event 4 means event 4 must start by day 7 = TL. Starting with event 1 takes 2 days and event 2 takes 2 days means that event 4 *could* start as early as day 4 = TE. Slack = TL − TE = 7 − 4 = 3.)

SUMMARY

All of the planning tools mentioned in this chapter are just that—tools. Like any tool they can be properly used or misused. The understanding of these and other planning tools can provide supervisors with helpful technical support to add to a "scientific" approach to the complex mission of supervision. The way in which the tools are used in harmony with other individuals is more nearly an art than a science. It remains for colleagues authoring the other chapters of this book to help supervisors add to their understanding of the art of supervision.

NOTES

1. K. Wiles, *Supervision for Better Schools* (Englewood Cliffs, New Jersey: Prentice-Hall, 1951); A.S. Barr, W. H. Burton, and L.J. Brueckner, *Supervision* (New York: Appleton-Century-Crofts, 1947); C.T. McNerney, *Educational Supervision* (New York: McGraw-Hill, 1951); T.H. Briggs, and J. Justman, *Improving Instruction Through Supervision* (New York: Macmillan, 1952).

2. To avoid the semantic dispute, assume that in this chapter *staff* refers to all school district employees except the professional educators.

3. See, for example, *Education and Urban Society*, vol. 13, no. 2 (February 1981); and "Interest Groups," in *School and Community Relations in Transition*, edited by Richard Saxe (Berkeley, Calif.: McCutchan, 1983), Ch. 4.

4. R.W. Saxe, *School and Community Relations in Transition* (Berkeley, Calif.: McCutchan, 1984), Ch. 8.

5. The force field technique is credited to Kurt Lewin. See his *Principles of Topographical Psychology* (New York: McGraw-Hill, 1936). The concept of force fields has since appeared in countless sources but see, for example, R.A. Schmuck et al., *The Second Handbook of Organization Development in Schools* (Palo Alto, Calif.: Mayfield, 1977), pp. 293–303.

6. Students of administration will have encountered this dilemma in their consideration of the need for administrators to "satisfice," settle for the best they can get, rather than "maximize," go for the ideal solution. These terms are credited to Herbert Simon, *Administrative Behavior*, 2d ed. (New York: Macmillan, 1957), p. xxv.

7. For an introduction to this from an educational point of view see American Association of School Administrators, *Educational Management Tools for the Practicing School Administrator* (Arlington, Va.: Author, 1979), pp. 27–40.

8. Readers are advised that the author of this chapter has coined acronyms for the various forms and instruments introduced. This is done for ease of reference and the acronyms are *not* standard professional usage . . . yet.

9. P.F. Drucker, *Management: Tasks, Responsibilities, Practices* (New York: Harper and Row, 1974), p. 182.

10. W.G. Cunningham, *Systematic Planning for Educational Change* (Palo Alto, Calif.: Mayfield, 1982), p. 146.

11. See for example, D.L. Cook, *Program Evaluation and Review Technique: Applications in Education* (Washington, D.C.: U.S. Government Printing Office, 1966).

12. Often for complex projects three time estimates are entered and a best estimate is secured by a simple formula.

ADDITIONAL READINGS

American Association of School Administrators. *Educational Management Tools for the Practicing School Administrator*. Arlington, Va.: Author, 1979.

Cunningham, W.G. *Systematic Planning for Educational Change*. Palo Alto, Calif.: Mayfield, 1982.

Delbecq, A.L., A.H. Van deVen, and D.H. Gustafson. *Group Techniques for Program Planning*. Glenview, Ill.: Scott Foresman, 1975.

Dusseldorp, R.A., D.E. Richardson, and W.J. Foley. *Educational Decision-Making through Operations Research*. Boston: Allyn and Bacon, 1971.

Granger, R.L. *Educational Leadership: An Interdisciplinary Perspective*. Scranton, Pa.: Entext, 1971.

Hartley, H.J. *Educational Planning-Programming-Budgeting: A Systems Approach*. Englewood Cliffs, N.J.: Prentice-Hall, 1968.

Hentschke, G.C. *Management Operations in Education*. Berkeley, Calif.: McCutchan, 1975.

Houston, W.R. et al. *Assessing School/College/Community Needs*. Omaha, Neb.: Center for Urban Education, University of Nebraska, 1978.

Kaufman, R. *Educational System Planning*. Englewood Cliffs, N.J.: Prentice-Hall, 1972.

———. *Identifying and Solving Problems: A Systems Approach*. La Jolla, Calif.: University Associates, 1976.

Kaufman, R.A., and F.W. English. *Needs Assessment: A Guide to Improve School District Management*. Arlington, Va.: American Association of School Administrators, 1976.

Landers, T.J., and J.G. Myers. *Essentials of School Management*. Philadelphia: W.B. Saunders, 1977, Ch. 16.

Knezevitch, S.J. *Administration of Public Education*, 3d ed. New York: Harper and Row, 1975. Ch. 7.

Schmuck, R.A. et al. *The Second Handbook of Organization Development in Schools*. Palo Alto, Calif.: Mayfield, 1977.

Tanner, C.K., and E.J. Williams. *Educational Planning and Decision Making*. Lexington, Mass.: Lexington Books, 1981.

ORGANIZING AND MANAGING TIME

3

Larry W. Hughes

Objective 1 To conduct a job analysis
Objective 2 To determine the difference between managing and doing, and to apply the Katz model to instructional supervision
Objective 3 To set personal goals and objectives and to develop strategies for achieving them
Objective 4 To conduct a personal time audit
Objective 5 To employ strategies to avoid interruptions
Objective 6 To employ techniques of good delegation
Objective 7 To plan and conduct effective meetings
Objective 8 To employ strategies for organizing productive committees and task forces

OVERVIEW

Your "mess is so big and so tall, we cannot pick it up, there's no way at all" (Dr. Seuss, The Cat In The Hat*)*

Supervisory loads are notoriously burdensome. Usually supervisors find themselves responsible for more teachers and activities than they can possibly cope with in an effective manner. Moreover, supervisors are often delegated ad hoc projects that take time from regularly assigned duties. Skillful organization and time management are important for all professionals, but given frequently excessive work loads, these skills are crucial for supervisors.

Setting professional and personal goals, job analysis, and systematic planning are fundamental to the process of getting and maintaining control of time. This chapter examines the direct application of these concepts to individual supervisor behavior. Making better use of discretionary time; developing skills in delegation; organizing more effective conferences, committees, and meetings; and avoiding interruptions are among other topics to be considered. The material in this chapter focuses on skill building and immediate application of the concepts discussed.

Time Laments

Have you ever felt this way?:

"I have so much to do, there is just not time to do it all."

or

"I'm harassed, overworked, tired, tense: I seem to be forever pushing myself and can't ever relax completely."

or

"I waste so much of my time doing things that are really not important, while my life is slipping away."

or

"I could manage OK if only all those other people would leave me alone once in awhile."

or

All of the above!

These are not uncommon feelings; most of us, at one time or another, have expressed the same or similar laments. But, if this describes a supervisor's usual state of mind, trouble is coming in the form of job dissatisfaction, undone necessary tasks, stress, illness, and poor performance reviews. Moreover, it is possible, except on rare days, to completely avoid the feelings expressed in the quotations above. No one's professional and personal life need be characterized by feelings of time frustration.

Taking Charge

Few of us live lives without the need to interact with others; neither are we free from the impingement of others' expectations of us. We live in an organized society and belong at once to a family, a work organization, professional associations, churches, self-help groups, and so on—all of which make demands on our time. Some of the demands are hierarchical—from bosses, colleagues, and subordinates; some obligatory—from spouses, children, and parents; some self-induced—from friends, salespersons, clients, and professors. All of these demands are controllable, *but control takes conscious effort.* Taking charge starts with answering two questions: Who are the people making demands on my time, and are the right people getting the right amount?

In my seminars on time management, I often discuss the four Ds. The first three Ds are *drifting*, *dreaming*, and *drowning*. One can drift through a work day accepting new assignments and other people's assignments, taking on more and more work irrespective of its importance, centrality, appropriateness, or personal interest, and at the end of a day, a week, a year one could dream that maybe tomorrow, next week, next year will be different. It won't, and if one drifts and dreams for long, one will drown in a sea of frustration, stress, and unrealized personal goals and ambitions.

The fourth D is *deciding*—making a conscious, goal-oriented effort to take charge of one's life. That's what this chapter is all about: attitudes and strategies to get the kind of control needed to get the job done well and on time, and to achieve a more satisfying personal and professional life.

A Perspective

A discussion of control, taking charge, goal setting, and deciding needs to be placed in proper perspective. Some readers may impute a negative, robotic approach to good organization and time management practices. Other persons may expect automatic productivity from putting into practice an array of time management techniques. Neither attitude is realistic.

On the first hand, the attitude about personal control and time management may be that it reduces one's personality and virtually all human interaction to conditioned responses and selfish activities. Not true, although if this attitude is implemented one will, of course, have few time management problems. One will also not have a family, friends, or, for long, a job. Organizing, planning, and good time management practices free, not constrain, a person. These practices are designed to allow more time to accomplish satisfying tasks. Slavish application of the practices and techniques described herein would be a foolish misuse and antithetical to the very concepts being expressed.

On the second hand, productivity is not an automatic result of good planning and time management. These practices are processes that will help a competent person work in the most efficient way, but will not make an incompetent or technically inadequate person better skilled at a job. Good time management practices will simply give the poorly skilled person more time to display incompetence.[1]

I assume that readers are at least on their way to technical competence; are operating from a conceptually sound supervisory perspective; and have the requisite human relations skills to perform adequately as supervisors. What this chapter endeavors to do is to provide ways for these skills to be more readily displayed and more effectively put into practice.

GOALS OF THE CHAPTER

This chapter strives to accomplish three goals:

To motivate the reader to modify present time management practices.

To help the reader identify ways personal and professional time is being used and misused.

To provide the reader with specific time management techniques.

Your Turn

You have just returned from a professional trip that has kept you out of the office for two days. It is now 7:00 A.M. and you have decided to spend some time planning your day so that you can get caught up. On your desk is a stack of materials and messages (listed in Figure 3.1). Your

_____ 1. Stack of mail that accumulated while you were gone.

_____ 2. Get theatre tickets—anniversary.

_____ 3. Schedule end-of-quarter activities to include personal conferences with each of the staff.

_____ 4. Eleven call-back phone calls which accumulated while you were gone.

_____ 5. Dr. Alex Johnson, the superintendent, left a note. He wants to see you as soon as you are free.

_____ 6. A note from your secretary that a Ms. Wilson has called twice about a problem and will be in to see you at 9:00 A.M.

_____ 7. The Phi Delta Kappa program planning meeting is at 2:00 P.M. (you are one of six members).

_____ 8. There is a staff luncheon meeting to discuss the new method for personnel evaluation.

_____ 9. Complete the evaluation of the ESAA project and revise the format for next year.

_____ 10. Call Ralph: tennis date for the weekend.

_____ 11. Deliver an overdue evaluation report to the assistant superintendent.

_____ 12. Read latest issue of *Educational Leadership*. Re: evaluation.

_____ 13. Jack Davis, the principal at Brown High School, wants to see you about the materials you were supposed to order two months ago. (They have not been delivered, he says.)

_____ 14. Advise director about your vacation schedule.

_____ 15. Develop the agenda for next week's supervisory council meeting.

_____ 16. Lunch with spouse.

_____ 17. Write the proposal for personnel development that was requested by Dr. Johnson last week just before you left town.

_____ 18. Gift for secretary—it's national secretaries' week.

_____ 19. Plan tomorrow's activities.

_____ 20. Write brief report about professional trip for file.

_____ 21. Note from secretary: There is an RFP for a federal grant for staff development. Deadline for submissions is next Monday.

_____ 22. Kiwanis Club called to remind you about your address at the luncheon tomorrow.

_____ 23. Note from Reverend Billings. Can you call him today about heading the membership drive? Said they really need you.

_____ 24. Note from secretary: Jack Davis called to talk about some teacher complaints and concerns, re: no feedback on your last visit.

_____ 25. Three of the principals in your district sent you a note wondering when you would be in their building next.

_____ 26. Wildwood PTA would like to have you come out tomorrow night to be on a panel about teacher evaluation.

FIGURE 3.1 Notes, in-basket items, and activities of the day.

immediate staff includes a secretary, a professional subordinate, and a part-time intern. Do the following:

1. Read over the list of items for your action.
2. Plan your day's activities by placing each item on the Daily Time Plan (in Figure 3.2).

Name ______________________ For the day of ______________________

The major *results* I would like to have accomplished by the end of today:

1. ______________ 3. ______________ 5. ______________
2. ______________ 4. ______________ 6. ______________

(A) Time	(B) Activity	(C) Priority*	(D) Type of Imposition**	(E) Method of Disposition***
7:00				
7:15				
7:30				
7:45				
8:00				
8:15				
8:30				
8:45				
9:00				
9:15				
9:30				
9:45				
10:00				
10:15				
10:30				
10:45				
11:00				
11:15				
11:30				
11:45				
12:00				
12:15				
12:30				
12:45				
1:00				
1:15				
1:30				
1:45				
2:00				
2:15				
2:30				
2:45				
3:00				
3:15				
3:30				
3:45				
4:00				
4:15				
4:30				
4:45				
5:00				
5:15				
5:30				
5:45				

* 1 = important and urgent, 2 = important, not urgent, 3 = urgent, not important, 4 = routine only

** 1 = self-imposed, 2 = system imposed, 3 = boss imposed, 4 = subordinate imposed, 5 = discretionary time

*** 1 = delegate to __________, 2 = train __________ to handle, 3 = consult __________, 4 = handle by myself, 5 = next time say "no," 6 = delay until __________

FIGURE 3.2 Daily time plan.

3. Complete also columns, C, D, and E.

Begin at once. Time is passing! You may be tempted at this point to skip ahead without actually attempting this exercise. If you do, you will be making a mistake. The exercises in this chapter are designed to give you practice in developing time management skills. If you just read the chapter without responding to the exercises you will not find out very much about your own strengths and weaknesses in this area. To really learn these materials you must interact actively with them. This particular exercise is quite similar to the final mastery test and will provide you with an opportunity to make pre-post comparisons, thus giving you some indication as to what you have learned over the course of studying the chapter.

Results

In doing this exercise you performed three fundamental acts of good time management: planning, scheduling, and priority setting. Review your work; what difficulties did you experience? There really weren't enough hours in the day to do all of those things. Which one's did you delay? Which did you delegate? Did you make use of your secretary? Did the attention given boss-related items differ markedly from other items? Did you cluster similar types of activities such as call-backs and appointments? How much time did you allocate to collect necessary information? Did you first review the entire list before starting your flurry of scheduling activities? Finally, how does the time you allocated and the nature of your scheduling relate to the major results you listed?

There are no right or wrong answers to this exercise. However, there are some right ways to go about managing such a day as that described in the exercise. And that's what the remainder of this chapter is all about.

OBJECTIVE 1 TO CONDUCT A JOB ANALYSIS

What is the job of the supervisor? The first step in getting control is to clearly identify the functions and tasks of the position—those things the supervisor gets paid for doing; those things for which the supervisor "has a carpet on the floor and a title on the door."

Probably no position is so variously defined as that of the supervisor. Textbook definitions are of only meager help; these tend to be general in nature, direction setting to a degree, but inadequate and often far too ambiguous to provide much analytic help. Moreover, individual school districts, even those with well-developed position descriptions, vary in the interpretation of the supervisor's operational role. Thus, there is a need to clarify what it is that the individual supervisor is supposed to accomplish.

An Exercise in Job Clarification

On a sheet of paper entitled "Tasks and Functions Central to the Job of the Supervisor," list the important functions of the job.[2] Be as specific as you can. List tasks that you feel are critical to the job—those for which the state has determined you must have a certificate. State these without worrying about grammar, syntax, or literary flow, allowing yourself 15 to 30 minutes.

Next, on a separate sheet of paper, list other tasks that accrue to you as you go about your job. These aren't central, perhaps, but they are routinely assigned, and while accomplishing them may not require specific training or great expertise, they are tasks that must be accomplished. Somebody has to do them in order for the school system to function, and that somebody is, more often than not, you. For the supervisor these tasks run the gamut from typing reports, to arranging for refreshments for an in-service workshop, to a myriad of administrative responsibilities that could be perceived as being outside of the central instructional or curricular supervisory role. There are few jobs that don't contain some of these kinds of tasks. Few organizations are so well or specifically staffed, that persons aren't assigned ancillary duties from time to time.[3] Allow yourself another 15 to 30 minutes for this, again being highly specific.

After compiling the two lists, review them and consider work life in the "best of all worlds"—the utopian school. What percentage of your work day or work week would you *ideally* allocate to each of the specific entries? Write this beside each entry. (It's usually best to consider work weeks or work months, because some of the tasks probably do not recur on a daily basis).

Having done this, you now have a list of activities, tasks, and/or functions that you believe define your job. Moreover, you have taken the first step toward the most important aspect of time control—priority setting. That's what results when you consider the ideal world and allocate time accordingly.

The Real World Alas, it's not the ideal world and you do not work in an utopian school district. Go back over your list and now make a considered estimate of how much time you perceive you are actually able to spend on those tasks you have in both lists. This is your *perceived actual* use of time.

Are there discrepancies between the ideal *(I)* and the perceived actual *(PA)*? Are many of the percentages skewed in the direction of spending too little time on central tasks and too much time on ancillary tasks? It would be a rare individual who would not find this to be true.

The third step in this initial exercise may provide some insights into why this is so. At least it will provide insights about external impingements. Title another sheet of paper "Things and People that Make the Ideal Different from Perceived Actual." (That is, what is getting in the way?)

After completing this you will be able to picture your job, the time it is taking for the several tasks, and the nature of external impingements. Figure 3.3 depicts one supervisor's completed exercise using a standard format I

	Ideal %	PA %	AA %
I. Functions and tasks central to my job:			
School visits, including direct observation of teachers.	30	15	
Develop curriculum materials.	15	0	
Staff development activities, including planning workshops.	15	20	
Budget preparation and administration.	5	10	
Selection of staff, including interviews.	5	15	
Personal professional development (reading, attending conferences, etc.).	10	5	
II. Other tasks I have to perform:			
Administrator meetings.	5	10	
Report writing—local, state, federal.	5	10	
Collecting information for surveys.	0	5	
Writing proposals to secure external funding.	10	10	

III. What gets in the way:

Meetings I am expected to attend but have no real part in.
Too many useless reports, correspondence, memos.
Last minute requests from administrators.
Telephone calls; interruptions from staff; clerical chores; junk mail.
My boss.
No time to plan; false starts; can't say no.

FIGURE 3.3 An example of a completed initial job analysis instrument for one supervisor.

have developed for time management seminars.[4] Note the discrepancies between the two columns. The supervisor is not able to spend nearly as much time on tasks felt to be important, and for which he is held accountable. Moreover, he perceives himself as spending 35 percent of his work life on less central tasks! You will note a third column in the job analysis format depicted in Figure 3.3. This column is labeled *AA* and stands for *actual actual*, the most critical assessment, but one most people are unable to make. *Without it*, time control is not really possible.

Research about time management practices reveals that while most persons are aware that they are not able to use time the way they would ideally, they aren't even using time the way they think they are! It is this lack of information that most often contributes to an unsatisfying work life.

If we assume that the individual has described the major responsibilities of the particular position accurately—and this is an essential assumption—then it is necessary to find out where the time is actually going. As noted, research tells us that ex post facto perceptions cannot be relied on, and the next step in the process of getting control is to discover where the time is actually being spent. To do this requires a time log.

The Time Log Doing a time log requires hard work and strict attention, but it is absolutely essential for the individual who wants to focus energies on important tasks and avoid time frustrations. It is a data collection process conducted several times during a three- or four-week period. Basically, one divides the work day into 15-minute segments and records specifically what is going on at those intervals. I recommend that the individual select a different day each week during the period of time the data are collected in order to get the most accurate depiction of typical time usage. Tuesdays have a way of being different from Fridays. Moreover, seasoned time managers monitor their time regularly at different times of the work year. But, to begin, select any relatively short span of a few weeks and complete a time log for some days, at least three, in that span.

Figure 3.4 is a sample format of a time log that is useful because it requires recording sufficient information to allow more insightful analysis.

TIME TIP

Why Do We Have Time Management Problems?

1. We do not regard time as precious.
2. We respond too much to the desires of others.
3. We rely on crisis to motivate us.
4. We do not establish specific objectives.
   And 1, 2, and 3 occur mostly because of 4!

Once you have completed the time log, list the activities under the major and minor categories identified in your initial job analysis. Not surprisingly, you may have a number of activities that do not fit, so there may be a need to create other categories, or simply list these activities by specific entry under an Other category. Do not leave out any of the things you did; they took time to do, do not be apologetic about it.[5] Compute your percentages. How much time is allocated specifically to each activity and each category. Compare this with your initial time allocation column. Any differences? It would be most unusual if there were not.

Two questions need to be addressed. First, was the job accurately described? Perhaps your position description needs to be further analyzed and discussed with your boss. Assuming this is *not* so, why are you not able to allocate time more nearly the way you feel it should be allocated?

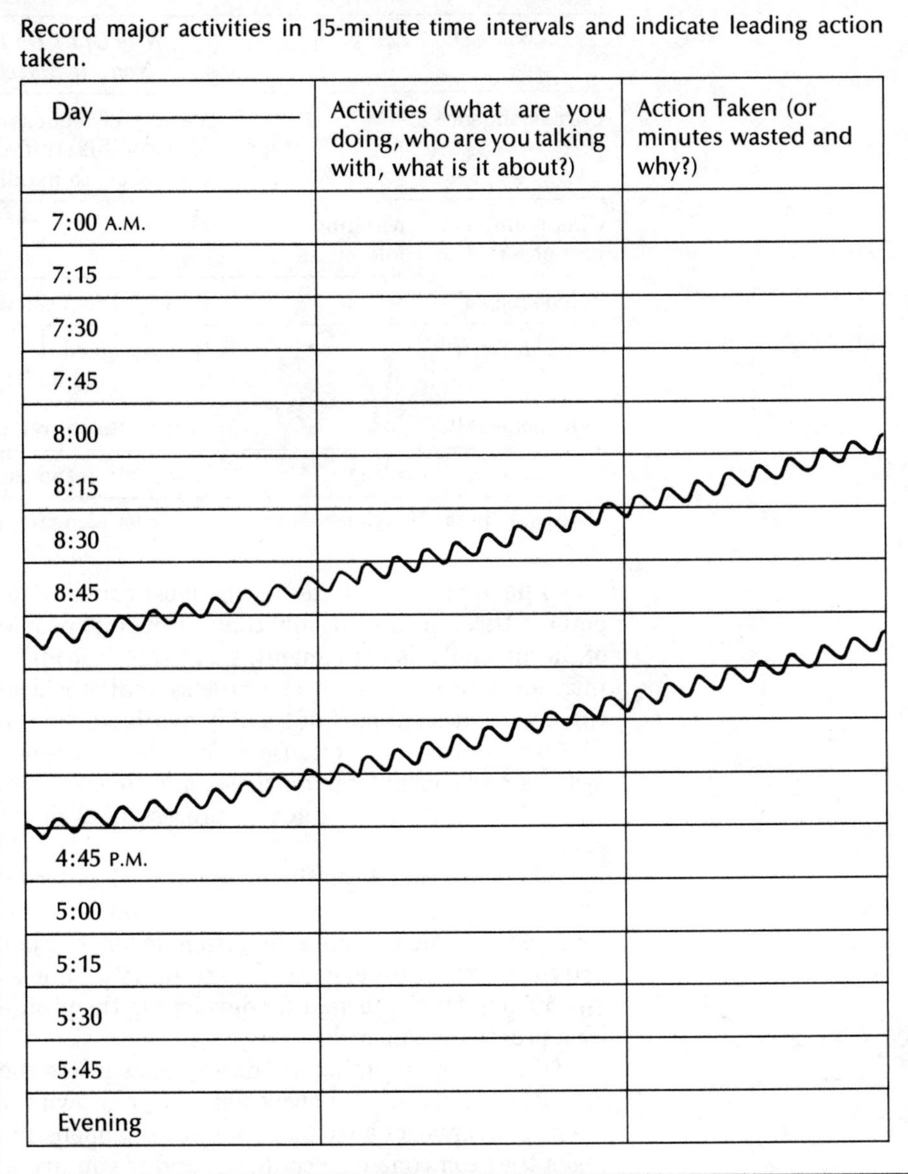
Record major activities in 15-minute time intervals and indicate leading action taken.

Day ________	Activities (what are you doing, who are you talking with, what is it about?)	Action Taken (or minutes wasted and why?)
7:00 A.M.		
7:15		
7:30		
7:45		
8:00		
8:15		
8:30		
8:45		
4:45 P.M.		
5:00		
5:15		
5:30		
5:45		
Evening		

FIGURE 3.4 Format for a time log.

TABLE 3.1 Sample Job Analysis Profile (Partial) Developed from Time Logs

What Did I Do?	*Why Did I Do It? Notes to Myself*	*Must It Be Me? Yes*	*No**
Attended personnel meeting	Office needs to be represented (could send asst.)		X
Open and sorted mail	Always have done it (secretary could handle)		X
Evaluation committee mtg.	Chair committee	X	
Reviewed evaluation reports	I'm responsible for recommending tenure	X	
Speech to Kiwanis	They asked me (next time suggest asst. or somebody else)		X

(Continued)

Table 3.1 *(Continued)*

What Did I Do?	*Why Did I Do It? Notes to Myself*	*Must It Be Me? Yes*	*No**
Correspondence	Variety of requests (some of this stuff routine; train secy. to handle)	X	
Classroom visits, including post-observation conferences	My job	X	
Telephone call	Principal requested lab	X	
Johnson report	Boss assigned it (Intern could do it)		X
Telephone call	Angry citizen, re: taxes		X
Staff in-service meeting	It was my responsibility	X	

*Every "X" in the No column means more time for high-priority tasks.

"I have too much to do" is the most common lament. Or, you may silently point to those organizational constraints and people you noted in the third part of the job analysis instrument. Don't say or do either of these things. This is an introspective process. In the professional world all of us have discretionary time, with at least part of the day available for self-determined central tasks. The problem is more often a failure to focus energies, to set reasonable objectives and concentrate on those, and to ask: "Why did I do that?" The final step in the initial job analysis process is to develop a personal job analysis profile.

Select any one day's time log. For each entry (What Did I Do?) answer two questions in order: Why did I do it? and Must it be me? The first question requires that you examine the rationale for your behavior; the second identifies activities you can delegate. Every no is a time-saving event. Table 3.1 (pp. 49–50) depicts the format for developing the profile with information supplied by a practicing supervisor.

Of course none of this will do any good unless you are willing to give up some activities. If you like to open and sort your own mail; if you like to have telephone conversations with anyone who happens to call; if you like to work on tasks that someone else could do; and if you are unwilling to risk delegation to others, then the development of a job analysis profile will simply be an interesting exercise.

THE TASK AND TIME ANALYSIS USUALLY REVEALS:

1. Others are consistently wasting our time (and vice versa!)
2. We consistently waste time because of inefficiencies in day-to-day activities.
3. We spend far too much time on unplanned and relatively unimportant activities rather than focusing on high-priority items.

Drawing the Job Circle Think of all of the tasks and functions that must be performed in order to have effective, well-managed instructional and curricular programs. Are you required to perform all of those tasks and functions? Of course not. Others, with other specialties, skills, and responsibilities have roles to play in accomplishing the program. There is a need, thus, to determine those tasks that are absolutely essential to the performance of your role. Draw a circle around those and let other people accomplish the less central activities that fall outside the circle. The other people may include secretaries, assistants, colleagues, and even bosses, if you are especially adroit and perseverant. More about this later in the chapter. Perhaps, too, some of those things you've been doing that fall outside the circle simply do not have to be done at all.

The concentric circle diagram depicted in Figure 3.5 may help. The inner circle of the target contains essential activities of the job—the things a particular supervisor is responsible for and must do. Even within this circle there may be aspects of various activities that someone else can attend to. For example, collecting background information and first-draft proposals, among other necessary beginning and supporting activities, might be delegated to others, even though final responsibility for a project is the supervisor's.

As one progresses outward from the inner circle the activities become less central to the supervisor's main responsibilities and more clearly must become someone else's, if they are to be done at all. The second circle contains things that you "could do." Of course you could do these—you're smart, have probably done those things yourself on your "way up;" *but* these are activities that should be delegated. Within the third circle are activities the particular supervisor must not do. These activities either belong in someone else's bailiwick, are activities for which you have no skills, or are things that are unnecessary for anyone to do. The supervisor must never do third-circle activities and only in emergencies do second-circle activities. If the supervisor's analysis reveals that much time is being devoted to second-circle activities, something is wrong.

The most frequent causes of devoting too much time to second- or third-circle activities are failure to focus energies and failure to delegate. In either case, the supervisor spends days (and nights and weekends) performing other people's work, or work that doesn't need to be performed at all, and is left at the end of the day, week, month, year with an underdeveloped staff and a mountain of deskwork that keeps getting larger.

Probably no professional group has been able to avoid functioning outside the first circle of responsibility as well as physicians. Even a cursory observation of persons as they go about their assigned activities in the typical physician's office is sufficient to illustrate the point. A series of questions may lend clarity.

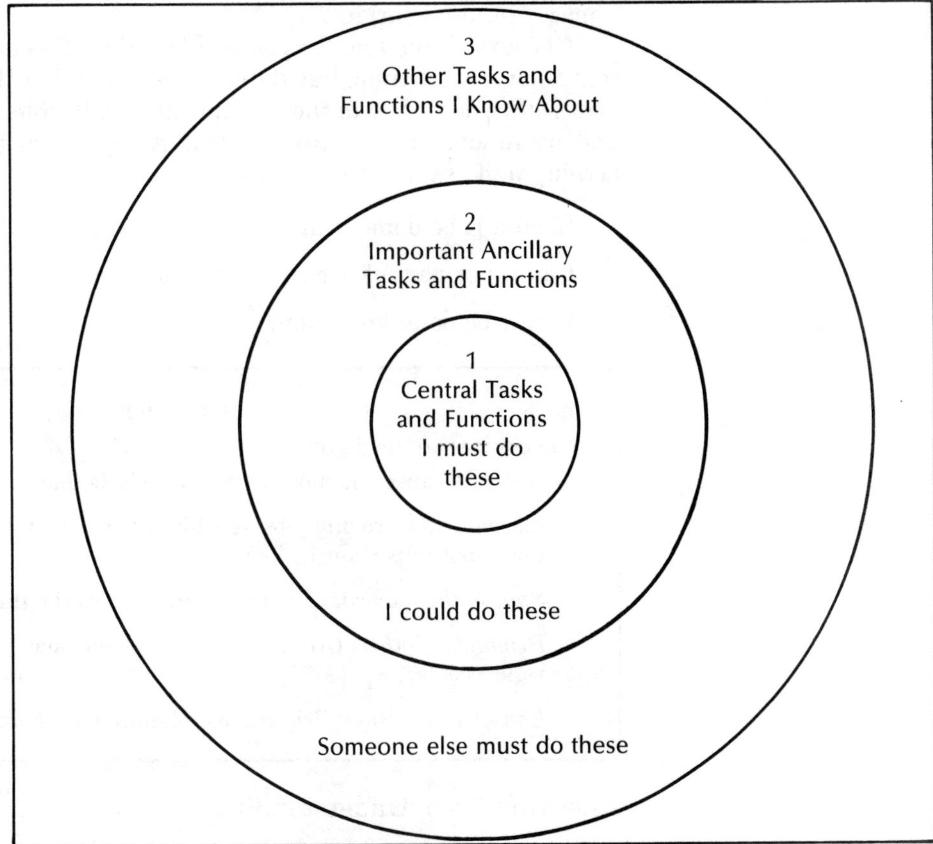

FIGURE 3.5 Responsibility circles.

1. *Does the physician take the initial phone call?* No, *and* the person who does also has the authority to determine *if* the physician can see the caller and *when.*

2. *When a patient arrives at the office, does the physician greet the person and invite the person in?* No, a receptionist does this and collects other information for the file to facilitate billing and continuing case history.

3. Ultimately, the patient is invited to an examining room. *Does the physician participate in this?* No; it is probably a nurse who also is responsible for further data collection. Questions such as "What seems to be the trouble?" "How long have you had it?" are asked and responses recorded for the file. Moreover, aspects about the patient's physical condition requiring specific technical skills are noted. For example the nurse may perform a blood test (later another medical specialist—a lab technician—will be involved in this), check blood pressure, take a body temperature reading, and record height and weight, among a number of other technical tasks. All of this is necessary for a good diagnosis and prescription but none of it has been performed by the physician. The patient has not been seen by the physician yet! After all of this occurs, the nurse places the folder outside the examination cubicle, at a convenient height and bids the patient farewell.

4. At this point, the patient is about to enter the physician's "inner circle," but it is not until all of the other specialists and support personnel have performed the tasks that are in their inner circle that the physician appears to do his or her specific task: diagnosis and prescription.

5. *Could the physician have answered the phone?* Yes, and as a result he or she would have been able to see one less patient that day or work later into the evening. *Could the physician have maintained the records?* Yes. *Could the physician have taken the patient's temperature, blood pressure, etc.?* Yes.

Because the physician in the example was able to organize the work, structure the tasks of others and focus energies only on the essential elements of his or her job, it was possible to see many more patients and maximize the impact of those energies.

Of course it may not be possible for all professionals to have this degree of control over worktime, but the principles guiding the operation of the physician's office described in the example are applicable to any professional setting and are fundamental to time control. A supervisor needs to examine each job activity and ask three questions:

Should it be done at all?

Can all or part of it be delegated and to whom?

Can it be done less often?

TIME CHOICES

Time choices are made by:

Habit (Because you have always done it, is that reason to continue doing it?)

Escapism (Overdoing jobs you like or socializing is a way of avoiding the tough but important tasks.)

Spur of the moment (The urgent overcomes the important.)

Demands of others (Are those demands legitimate; are you responding to the right people?)

Conscious decision (Prioritizing, planning, organizing, implementing.)

Assessing Your Understanding

In the normal format of this book you would now be asked to take a mastery test to assess your understanding of Objective 1. However, because of the highly integrated nature of the chapter objectives and the chapter's emphasis on application to your own job situation rather than test situations, mastery tests after each objective do not appear. Instead, there is one final mastery test at the end of the chapter. To assess how you are doing along the way before you reach the mastery test, compare your responses to the various simulations and exercises that you are asked to complete with the guidelines and examples presented in the chapter.

OBJECTIVE 2 TO DETERMINE THE DIFFERENCE BETWEEN MANAGING AND DOING, AND TO APPLY THE KATZ MODEL TO INSTRUCTIONAL SUPERVISION

A fundamental concept of management and supervision is that executives must not confuse managing with doing. The essence of supervision (and management) is to structure work in such a way that others are performing the routine, though essential, operational tasks. Managing, thus, is not doing; it is seeing to it that things get done.

Frequently, efficiency is confused with effectiveness. Efficiency is doing things well; effectiveness is getting the *right* things done well. There is little sense in doing something well that does not need to be done at all or that can be done by someone else. The supervisor who insists on doing as opposed to organizing, planning, and structuring the work of others is in danger of confusing sheer activity with productivity.

Household heads of happy large families have intuitively followed good management practices, and there are practical lessons for the supervisor or administrator to be learned from these household managers. Even small children in such families are given important chores to perform with mother and/or dad performing overseer roles and doing those things the children are not able to do until they are older or are trained. Of course it does require a willingness to take time to train others and to accept less than the "perfect" job the overseer would do. But, such practices do result in getting the right things done.

One of the hardest things most supervisors have to do is relinquish some of their activities—activities that someone else could and should do but which the individual enjoys doing and is also good at performing. This is not surprising. Individuals are frequently promoted in organizations because they have come to the attention of others by being skilled at tasks that are *not* central to success in the new job. The old tasks become like old, comfortable shoes. But continuing to perform them in addition to meeting the demands of the new job limits time to acquire essential new skills. Such an unwillingness to let go also leaves one with an underdeveloped staff and burdensome overtime activities.

> TIME TIP
>
> One Hour of Planning Will Save Hours in Execution
>
> The first 30 to 60 minutes of every day should be spent in planning activities by oneself or with a secretary. The upcoming day and remainder of the week should be organized with specific time allocations. Revisions in previous plans can be made at this time. Look for and allocate those large blocks of time needed for big projects. And follow the plan!
>
> If it's impossible to work uninterrupted in your office space, find a "hideaway." People will "muddle through" without you, for awhile.

An examination of the Katz Model will clarify the difference between managing and doing. Analyzing supervisory activities, Katz identified three general categories of supervisory skills: conceptual, technical, and human.[6]

Conceptual skills relate to the need for problem-sensing, problem-solving capabilities as a part of good supervisory performance and the need to perceive the relationship of seemingly disparate data as one engages in problem solving and futuristic planning. These activities involve organizing and planning, structuring the work of others, evaluating, allocating resources, and conducting research and development programs among other activities essential to the efficient and effective application of technical skills at the operational level of the organization. The need for and ability to see the "big picture" is how one supervisor described it.

Technical skills, as used here, relate to those specific tasks that have to do with the operational side of the enterprise. Into this category fit the specific "doing" activities that directly apply the technology of the business at the points of production. In schools, technical skills refer to the instructional skills that a well-educated, well-trained teacher employs with learners. It requires knowing how to make direct interventions that affect learner outcomes. (These skills are analogous to those of the graduate engineer who makes the line drawings and blue prints that translate a conceptualization of space relationships into a plan of action that ultimately results in a 75-story building.)

Human skills loom large in all aspects of supervisory endeavors and at all levels of the organization. To be sensitive to the needs of others; to be skillful in communication; to employ appropriate rewards; to stimulate and motivate one's colleagues, subordinates, superordinates, and clients are fundamental skills of good supervisory practice.

Figure 3.6 depicts a rendition of the Katz Model applied to instructional supervision. As a supervisor accepts broader and broader responsibility—for instance when one leaves direct classroom teaching and moves to an instructional supervisor's position, working with teachers rather than pupils—the need for the relative use of skills in two of the skill areas changes. The nature of the job responsibilities requires this. Supervisors who spend time applying or developing refined technical skills of teaching limit the amount of time available for planning, appraisal, and development and research activities, which are essential aspects of the supervisor's job.

Look at it this way. Being able to teach a child to read (a technical teaching skill) is less important to a supervisor than knowing about new developments in the field and being able to get help to teachers (conceptualizing) who do need to know how to teach a child to read.

To be sure, even as one assumes broader organizational responsibilities, there remains some degree of need for continued use and development of technical teaching skills. (For example, demonstration teaching, an activity in which supervisors frequently engage, requires very well refined technical skills.) Similarly, some use of conceptual skills is important at the operational level.

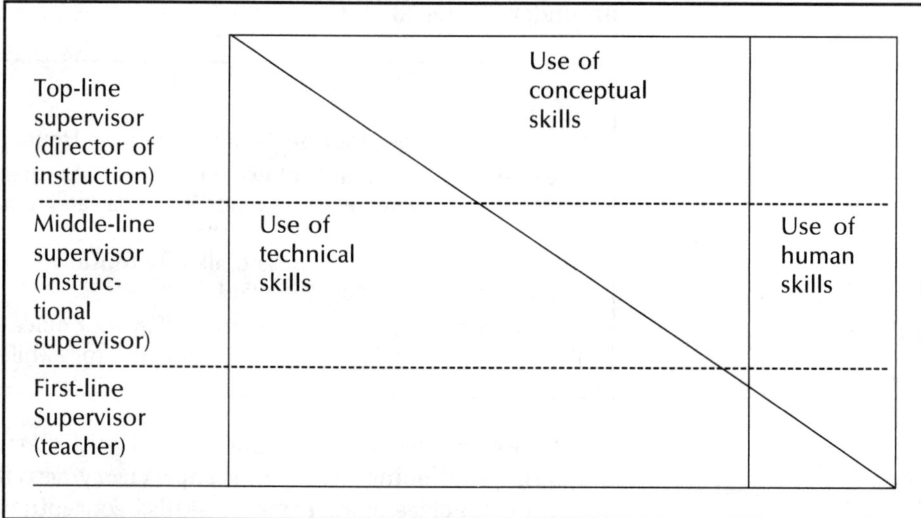

FIGURE 3.6 A rendition of the Katz model of supervisory skills.

The model depicts this, as well. There is never a complete absence of the need for either technical or conceptual skills. Rather, instructional supervisors must allocate their energies more in the conceptual and less in the teaching skills category if they are to be maximally effective and time efficient.

The human skills aspect of the model does not change in size regardless of the level at which the individual is functioning. While the persons with whom one must interact or be accountable to do change, the need to employ good human relations skills does not change. The specific practices required to motivate, stimulate, and communicate with children may differ from those necessary to motivate, stimulate, and communicate with subordinates, colleagues, superordinates, and parents; but the need to devote energy to this, and have well-honed human relations skills, does not change, irrespective of the position a person has in the organization.

Effective managerial and supervisory practices require the conscious application of the Katz Model if time is to be used maximally to meet the responsibilities of the job.

OBJECTIVE 3 TO SET PERSONAL GOALS AND OBJECTIVES AND TO DEVELOP STRATEGIES FOR ACHIEVING THEM

Few persons simply drift through life. Most have at least some general goals that guide behavior and the manner in which time is allocated. But for too many the goals are ambiguous and, moreover, too little effort is directed to maximum use of both nondiscretionary and discretionary time in the achievement of these.

Discretionary Time

To some degree, all of us have to do things that are requested by others, but no professionals that I can think of are required at all times to work at tasks others assign. And, no one's personal life needs to be completely reactive. It is with the planned use of discretionary time that the greatest control can be achieved, and it is in this dimension that many people reveal themselves to be their own worst time enemy. Discretionary time is often spent in random movement from task to task with little effort directed toward systematically accomplishing things that will make a difference in work and personal life. Moreover, the very manner in which work or personal activities are arranged often is contrary to good time management practices.

Interruptions rank high as an external factor that can destroy the best laid plans—yet many people spend a great amount of time interrupting themselves by failing to focus energies on the most important tasks.

The Pareto Principle Over a century ago the Italian economist Pareto made an observation that has been applied to virtually all aspects of human endeavor. He observed that 80 percent of Italy's wealth was in the hands of 20 percent of the population. Thus was born the 80/20 rule. So much of worldly activity can be observed to relate to the Pareto 80/20 rule that it provides a very useful time management concept.

For example, from a list of any ten items, pick the two most important to address and focus energy on accomplishing these. It won't matter much if the other eight do not get done because doing the most important two will accomplish 80 percent of the day's work. Not persuaded by this example? Examine the Time Tip box following to see if the other examples "strike home."

The point is that all of the activities one engages in *do not have to be done* in order to make one an effective person. Why spend time on low-output tasks? However, an individual is required to devote some initial time to arranging the tasks in order to make a considered judgment about which ones are more important. That is why one needs to spend the first 30 minutes or so of every day planning.

TIME TIP

The 80/20 Rule for More Effective Use of Time

80% of the file usage is in 20% of the files. (Keep these files handy, put the others in the basement.)

80% of the phone calls are from 20% of the callers. (Are they the ones you should be talking to?)

80% of the value of the meeting will occur in the first 20% of the time allocated for the meeting. (Does the agenda reflect this, i.e., are important items up first?)

80% of the interruptions come from 20% of your staff. (Are they the ones who should be seeing you?)

20% of the paper that crosses your desk yields 80% of the benefit. (Keep that other stuff out of sight.)

80% of the sick leave is taken by 20% of the staff. (Find out what is making them ill.)

And for Homemakers

20% of the carpet gets 80% of the wear. (Sweep that part; leave the other 80%.)

What's Important Anyhow?

"I have so much to do, there just is not time to do it all." This statement expresses a common lament. Unquestionably, there are periods in any person's life when this seems to be true, but even during the most frantic times a way exists to keep things in perspective and insure that at least the important things will get done. Each individual decides what the important things are! It requires that one keep the Pareto Principle (see Figure 3.7) brightly burnished, *and* that there be a basis on which the 80/20 rule can be applied. It takes planning and conscious effort.

Establishing the Framework Think about the rest of your professional career. What would you like to accomplish? What would you like to experience? Where would you like to go? What persons would you like to see? Take five minutes to think about this, and without worrying about syntax, grammar, or style jot these down on a piece of paper. This is a brainstorming exercise, so do not fetter yourself unnecessarily with real-life constraints or considerations about practicalities, probabilities, or "how's." Think expansively, get as many things down, large and small, as you can.[7]

Now set this list aside. It is the beginning of a lifetime professional goal statement, and you will be returning to it later. Using a separate sheet of paper and without referring to the first sheet, think about the next five years of your professional life. Where would you like to be? What would you like to accomplish in five years' time? What experiences would you like to have? Brainstorm this for five minutes. Don't be concerned if some or even many of the entries are similar to the previous list; many will not be, because you are focusing on a much shorter span of time. (You may notice a greater degree of specificity, as well.)

Set the five-year goal statements aside and turn to a third sheet of paper. Assume that this is the final year of your professional life and taking no more than five additional minutes, list all of the things you want to accomplish by the end of the year, big and small. Write quickly without concern for style. What would you do? What would you like to leave behind as your professional epitaph? The purpose of the final goal-setting brainstorm is to try to discover things that are really important to you—things that you feel would really make a difference.

Now go over all three lists. Circle the most important two or three on each list. Through a process of combining, modifying, and synthesizing arrive at 6 to 9 high-priority goals and restate these on another sheet of paper. You now have developed a series of professional and/or personal goal statements.[8]

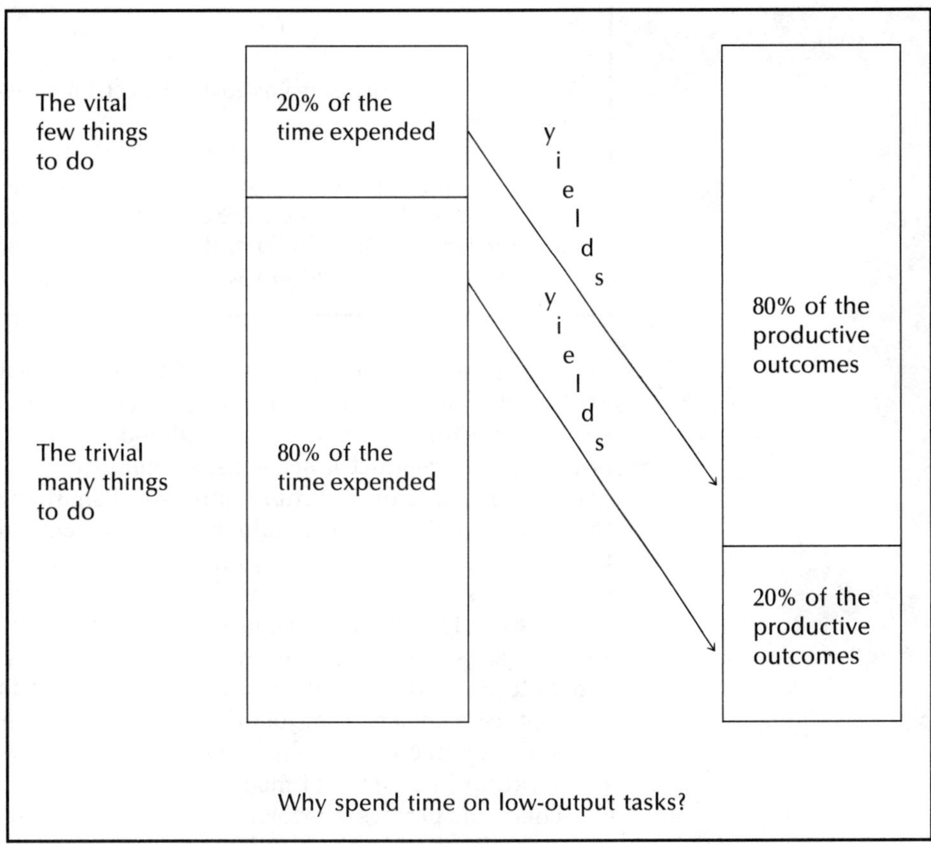

FIGURE 3.7 Pareto principle.

Achieving Goals But, stating a goal is not the same as achieving a goal. Without further steps at this point, you have simply uncovered some desired attainments. Goal achievement requires further analysis and a series of conscious self-directed activities.

For each goal you have determined generate a list of specific activities you believe will help attain the particular goal. (If this seems too much to do all at once, simply focus on one of the goals; you can return to the others later. But, do at least one goal, now.) Allow yourself 10 minutes for each goal to develop several activities that you think will get you there. (These are, in a sense, hypotheses: you think doing these things will result in movement toward the goal.) Accomplishing these activities shows benchmarks of progress and develops a sense of real movement toward a desired end.

For each goal, select three or four activities that you could reasonably accomplish in the next three months. Schedule on a calendar when it is that you will do those things—weekly, monthly, daily. These are high-priority activities. When you had a chance to think about it you determined these goals and activities. You realized the activities were important and would result in desired attainments. These are activities that have maximum payoff for you. Schedule them as you would any important To Do activity that is externally imposed by your boss or your colleagues. And, do not violate the schedule. A commitment you make to yourself is just as important—probably more so—than externally induced commitments.

For example, suppose you really want to become a director of instruction. You decide this is an important professional and personal goal—a high priority, so to speak. How will you go about addressing this goal.

What will it take? It will take some self- and organizational analysis and a determined list of activities, the accomplishment of which might get you there. If you need a requisite state credential to be eligible for a desired position, planning a university program could become one of several activities designed

TIME TIP

Big project to complete; major goal to be accomplished? But, not enough time at once to get going?

SWISS CHEESE IT!

Break large projects out into a series of manageable components that will ultimately result in the project's being accomplished. Specify when you will do these, put it on the calendar, and do it. (Include some 10- and 15-minute tasks, so that "waiting time" can be put to use.)

to achieve the goal. Or, you may decide that the way to acquire the necessary skills and organizational visibility is to develop a new curriculum or teaching strategy in your specialty area, to publish a journal article about an in-district practice, or to conduct a needs assessment.

Divide such a project into a number of smaller tasks and set deadlines for their accomplishment. Schedule these on your calendar during periods of discretionary time and you are on your way. Each week (Sunday night or Monday morning) list those tasks or events to be completed in order to meet your deadlines and make time estimates about how long it will take to accomplish the specific tasks. Examine your weekly calendar. When is this time available? Schedule the activity and do not violate the schedule.

A process such as that just discussed will get the important things accomplished and will create a self-motivating work environment. No longer will you be operating in a survival mode.

This same process of priority setting and time scheduling should be used for the supervisory tasks that are imposed by others; organizational priorities that the supervisor may or may not see as central to his or her development but are important to the school system and part of the job. For this, one returns to the initial job analysis form (see Figure 3.3). The functions and tasks detailed therein are disaggregated into a series of activities the accomplishment of which will meet the function. These are labeled "H," are scheduled on the calendar as commitments, and become the focus of the day's, week's, and month's energies.

Your task now is to reflect about the job analysis instrument completed earlier. Do the following:

1. Determine the important tasks that need to be accomplished in the next month or so as these relate to your job (relate these to a major job function or goal.)
2. If necessary, because of the overall complexity of the task, break down any of these events into steps that will result in the completion of the overall task.
3. Estimate the amount of time that will be required to accomplish these tasks or events.
4. Examine your weekly and monthly calendar. When is time available to do these things? Block it in. You now have a commitment (and a basis for saying no to any or all who come in with a spur of the moment demand on your time). Be sensible about this. Don't schedule events too tightly. Allow some "glide time" between events or appointments—15 minutes at least, so that there is opportunity for clean-up tasks, and to get ready for the next activity.
5. Determine where you will perform this work. Frequently the usual work station is the worst of all places to accomplish important time-consuming projects because one is too readily interruptible—by phone calls, by colleagues passing by, because there isn't a door to close—so find a hideout. A school library, an unused office, home, any place where

you are not accessible will provide the relief from interruptions that characterize most office activity.[9]

The Daily To Do List Most people are familiar with the To Do list—lists of specific daily items that one wants to get done or thinks should be done. Where many people go astray in the development of these lists is in failing to employ the Pareto Principle; that is, in failing to recognize that all things are not of equal importance. The only way to avoid the "activity trap" is to prioritize the daily action items.

> Most people get caught in the activity trap! They become so enmeshed in activity they lose sight of why they are doing it, and the activity becomes a false goal, an end in itself. Successful people never lose sight of their goals; the hoped for outputs.[10]

Label items on the To Do list according to their overall importance, given weekly and monthly goals and legitimate pressing organizational demands. During the daily planning period label and record those items of maximum importance H (high priority), those many remaining items M (medium priority) or L (low importance, less pressing, or could be delegated). Work only on H items and never work on an M until all of the high-priority items have been addressed. Most of Ls will probably never be addressed because you won't have time, and it won't matter—some of those things will never need doing; a few items will elevate in importance and become H. *Never* spend time on low-priority items; if you have only a few minutes before a meeting or before lunch and all of the high-priority items will require longer than that, it is better to spend that time just thinking about an H, planning or jotting notes, than to do a lower-priority item.

Figure 3.8 (p. 60) depicts one kind of daily organizer that capitalizes on the concept just discussed.

TIME TIP

The "Due/Do" Box

For those onerous, dull, routine things that must be done (time-and-effort reports, expense accounts, minutes, etc.) create a special drawer, file folder, or box. As these things come in put them in the "Due/Do" box and once a week schedule these to be done all at once—whatever time of week you are at your least creative—schedule it, do it, and forget it, until next week. Focus, don't spray your activities.

The Tickler File Many persons are afraid they will forget to accomplish certain job responsibilities in a timely manner and burden themselves with terribly long lists of future To Do's, writing and rewriting each day's activities to be accomplished in the weeks and months ahead; or worse, keep as constant reminders (interrupting spectres, really) all of those future To Do's out on the desk top. Aside from the psychologically devastating nature of such practices (How will I ever get all of that stuff done?) this is unwise because it serves only to interrupt current thought processes. "But, if I get it off my desk, I'll forget it" is the fear.

Judicious and systematic use of the *tickler file*, sometimes also called the *1–31 file*, will avoid the problem. The tickler file is simply a system for reminding a person of when a project or activity's time has come, and keeps these out of sight and mind until that time.

For example, you are advised of an upcoming responsibility or you receive a new job request—a report to write, an evaluation conference that will require analysis of a personnel folder, a speech to be made, or similar future activity. It doesn't have to be done now but will probably have to be addressed sometime.

TO DO TODAY DATE: ______________

Priority	Current Work	Deadline	Estimated Time	Results & Actual Time

When can it be done

Long-range goals

Personal, family

Phone Calls (name, purpose, number, address)	Correspondence

FIGURE 3.8 Daily organizer.

Make a judgment about how long it will take to prepare the item and put it along with any supportive materials into a folder marked for that day. The 1–31 label simply refers to 31 folders, one each for the days of the month. (Some persons also have a 1–12 series for subsequent months.) Each day as the supervisor arrives at the office, or late afternoon the day before if that is when the supervisor has the planning period, the file of the day is reviewed, transferred to the To Do list, and appropriately prioritized.

Sometimes a further, unanticipated benefit of this practice develops. It is not uncommon that some of these activities will never have to be done at all. Plans change, meetings get cancelled, "critical" issues often fade away and the supervisor may discover that it is no longer necessary to devote any energy at all to an activity that several weeks before appeared important.

The tickler file is simply a way of delaying action on an item until a more appropriate time, without running the risk of forgetting it. Estimated completion times require good judgment, of course, but judgments of this nature are fundamental to successful management.

OBJECTIVE 4 TO CONDUCT A PERSONAL TIME AUDIT

Our discussion to this point shows that to be an effective supervisor requires conducting a *personal time audit.* Figure 3.9 depicts the four steps contained in a personal time audit:

1. Identify and clarify the important job functions and record (time log) what you are actually doing. This is the essential first step. It is impossible to get control unless you know just where time is being spent.
2. Determine how the way you are spending time relates to the major functions of the job. This requires a job and time analysis. It requires honest answers to the questions: What am I doing? Is it what I should be doing? Am I the one who must do these things?
3. Identify crucial personal, professional, and organizational goals. Set and write down high-priority goals and the activities necessary to

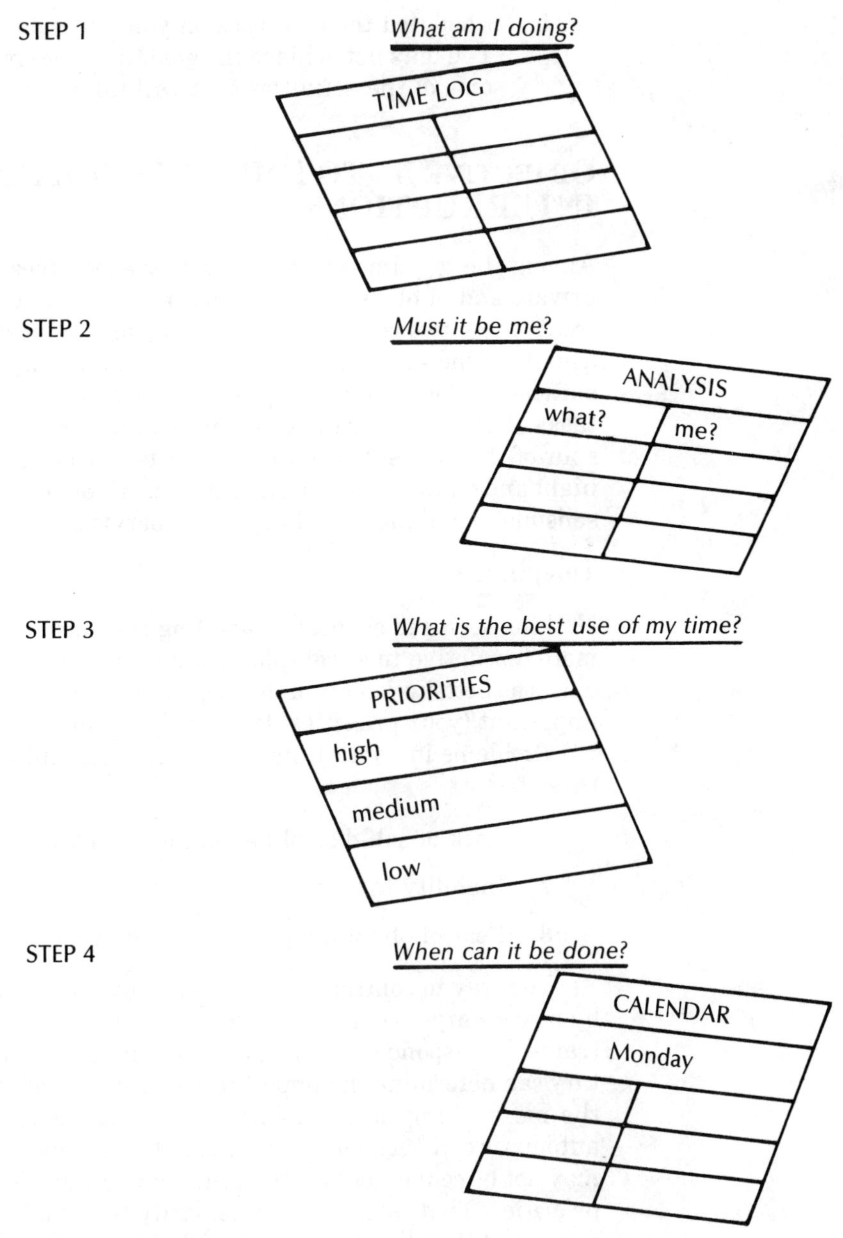

FIGURE 3.9 The personal time audit.

accomplish these goals. The focus is on high-priority goals only; use the Pareto Principle.

4. Calendar in high-priority activities. Relate these activities to the goals. Set time bench marks for completion and live by that calendar.

The remaining objectives of this chapter will focus on techniques and strategies for implementing these fundamental concepts. Before proceeding it is important that you have:

1. Completed the initial job, task, and time analyses, including at least three time logs.
2. Reached agreement with your immediate superordinate about the accuracy of your perceptions of your job.
3. Conducted the goal and activity development exercise.
4. Developed at least one of these goals with supportive activities.
5. Scheduled the activities on your calendar for the next several weeks. (You may not achieve the goal this quickly but you will have scheduled some of the activities that will take you there.)

OBJECTIVE 5 TO EMPLOY STRATEGIES TO AVOID INTERRUPTIONS

Among the top time wasters listed by executives and supervisors in both the private and public sector are drop-in visitors and telephone calls. Objective 5 treats these two common time impingements together because they are really aspects of the same general problem: an inability to control one's time so that sufficiently long, uninterrupted periods can be spent on the major supervisory tasks. Entire days can be spent reacting and responding to other people's spur-of-the-moment needs and requests, with little or no time left over except at night and on weekends for the supervisor's own proactive tasks. Applying a few sensible techniques will keep the supervisor in control.

Telephones

Nothing seems to be more compelling than a ringing telephone, and nothing is more disruptive to a well-planned day than a series of telephone calls. There exists no better example of the urgent (other people's urgencies) overcoming the important (your priorities) than indiscriminate telephone responses.

Problems in controlling telephone interruptions usually occur because of three factors:

1. Lack of self-discipline manifested by insistence in taking all calls.
2. Inability to terminate telephone conversations.
3. Fear of offending people by having calls screened.

The way to control most telephone interruptions is to provide intercession by a secretary/receptionist. Even a secretary shared by several people can be trained to respond to individual preferences regarding telephone calls. A secretary can determine the importance or urgency of the call and will know who is the most appropriate person to return it. Generally speaking I suggest an automatic call back for everything but emergencies. The timing of the call back may not be convenient for the initial caller but it's really a matter of balancing priorities. That is, it is not necessarily true that the caller's message is more important than the activity in which the supervisor is currently engaged. If it is an emergency the secretary's best response is, "Let me see if I can interrupt her."

This will tend to keep the conversation brief and provides a good exit line as well: "I must be getting back to my meeting."

Frequently, calls from superordinates have an assumed urgency, simply because those persons are bosses. A good secretary/receptionist can handle this adroitly by responding to the boss or the boss's secretary: "Dr. Witherspoon is in conference at the moment, would you like to have me interrupt her?" The ball is now in the superordinate's court; most frequently the response will be that the call is not that urgent and will elicit a "Just have Dr. Witherspoon call me when she's free."

It is best, where at all possible and sensible, to schedule call backs during two times per day: the half hour just before lunch for morning calls and the half hour just before closing time for afternoon calls. Aside from the focusing nature of such a practice, these are periods of time when one is less likely to get involved in long-winded conversations. The person being called will probably be eager either to go eat or go home.

When operating on the call-back basis it is good practice for the secretary to indicate to the caller that he or she will be called back *before* asking for the caller's name and number. This will help assure the caller that he or she is not simply being screened out as unimportant. And, it is fundamental that the supervisor call back! Personal policy, if not organizational policy, should be that all calls are returned within a 24-hour period. Anything less will result in a reputation of absolute inaccessability, inappropriate for any person but absolutely unconscionable for persons in the public sector.

TIME TIP

Analyze Your Telephone Interruptions

Each time you are interrupted by a telephone call, note the following:

1. Who was it from?
2. What was it about?
3. Did it need immediate attention?
4. Were you the one to whom the party should be speaking?
5. How long did the call take?

Such a practice, if employed routinely, will probably persuade you to:

1. Operate mostly on a call-back basis.
2. Train your secretary in the nature of your work, your work day, and how to refer callers to others.
3. Invest in a telephone answering device, if you work at home.

Drop-In Visitors

"Hi, gotta minute?" And, you are just about to lose the last half hour before lunch—time scheduled to complete the agenda that is due first thing tomorrow. Good time managers avoid the "gotta minute" syndrome with a variety of techniques including saying, "Gee, I'm sorry I don't really have time now; I've simply got to finish this by noon. Can I see you at lunch?" (Not a bad, albeit direct, approach, and the refusal was softened by setting up a later time to talk.)

Supervisors often unintentionally encourage interruptions by not following an "appointments mostly" policy and enlisting the assistance of secretary, subordinates, and colleagues in following it. Moreover, interruptions are invited by such practices as keeping the office door always open and the desk situated in such a way that eye contact is unavoidable when someone passes by. (Eye contact is the same as touching a person—it invariably requires verbal acknowledgement).

The following suggestions are time tested:

1. Give a secretary or assistant the authority and responsibility to handle all of your appointments. And don't interfere—have all requests referred to this person.
2. Close the door to your office. If the culture of your organization is such that closed doors are viewed with distaste, then schedule certain hours when the door will be closed and leave it open at other times. If your desk is in an open space or separated only by a divider, arrange the furniture so that eye contact is not automatic when you look up from your work.
3. Find a "hideaway" if privacy is not possible in your work space, and go there when you have a complex project to complete. (Many supervisors use the professional library for such purposes, but any out-of-the-way place will do.)
4. Note on the calendar the nature of a meeting so that you can be adequately prepared to handle a visitor's concerns without need for a file search or a follow-up meeting. If a secretary makes your appointments, have that person do this.
5. Have the secretary or an assistant (or a colleague) automatically interrupt any visit that has lasted longer than 15 minutes to remind you of another appointment. Learn some good closing lines and bring the meeting to a halt. One good way is to summarize briefly the content of the meeting, arrange for any needed follow-up, assign a responsibility, and then stand up.
6. Stand up immediately anytime you are interrupted with a "gotta minute." Keep standing and don't offer a chair. Shake hands and walk to the door with the visitor, keep walking out of the office with the visitor, and use the break to continue to the restroom. Make arrangements if necessary to continue the conversation at lunch time.

TIME TIP

Controlling Unscheduled Visitors

1. Keep a log of everyone who enters your work space to talk to you. Record the name of the person, the nature of the visit, the time it took, and whether the visit was a scheduled appointment.
2. Analyze this log daily or weekly to determine the pattern of and the reasons for the interruptions. Are the patterns of the unscheduled interruptions related to a time of the day or week? Close your door or be absent from the office in a work hideaway during these periods.
3. Are you violating your own "appointments mostly" policy?

The Conference Planner

Probably no other technique is so effective a time saver as the conference planner. It's quite simple to employ and its regular use will encourage others to use it as well. Figure 3.10 depicts a blank planner.

The names included on the conference planner are those persons you need to see regularly and frequently, either in the usual course of your work, or because of some current project. Each time during the day when an item arises requiring contact with that person, instead of running down the hall to see them or calling them on the telephone, record the item in their box on the planner. Usually such items are not urgent but something that has to be taken care of soon, and you do not want to forget it. Resolve not to interrupt that person until you have a minimum of three items in the box. At that point you make an arrangement

I need to see these people:		
Name:	Name:	Name:
Item 1 Item 2 Item 3 Item 4 Item 5	Item 1 Item 2 Item 3 Item 4 Item 5	Item 1 Item 2 Item 3 Item 4 Item 5
Name:	Name:	Name:
Item 1 Item 2 Item 3 Item 4 Item 5	Item 1 Item 2 Item 3 Item 4 Item 5	Item 1 Item 2 Item 3 Item 4 Item 5

FIGURE 3.10 The conference planner.

with them and *take care of all items at once*, making one interruption or visit take the place of three or more.

OBJECTIVE 6 TO EMPLOY TECHNIQUES OF GOOD DELEGATION

Delegation is nothing more than organizing self, subordinates, colleagues, and bosses to accomplish necessary work in the most efficient way possible. (Organize bosses and colleagues? Yes, it can be done—the previously discussed conference planner is one way.) Keeping the principles manifest in the responsibility circle depicted in Figure 3.5 clearly in mind it is possible to develop a network of mutually supportive working relationships.

Working with Subordinates and Secretaries

Earlier in this chapter you were assigned an initial job analysis task (see Figure 3.3 for example of this format). There is no better place to begin working with subordinates, including your secretary and any other support staff such as interns and paraprofessionals, than by having them complete this same instrument and share it with you. Complete one yourself for each of your subordinates and compare theirs with yours.

Doing the preceding will accomplish three important things. One, it will provide the supervisor with a picture of how the subordinate sees the job and may uncover some heretofore unexpressed interests and abilities. Two, it will uncover any discrepancies between the expectations the supervisor has for the subordinate and the subordinate has about the job's major functions and perfunctory duties. Three, it provides a basis for a good interchange of ideas about what needs to be done to get the work out.

Your Turn

List those major and minor expectations you have of your subordinates. (Use the initial job analysis instrument.) Have your subordinate do this for themselves as well. Is there a fit? If not, where is there not a fit and why not? Develop a joint plan about how a fit may be achieved and how to get the ideal and the real closer together. Pay particular attention to the third part of the initial job analysis instrument. Are there things you both could do to eliminate or mitigate the things that "get in the way?"[12]

It is not uncommon for supervisors and other mid-managers to share the services of support personnel and subordinates. This should in no way inhibit engaging in this exercise or the process described. Whether or not your fellow colleagues follow this practice is also irrelevant. Any secretary or subordinate will appreciate the clarity the process provides and it will help establish a most effective and rewarding working relationship. The supervisor's own satisfaction with the subordinate will increase—and that person's job satisfaction will increase as well. Job clarity, individual attention, and more responsibility are all motivators. And, importantly, the supervisor will find the work getting out faster.

TIME TIP

How to Handle Incoming Mail

The secretary should open and sort your mail into five folders:

1. Needs a response
2. Needs to be signed or otherwise important.
3. Other first class.
4. Informational and routing.
5. Third class, ads, conferences, magazines.
   Resolve to look at 4 and 5 no more than once a week

Keys to Delegation

First of all it must be established that delegation is not the indiscriminate dumping of unpleasant tasks. It requires the job analysis previously described as well as a willingness to train others to perform some tasks that fall outside the first circle, let go of what may have become pleasurable activities, and perhaps accept less than the "perfect" job that you would have done.

Essentially, good delegation is a three-step process: (1) find a capable person (subordinate or colleague); (2) set objectives to be accomplished by the task and explain how the task fits into an overall project; and (3) set a realistic time line and check back from time to time to see how things are going (but don't hover). Engaging in such a process requires trust that other people can perform competently and an understanding that they will be held accountable once they have accepted a responsibility. Within such a framework it is possible to delegate widely and frequently.

To get started in this sort of relationship with one's subordinates and colleagues, it may help to think of the different degrees of delegation that are open to the supervisor. The degrees of delegation extend from a very modest request that an individual look into a particular issue and provide information about it (this is a step in the right direction and it does save a little time), to describing an issue or problem and turning the entire matter over with no requirement that the individual check back. Figure 3.11 illustrates these two extremes and the degrees in between.

The supervisor's relationship with a subordinate or colleague will depend on individual abilities previously displayed on other tasks, the specific situation, and the overall risks. But one should never become immobilized by these criteria; the development of others is a prime responsibility of the supervisor. This requires some risk taking and a willingness to let others learn by doing. One will never know the degree to which others are ready for more responsibility without risking delegation.

Taking on the entire workload leaves one with mountains of paperwork, a full briefcase to be taken home, a packed office, a sweaty brow, an underdeveloped staff, and an early retirement. However, *the organization survives even if the supervisor doesn't.*

As tasks accrue to the supervisor and delegation appears to be the most appropriate action, it may help to subject the issue to an eight-point intellectual process:

1. What is the activity to be delegated: what are the objectives being sought and what are the minimum performance standards that are acceptable?
2. To whom might this activity be delegated?
3. Is that person able and willing to do it?
4. Is it to be a 100 percent delegation. If not, to what degree can it be delegated? How much feedback will be required?
5. What are the time frames relative to the activity being delegated?
6. Is there more concern with results than with method?
7. How much margin for error is there in results or time frame, or both?
8. What counseling procedures will be followed when mistakes are made?

Again, it must be said, delegation is not dumping, and managing is not doing. Putting these two concepts into proper perspective and applying in a sensible and sensitive way the practices discussed in this section will result in getting work out well done and in a timely fashion. It will also result in a supervisory team composed of productive, satisfied individuals capable of even greater achievement.

Upward Delegation

It is even possible to engage in *upward delegation*, at those times when the workload gets impossibly burdensome. Consider: A particularly troublesome curriculum problem occurs, leaving you as supervisor with little time for other essential tasks. You pass the boss in the hall or make a quick visit to the executive office. "Hi, Dr. Fishbaugh. You ought to know we've got a problem developing with the new seventh-grade social studies unit on Hispanic culture. The approved textbooks are not adequate and the ones that are adequate are not on the approved list. We'll need some policy guidance and help on this one. Jack has the information." (You exit.) Fishbaugh will have to look into the issue herself and the problem is now in her tickler file. (On the other hand, if you are Fishbaugh and one of your people does this to you, your immediate response must be, "Let me have your thoughts on this in some sort of written form by Thursday noon," and note that in your tickler file, remembering that: it is an important issue and your subordinate is responsible for delivering the goods to you by Thursday. Don't let that due date pass without accomplishment or acknowledgement.)

1. Look into this and give me the particulars. I will then determine the course of action.
2. Give me your analysis and recommendation for my review.
3. Decide and let me know your decision *but* wait for my go ahead.
4. Decide and let me know your decision. Take action unless you hear from me by. . . .
5. Decide and take action but let me know what you did.
6. Decide and take action. There is no need to check back with me.

FIGURE 3.11 Degrees of delegation.

There are times in a work year, too, when one does become overcommitted. When this happens as a result of too much delegation *from* the boss, or one more project is assigned and further delegation by you is not possible, there is no alternative but to secure help from the superordinate. The chances are great that the superordinate is largely unaware of the amount of work or the complexity of the delegated projects. (Following good practices of delegation, the boss has simply been locating capable people and showing a high degree of confidence in subordinate abilities).

An approach that is often used effectively is to go to the superordinate, indicate the several ongoing projects, and ask which one of them should be put on the back burner, if this new project is to be accepted. This engages the boss's participation in a priority-setting activity while reminding him or her of the other things that you are doing. It's a simple and effective technique, and will provide a basis for the right things getting done. It is not a way to avoid doing necessary work however and can be employed effectively only when in fact there is a serious overload problem.

There are also times in a career when one does have to work late and work weekends because of an array of crucial projects and extremely tight deadlines. The need to seize an unusually attractive opportunity for some external funding among a host of other fast-breaking issues or simple faulty organizational planning, will cause this. When this happens one addresses the issue and invests the time and energy necessary to get the job done.

Once through such a situation, however, there is a need to reflect about how such crisis management can be avoided next time. An organization (or an individual) that is continually operating on an overload basis is dysfunctioning. Moving from crisis to crisis is symptomatic of poor planning and a serious lack of priority setting.

OBJECTIVE 7 TO PLAN AND CONDUCT EFFECTIVE MEETINGS

Say the word *meeting* and listen for the sighs and groans from colleagues. Probably nothing is so frustrating to the instructional supervisor as the seemingly endless series of meetings to be attended. Three things are especially frustrating about meetings: they tend to be too frequent, too long, and too inclusive. Rather than facilitating work accomplishment, meetings too often become unwanted and unwarranted interruptions in what might otherwise have been a productive day.

Does it have to be this way? No. The prime purpose of every meeting ought to be to increase teamwork to improve output. By harnessing and focusing the diverse talents and considerable energy resident in the school organization synergy can be achieved. This can be accomplished by adhering to a few simple rules and procedures.

First of all, most meetings are too long, fail to exhibit the use of the Pareto Principle, and are not characterized by common sense about the nature of human interaction. Applied to meetings, the Pareto Principle simply means that 80 percent of the benefit of the meeting will occur in the first 20 percent of the time allowed for the meeting. It won't really matter much if the meeting is halted after that time, *if*, and it's a big if, the agenda is constructed in such a way that the two or three most important items are up first. Leaving important items until after the routine or mundane matters are discussed is the same trap an individual gets into by focusing energies on the low-priority items in an effort to "get all these little things out of the way, so I can really get down to work with a clean desk." That is nonsense, and results from a failure to set priorities.

Second, required attendance at meetings is too often indiscriminate. Does everyone in the shop really have to go? Does the supervisor have to go or would it be sufficient to send a representative? And, is it necessary for all participants to be there for the entire meeting or can some speak and leave? Only those people directly concerned with the subject or who have a need to know should be required to attend. Others may be welcome to come for all or part of the meeting, of course, but requiring them to do so reveals little concern for their other important duties. An announcement such as that depicted in Figure 3.12 should be sufficient. It keeps any interested parties informed, invites participation of any who are interested, but does not require attendance beyond the principal participants. It also clearly establishes the intended outcome of the meeting.

Third, a time limit should be set and adhered to. Meetings should start on time, end on time, and individual agenda items should each have an estimated time for discussion before the chair requests action. Nothing is so frustrating as 1:30 meetings that begin at 1:45 or later, while those who were prompt await those who are late. The chair's responsibility is to call the meeting to order at the appointed hour, no matter if all or even most are not there. Doing otherwise encourages late coming and violates the time of those who come as scheduled. (One must be sensible about this, of course; if most are not in attendance at the scheduled time, perhaps 1:30 is not a good time for a meeting.)

Fourth, any meeting worth having requires a printed agenda sent out a few days in advance. This will help insure that those persons involved have time to prepare any needed materials and do some thinking about the issues so that the discussion time will not be lost while participants collect their thoughts. The announcement of the meeting should include (a) the purpose of the meeting; (b) the date, place, starting, and ending time; (c) the agenda with any supportive informational material; and (d) the role each participant is to play.

Fifth, a brief report of the meeting, decisions made, and responsibilities assigned and accepted should be in participants' hands no later than 48 hours after the meeting. Copies of this should be placed in the tickler file of the chair according to deadlines set so that there can be appropriate follow-up. When a brief summary of the meeting, with assignments by name, is circulated in such a manner the chair will hear almost immediately if an error has occurred. Otherwise one must wait until the next meeting to find out that Sally thought "Bill was going to take care of that," and an important deadline may be missed.

The chairperson's role is critical. As designated leader of the meeting this person's behavior will determine the effectiveness of the meeting. If the chair is weak, does not adhere to time lines, allows rambling discourse, or violates the agenda by entertaining extraneous spur-of-the-moment changes, then the meeting is doomed. Figure 3.13 (p. 70) illustrates the fundamental rules for leading a productive meeting and summarizes this discussion.

To: Staff
From: John Croft
Subject: New teacher evaluation format: primary grades

All grade-level chairs will be meeting with me on Thursday from 3:00 until 4:30 in the conference room to discuss the need for an improved teacher evaluation process for the primary grades. The intended outcome of this meeting is an initial schema for such a process.

You are welcome to attend if you are interested in or have information about new teacher evaluation processes.

In any case, all will be kept informed.

FIGURE 3.12 Meeting announcement.

1. Plan and distribute an agenda ahead of the meeting (and stick to it).
2. Set a starting time, a time limit on discussion of items, and an adjournment time.
3. Start on time and stop on time.
4. Follow a format of (a) data presentation, (b) discussion, and (c) decision, and stay on the topic.
5. Control the meeting and keep the pace going.
6. Don't distribute a printed report or summary before an oral presentation. (If such a report is distributed, participants will read it rather than listen to the presentor make the important, salient points. Conversely, if the written report is sufficient, why take time with an oral presentation?)
7. Recap each issue and summarize action before moving to the next item on the agenda.
8. The chairperson's role is to force the group to a conclusion.
9. After the meeting, compile a brief outline of all action taken, who was assigned what and the deadlines set. Distribute within 48 hours.

FIGURE 3.13 Nine rules for leading a productive meeting.

OBJECTIVE 8 TO EMPLOY STRATEGIES FOR ORGANIZING PRODUCTIVE COMMITTEES AND TASK FORCES

A committee is a collection of individuals who, because of expertise and/or interest, have come together to develop action plans for resolving important issues. Whether the issue is the annual holiday party or a new curriculum, the emphasis in the definition is *action*. A currently popular term for a committee is *task force* and this is generally used because it seems to suggest action. Some organizations use both terms and in a definitive sense. Committee is used to denote certain continuing bodies of a policy-making or legislative nature; task force to indicate an ad hoc group, single focused in purpose and temporary in nature.

Structuring individual staff members into a work group to solve problems can be an efficient and effective way to move an organization forward. The rich diversity of talents resident in a school system needs to be capitalized on if creative solutions to troubling issues are to be realized in a timely manner. A few common-sense guidelines will insure productive efforts. The focus here is on ad hoc task forces although these same guidelines are also appropriate for more permanent deliberative bodies, and when applied with attention to the principles of conducting good meetings they will result in a good product and group member satisfaction.

First, before a task force is asked to begin its work, the group needs to carefully define its mission. At this time also the supervisor or whoever is convening the group needs to define the essential conditions the task force must meet and to identify any real world constraints. Real world constraints might include legal concerns, board policies, community mores, and budgetary restrictions, among others. Few task forces can operate completely unfettered, but failing to specify these important conditions and constraints up front may result in much misspent energy and time on a solution that cannot be implemented.

Second, the group needs to establish a time line for completion. This requires setting cooperatively some realistic target dates concerning the amount of time required for collecting data, generating alternatives, preparing final recommendations, and setting anticipated implementation dates. As a part of this activity certain responsibilities may also be assigned.

Third, the task force needs to know the extent of the resources available for the completion of the project. Possible line items here would be released time costs, materials costs, transportation costs, and any general budgetary commitment to new programs.

Fourth, the group should be fully informed about the expected outcome and establish the limits of the task force's authority. If the task force is advisory only this needs to be clearly indicated; similarly, if the task force will have wide decision-making authority, this too should be made clear.

TIME TIP

Shouldn't You Just Say No?

Does the request to take on one more task pass the following test:

1. How important is this, really (to me; to the organization)?
2. Can someone else do it with equal facility?
3. Is there a more appropriate person who should do it?
4. Does it need immediate attention from me or someone else (is it urgent)?
5. What kinds of information will be required to get the job done and from whom or where is this information available? (that is, how complex is this task going to be?)
6. What will happen if nothing is done?

SUMMARY

This chapter has focused on fundamental concepts of time management and the techniques by which the concepts can be put into daily operation. Not one of these techniques should be used slavishly, with the important exceptions of priority setting and the application of the 80/20 rule. Priority setting activities and the Pareto Principle are basic. Time management provides a framework for a productive personal and professional life and allows people to participate fully and richly in those activities that are really rewarding and stimulating.

A good time manager deplores mechanical behavior and great rigidity. Resoluteness should not be confused with unthinking robotic behavior; good time management practices are to release, not to constrain, the individual. These practices should provide more opportunities to work in a relaxed manner with colleagues, teachers, bosses, and students; to feel the pulse of the school system; to see and be seen. Time consciousness is not license to disappear behind a closed office door and not be seen again until the next working day.

The effective instructional supervisor organizes time in such a way that the important and satisfying things get done in a timely way by those best suited to do them.

The concepts and techniques that have been detailed in this chapter are "time tested," but my experience as both a practitioner and a seminar director is that if these techniques are not put to immediate use, they will not be put to use at all. That is, while almost all individuals can quite readily accept the principles of good time management in theory, there is still recidivism for many. The key is to put the concepts and techniques into practice immediately. Don't fall victim to the behaviors manifest in the following statements

- I have too much to do right now; I'll start next week.
- I do the same stuff, but I do it in my head.

- I could change my way of behaving but it wouldn't help—my boss is the problem.
- I don't have time to write all those things down.
- It sounds great, but no one else does it, so how can I.
- It's o.k. in theory, but it won't work in practice.

This list could go on, but the point has been made. Rest assured, these statements are just excuses and nothing more. Time *can be* managed. The time to start is *now*.

Performance Checklist

During the course of this chapter a series of tasks were assigned. These tasks are intended to be developmental in nature with each one leading to the next time management concept or series of concepts. All of these tasks are to be completed. Use the checklist below to indicate your progress.

Simulation activity	____
Initial job analysis	____
Conference with boss ("This is the way I see my job.")	____
Three time logs	____
Job analysis document ("Must it be me?")	____
Lifetime, five-year, six-month goal list	____
Goals prioritized	____
Activities established for at least three goals	____
Monthly plan calendared	____
Tomorrow's (and next week's) plan developed	____
Entire personal time audit completed	____
Project document developed	____
Subordinate's job analysis in and discussed	____
Tickler file established	____
Conference planner developed	____
Desktop cleaned	____

If all of these steps are not completed, you are not completely in control. Perhaps a start has been made, but the important practices are not being sufficiently applied in a manner that will sustain the long-term usefulness of good time management.

Mastery Test

OBJECTIVES 1–8

You have just returned from a professional trip that has kept you out of the office for two days. It is now 7 A.M. and you have arrived at your office. On your desk is a stack of messages, requests, and other materials. These are noted in Figure 3.14. Your immediate staff includes a secretary, a professional subordinate and a part-time intern. Do the following:

1. Review the material and take action.

_____ 1. Stack of mail that accumulated while you were gone.

_____ 2. Get theatre tickets—anniversary.

_____ 3. Schedule end-of-quarter activities to include personal conferences with each of the staff.

_____ 4. Eleven call-back phone calls which accumulated while you were gone.

_____ 5. Dr. Alex Johnson, the superintendent, left a note. He wants to see you as soon as you are free.

_____ 6. A note from your secretary that a Ms. Wilson has called twice about a problem and will be in to see you at 9:00 A.M.

_____ 7. The Phi Delta Kappa program planning meeting is at 2:00 P.M. (you are one of six members).

_____ 8. There is a staff luncheon meeting to discuss the new method for personnel evaluation.

_____ 9. Complete the evaluation of the ESAA project and revise the format for next year.

_____ 10. Call Ralph: tennis date for the weekend.

_____ 11. Deliver an overdue evaluation report to the assistant superintendent.

_____ 12. Read latest issue of *Educational Leadership*. Re: evaluation.

_____ 13. Jack Davis, the principal at Brown High School, wants to see you about the materials you were supposed to order two months ago. (They have not been delivered, he says).

_____ 14. Advise director about your vacation schedule.

_____ 15. Develop the agenda for next week's supervisory council meeting.

_____ 16. Lunch with spouse.

_____ 17. Write the proposal for personnel development that was requested by Dr. Johnson last week just before you left town.

_____ 18. Gift for secretary—it's National Secretarys' Week.

_____ 19. Write brief report about professional trip for file.

_____ 20. Note from secretary: There is an RFP for a federal grant for staff development. Deadline for submissions is next Monday.

_____ 21. Kiwanis Club called to remind you about your address at the luncheon tomorrow.

_____ 22. Note from Reverend Billings. Can you call him today about heading the membership drive? Said they really need you.

_____ 23. Note from secretary: Jack Davis called to talk about some teacher complaints and concerns, re: no feedback on your last visit.

_____ 24. Three of the principals in your district sent you a note wondering when you would be in their building next.

_____ 25. Wildwood P.T.A. would like to have you come out tomorrow night to be on a panel about teacher evaluation.

FIGURE 3.14 Notes, in-basket items, and activities of the day.

2. Describe how you would handle these requests and notes. Display this using the calendar in Figure 3.15.
3. Develop any other forms or formats that you think will be useful.

Begin at once.

Time	Notes
7:00	
7:15	
7:30	
7:45	
8:00	
8:15	
8:30	
8:45	
9:00	
9:15	
9:30	
9:45	
10:00	
10:15	
10:30	
10:45	
11:00	
11:15	
11:30	
11:45	
12:00	
12:15	
12:30	
12:45	
1:00	
1:15	
1:30	
1:45	
2:00	
2:15	
2:30	
2:45	
3:00	
3:15	
3:30	
3:45	
4:00	
4:15	
4:30	
4:45	
5:00	
Evening	

FIGURE 3.15 Calendar for the morning, afternoon, and evening.

Answer Key

Mastery Test, Objectives 1–8

Consider your responses to the task in light of the following.

1. Does your calendar reflect that the first 30 minutes or so of your day was spent planning the remainder of the day and week?
2. Were your call backs grouped for two appropriate times of the day? Give yourself an extra pat on the back if these two times were immediately prior to lunch and immediately prior to leaving for the day.
3. Did you develop a conference planner and fill it in? Was your secretary's name on the planner?
4. Does your initial To Do list reflect priority setting?
5. Do your calendar or other forms indicate how you used your subordinates? How did you decide on these assignments. How did you make use of the supervisor's delegation chart and the degrees of delegation chart? Explain.
6. Did you ask your secretary to tell you what all of those people wanted to talk to you about *before* calling back or seeing them?
7. Did you develop a tickler file for the items you were delaying or delegating?
8. Did you have your secretary open and sort your mail according to the system described in the time tip about incoming mail?
9. What use did you make of the "swiss cheese" approach; the "due/do" box?
10. How did you handle the Phi Delta Kappa meeting? Did you go? Send a representative? Cancel? Arrange to speak and leave? Why did you do what you did?
11. How did you decide about the luncheon conflict? Was this consistent with your priorities?
12. Did you ensure taking care of important personal needs such as the tennis date; the theatre?
13. Did you allocate time to work on the proposal for personnel development (item 17) *before* you met with Dr. Johnson (item 5)? Too bad. Johnson wanted to see you to tell you he had assigned it to someone else in your absence.
14. Did you schedule evening activities on this day? If so, maybe it was necessary, but don't make a habit of it.
15. Finally, compare and contrast your responses to this exercise with the responses you made when you first completed it at the beginning of the chapter.

What It All Means

The responses to these questions with supportive documentation will tell you the degree to which you have assimilated and can use the concepts presented in the chapter:

1. If you made little or no use of your subordinates, you should reread the section on delegation, rethink this process, reanalyze the day's activities, and amend your calendar accordingly.
2. If no priority setting is apparent on your calendar or To Do list—or if you did not develop a To Do list—return to the sections of the chapter where these important concepts were discussed, read those sections again, and prepare such a priority list.

3. If you did not establish a tickler file, reread that section and prepare such a file, indicating which items you are putting in it and to what date these items are being delayed and why.
4. If you did not develop a conference planner do some rereading and develop such a planner for this day. Fill it in.

NOTES

1. Nevertheless, while this chapter will not endeavor to provide more technical skill and professional knowledge about the jobs of the supervisor, implementing the practices will provide more time for professional study and skills development.

2. If you are not now a supervisor, do this same exercise for the job you do hold. The concept to be explored is applicable to any position.

3. Teachers, for example, keep attendance and other records, collect money for this or that activity, supervise lunch rooms and play grounds, and so forth, none of which is central to the task of helping children learn or would require a degree and certificate to perform adequately.

4. It is useful for many at this stage to verify their perception of their job with a superordinate and a colleague. Is your perception of the job in the ideal setting consistent with your boss's? If not, you need to address this immediately and to clarify organizational expectations. There is little sense in performing tasks the organization does not expect you or pay you to perform. Achieving congruence between superordinate and self expectations is essential to a productive work life.

5. It is likely that at least some part of each day you were occupied in socializing or taking care of personal needs and these will appear in your log. These activities are normal; one spends time with colleagues or personal activities in the usual course of any day.

6. R. L. Katz, "Skills of An Effective Administrator," *Harvard Business Review* (Jan.-Feb. 1975).

7. This exercise can be employed in all aspects of life, not just the professional side. One should set long-range goals for whatever phases of life one deems important—career, family, financial success, spiritual, and so forth. In fact you may care to approach this exercise from the broad perspective, rather than limiting it to just your professional side. Conceptually, this process is based on the process suggested by Alan Lakein in his book *How to Get Control of Your Time and Life* (New York: Peter H. Wyden, 1973).

8. This process should be a regular yearly activity. Goals are achieved or change; interests change. The list should be subject to modification over time.

9. Research has shown that the average amount of time a professional works uninterrupted is eight minutes! (Secretaries get three minutes—and bosses do it to them.) This is not sufficient time to accomplish much of anything, and getting back to the task at hand after being interrupted often requires a few minutes, all of which means there aren't even eight minutes left until the next interruption.

10. G. S. Odiorne, *Management and the Activity Trap* (New York: Harper and Row, 1974), p. 6.

11. Telephone courtesy is a two-way street. When calling another person, avoid the conventional opening line, "Are you busy?" The only polite response to this is "No." Instead ask, "Are you in a meeting?" This direct question provides the respondent with an out and an opportunity to set up a call back.

12. Once again, even if the reader is not yet a supervisor or manager and has no subordinates, this exercise still can be completed using either colleagues or family members. Any continuing situation where roles differ and expectations vary may be analyzed this way.

REFERENCES

Ashkenas, R. "Managers Can Avoid Wasting Time." *Harvard Business Review*, vol. 60, no. 3 (May-June 1982): pp. 98–104.

Cross, R. "How to Beat the Clock: Tips on Time Management." *National Elementary Principal*, vol. 59 (March 1980): pp. 27–30.

Halverson, D.E. *Time Management.* Redwood City, Calif.: San Mateo County Office of Education, 1981.

Hughes, L.W. "Time Management Problems of Instructional Supervisors." *Catalyst for Change*, vol. 13, no. 1: 21–25.

Hughes, L.W., and G. C. Ubben. "The Effective Management of Time." In *The Secondary Principal's Handbook: Guide to Executive Action*. Boston: Allyn and Bacon, 1980. Ch. 24.

Hughes, L. W., and G. C. Ubben. "Managing Executive Time." In *The Elementary Principal's Handbook: Guide to Effective Action*. Boston: Allyn and Bacon, 1984. Ch. 23.

Lakein, A. *How to Get Control of Your Time and Life*. New York: Peter H. Wyden, 1973.

Lane, J.J. "Is this Meeting Necessary? An Application of Decision Theory." *NASSP Bulletin*, vol. 65, no. 446 (September 1981): pp. 85–89.

Ordione, G. *Management and the Activity Trap*. New York: Harper and Row, 1974.

Scott, D. *How to Put More Time in Your Life*. New York: Rawson Wade, 1980.

Spillane, R.R. "Management by Objectives (or) I'll Try to Find Time to Observe More Teachers Next Year." *Phi Delta Kappan*, vol. 58, no. 8 (April 1977): pp. 624–626.

Wedman, J. "Time Management and Instructional Supervision. *The Clearing House*, vol. 55, no. 7 (March 1982): pp. 287–299.

Youngs, B.B. "With Time Management Skills Schools Can Offer More Instructional Time at No Cost." *NASSP Bulletin*, vol. 66, no. 454 (May 1982): 49–51.

OBSERVATION SKILLS

4

James M. Cooper

Objective 1 To identify potential problems related to classroom observation
Objective 2 To develop behavioral indicators for a given area of teacher interest or concern
Objective 3 To distinguish between descriptive and judgmental statements
Objective 4 To identify different techniques for collecting observational data, and to describe the strengths and weaknesses of each
Objective 5 To identify the functions of three different types of observation instruments, and to identify how specific examples of each type are used
Objective 6 To select or construct appropriate observation instruments for a given area of teacher interest or concern

INTRODUCTION

One of the most commonly accepted functions of supervisors is the observation of teachers. Supervisors observe teachers for two purposes: (1) to collect descriptive data on classroom behavior to help teachers make decisions about aspects of their teaching that they want to maintain or change; and (2) to evaluate teachers' effectiveness. The first purpose will be the focus of this chapter, while the second purpose will be considered in Chapter 6, "Teacher Evaluation Skills."

If supervisors are to help teachers improve instruction by modifying their behaviors, then teachers need to examine data that reflect their classroom actions and those of their students. Because teachers have personal concerns regarding their teaching, the data collected must be relevant to these concerns. Supervisors must collect data that describe as validly and reliably as possible what happens in the classroom, allowing teachers to make judgments and decisions regarding their effectiveness as teachers. Supervisors, therefore, must be skilled in using different observational techniques and in developing observation instruments that will yield those data pertinent to the teacher's interests and concerns.

The observation of teaching does not occur in a vacuum; it is usually preceded by certain actions and followed by others. Ideally, the supervisor and the teacher meet prior to the actual classroom observation to discuss the lesson to be observed, identify the teacher's intentions, areas of interest or concern; and decide what kind of information or data are needed. Following the observation, the supervisor and the teacher meet again to examine the observational data, analyze their meaning, and determine what actions the teacher wants to take next. In this process the supervisor must demonstrate knowledge and skill in the areas of human relations, interpersonal communication, motivation, leadership, and planning, as well as observation, if the process is to operate effectively. While these other areas are treated in other chapters, we now turn to the knowledge and skills necessary for effective observation of classroom behavior.

OBJECTIVE 1 TO IDENTIFY POTENTIAL PROBLEMS RELATED TO CLASSROOM OBSERVATION

Classroom observation is a deceptively complex process, although at first glance it may seem rather simple. After all, the supervisor only has to go into the classroom, observe what is going on, and then tell the teacher what he or she saw, right? Stripped to the bare bones, this is what supervisors do when they observe teachers. However, in reality, the process is much more complicated than that. How does the supervisor know what to look for? How does the supervisor take notes or collect information? What if the teacher disagrees with what the supervisor believes occurred in the class? How can the supervisor or teacher discern the important from the unimportant happenings? These and many more questions can be asked about the observational process, each one revealing that classroom observation is not so simple as it might first appear.

In any process as complex as classroom observation, problems and puzzles are bound to occur as supervisors try to collect information. Knowing some of these problems in advance may help you to avoid them, or at least take precautionary steps to reduce their effect. To be forewarned is to be forearmed.

1. *Lack of agreement regarding what is to be observed.* Unless the supervisor and teacher discuss the particular lesson and reach an accord regarding what the supervisor is going to be observing and what information will be collected, problems will almost certainly arise during their postobservation conference. A preobservation conference, in which these issues are discussed and agreed upon, is critical to the success of the whole supervision process. It is difficult to see how much can be accomplished if the supervisor and teacher each have different agendas, goals, and expectations regarding the observation. As

self-evident as this may seem, the number of times that this problem arises probably makes it the most serious problem related to observation.

2. *Achieving a reasonable degree of objectivity.* The first point to recognize is that there is no such thing as complete objectivity. Each of us sees the world according to individual glasses whose lenses have been ground from our unique experiences, values, biases, and emotions. It is impossible to eliminate these factors completely. Also, many events occur simultaneously in classrooms and what we choose to perceive and attend to is, at least partially, the result of our past experiences and who we are. Having said this, should we just give in to the inevitable biases, prejudices, and values that each of us has? The answer is no, and the rest of this chapter spends considerable space trying to show you how some of these factors can be partially controlled. The point made here is that we should be aware that some subjectivity is always present and not treat our observations and collected information as if they were pure as the wind-driven snow and untainted by human frailty. What we see as truth may not always be perceived as such by others.

3. *Effect of observer or observational equipment on behavior of teacher and students.* Anytime someone or something new and different enters a classroom, that person or thing affects the dynamics of the group in some way. Your presence may cause the teacher to be somewhat more nervous, thus affecting his or her behavior. The students, aware of your presence, may turn their heads to see what you are doing. If you are collecting data using a piece of mechanical equipment, such as a video tape recorder, the teacher's and students' behavior will be affected. Therefore, you can never observe or collect information completely free from the effects of your presence. What you can do, however, is to become a frequent enough visitor to the classroom that your presence will not produce extreme shock waves among the regular participants in the classroom. You can also locate yourself physically in the room to reduce your obtrusiveness and to stay out of the students' direct line of sight.

4. *Improper preparation for observation.* Even if the supervisor and teacher have reached agreement on the focus of the observation, the supervisor may find that once in the classroom he or she is unprepared for what happens. For example, the supervisor may have thought he or she knew what to observe and what data to collect, only to discover that the agreement had been too general. Or the supervisor may realize that he or she had agreed to collect too much data and had overcommitted him- or herself. Before going into the classroom to collect data be certain that you know the specific behaviors you will be observing, how you are going to collect those data, and your own capabilities in terms of how much information you can reasonably collect.

5. *Generalizing from an inadequate sample of behavior.* Supervisors are busy people, and often their visits to individual teachers' classrooms do not occur as frequently as they might like. As a result, supervisors may be tempted to treat the times they do visit as being typical of what happens in the classroom all the time, which may or may not be the case. Before coming to a conclusion that the sample of classroom behavior you saw was typical, you should try to visit on other occasions to collect additional data to see if patterns of behavior exist. There is no sense spending valuable time examining data and working with the teacher on a problem or issue that is unlikely to occur again.

Mastery Test

OBJECTIVE 1 TO IDENTIFY PROBLEMS RELATED TO CLASSROOM OBSERVATION

Identify five potential problems related to the process of classroom observation.

Answer Key

Mastery Test, Objective 1

1. Nonagreement between supervisor and teacher regarding what is to be observed.
2. Achieving a reasonable degree of objectivity in seeing and describing classroom events.
3. Minimizing the effect an observer in the classroom has on the teacher and students.
4. Being unprepared to collect data once in the classroom.
5. Generalizing about the teacher's or students' behaviors based on an inadequate sample of their behavior.

OBJECTIVE 2 TO DEVELOP BEHAVIORAL INDICATORS FOR A GIVEN AREA OF INTEREST OR CONCERN

One of the most threatening things a supervisor can do is to go into a teacher's classroom for an unannounced observation without negotiating beforehand with the teacher what will be observed. The teacher's anxieties are raised because of the uncertainties of the situation. A key assumption of effective supervision is that if teachers are to assume responsibility for their own growth then they must be the major determiners of what will be the focus of observations. It will accomplish little if the supervisor manipulates, cajoles, or threatens the teacher into accepting an observational focus of interest only to the supervisor. Starting with the teacher's area of interest or concern will be much more fruitful in the long run.

Some teachers make the supervisor's work very easy by clearly and specifically communicating to the supervisor those areas in which they are interested or concerned. These teachers have already spent considerable time thinking and analyzing their teaching and both the teacher and supervisor benefit from this advance introspection. However, it is often the case that teachers have not defined clearly what interests or concerns them. These teachers may know that a problem exists but may be unable to pinpoint the specific problem or concern. When this is the situation, then the supervisor must be able to ask appropriate analytical questions to help the teacher clarify as specifically and behaviorally as possible the problem or interest area. Unless the teacher and supervisor can define accurately the problem, concern, or interest area, any observation is unlikely to yield relevant data. The first and most crucial task of the observational process, then, is to agree upon the most useful and specific indicators of the interest or concern area. This is called *behaviorally defining the area of concern.*

Suppose, for example, that a teacher says, "I'm having problems with classroom discipline." The teacher might be referring to any one of many possible problems: there might be two or three specific students who continually bother their classmates; most of the students might be refusing to do their assigned work; there might exist a classroom clown whose antics disrupt discussions—and on, and on. . . . While the teacher may be very aware of the general area of concern, initially he or she may be unable to describe the specifics. The supervisor's first task, therefore, is to help the teacher obtain a behaviorally precise definition of the concern.

Instructional concerns typically involve two types of behavior: pupil and teacher. Sometimes pupils are doing things the teacher doesn't want them to do (negative behavior), or they may not be doing what the teacher wants them to do (absence of positive behavior). Similarly, the teacher may be doing something he or she doesn't want to do (negative behavior), or not doing something he or she believes ought to be done (absence of positive behavior). Questions such as the following[1] may help the teacher and supervisor focus attention on observable actions and determine behaviorally what the specific concern is:

1. What are the pupils doing that you don't want them to do? (What are you doing that you don't want to do?)
2. What should the pupils be doing instead? (What should you be doing instead?)
3. What are students not doing that you would like them to do? (What are you not doing that you would like to do?)
4. How many students are or are not doing it?
5. How often should the students be doing this? (How often should you be doing this?)

By asking questions such as these, the supervisor can assist the teacher to develop a behavioral definition of the concern or interest area. The specific pupil and teacher behaviors related to the area of concern can be identified and agreed upon. Please note that in this process the teacher must be satisfied that the behavioral definition accurately defines the area of concern. Only the teacher can make this judgment. The supervisor, on the other hand, should assume responsibility for assuring that the definition arrived at is a behavioral one.

Most educators have had some training in how to write objectives that are behavioral and observable. However, it is sometimes difficult to tell if the problem definition is behavioral. If you are uncertain, check the behavioral definition against these criteria:

- Are the behaviors specific, so they can be measured?
- Are the behaviors observable at the time they are being measured?
- Are the behaviors free of any evaluative component; that is, are they descriptive rather than judgmental?

When these criteria are met, you can be reasonably certain that you have defined the problem area behaviorally. If you must still ask the question, "What do you mean by. . . ?" about the behaviors to be measured, then your definition is still not behavioral enough. Further refinement is probably necessary if you and the teacher are to insure a clear understanding.

Let's take a look at an example of behaviorally defining a general area of concern. In the preobservation conference a teacher stated that he was worried that the students weren't understanding his explanations of new ideas and concepts. Furthermore, he noted that the fault was his, not the students'. The students did well in other classes, but in his class they made comments about how they didn't understand his explanations and how they always seemed to be confused. After some discussion the supervisor had ascertained that the teacher's basic concern was why his explanations were not clear to the students.

The supervisor asked the teacher to think of a hypothetical situation in which a teacher was explaining a new concept or theory to a group of students and in which the teacher was explaining the concept as well as could be imagined. The supervisor then asked the teacher to describe all the things he was seeing happen in this hypothetical situation. What was the teacher doing? What were the students doing? How were they interacting? As the teacher described the behaviors occurring in the situation, the supervisor jotted down notes. After a few minutes, the supervisor's list of teacher's behaviors looked something like this:

- Pronounces words distinctly
- Uses common words

- Gives examples and explains them
- Writes important things on the blackboard
- Repeats questions and explanations if students don't understand them
- Asks questions to determine if students understand what he has told them
- Lets students ask questions
- Talks only about things related to the topic he is teaching

Although this list could be expanded, it does reflect the behaviors that the teacher thought were important in explaining new concepts clearly. Note that each of these teacher behaviors is observable and measurable, and from this list the teacher and supervisor can develop a focus for a classroom observation. Acheson and Gall suggest that a supervisor can judge success in translating concerns into behaviors by considering the following questions: "Do I have enough information so that I can clearly observe the teacher's concern as it is expressed in his classroom?" and "Do the teacher and I mean the same thing when we use the term __________?" If the answers to both questions are yes, then the supervisor is probably using the technique properly.[2]

Mastery Test

OBJECTIVE 2 TO DEVELOP BEHAVIORAL INDICATORS FOR A GIVEN AREA OF CONCERN

For each of the following teacher concern statements identify behavioral indicators that might reflect the concern.

1. The teacher expressed concern about keeping the students interested and involved in the lesson. Identify five behavioral indicators of student interest and involvement. (The first two are completed for you).
   a. Students maintain eye contact with teacher.
   b. Students raise hands to be called on.
2. The teacher was concerned about keeping good classroom control. Identify five behavioral indicators of effective classroom control.
3. The teacher is worried that she is not being supportive or friendly enough to the pupils. Identify five behavioral indicators of teacher supportiveness and friendliness.

Answer Key

Mastery Test, Objective 2

The answers provided are only exemplary and not exhaustive. You may have developed different indicators. If so, check your answers to be certain that they are specific, observable, and free from any evaluative component.

1. c. Students volunteer answers.
   d. Students respond to other students' comments.
   e. Students work on assignments without distraction.
   f. Students answer teacher's questions correctly and promptly.

2. a. Students perform teacher-directed tasks and assignments promptly without back-talk.
   b. Students remain in seats unless teacher gives permission to leave them.
   c. Absence of teacher statements urging students to be quiet.
   d. Students remain on-task when teacher is called out of the room.
   e. Students raise hands when they want to contribute to class discussion.
3. a. Teacher praises and encourages students.
   b. Teacher smiles at students.
   c. Teacher rewards students for appropriate behavior.
   d. Teacher accepts and uses students' ideas and contributions.
   e. Teacher volunteers to work after class with students who need extra help.

OBJECTIVE 3 TO DISTINGUISH BETWEEN DESCRIPTIVE AND JUDGMENTAL STATEMENTS

"You spent too much time with Bobby during the lesson."

"In the 40-minute lesson you spent 15 minutes with Bobby."

If you were a teacher hearing these statements from a supervisor, is one of them likely to be more threatening to you or produce defensive reactions? If so, which one? What is the difference between these two statements?

The chances are you identified the first statement as being more threatening or defense producing. The second statement is a piece of information, while the first statement is a judgment. A judgmental statement is a personal evaluation, usually containing terms that are defined subjectively by the speaker. In the first statement, the term "too much time" represents an opinion, not a statement of fact. The teacher may disagree that he or she spent too much time with Bobby. Perhaps, in the teacher's opinion, Bobby needed the amount of time spent with him. Whose opinion is correct? The second statement, on the other hand, simply describes how much time the teacher spent with Bobby, making no attempt to imply whether 15 minutes was too much, not enough, or just the right amount of time. Furthermore, the second statement allows the teacher the opportunity to make his or her own judgment about whether 15 minutes with Bobby out of a 40-minute lesson was appropriate or not.

Separating the information or facts from their interpretation is a critical skill for supervisors who want to help teachers improve their instruction. Supervisors who do not make this distinction and who tend to be judgmental in their descriptions of classroom occurrences, do not usually succeed in developing a trusting, compatible relationship with the teachers with whom they work. This type of supervision often makes teachers feel that they are on trial, awaiting the verdict to be pronounced by the supervisor-judge. Keep in mind that if the observational report is stated in descriptive terms, a judgment about effectiveness or appropriateness can always be made later. However, if the report is judgmental rather than descriptive, the information or description is lost. Descriptive statements are much more objective and useful for supervisory purposes than judgmental statements.

Judgmental statements usually contain terms or phrases that are nonspecific or undefined. Some judgmental statements refer to a quantity, using terms such as *a lot*, *many*, *more*, or *enough*. Other judgmental statements refer to a period of time, for example, *often*, *frequently*, *seldom*. Still others refer to a quality that requires personal judgment, for example, *good*, *fair*, *warm*, *encouraging*.

Descriptive statements, on the other hand, are specifically defined. They state a measured quantity, such as a percentage of the students, all, or none; a measured time, such as 10 times in one-half hour, always, or never; or specific identification of what/who was involved, such as, "The principal stated . . ." or, "The test scores showed that. . . ."

Although this objective is concerned with the distinctions between descriptive and judgmental statements, there will always be gray areas. In fact, the distinctions between descriptive and judgmental data are not always clear. In many instances, descriptions and judgments represent opposite ends of a continuum, with some statements reflecting a "middle ground" or one that contains characteristics of both statements. The following examples illustrate this point.

DESCRIPTIVE	MIDDLE GROUND	JUDGMENTAL
Every student volunteered at least twice.	The students were on-task 85 percent of the time.	The teacher involved the students in the lesson.
Teacher said, "good thinking" or "nice try" 10 times during lesson.	Teacher praised students during the lesson.	Teacher was warm and supportive.

Keep in mind that our view of the world comes from our perceptions, conceptual frameworks, and previous experiences. There is no such thing as completely objective data. However, what we need to strive for is to make the data and information we collect as objective and descriptive as we possibly can, knowing that complete objectivity can never be achieved.

Your Turn

Read each statement and identify at which end of the continuum the statement most likely fits by placing a D (descriptive) or a J (judgmental) in the space provided. Also, circle the word or words in the statement that most influenced you in making your decision.

______ 1. The teacher is chastising the child.

______ 2. The boy is staring out the window while resting his head on his hand.

______ 3. The boy does not like the lesson.

______ 4. The teacher has his back to the class.

______ 5. The girl is confused by the teacher's explanations.

______ 6. The teacher was in a bad mood four of the seven days he was observed.

Answer Key

Your Turn

1. Judgmental. *Chastising* is one person's opinion of what the teacher is doing. The teacher may believe she is giving the child corrective feedback.
2. Descriptive. The only word slightly open to interpretation is *staring*. If the boy is gazing out the window with little head or eye movement and infrequent blinks, it is descriptive to say he is staring.

3. Judgmental. How does the observer know that the boy does not *like* the lesson? What is he doing? If he is making faces or talking to a neighbor, these behaviors should be described rather than inferring from them that he doesn't like the lesson.
4. Descriptive. Everything in the sentence is observable.
5. Judgmental. The judgmental word is *confused*. How does the observer know that the girl is confused? Instead of making this judgment, the observer should describe what the girl is doing, for example, asking a neighbor a question about what the teacher said, or scratching her head while making a quizzical face.
6. Judgmental. Stating that the teacher was in a *bad mood* is certainly a judgment. A numerical count does not make judgmental statements descriptive.

If you got five out of the six statements correct you are probably ready to take the Mastery Test. If you missed more than one statement, reread this section and/or discuss the objective with a teacher or peer.

Mastery Test

OBJECTIVE 3 TO DISTINGUISH BETWEEN DESCRIPTIVE AND JUDGMENTAL STATEMENTS

Read each statement and categorize it as being primarily a descriptive or judgmental statement by placing a D or a J in the space provided. Also, circle the word or words in the statement that most influenced you in making your decision regarding judgmental statements.

______ 1. The teacher talked to 14 students during the first 20 minutes of the lesson.

______ 2. The teacher didn't move around the room enough.

______ 3. The teacher was too harsh with Mike.

______ 4. The student went to the table, picked up a pair of scissors, and returned to her desk without speaking to anyone.

______ 5. The teacher spent time helping those students who needed help.

______ 6. According to the student survey, the students like science class best of all.

______ 7. The teacher's comments made Jane feel put down.

______ 8. No student wanted to be the first to answer.

______ 9. The substitute teacher did a good job of managing the class.

______ 10. The teacher did not ask any questions.

Answer Key

Mastery Test, Objective 3

1. Descriptive. Only facts are reported, no opinions.
2. Judgmental. *Enough* is an opinion, not a description.
3. Judgmental. *Too harsh* is an opinion, not a description.

4. Descriptive. Only facts are described.
5. Judgmental. *Needed help* is the terminology that makes the statement judgmental. How did the observer know this? A more descriptive statement might have been, "The teacher spent time helping those students who raised their hands."
6. Descriptive. Although saying that the students like science class best does state a judgment, by referring to the source of the judgment the statement is descriptive. It is a statement of fact that according to the survey the science class is what the students liked best.
7. Judgmental. *Made Jane feel put down* is the key phrase. How does the observer know this? Inferring how a student feels is a judgment.
8. Judgmental. How does the observer know that no one wanted to be the first to answer? A more descriptve statement might be, "No student raised his hand to volunteer to answer."
9. Judgmental. *Did a good job* is a judgment.
10. Descriptive. Whether the teacher did or did not ask any questions is certainly observable.

OBJECTIVE 4 TO IDENTIFY DIFFERENT TECHNIQUES FOR COLLECTING OBSERVATIONAL DATA, AND TO DESCRIBE THE STRENGTHS AND WEAKNESSES OF EACH

The primary purpose for supervisory observation is to collect information. There are a number of observation techniques and methods for collecting classroom information. The purpose of this section is to acquaint you with some of these techniques and to make you aware of their relative strengths and weaknesses.

Audio Recorders

Since so much instruction in classrooms is oral, audiocassette recordings can be analyzed to yield such information as teacher patterns in speaking, clarity in explanations or giving directions, and questioning strategies. One of the strengths of the audio recorder, however, is also a weakness: because it records so much information it is necessary to sift through the recording to identify specific information that will be useful to you and the teacher in examining the stated areas of interest.

Any effort to collect information affects the dynamics of the classroom in some way. The presence of a person or machine will affect how the teacher and students behave, but repeated observations will lessen the influence. If the method of collecting data is relatively unobtrusive then you can have more confidence that the information will be more valid and reliable. Because of its smallness, the audiocassette recorder is relatively unobtrusive, and thus an advantage of this technique. Other strengths are its relative cheapness, and its portability.

On the negative side, if only one microphone is available then it is often difficult to hear persons who are not located close to the microphone. Since the microphone is usually placed near the teacher, the voices of many students may be indiscernible. The microphone is also very sensitive to nearby extraneous noises such as chalk on the board or accidental bumping. Care must be taken to place the microphone in a position where background noise will not interfere. Given its availability, relative operative simplicity, and flexibility, the audiotape recorder seems a particularly underutilized mode of recording classroom events.

Video Recorders

Since the first portable videotape recorder made was purchased by Stanford University for use in its teacher education program in 1961, tremendous technical advances have been made, along with dramatic cost reductions. Today's videocassette recorders (VCRs) are very portable, usually weighing 20 to 25 pounds, and record on color cassettes. This equipment is the most comprehensive means available for recording classroom happenings, including the collection of both verbal and nonverbal behaviors of teachers and students. Operating the equipment is relatively easy, usually requiring no more than one hour or so for training. Special lighting equipment is usually not needed.

The main advantages of the VCR are its capability to be replayed at a time convenient to supervisor and teacher, its capability to stimulate a comprehensive recall of the classroom events, and its relative objectivity. The machine can be started, stopped, and replayed as supervisor and teacher examine instances when behavior under consideration occurred. Data can be stored on the cassettes for as long as is needed, or erased, and the cassettes can be used over and over again.

In spite of its capability to record so much, the VCR cannot record everything. Decisions must be made by the operator whether to focus on the teacher, the class, or individual students. The decisions should be prompted, of course, by the agreed-upon focus of the observation.

As with the audiotape recorder, VCRs provide so much information that supervisor and teacher must be selective as they view the cassettes. Additionally, the same sound limitations that applied to audiotape recorders also apply to videocassette recorders.

While audiotape recorders are relatively unobtrusive, the same is not true for videocassette recorders, which are usually very noticeable in the classroom. Children will be extremely curious about the machine and its purpose. The supervisor and teacher are well advised to allow some time for the children to become acclimated to seeing the equipment and to ask any questions that they might have. Repeated use of the equipment will diminish its obviousness in the room, but it will always affect the participants' behaviors in some way.

Verbatim Transcripts

As noted earlier, if you and the teacher are interested in some aspect of the verbal behavior in the classroom, the audiotape recorder is a most useful tool. However, because words often flow quickly in the classroom and never hold still, transcribing an audiotape into a written typescript has some advantages. Transcribing a 10- or 15-minute segment of verbal interaction allows you and the teacher to scan the transcript quickly to see what may interest you. Verbal patterns of teacher and student behavior are also identified more easily from a transcript than from the audiotape itself because you can move quickly from one segment of dialogue to another, identifying, affirming or denying the existence of patterns of behavior. Using an audiotape alone you must commit to memory what has already transpired, hoping to recognize new instances of behavior that also indicate the existence of patterns. Transcripts can also be examined to ascertain: logical order of statements, content errors, positive and/or negative statements by the teacher toward learners, grammatical errors, and so forth. (See the next chapter on analysis skills for other frameworks for analyzing transcripts.)

The major drawback of complete verbatim transcripts is the obvious one: getting the audiotapes transcribed and typed. Most supervisors do not have extensive secretarial help, so any typing that needs to be done will probably have to be performed by either the supervisor or the teacher. Because of this serious limitation, complete transcript analysis is not usually possible more than once or twice with any given teacher. Depending on the pace of the lesson, a 15-minute segment will usually become five to six pages of transcript, and five pages of transcript will usually reveal a great deal of information.

Some people who have developed shorthand or fast writing skills are able to capture most of the dialogue while observing in the classroom. An audiotape recorder might also be used to supplement the note-taking process for times when the supervisor is unable to record everything by hand. There are also techniques and tricks that can help speed up the note-taking process, including: indent all student comments to keep them visually separate from the teacher's statements; use abbreviations (T = teacher, Q = question, wrtg = writing, and so forth); use symbols, such as arrows to indicate direction, a square with a T in it to represent the teacher at his or her desk, or the use of subscripts to designate particular students (S_6). Reliably and validly recording everything that is said in a classroom requires a great deal of practice. The skill is not one that is easily mastered.

Selected Verbatim Notetaking

As the name of this category implies, the supervisor records exactly what is said, but not all verbal statements are recorded. The supervisor selects certain categories of verbal behaviors to record, ignoring other categories. The choice of which categories to record and which to ignore is determined by the preobservation agreement between supervisor and teacher and reflects the areas of teacher interest or concern. Suppose, for example, that the teacher has expressed concern about the kinds of questions she asks during classroom discussions. The supervisor and teacher agree that it would be helpful if they knew exactly what questions the teacher asked so they could examine them to identify if any problems are evident. The supervisor might decide to use the selected verbatim technique to record the exact wording used by the teacher for every question the teacher asked. Other categories of teacher behavior, such as praise statements, criticisms, and lecturing, would be ignored.

The selected verbatim note-taking technique has several advantages. First, because it is selective the observation and subsequent conference can focus solely on the information relevant to the teacher's interest or concern area. As a result, neither the teacher nor supervisor becomes overwhelmed by too much information, thus making it easier for the teacher to concentrate on a few behaviors at a time if he or she decides change is required.

Second, the technique is relatively easy to use. A pen or pencil and a pad of paper is all that is needed. Furthermore, no additional transcription is required. Third, the technique is relatively unobtrusive since only the supervisor is present in the classroom, and he or she can be positioned in such a way as to be out of the students' natural line of sight.

On the negative side, there is a danger that teacher and supervisor will focus on relatively trivial verbal behaviors, either because they are less threatening or because they are easy to collect. Sensitivity to this issue should preclude the problem from developing. Sometimes the verbal flow goes so quickly that the supervisor may be unable to record the selected verbatim statements accurately. If this occurs, the supervisor should be certain that what is recorded is accurate, and let the rest go unrecorded. See Figure 4.1 for an example of a selected verbatim transcript.

Anecdotal Records

Anecdotal records are written descriptions of the observations supervisors make in the classroom. These descriptions are factual records rather than interpretations of what happened. They are different from verbatim or selective verbatim records in that they do not attempt to use exclusively the exact words of teachers and students. Rather, the supervisor summarizes or paraphrases what he or she sees occurring, stating everything in descriptive or behavioral terms. The supervisor writes what is seen or heard, but does not make any interpretive statements about what he or she thinks is happening or about what he or she feels are the reasons for the behaviors.

Ancedotal records permit the development of a broad view of what is happening in the classroom, rather than a narrower, more selective view. The notes that the supervisor makes form a *protocol* of what happened. This technique of

10:05	1. Do you want to close the door?
	2. What were we talking about yesterday?
	3. Give me something that could help to stop the vicious circle.
	4. What else?
	5. What do we consider to be the main problems?
	6. What is one of the problems that stems from this?
	7. Why?
	8. What's the word?
	9. What does THAT mean?
	10. From the word "convict" what comes out?
	11. What else?
	12. What are they classified as?
10:17	13. What does ostracized mean? (No answer)
	14. They immediately lose what?
	15. What else?
	16. What's a deviant?
	17. They become hard-core criminals more or less because why?
	18. Who do they associate with?
	19. What do they receive from this? (Student: I don't understand what you want.)
	20. What do they get from these people?
	21. What do they get from these people?
	22. They get acceptance from whom?
	23. Any questions on this? Is it understandable?
	24. What other restrictions do they place on them?
	25. What shows they aren't considered acceptable?
	26. What else?
	27. The custodial prison does what?
	28. What is the idea behind prison?
	29. Wouldn't you agree? (No answer)
	30. Who should be giving the criminal leadership?
	31. What's going to happen as soon as he gets back?
	32. Would that be a good assumption? (No answer)
10:29	33. Would you agree? (Student: Yeah.)
	34. Do you know anything ________ ? What do you think?
	35. What kind of programs should these be?
	36. Where is Marianna? (No answer)
	37. Does anyone know where Okeechobee is?
	38. What was that?
	39. They wouldn't take a guy right after he committed a crime and put him on a job, would they?
	40. Do you remember what we talked about yesterday?
	41. What happens when he's been ostracized from society when he goes over to the hard core group when he's been pushed so far to one side when a program comes up?
	42. Why?
	43. So what would be considered if he broke away from his peers which he'd be unlikely to do when he takes advantage of such a program?
	44. So what happens when the relationship breaks down when he still has two years to go?
	45. How can you do this?
	46. Is that your only solution?
10:35	47. Do you want to bet on that?

FIGURE 4.1 Teacher questions to high school sociology class on penal problems and reforms. (From J. Hansen, "Observation Skills," in J. M. Cooper, ed., *Classroom Teaching Skills: A Handbook*, Lexington, Mass., D. C. Heath, 1977.)

data collection is used often by anthropologists who make notes as they study new or different cultural settings. The technique is a useful one when the teacher and the supervisor cannot agree on any specific area of interest or concern, a situation most often occurring during the early stages of supervision when the teacher and supervisor are still exploring their relationship. You and the teacher must decide, however, whether you are going to observe the teacher, one student, a group of students, or the whole class. The more focused the observation, the more details you can include, thus making the description more intensive.

The key to collecting useful anecdotal records is to write descriptive rather than judgmental statements. Objective 2 in this chapter provided you with practice in distinguishing between descriptive and judgmental statements. Yet, distinguishing between these two types of statements is definitely easier than observing classroom events and writing descriptive rather than judgmental statements. To accomplish this requires considerable practice. Objectivity, then, is the greatest weakness of this technique. Unless you are willing to practice writing descriptive statements as you observe, and receive critiques from someone with expertise in this skill, you are probably better off not using this technique. On the other hand, if you do develop this skill to a competent level, you will find it quite valuable.

One additional point should be made: unless your handwriting is quite legible you may find it necessary to have your notes typed so the teacher can read them. This results in additional costs and a time delay. The moral of the story is to write neatly! See Figure 4.2 for an example of an anecdotal record.

Observation Instruments

There are literally thousands of different classroom observation instruments that have been developed to collect data on everything from classroom verbal interactions to teacher and student movement. It is beyond the scope of this chapter to acquaint you with even a small fraction of the instruments, but the next section in this chapter will focus on a few useful and easy-to-use instruments, as well as helping you to develop the skill of constructing your own observation instruments.

What are the advantages of observation instruments? Their greatest advantage is that they are constructed to collect data of a particular nature, so they are focused instruments. Another advantage of an observation instrument is that frequently the data are categorized or organized in such a way that analysis of the data is quantifiable; that is, the number of times that a particular behavior or set of behaviors occur can be counted, allowing the data to be analyzed more easily. Similarly, once an instrument has been developed, the same or a modified version of the instrument can be used again if a similar concern is expressed by a teacher. Thus, a professional supervisor can develop a catalogue of instruments that will yield information relevant to specific problems or issues. Having a variety of instruments is useful when working with teachers who aren't certain what their areas of concern or interest are. The supervisor can suggest areas from among the different instruments in the supervisor's possession, allowing the teacher to choose any of interest.

Some existing instruments are simple and easy to use, while others are very complex and require considerable training to use effectively. This chapter will discuss only those that are relatively easy to use, believing that instrument simplicity and ease of utility are important virtues in working with teachers. Your time as a supervisor is probably better spent learning how to use a large number of easy-to-use instruments, rather than concentrating on mastering one or two complex observation instruments. You are also likely to encounter many situations in which no existing instrument is appropriate, and it will be necessary for you to construct a new instrument or modify an existing one to focus precisely on the area of interest.

Most of the complex and elaborate classroom observation instruments were

Teacher Number: 202
Date of Observation: October 11, 1976—Segment C
Researcher Number: 3
Protocol Number: 49

Time: 10:50.

The bell rings and the students line up to return to the classroom. They quickly come in and take their seats. The teacher nods to Joe and he rings

Noise level 1.

the chimes. Lucy and Billy pass out listening skills folders. The teacher stands in zone 1 near the chalkboard. She has her arms folded and is pressing her lips tightly together. She says after all of the folders are passed out, "All right, who are the 3 people responsible for passing out these booklets on Mondays and Wednesdays?" Terry, Billy and Lucy raise their hands. The teacher glances around the room and says, "All right, that's why it took so long for us to get ready. Some of you who are responsible for passing these out forgot." The teacher walks over to zone 1 and turns on the tape

Time: 10:55. Noise level 0.

recorder. The kids listen to the

Time: 11:00. Noise level 0.

taped lesson. The taped voice mentions that the pledge of allegiance originally was written on October 11, 1892. John gets very excited and looks over at the teacher. He says in a very enthusiastic voice, "It's a holiday. It's Columbus Day." The teacher smiles at John. The teacher's aide walks in the classroom and the teacher smiles at her. They talk with their backs to the class. Sharon looks over and sees that the teacher has her back turned toward the class. She gets out of her desk, walks over and picks up a pencil on the floor. She says something to Joe who is sitting across from her. Ted gets up out of his seat in the back of zone 1, runs up to the center of the table and looks over at the teacher. When he sees she isn't looking, he grabs a stapler and scurries back to his desk. Joe and Roger, who are sitting

FIGURE 4.2 Anecdotal record. (From P.K. Buckley, *An Ethnographic Study of an Elementary School Teacher's Establishment and Maintenance of Group Norms*. Unpublished doctoral dissertation, University of Houston, Houston, Texas, 1977.)

developed primarily for research purposes, rather than as helpful feedback instruments for teachers. If you are interested in learning more about some of these systematic observation instruments, consult the additional readings at the end of the chapter.

Mastery Test

OBJECTIVE 4 TO IDENTIFY DIFFERENT TECHNIQUES FOR COLLECTING OBSERVATIONAL DATA, AND TO DESCRIBE THE MAJOR STRENGTHS AND WEAKNESSES OF EACH

Identify six different techniques for collecting classroom observational data, listing the strengths and weaknesses of each.

Answer Key

Mastery Test, Objective 4

1. Audio recorders. *Strengths*: relatively unobtrusive; portable and easy to use; record a great deal of information; inexpensive. *Weaknesses:* record a great deal of information so that much of it could be unrelated to teacher's concern; difficult to hear all participants, particularly the students distant from the microphone; microphone often picks up background noise.
2. Video recorders. *Strengths:* record classroom events more accurately and comprehensively than any other method; replayable at a time and place convenient to supervisor and teacher; cassettes can be reused many times. *Weaknesses:* very obtrusive; record a great deal of information so that much of it could be unrelated to teacher's concern; same sound difficulties as the audio recorder; although prices have dropped considerably, they are still relatively expensive.
3. Verbatim transcripts. *Strengths:* easy to identify verbal patterns; easy to scan back and forth quickly. *Weaknesses:* time and cost in getting audiotapes transcribed; need for shorthand or speedwriting skills if an audiotape is not used.
4. Selected verbatim note taking. *Strengths:* exact words are recorded but only in the area of interest or concern; can help teacher become more sensitive to the verbal aspects of teaching; relatively easy to use; unobtrusive. *Weaknesses:* speed of dialogue may cause supervisor to miss some things that are said; danger of focusing on trivial verbal behaviors.
5. Anecdotal records. *Strengths:* summarize and describe considerable information; permit a broad view of classroom happenings. *Weaknesses:* difficult to maintain objectivity; difficult to write descriptions rather than judgments; require legible handwriting or typed notes.
6. Observation instruments. *Strengths:* focus on a prespecified area of interest; often yield quantifiable data; a catalogue of instruments can be accumulated. *Weaknesses:* supervisor must be trained in using and/or developing observation instruments.

OBJECTIVE 5 TO IDENTIFY THE FUNCTIONS OF THREE DIFFERENT TYPES OF OBSERVATION INSTRUMENTS, AND TO IDENTIFY HOW SPECIFIC EXAMPLES OF EACH TYPE ARE USED

Although there are many different ways to label or categorize observation instruments, we will examine a number of specific instruments that can be categorized according to one of three format types: seating charts and diagrams, frequency counts, and checklists.

Seating Charts and Diagrams

Several different instruments specify the use of seating charts or diagrams as ways to collect information about classroom events. The seating chart has several advantages as a format for data collection. First, because seating charts are commonly used by teachers they are familiar rather than foreign looking. This familiarity can ease some of the discomfort a teacher might experience in the data interpretation process. Second, the types of data yielded from a seating chart or diagram are usually easy to collect and interpret. Third, observational instruments based on seating charts and diagrams can examine important aspects of classroom behavior, such as pupil attentiveness or the distribution of teacher attention to specific members of the class. Fourth, seating charts enable the supervisor and teacher to examine the actions of individual students as well as the class as a whole.

Among the possible disadvantages of seating charts and diagrams is the potential for seeing the trees but not the forest. That is, the focused nature of data collected for the seating charts or diagrams may cause the observer not to grasp the gestalt, or the overall sense of what was happening in the classroom. And like other data-collecting techniques, there is also a possible danger that trivial, rather than important, behaviors could be recorded. The potential drawbacks are slight, however, in comparison to the strengths of the format.

Pupil On-Task Behavior During the 1970s the National Institute of Education (NIE) funded numerous research studies in an attempt to identify the basic skills of effective teaching. One of the strongest variables emerging from this research has acquired the name *academic learning time*. Academic learning time is the time a student spends engaged in academically relevant material that for him or her is of a moderate level of difficulty. These research studies indicate that academic learning time in reading or mathematics, more than any other coded teacher or student behavior, is most highly related to achievement in those respective subjects at the elementary-grade level. Simply put, the more time elementary students spend working on reading or mathematics activities, the more likely they are to achieve in those areas. Although this finding may seem obvious, classroom observations indicate that tremendous variations exist in the amount of time individual students spend engaged in academic activities, both within the same classroom, and from one teacher's classroom to another's.

The research on academic learning time clearly indicates that a primary goal of elementary teachers (and possibly secondary teachers, although the research has been limited to elementary schools) should be to keep students on-task. Because pupil work involvement or on-task behavior is a concern of the teacher, this observation instrument should provide useful data in which students are involved.

Ideally, if you wanted to know which students were on- or off-task you might take a videocassette recording of each individual student. The data gathered would provide you with a continuous record of each student's behavior. However, as is well recognized, this would be logistically and financially impossible. Instead of taking a continuous record, pupil on-task instruments allow you to sample the students' behavior periodically during the lesson.

Let's examine Figure 4.3 (p. 96) to see how one instrument works. Each box represents a student, with the boxes located on the paper to reflect the student's physical location in the classroom. Within each box there is a sequence of numbers, each representing one observation of the student. Depending on the length of the observation time period, there may be fewer or more than the 15 observations represented in this instrument. A list of categories with their code symbols, a legend, is also listed. The on-task (or at-task) behaviors may be symbolized by the letter A, or the behaviors that the teacher considers at-task for the given lesson may be listed and coded separately. The developer of this instrument lists the on- and off-task behaviors separately because more information can be derived from the separate categories than from just one, global category of on-task. These instruments are flexible and can be adapted to fit the observer's and the teacher's needs. If you like, one global on-task category, can be used; if you like to code behaviors using separate categories, use them. The off-task behaviors that might be expected from the students can also be

Purpose: To determine which students are on- or off-task during a lesson, and what specific behaviors they are engaged in.
Lesson Type: Teacher-led discussion in eighth-grade social studies.

Note:

On-Task	*Off-Task*
L = listening	R- = reading (nonclass related)
TN = taking notes	T- = talking (nonclass related)
H = hand raised	WS = working on another subject
T+ = talking (discussion related)	OS = out of seat
	O = other

Teacher

Time

1	9:15
2	9:17
3	9:20
4	9:22
5	9:25
6	9:27
7	9:29
8	9:32
9	9:34
10	9:37
11	9:40
12	9:42
13	9:44
14	9:47
15	9:50

Corrine	Mike	Jim	Nancy	Jo
1 6 11	1 6 11	1 6 11	1 6 11	1 6 11
2 7 12	2 7 12	2 7 12	2 7 12	2 7 12
3 8 13	3 8 13	3 8 13	3 8 13	3 8 13
4 9 14	4 9 14	4 9 14	4 9 14	4 9 14
5 10 15	5 10 15	5 10 15	5 10 15	5 10 15

Mary Kay	Will	Mildred	Carlos	James
1 6 11	1 6 11	1 6 11	1 6 11	1 6 11
2 7 12	2 7 12	2 7 12	2 7 12	2 7 12
3 8 13	3 8 13	3 8 13	3 8 13	3 8 13
4 9 14	4 9 14	4 9 14	4 9 14	4 9 14
5 10 15	5 10 15	5 10 15	5 10 15	5 10 15

Frank	Betty	Marilyn	Fran	Howie
1 6 11	1 6 11	1 6 11	1 6 11	1 6 11
2 7 12	2 7 12	2 7 12	2 7 12	2 7 12
3 8 13	3 8 13	3 8 13	3 8 13	3 8 13
4 9 14	4 9 14	4 9 14	4 9 14	4 9 14
5 10 15	5 10 15	5 10 15	5 10 15	5 10 15

Jack	Bob	Maria	Vince	Chet
1 6 11	1 6 11	1 6 11	1 6 11	1 6 11
2 7 12	2 7 12	2 7 12	2 7 12	2 7 12
3 8 13	3 8 13	3 8 13	3 8 13	3 8 13
4 9 14	4 9 14	4 9 14	4 9 14	4 9 14
5 10 15	5 10 15	5 10 15	5 10 15	5 10 15

FIGURE 4.3 Pupil on-task behavior.

listed and a code symbol assigned to each. Many of these off-task behaviors can be anticipated in advance of the actual observation, but should one occur that was not anticipated, just add it to the legend.

When you are ready to begin the observation, identify the time you begin and then observe the first student. What is he or she doing? Code the behavior appropriately and place the code in the box next to the number 1. Then move quickly to the next student and repeat the process, again placing the code next to the number 1. Continue until you have observed all the students (or at least the ones that you and the teacher agreed to observe), and then start your second round of observations with the first student and repeat the sequence. Each time you get ready to begin a new observation cycle, record the time you start. The times that you see listed on the instrument in Figure 4.3 are not placed there in advance of the actual observation. They are there simply to remind you to record the time so you will know how much time was required for each observation cycle.

With some practice and familiarity with the instrument you will soon be able to move quickly from student to student while coding their behavior. Remember, you are sampling the students' behavior. The more observations you make, the greater the confidence you can have that your sample validly and reliably represents the full set of behaviors the students demonstrated.

Physical Movement A teacher may express concern about how much time he or she spends with individual students or groups of students. The teacher

NORMA	SAM ① 1:30–1:31	WILLA	JODY *(M)* ⑧ 1:51–1:52	STEVEN ⑨ 1:52 (20 secs.)
DICK	WALT ⑪ 1:59 (30 secs.)	CHRIS *(F)*	JEFF ② 1:33 (30 secs.) ⑫ 2:00–2:02	CRAIG ③ 1:34–1:37 ⑥ 1:44–1:46 ⑩ 1:53–1:58
LYN 1:40 Goes to bookshelf 1:55 Returns from bookshelf	MICKEY	CAROL	DELL *(F)*	MARTHA
MARVIN ④ 1:40–1:41	CINDY 1:48 Raises hand	SUE Raises hand at 1:35 ⑤ 1:41–1:42	JANET	SHARON ⑦ 1:48–1:50

Note: ① teacher-student conference at student's desk (number indicates sequential order); 1:30—1:31 time at which conference took place and its duration

FIGURE 4.4 Observation of physical movement using seating chart.

may question whether certain students receive an undue amount of attention, while other students are neglected. Do certain sections of the room regularly receive more attention than other sections? Does physical location seem to be related in any way with students' off-task behavior or misbehavior? When teachers express these kinds of concerns, physical movement observation instruments are often appropriate.

Physical movement data can be collected on seating charts or on diagrams that reflect the layout of the classroom. Figures 4.4 (p. 97) and 4.5 are examples of two different techniques that can be used to collect physical movement data. Figure 4.4 is a seating chart on which each teacher-student conference during seatwork is recorded. Each conference is recorded sequentially along with the time when the conference occurred and its duration. For example, the 1 indicates the first conference held; it lasted from 1:30 until 1:31. These data can tell you who the teacher is conferencing with, how often, and for what duration. In addition, an experienced observer can record in anecdotal form any additional data (for example, "raises hand") if this information is desired.

Figure 4.5 is a somewhat simpler diagram in which the room is divided into quadrants, and the teacher's location is recorded every 30 or 60 seconds. Again, the teacher's location is numbered sequentially. If the teacher doesn't move during the 30- or 60-second time interval, make a mark on the edge of the circle and continue to do so at the chosen interval until the teacher moves, for example, ④ʹ. At the end of observation period you and the teacher can determine how often the teacher was in each quadrant of the classroom. If this procedure is repeated several times the data can be analyzed to see if certain patterns of movement exist. It is also helpful during the preobservation conference to ask the teacher to state what kind of distribution of movement he or she would like to see during the lesson. The collected data can then be used to determine if there is congruency or discrepancy between what the teacher intended and what actually occurred. If there is a discrepancy, then the teacher and supervisor can explore possible reasons for it.

Purpose: To determine teacher mobility and attention to learners with respect to physical location in the classroom.

Directions: (1) Draw a seating diagram of the classroom and divide the room into four quadrants. (2) After noting time at the top of the observation sheet, begin to track the teacher's position. (3) After 30 seconds, note the teacher's position and record this on observation sheet with a ①. (4) Take additional observations at 30-second intervals. If 30 seconds pass and the teacher remains stationary, record this by placing a mark on the circle (⑭ʹ). Continue this procedure as long as the teacher remains in one location. (5) Continue the procedure noting position and coding it on the observation sheet for the remainder of the period. (6) At the conclusion of the observation, determine how often the teacher is in each quadrant of the classroom.

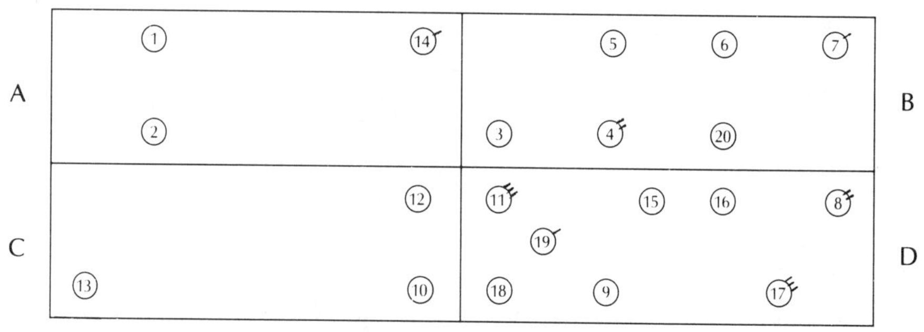

FIGURE 4.5 Observation of physical movement data using diagram.

Verbal Flow Seating charts can also be used to record teacher and/or student verbal behavior. Verbal flow observation techniques record who is talking to whom, the initiators and recipients of the verbal communication, and the kind of communication in which they are engaged. This technique can be used to determine which students the teacher calls on to answer questions, which students volunteer to answer questions, which students actually contribute to the discussion, which students the teacher praises or criticizes, and/or which students ask questions. The observer can also record personal characteristics of each student, for example, race and sex, to see if any verbal flow patterns may be related to these or other variables such as physical location in the classroom.

The basic technique is to identify those verbal behaviors you and the teacher wish to record, select codes or symbols to represent each type of behavior, and record the symbols or codes on the seating chart as the behaviors occur. If a sequence of the behaviors is also desired, then numerical subscripts can be added to the symbols as they are entered on to the seating chart.

Some supervisors and teachers like to use arrows and lines as the symbols to represent the various types of behavior. For example:

T ↓	teacher calls on student
T ↓ +	student responds to teacher correctly (a minus sign would be incorrectly, and a zero would be no response)
|	student raises hand
↑ +	student is recognized and makes contribution (+, −, and 0 can be used in the same way as above)
? ↑	student question

If any of the behaviors are repeated for a given student, instead of drawing the symbol again simply draw a line through the symbol to indicate each time the behavior was repeated. For example, indicates that the student asked four questions, the original symbol plus the three crossmarks. Also recognize that some of the symbols are designed so you can add to them to create a new meaning, rather than drawing another symbol. For example, if the student raises his hand (|), and then is called on and makes a positive contribution, instead of having two symbols in the student's place on the seating chart (| and ↑ +), by simply adding the arrow and the + symbol to the original straight line the same meaning is created (↑ +). Figure 4.6 illustrates a verbal flow observation instrument that uses these symbols of lines and arrows.

Some supervisors and teachers prefer to use an alphabetic notation system rather than arrows. Letters of the alphabet indicate separate categories of verbal behavior; for example:

P	teacher praise
Q	teacher question
C	teacher criticism
I	teacher used student's idea
q	student question
v+	student volunteered a relevant or correct response
v−	student volunteered an irrelevant or incorrect response
a	student added to comment of previous student

By recording teacher verbal behavior in capital letters and student comments in

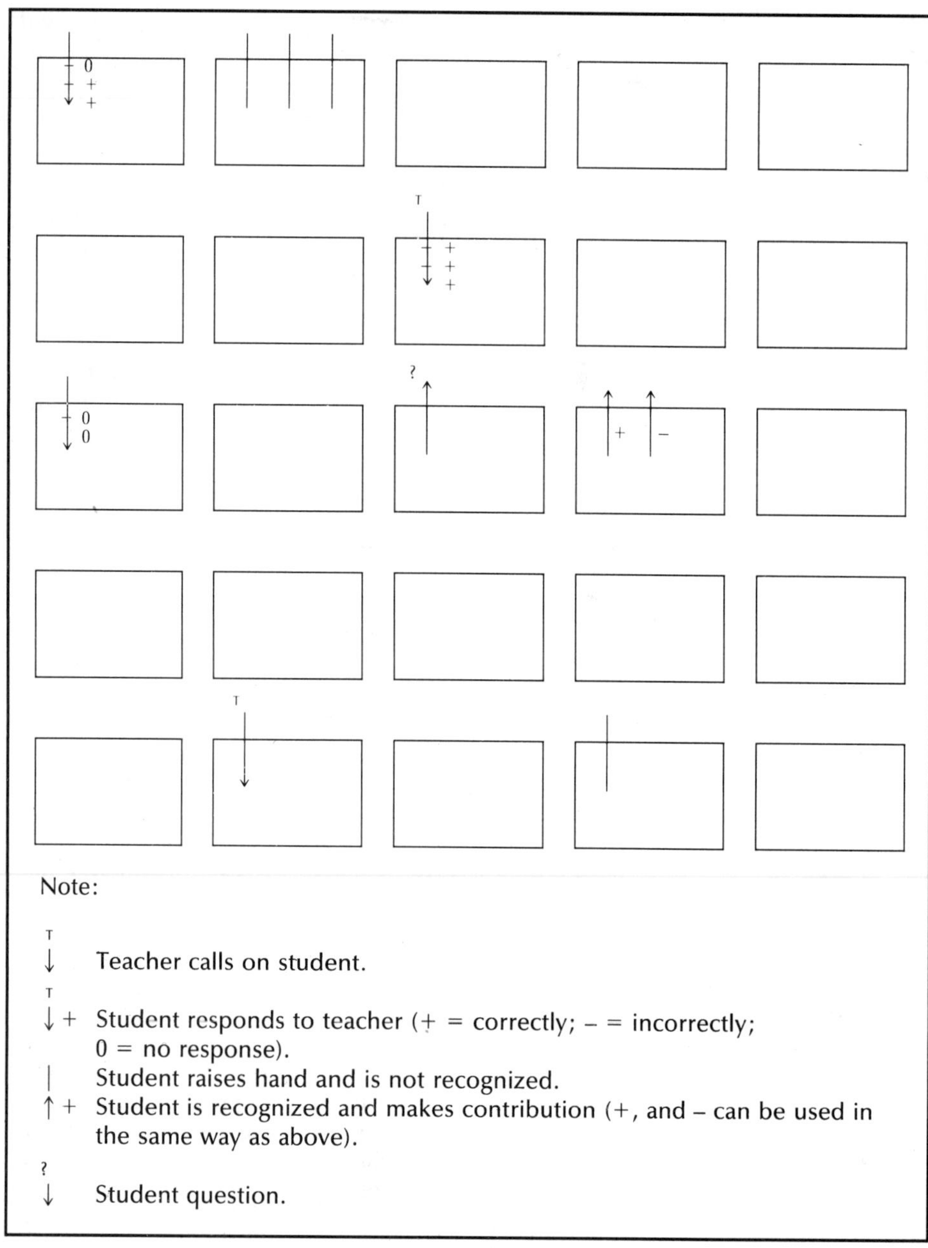

FIGURE 4.6 Verbal flow observation instrument using arrows as symbols.

lower case, it is easier to keep from confusing the two. Figure 4.7 illustrates a verbal flow instrument that uses this set of alphabetical symbols.

Frequency Counts

A frequency count is a record of the total number of times a behavior has occurred during any given period. If, for example, you and the teacher are interested in how many times the teacher praised children using the expression "very good" as compared with all other expressions of praise, you could tally each time "very good" was said, and also tally each time any other praise statement was uttered. Over a 15-minute period your tallies might look like this:

Very good (VG) 𝍸 ||

Other praise statements (P) ||||

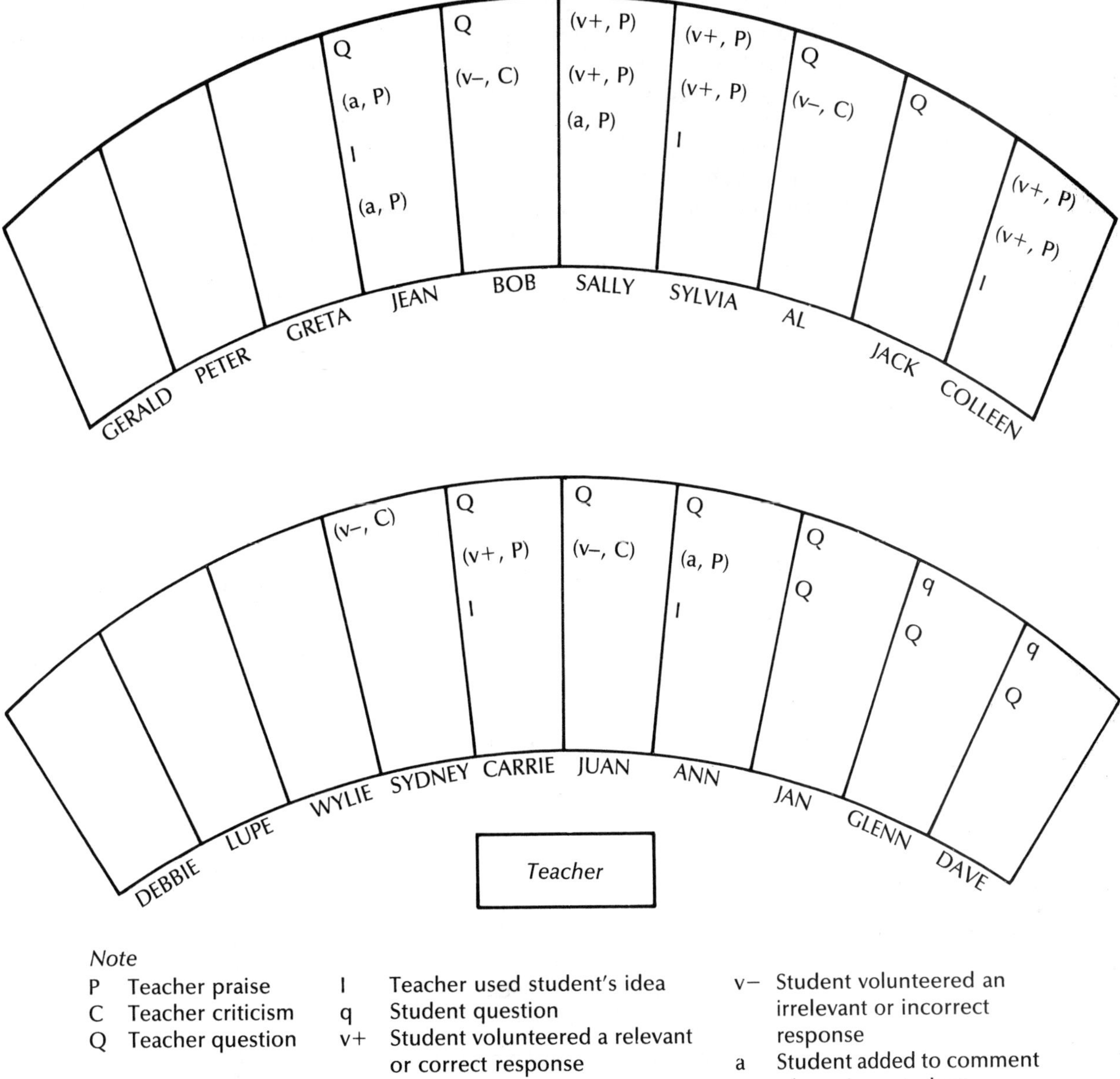

FIGURE 4.7 Verbal flow observation instrument using alphabetical symbols.

This example is, of course, a very simple one. Much more elaborate frequency count observation instruments exist. But if simply knowing how many times certain behaviors occur is important then using a simple frequency count system is most appropriate.

Sometimes you might also want to know the sequence in which certain behavior categories occur. In the example above, if you assigned the letters VG to mean very good and P to represent other praise statements, then you might record these behaviors in the following manner:

VG | VG | P | VG | P | VG | VG | P | VG | VG | P

Note that if recorded in this fashion, you can then summarize these data to produce the frequency counts given in the first example above: very good (7) and other praise statements (4). However, if you originally recorded the data in the form of frequency count tallies, you are not able to reconstruct the sequence in which the behaviors occurred, unless you use some form of numerical notation such as subscripts. If sequence is important, then you must record the data in such a way to preserve the sequence, knowing that you can always summarize the data in frequency count form later.

One format for preserving sequence is illustrated in Figure 4.8. This instrument provides information about a very common classroom dilemma for the teacher: when a student fails to answer a question correctly, what does the teacher do? The behavior categories include many of the most common teacher reactions. The open-ended *other* category allows the observer to add any other reactions that may not have been anticipated. Under the category labeled *codes*, is a sequence of numerals from 1 to 50, representing simply the order in which the behaviors are recorded. For example, in the first space the number 2 is recorded, indicating that after a student had failed to answer correctly this

Use: In discussion and recitation situations when students are answering questions.
Purpose: To see if teacher is giving appropriate feedback to students about the adequacy of their responses.
When a student is unable to answer a question, or answers it incorrectly, code as many categories as apply to the teacher's feedback response.

Behavior Categories

1. Criticizes
2. Says "No," "That's not right," etc.
3. No feedback—goes on to something else
4. Ambiguous—doesn't indicate whether or not answer is acceptable
5. Asks a student or the class whether answer is correct
6. Asks someone else to answer the question
7. Repeats question to same student, prompts ("Well?" "Do you know?" etc.)
8. Gives a clue
9. Rephrases question to make it easier
10. Asks same student an entirely new question
11. Answers question for the student
12. Answers question and also gives explanation or rationale for answer
13. Gives explanation or rationale for why student's answer was not correct
14. Praises student for good attempt or guess
15. Other (specify)

Codes

1. 2	26. ____
2. 2, 6	27. ____
3. 2, 8	28. ____
4. 2, 10	29. ____
5. 2, 10	30. ____
6. 2, 12	31. ____
7. ____	32. ____
8. ____	33. ____
9. ____	34. ____
10. ____	35. ____
11. ____	36. ____
12. ____	37. ____
13. ____	38. ____
14. ____	39. ____
15. ____	40. ____
16. ____	41. ____
17. ____	42. ____
18. ____	43. ____
19. ____	44. ____
20. ____	45. ____
21. ____	46. ____
22. ____	47. ____
23. ____	48. ____
24. ____	49. ____
25. ____	50. ____

FIGURE 4.8 Feedback when students fail to answer correctly. (Adapted from T.L. Good and J.E. Brophy, *Looking in Classrooms*, 3rd ed., New York, Harper and Row, 1984.)

teacher had said, "No; that's not right," or some similar phrase. In the second space there are two numerals recorded, a 2 followed by a 6. This means that the next time a student failed to answer a question correctly, the teacher again responded with a similar phrase (2), and then asked someone else to answer the question (6). Each time a student gives an incorrect response the numeral of the behavior category that best describes the teacher's reaction is recorded in sequence. Maintaining a record of the sequence for these behaviors may be important if valid interpretations are to be made from the data.

Two other points might be made about this particular instrument and others like it. First, if identifying the student who received each form of reaction from the teacher is important, then the student's name could be recorded next to the data, as shown below.

Mary	1.	2
Franklin	2.	2,6
Juan	3.	2,8

By recording the students' names you and the teacher can determine if some students tend to receive certain types of reactions and feedback from the teacher, while other students receive reactions of a different nature.

The second point focuses on the general question of how do you know which teacher reactions are appropriate and which are less desirable? In some cases research findings may serve as a guide. Lacking research evidence, in the preobservation conference you can try to get the teacher to express his or her values regarding the type of responses that he or she deems to be more beneficial to the student. For example, regarding Figure 4.8, the teacher may say that it is important to let the students know that the answer given is incorrect so students don't acquire incorrect information. But, on the other hand, the teacher doesn't want to abandon that student, so the teacher would like to give the student a clue (8) or rephrase the question (9). And, the teacher may add, he or she doesn't want to answer the question him- or herself (11 and 12). At this point, the supervisor and the teacher have some criteria against which to judge the adequacy of the teacher's reactions when students answer incorrectly. Without such a platform stated in advance, the postobservation conference may become simply a rationalization for why the data look the way they do.

Figure 4.9 (p. 104) uses basically the same format as Figure 4.8 to collect information on the teacher's response to unexpected answers. Students often surprise teachers by giving answers that teachers do not anticipate. How the teacher reacts when this happens may give some indication of the teacher's willingness to accept divergent thinking, encourage individuality, and be flexible in his or her thinking. As mentioned previously, having the teacher identify the desired behaviors that he or she would like to demonstrate prior to the observation allows for some criteria to be used in judging the data obtained from the observation.

Checklists

Sometimes the supervisor and the teacher are interested in knowing only whether or not certain behaviors have occurred, not in how often they occur. When this is the circumstance then checklists are appropriate instruments. Checklists provide "it's there–it's not there" kind of information. If you or the teacher can ask yourselves whether there are some behaviors that are so important during a given activity that it is valuable simply to know whether or not they occur, and answer yes, then consider using a checklist. Figure 4.10 (p. 105) illustrates the use of a checklist to determine which resources students used during a self-paced program. Figure 4.11 (p. 106) is a checklist used to evaluate the construction and administration of tests.

Use: When a student answers the teacher's question in a way that is reasonable but unexpected.

Purpose: To see if teacher models respect for good thinking when a question doesn't lead to the expected response.

For each codable instance, code each applicable behavior category shown by the teacher in reacting to a reasonable but unexpected answer.

Behavior Categories

1. Compliments ("Why, that's right! I hadn't thought of that!")
2. Acknowledges that the answer is correct or partially correct
3. Gives vague or ambiguous feedback ("I guess you could say that. . . .")
4. Responds as if the answer were simply incorrect
5. Criticizes the answer as irrelevant, dumb, out of place, etc.
6. Other (specify)

Notes:

Student Name	*Codes*
John	1. 3
Sam	2. 4
Mary	3. 3
Rosemary	4. 3
Nancy	5. 4
Abel	6. 3
Saul	7. 3
Saul	8. 3
Connie	9. 4
George	10. 3
Billie	11. 4
Bob	12. 4
Margaret	13. 3
______	14. ____
______	15. ____
______	16. ____
______	17. ____
______	18. ____
______	19. ____
______	20. ____
______	21. ____
______	22. ____
______	23. ____
______	24. ____
______	25. ____

FIGURE 4.9 Teacher's response to unexpected answers. (Adapted from T.L. Good and J.E. Brophy, *Looking in Classrooms*, 3rd ed., New York, Harper and Row, 1984.)

There are five steps to follow in constructing a checklist:

Step 1: Specify an appropriate performance or product

Checklists can be used to provide data on either performances or products, such as tests or materials. For example, introducing or closing a lesson may call for certain steps to be performed by the teacher. Using a checklist would enable you to determine whether those behaviors occurred. Explaining and demonstrating how a microcomputer works may require that certain critical information be given to the students. Again, a checklist of those important points would reveal whether or not the teacher included the critical information. Products such as tests can be scrutinized to see if certain desired characteristics are present or absent. The first step, then, is to identify the performance or product about which you want information.

Use: Small groups and independent study activities when some concern exists about the involvement of learners in a self-paced instructional setting.
Purpose: To determine the variety of resources used by the students during the course of one period in a self-paced program.
Directions: Observe and record the materials each student is working with at the beginning, the middle, and the end of an instructional period.

Codes	*Student*	*Observation*		
A—Audio recording	1	____	____	____
B—Audiotape with worksheets	2	____	____	____
C—Audio-tutorial station	3	____	____	____
D—Record (phonograph)	4	____	____	____
E—Videotape	5	____	____	____
F—16 mm movie	6	____	____	____
G—8 mm film loop	7	____	____	____
H—Slide-audio tape	8	____	____	____
I—Slides	9	____	____	____
J—Photographs	10	____	____	____
K—Graphics (graphs, maps, charts)	11	____	____	____
L—Filmstrip	12	____	____	____
M—Cartoons	13	____	____	____
N—Supplemental text	14	____	____	____
O—Text	15	____	____	____
P—Periodical	16	____	____	____
Q—Magazine	17	____	____	____
R—Simulation/games	18	____	____	____
S—Workbook/worksheet	19	____	____	____
T—Laboratory activity	20	____	____	____
Z—Not working	21	____	____	____
	22	____	____	____
	23	____	____	____
	24	____	____	____

FIGURE 4.10 Variety of teaching techniques and materials. (From J. Denton, *Classroom and School Data Collection Procedures*, School Based Teacher Educator Series, Houston, University of Houston, College of Education, 1977.)

Step 2: List the important behaviors or characteristics

The next step is to list those important behaviors or characteristics that are associated with the performance or product. In the supervisory cycle, this step should be performed jointly by both the supervisor and the teacher so they are in agreement about the specific behaviors.

Step 3: Add any common errors

Frequently it is important to know not only whether the teacher has included the appropriate behaviors in a performance, but also whether particular errors have been made. For example, if an industrial arts teacher were demonstrating the proper application of varnish, an error that he or she might want to avoid would be to pour the excess varnish back into the can. "Does *not* pour excess varnish back into can" might be an item included in the checklist developed. It is a good rule not to add a large number of undesirable traits to your checklist; add only those that are serious and very common.

Step 4: Arrange the list of behaviors and/or products

Arrange the behaviors to be observed in the order in which they are likely to occur. To develop checklists focusing on products, the characteristics should be

Use: When a test is administered to students.
Purpose: (1) To determine the quality of the instrument used, and (2) To evaluate procedures of using cognitive assessments.
Directions: Compare examination to the stated objectives for the unit. Then during test administration, observe class for the following behaviors. In addition, code any feedback provided as tests are turned in.

Category *Test Construction*	*(Check)* *Yes*	*(✓)* *No*
1. Criterion-referenced for scoring purposes (score/objective)	______	___
2. Norm referenced for scoring purposes (total score)	______	___
3. Items clearly related to unit objectives	______	___
4. Essay items used only for higher cognitive processes	______	___
5. Objective type items (true-false, multiple-choice, matching) used for memory level objectives	______	___
6. Balance between lower and higher order thought processes	______	___
7. Tests are printed for each learner in class	______	___
8. Attention of class obtained before test is distributed	______	___
9. Pre-administration advice and special directions are provided for clarification	______	___
10. Class is reminded of ground rules before test is distributed	______	___
11. Test items are presented with a separate answer sheet(s)	______	___
12. Teacher serves as a proctor during the examination period	______	___
13. Test is reviewed by class immediately after all tests are turned in	______	___
14. Test is reviewed by class the following day	______	___
15. Test is scored and scores are posted but feedback is not provided	______	___

FIGURE 4.11 Use of learner assessments. (From J. Denton, *Classroom and School Data Collection Procedures*, School Based Teacher Educator Series, Houston, University of Houston, College of Education, 1977.)

arranged in some logical order, either by location of the characteristics on the product or by sequence in which the examiner is likely to encounter the characteristics.

Step 5: Provide a way to use the list

To use the checklist there must be a convenient place to check each behavior as it occurs (or each characteristic present). The best way to do this is to leave blanks along the side of the page next to each characteristic being checked. A check mark is then made in this blank when the behavior occurs. If the sequence of the occurrences is important, a numeral indicating the sequential steps can also be placed in the blanks.

Mastery Test

OBJECTIVE 5 TO IDENTIFY THE FUNCTIONS OF THREE DIFFERENT TYPES OF OBSERVATION INSTRUMENTS, AND TO IDENTIFY HOW SPECIFIC EXAMPLES OF EACH TYPE ARE USED

1. Identify three different types of classroom data that can be collected using seating charts or diagrams.

2. Name at least four categories of classroom behavior (either teacher or pupil) for which an observation instrument using frequency counts would be appropriate.
3. Name at least three teacher performances for which a checklist would be an appropriate observation instrument.
4. For Figures 4.3, 4.5, 4.7, 4.9, and 4.11, describe how each instrument is used to collect data.

Answer Key

Mastery Test, Objective 5

1. a. On-task or off-task behavior of pupils
   b. Physical movement
   c. Verbal flow
2. Any of the following categories of classroom data would be appropriate: teacher praise statements, teacher criticisms, teacher questions, teacher responses to students' answers, teacher-student verbal interactions, student behaviors that draw praise or criticism from teacher, or any other type of teacher or student behavior which can be counted.
3. Numerous answers are possible, among which are: introducing a lesson, closing a lesson, demonstrating a skill, performing an experiment, giving directions, explaining a new concept, or any teacher performance where the presence or absence of particular behaviors is important and can be identified.
4. Reread the apprcpriate explanations that accompany each figure to determine how closely your explanation fits that of the text.

OBJECTIVE 6 TO SELECT OR CONSTRUCT APPROPRIATE OBSERVATION INSTRUMENTS FOR A GIVEN AREA OF TEACHER INTEREST OR CONCERN

Objective 5 of this chapter acquainted you with different formats for observation instruments and provided example instruments for each format. You should have a working knowledge of the kinds of information that can be gathered using classroom observation instruments. The observation instruments that you studied in Objective 5 may be exactly what you need when you work with teachers in behaviorally defining their areas of interest or concern. If so, then knowing that these instruments, and others like them, exist and being able to use them effectively provide you with a very important supervisory skill. But what if the teacher expresses a concern that calls for a unique data gathering instrument? What do you do? The answer, of course, is that you construct an instrument that will give you and the teacher the information that you need.

Constructing an instrument is not as difficult as it might seem, but it does require practice and familiarity with other observation instruments and their formats. Consequently, this objective should not be attempted unless you successfully passed the mastery tests of the previous objectives.

Selecting or Constructing an Observation Instrument

Step 1: Develop behavioral indicators for area of interest or concern

The first step in constructing or selecting an observation instrument is to develop behavioral indicators for the given area of concern (Objective 1). By doing this you and the teacher will be able to choose those behaviors (pupil or teacher) about which you want more information. These behaviors can become the observable categories of the instrument.

Let's suppose, for example, that the teacher has expressed concern about one student (Fred) who frequently is off-task and often bothersome to other students when they are trying to do their work. After some discussion, the two of you wonder what the teacher is doing and where she is located when Fred gets off-task. The concern basically is: Does there appear to be any pattern between Fred's off-task behavior and the teacher's actions and location? Information is needed about Fred's off-task behavior and the teacher's activity and location in the classroom. The two of you decide that indicators of Fred's off-task behaviors could be:

- Talking to another student
- Out of seat
- Drawing or doodling
- Gazing or daydreaming
- Doing nonclass-related work

His on-task behavior would be:

- Requesting help from the teacher
- Reading class-related material
- Doing assignment

Further, the two of you identify the following teacher behaviors as being appropriate for the lesson:

- Teacher sitting at desk
- Teacher working with student or small group within eight feet of Fred
- Teacher working with student or small group away from Fred (more than eight feet away)

Step 2: choose those behavioral indicators on which data will be collected

It may happen that in the process of developing behavioral indicators for the area of concern more are generated than can possibly be observed, or some of the indicators may be much more important than others. In other words, you may need to make selections. In the hypothetical example of Fred, it is determined that data would be collected on all of the behavioral indicators that had been generated.

Step 3: Select the format for the observation instrument

The next step is to choose a format for the instrument that is compatible with the kind of information you are seeking to collect. Often the choice will be simply a preference for one format over another because of familiarity or ease of use. Sometimes the teacher will prefer looking at the data in one format rather than another. At other times, however, one particular format will be clearly the best choice in terms of ease of use and interpretability.

Staying with our example of Fred, either a diagram/seating chart or a type of frequency count format would work. Because the seating chart might tend to become messy if there is a great deal of movement, it is decided to use the frequency count format.

Step 4: Construct the instrument

In constructing the instrument keep in mind the following points:

- Keep the instrument as simple as possible—don't include more behaviors than you can comfortably observe

- If you use a coding system, use symbols that are abbreviations of the actual behaviors rather than arbitrary symbols (the coding is easier to remember)

- Organize the instrument so it is easy to use

- Establish any directions or rules for its use and follow the rules consistently, for example, record the teacher's or Fred's behavior every 20 seconds or whenever a behavior change occurs

Following these guidelines, Figure 4.12 is an instrument developed for the example with which we have been concerned. To use the instrument the observer records the student's (Fred's) on-/off-task behaviors every 20 seconds or whenever a change in the behavior occurs. At the same time the observer also records the number that represents the appropriate teacher behavior categories (1, 2, or 3). Using the data provided in Figure 4.12 we see that at the first observation Fred was talking to another student (T) and the teacher was sitting at the desk (1). The information was recorded 1−T in the first observation space. (Note that T−1 would give the same information if you chose to write down the student's behavior first and the teacher's second.)

Use: To describe the kinds of off-task behaviors one particular student engages in, and to describe the activity and location of teacher simultaneously.
Purpose: To see if the teacher's physical location in the classroom appears related to the student's on-off-task behavior.

Teacher Behavior Categories

1 Teacher sitting at desk
2 Teacher working with student or small group close to Fred (within eight feet)
3 Teacher working with student or small group away from Fred (more than eight feet away)

Student Behavior Categories

On-Task behaviors
- H requesting help from teacher
- R+ reading class-related material
- W+ working on assignment

Off-Task Behaviors
- T talking to another student
- OS out of seat
- D drawing or doodling
- G gazing or daydreaming
- W– working on nonclass-related assignment
- O other

Code

1.	1—T	19.	______
2.	1—T	20.	______
3.	1—T	21.	______
4.	3—G	22.	______
5.	3—G	23.	______
6.	3—D	24.	______
7.	2—H	25.	______
8.	2—W+	26.	______
9.	2—W+	27.	______
10.	2—W+	28.	______
11.	3—G	29.	______
12.	3—OS	30.	______
13.	3—T	31.	______
14.	1—T	32.	______
15.	1—T	33.	______
16.	3—W+	34.	______
17.	3—W+	35.	______
18.	3—W+	36.	______

FIGURE 4.12 Teacher location/student off-task behavior analysis.

Mastery Test

OBJECTIVE 6 TO SELECT OR CONSTRUCT APPROPRIATE OBSERVATION INSTRUMENTS FOR A GIVEN AREA OF TEACHER INTEREST OR CONCERN

For each of the following items design an observation instrument that will yield the called-for information.

1. Context: Ms. Williams is working with 20 third-grade pupils. During the preobservation conference she indicated that the lesson you will be observing will be a 20-minute teacher-led discussion on a story the students have read. She expressed a concern over increasing the involvement of students in teacher-led discussions. She particularly wants to know which students do and don't participate, and how student-volunteered comments and questions compare in number with teacher-directed student responses.

   Task: Design an observation instrument to collect appropriate data for this context, focusing on student behavior.

2. Context: Mr. Ramirez seems to have difficulty getting lessons started on time with his tenth-grade English students. Instructional activities don't begin until 5 to 10 minutes after the bell rings.

   Task: Design an observation instrument to collect data on how the teacher spends the first 5 to 10 minutes of class.

3. Context: Mrs. Franklin has not been able to establish the type of socioemotional climate in her classroom that she would like. She suspects that she does not send positive affective messages consistently, she may even be sending hostile messages to the children.

   Task: Design an observation instrument that will gather data on supportive teacher behavior and hostile teacher behavior. Identify the grade level and subject (if relevant) that Mrs. Franklin teaches.

Answer Key

Mastery Test, Objective 6

1. The observation instrument could take many different forms. One form is the use of a seating chart to code which students: (a) volunteer and are called on; (b) volunteer and are not called on; (c) are directed by the teacher to answer. The volunteered statements could be further differentiated between comments and questions, if desired. The same information could be collected using frequency counts of the above-named behavior categories without using a seating chart. In both cases the data could be tabulated for individual students and for the class as a whole.
2. Working with the teacher, the supervisor should identify teacher behaviors and activities that may occur during the first ten minutes of class. These activities are behavioral categories which could be tallied in terms of frequency counts. The observed behaviors could be recorded by category at fixed intervals, say every ten seconds. Another way would be to time the duration of each behavior category as the teacher engages in each activity. Either way you will have an indication as to what activities the teacher engaged in, and either the time or the proportion of time spent in each activity. Some example behavior categories might include:

(a) talking to students; (b) talking to peer(s); (c) organizing for lesson; (d) handling late passes; (e) distributing papers; (f) taking attendance. If you chose not to use an observation instrument, taking anecdotal records would also yield relevant information.

3. A frequency count format might work well with this concern. The supervisor and teacher should identify supportive teacher behaviors and hostile teacher behaviors. Among the supportive behaviors might be: (a) the number of statements of endearment made by the teacher, such as *dear, honey*, and so forth; (b) the number of supportive statements made by the teacher, such as *that's right, very good*, and so forth; (c) the number of nonverbal supportive teacher behaviors, such as smiles, nods of approval, pats on the back. Examples of hostile teacher behavior might include: (a) the number of sarcastic comments; (b) the number of times the teacher yells; (c) the number of reproving statements the teacher makes, such as "Don't do that!" "No, that's wrong"; (d) the number of nonverbal hostile behaviors, such as frowns, scowls, glares, slapping the student. As each of these behaviors occur a tally is recorded. If you and the teacher were interested in knowing which students received supportive and hostile behaviors from the teacher, each behavior category could be coded on a seating chart.

Acknowledgments

The author wishes to thank Howard L. Jones for his editorial comments on an earlier draft of this chapter.

NOTES

1. These questions were adapted from N.J. Boyan and W.D. Copeland, *Instructional Supervision Training Program* (Columbus, Ohio: Charles E. Merrill, 1978), pp. 54–55.

2. K.A. Acheson, and M. D. Gall, *Techniques in the Clinical Supervision of Teachers* (New York, Longman, 1980), p. 47.

ADDITIONAL READINGS

Acheson, K.A., and M.D. Gall. *Techniques in the Clinical Supervision of Teachers*. New York: Longman, 1980.

Beegle, C.W., and R.M. Brandt, eds. *Observational Methods in the Classroom*. Washington, D.C.: Association for Supervision and Curriculum Development, 1973.

Boyan, N.J., and W.D. Copeland. *Instructional Supervision Training Program*. Columbus, Ohio: Charles E. Merrill, 1978.

Champagne, D., and R.C. Hogan. *Consultant Supervision: Theory and Skill Development*. Wheaton, Ill.: CH Publications, 1981.

*Flanders, N.A. *Analyzing Teacher Behavior*. Reading, Mass.: Addison-Wesley, 1970.

Good, T.L., and J.E. Brophy. *Looking in Classrooms*, 3rd ed. New York: Harper and Row, 1984.

Hansen, J. "Observation Skills. In *Classroom Teaching Skills: A Handbook*, edited by James M. Cooper. Lexington, Mass.: D.C. Heath, 1977.

*Simon, A., and E.G. Boyer, eds. *Mirrors for Behavior: An Anthology of Observation Instruments*. Philadelphia: Research for Better Schools, vols. 1–6, 1967 vols. 7–14, 1970. ERIC No. ED 029 833, 031, 613, 042 937.

*Stallings, J.A. *Learning to Look: A Handbook on Classroom Observation and Teaching Models*. Belmont, Calif.: Wadsworth, 1977.

Turney, C. et al. *Supervisor Development Programmes: Role Handbook*. Sydney, Australia: University of Sydney Press, 1982.

* These references are useful for examining more complex, elaborate observation instruments.

ANALYSIS SKILLS

5

James M. Cooper

OBJECTIVE 1 To organize and display observational data
OBJECTIVE 2 To analyze and interpret data generated by given observation instruments
OBJECTIVE 3 To identify patterns of teaching behavior from verbatim data, and to hypothesize about the possible effects of those patterns on pupils

INTRODUCTION

In order to meet the objectives of this chapter the reader should have successfully completed the previous chapter on observation skills, as the knowledge and skills gained in that chapter are prerequisites for this chapter.

Observation and analysis are closely related; in fact, the division of these two topics into separate chapters is based more on organizational considerations than on conceptual distinctions. Observations flows into analysis naturally and easily in the supervision process. Having collected descriptive data via different observational techniques and instruments, the supervisor and teacher are faced with interpreting the data and making sense of them. In many ways the analysis process is more demanding than the data collection process. Developing observation skills requires the supervisor to be aware of and to control, as well as possible, personal biases and perceptual selectivity, use observation instruments already in existence, develop new instruments when the situations call for them, and employ a variety of other techniques to collect information. Although not easy to master, in my experience, beginning supervisors have less difficulty with these skills than they do with those of analysis. It is not uncommon for beginning supervisors, for example, to examine data and either fail to identify certain relationships and implications that appear in the data, or to identify only the most obvious, and in many cases superficial, patterns of behavior.

Analyzing classroom data is a highly intellectual process that demands good, logical reasoning; familiarity with multiple ways of categorizing and viewing classroom events; and the ability to recognize from the data implications for students' learning. It is well beyond the scope of this chapter to help you develop proficiency in these areas. What this chapter will do, however, is to provide you with some skills and some practice in these areas. The single most important step you can take to develop analysis skills, in my opinion, is to immerse yourself in the literature related to the study of teaching and teacher effectiveness. Discover how researchers and students of teaching effectiveness analyze and describe teacher and student behavior, what categories they use to classify behavior, and what findings they have discovered regarding effective teaching behavior. By doing so you will begin to develop new concepts and theories that will assist you to analyze and interpret the information you collect. You will also discover that these new concepts and conceptual frameworks will assist you in developing observation instruments. Both your observation and analysis skills will benefit. Books such as Thomas L. Good and Jere E. Brophy, *Looking in Classrooms, 3rd edition*, and Michael J. Dunkin and Bruce J. Biddle, *The Study of Teaching*, are good places to start. Remember, the better you understand classroom behavior and the more conceptual tools you have to explain the behavior, the better you will be able to analyze observational data.

OBJECTIVE 1 TO ORGANIZE AND DISPLAY OBSERVATIONAL DATA

A supervisor I know likes to joke about the confidentiality of the notes he takes when visiting classrooms. The confidentiality exists because no one else can read his handwriting. Although he likes to joke about it, this situation illustrates a familiar phenomenon concerning supervisors: the raw data collected during an observation are often difficult to interpret as such. Sometimes the data are too messy; sometimes more data have been collected than can be used; and sometimes the data lack organization. To present such data to the teacher may only serve to confuse rather than enlighten. Observational data are more understandable when they are organized into meaningful units and presented in a clear manner. Several different modes and formats for presenting data will be discussed in this objective.

Frequency Distributions

In the last chapter on observation skills one of the formats for collecting data was using *frequency counts*. Figures 4.8 and 4.9 in that chapter were examples of observation instruments based on frequency counts. The raw data from Figure 4.9 are displayed in Figure 5.1. By tallying the incidence of each category, the raw data can be collapsed into a frequency distribution, which merely represents the number of times each behavior was observed (Figure 5.2). A different perspective can be achieved by converting the frequencies to percentage values, as is done in Figure 5.3.

Percentage values are useful when you want to compare different administrations of the same instrument. Because it is likely that the number of incidences of behavior will differ from one administration to another, comparing the frequency distributions from the first to subsequent administrations does not provide a useful basis for comparison. Comparing percentage values, however, makes more sense. Frequency distributions can be used with all observation instruments where the number of times certain behaviors occurred can be determined.

Graphs

Graphs can present similar information as frequency distributions, but provide visual data instead of numbers. For teachers who are pictorially oriented,

Behavior Categories	*Student Name*	*Code*
1. Compliments	John	1. 3
2. Acknowledges answer as correct	Sam	2. 4
3. Gives vague feedback	Mary	3. 3
4. Responds as if answers were incorrect	Rosemary	4. 3
5. Criticizes	Nancy	5. 4
6. Other	Abel	6. 3
	Saul	7. 3
	Saul	8. 3
	Connie	9. 4
	George	10. 3
	Billie	11. 4
	Bob	12. 4
	Margaret	13. 3

FIGURE 5.1 Teacher's response to unexpected answers.

Code	*f* (frequency)
1	0
2	0
3	8
4	5
5	0
6	0

FIGURE 5.2 Frequency distribution by code. (*Note:* Each student gave only one unexpected answer except Saul who gave two.)

Code	Frequency	Percentage
1	0	0
2	0	0
3	8	61.5
4	5	38.5
5	0	0
6	0	0

FIGURE 5.3 Percentage distribution of frequencies. (*Note:* The percentage distribution for each student was 8.3 except for Saul for whom it was 16.6.)

graphs may present the data in a more understandable and persuasive manner than frequency distributions. However, graphs do take longer to develop than frequency distributions.

The data in a frequency distribution can be shown graphically by a *bar graph* (also known as a histogram) or by a *frequency polygon.* When using graphic methods to present data, two axes are drawn at right angles to one another. The Y axis (vertical) should be approximately two-thirds the length of the X axis (horizontal). Thus, the graph should be rectangular in shape, two units high and three units wide.

Suppose, for example, that using a diagram of a classroom you collected data on the teacher's location and the amount of time spent in each quadrant of the room similar to Figure 4.5. After tallying the time spent in each quadrant, you created the following frequency distribution:

QUADRANT	FREQUENCY (IN MINUTES)
A	2
B	4.5
C	1.5
D	8.5

To graph these data using a bar graph (Figure 5.4), the room quadrants are identified along the X axis, while the Y axis designates time of location in minutes. The amount of time the teacher spent in each quadrant is represented by the rectangular columns, each with a width designated by the quadrant identification and a height equal to the number of minutes the teacher spent in that part of the room.

Using the same information, Figure 5.5 illustrates the frequency polygon form of representation. If instead of drawing bars, you located the middle point of each interval (quadrant) and drew lines connecting those midpoints, you would create a frequency polygon. For sake of convention, frequency polygons begin and end on the X axis.

One limitation of graphs is that only one independent variable can be treated per graph. If you use an instrument that produces information on

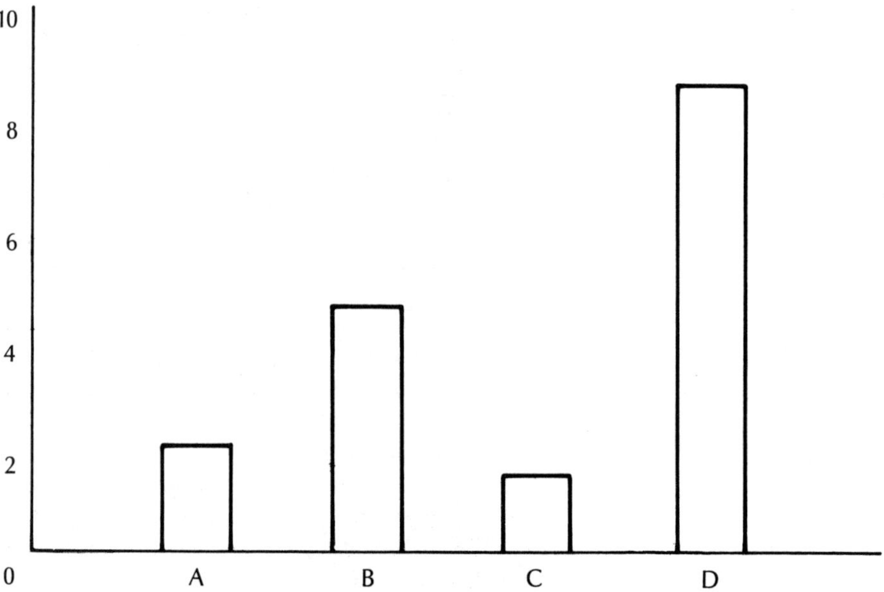

FIGURE 5.4 Teacher location data.

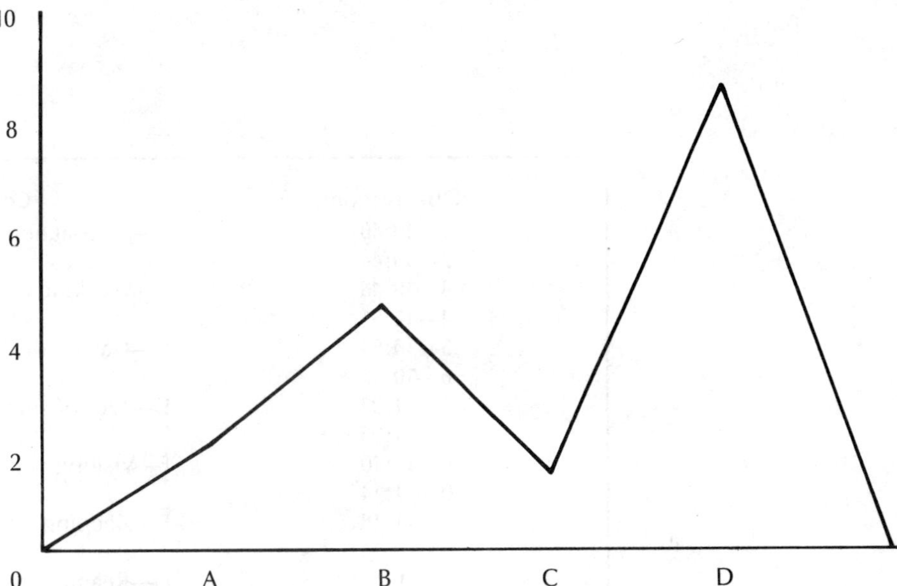

FIGURE 5.5 Frequency polygon for teacher location data.

several variables at once, you might not want to select graphs to illustrate the data summaries. On the other hand, an advantage of graphs is that different observations of the same variable can be displayed on the same graph.

Matrices

Matrices are often useful for displaying two-dimensional grids such as that obtained using student on-task seating charts. Figure 5.6 shows an example of such an instrument and the data obtained from using it. Note that while it is easy to obtain an idea of what each individual student's on-task record was by looking at each box, it is much more difficult to grasp the broader picture of the total class's on-task behavior. By developing a matrix with the type of tasks listed along one dimension and the time intervals along the other dimension, the overall view of the class can be obtained (Figure 5.7).

A matrix displays clearly and simply the relation between two or more variables. Matrices are easy to construct, with the cell values representing the number of instances or learners that meet the conditions designated by the two dimensions of the matrix. This characteristic makes the matrix an appropriate display technique for data gathered through the use of observation instruments.

Other Display Techniques

Some observation instruments, such as seating charts and diagrams, are conducive to the display of raw data. As long as the data are not messy and are relatively easily understood, showing the raw data directly on the observation instrument is appropriate. At times, such as with student on-task behavior, seeing both the raw data and some form of summary matrix will permit maximum interpretation.

Data-gathering techniques, such as verbatim, selective verbatim, and anecdotal records, are probably presented best in their raw form. As long as the writing is legible, which may mean the necessity of typing the data, working directly from the transcript or notes is a preferred procedure. As the analysis of the data proceeds, various types of summary charts or lists can be developed to focus on the pertinent data. Pattern analysis charts, which will be discussed later in the chapter, would be an example of this type of summary emanating from a transcript.

Observations	Codes
1—10:40	A—At assigned task
2—10:44	
3—10:48	B—Working on another subject
4—10:51	
5—10:54	C—Gazing or daydreaming
6—10:58	
7—11:02	D—Out of seat
8—11:06	
9—11:10	E—Visiting with neighbor
10—11:14	
11—11:18	F—Sleeping
	G—Reading magazine

A	B	C	D	E	F
1-A 6-A 2-A 7-A 3-A 8-A 4-A 9-A 5-A 10-A 11-D	1-E 6-A 2-E 7-E 3-B 8-E 4-B 9-E 5-E 10-E 11-E	1-E 6-A 2-A 7-A 3-A 8-A 4-A 9-A 5-A 10-A 11-D	1-E 6-D 2-D 7-A 3-D 8-A 4-A 9-A 5-A 10-E 11-E	1-B 6-D 2-A 7-A 3-A 8-A 4-A 9-A 5-A 10-E 11-D	1-A 6-A 2-A 7-D 3-A 8-A 4-A 9-A 5-A 10-A 11-A
1-A 6-A 2-A 7-A 3-A 8-A 4-A 9-E 5-A 10-D 11-E	1-A 6-A 2-A 7-A 3-A 8-A 4-A 9-A 5-A 10-A 11-A	1-B 6-A 2-B 7-A 3-B 8-A 4-D 9-D 5-A 10-A 11-A	1-A 6-D 2-A 7-A 3-A 8-A 4-A 9-A 5-A 10-A 11-A	1-A 6-A 2-A 7-D 3-A 8-D 4-D 9-A 5-A 10-E 11-F	1-E 6-A 2-A 7-D 3-A 8-C 4-A 9-A 5-A 10-A 11-A
1-B 6-A 2-A 7-A 3-D 8-A 4-A 9-A 5-A 10-A 11-A	1-A 6-A 2-A 7-A 3-A 8-A 4-A 9-D 5-E 10-E 11-A	1-B 6-A 2-D 7-A 3-A 8-A 4-A 9-D 5-A 10-A 11-D	1-A 6-A 2-A 7-A 3-A 8-A 4-A 9-A 5-A 10-A 11-A	1-A 6-A 2-A 7-A 3-A 8-A 4-E 9-A 5-A 10-A 11-D	1-C 6-D 2-C 7-D 3-C 8-E 4-C 9-C 5-E 10-E 11-D
1-A 6-A 2-A 7-E 3-A 8-E 4-A 9-A 5-C 10-E 11-E	1-A 6-A 2-B 7-A 3-A 8-A 4-A 9-A 5-A 10-A 11-A	1-A 6-A 2-A 7-A 3-E 8-A 4-A 9-A 5-A 10-A 11-A	1-A 6-A 2-A 7-A 3-A 8-E 4-A 9-A 5-A 10-A 11-A	1-A 6-A 2-A 7-D 3-A 8-D 4-E 9-A 5-D 10-D 11-F	1-D 6-A 2-A 7-A 3-A 8-A 4-A 9-A 5-A 10-A 11-A
	1-C 6-D 2-A 7-A 3-A 8-A 4-A 9-E 5-A 10-A 11-A	1-A 6-A 2-A 7-A 3-D 8-E 4-A 9-D 5-A 10-A 11-A	1-A 6-A 2-A 7-A 3-A 8-E 4-A 9-F 5-A 10-F 11-F		1-A 6-A 2-D 7-A 3-A 8-A 4-E 9-A 5-A 10-A 11-E

FIGURE 5.6 Classroom observation sheet—Time on-task. (From J. Denton, *Data Presentation and Analysis*, School Based Teacher Educator Series, Houston, Texas, University of Houston, College of Education, 1977.)

TASKS	10:40	10:44	10:48	10:51	10:54	10:58	11:02	11:06	11:10	11:14	11:18
A. At assigned task	17	21	21	21	23	23	21	18	19	18	14
B. Working on another subject	4	2	2	1	—	—	—	—	—	—	—
C. Gazing/Daydreaming	2	1	1	1	1	—	—	1	1	—	—
D. Out of seat	1	3	3	2	1	5	5	3	4	2	6
E. Visiting with neighbor	4	1	1	3	3	—	2	6	3	7	5
F. Sleeping	—	—	—	—	—	—	—	—	1	1	3
G. Reading magazines	—	—	—	—	—	—	—	—	—	—	—
Percentage of students at task	61	75	75	75	82	82	75	65	68	65	50

FIGURE 5.7 Time-task matrix showing frequency of students engaged in various tasks during a class period. (From J. Denton, *Data Presentation and Analysis*, School Based Teacher Educator Series, Houston, Texas, University of Houston, College of Education, 1977.)

Mastery Test

OBJECTIVE 1 TO ORGANIZE AND DISPLAY OBSERVATIONAL DATA

1. Arrange the following raw data from an observation instrument on teacher praise into a frequency distribution. Also, for each code, compute a percentage distribution as well.

BEHAVIOR CATEGORIES	STUDENT NAME	CODE
A Perseverance or effort	Marge	1. C
B Progress toward achievement	John	2. E
C Success achievement	Pat	3. C
D Good thinking	Frank	4. G
E Imagination or creativity	Joanne	5. F
F Neatness	John	6. E
G Compliant or good behavior	Jeff	7. B
H Thoughtfulness	Cindy	8. A
	Becky	9. C
	Marge	10. F
	Frank	11. G
	John	12. E
	Becky	13. C
	John	14. C
	Cindy	15. A

2. Using the same data supplied for Question 1, display the data in both bar graph and frequency polygon format.

3. Using the following raw data, construct a matrix that will easily permit the comparison of boys versus girls.

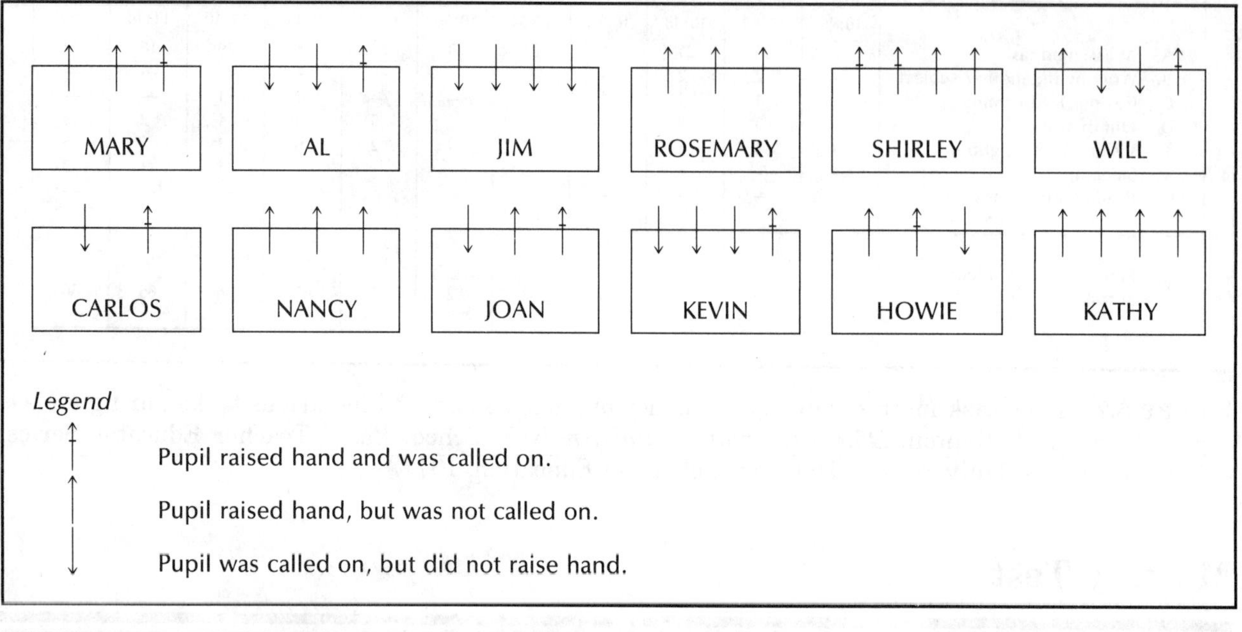

Answer Key

Mastery Test, Objective 1

1. Frequency distributions can be developed for code categories. These distributions would look like this:

CODE	FREQUENCY	PERCENTAGE
A	2	13.3
B	1	6.7
C	5	33.3
D	0	0
E	3	20
F	2	13.3
G	2	13.3
H	0	0

If you want to determine how many times each student received praise for each category of praise, then you would construct a matrix with one axis being the code categories and the other axis being the students' names. The instances that each student received a specific category of praise would fill in the cells created by the matrix.

2.

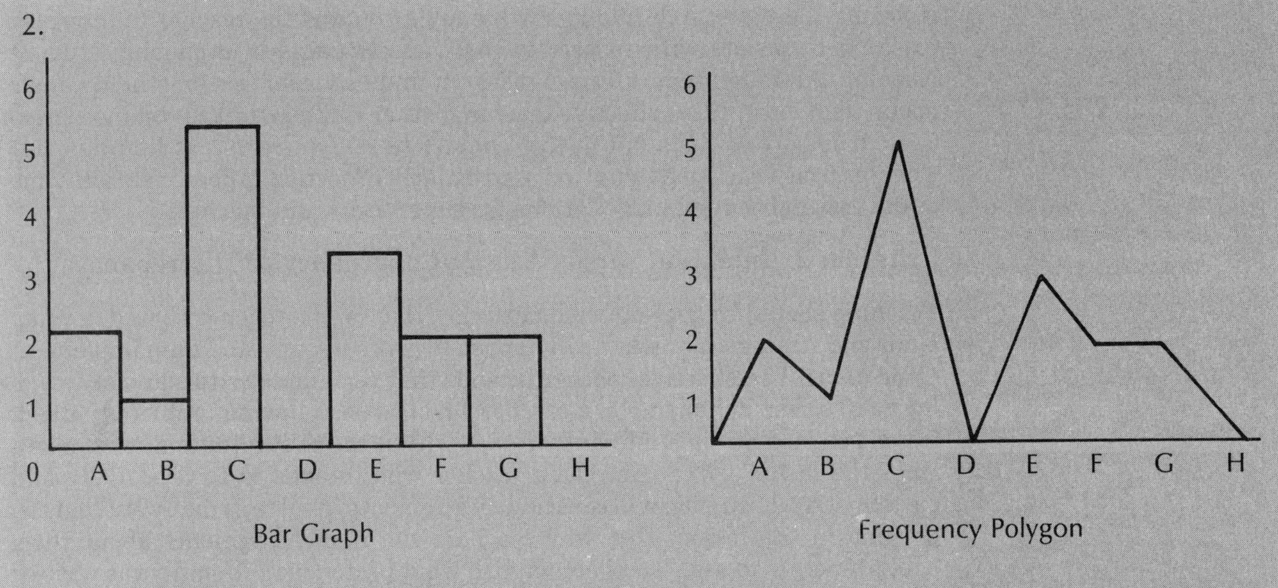

Bar Graph

Frequency Polygon

3. A matrix might look something like this:

	GIRLS							BOYS						
	M	R	S	K	J	N	TOTAL	A	J	W	C	K	H	TOTAL
Raised hand: Called on	1		2		1		4	1		1	1	1	1	5
Raised hand: Not called on	2	3	2	4	1	3	15			1			1	2
Called on: Hand not raised					1		1	2	4	2	1	3	1	13

OBJECTIVE 2 TO ANALYZE AND INTERPRET DATA GENERATED BY GIVEN OBSERVATION INSTRUMENTS

Up to this point you have developed some skill and knowledge in how to use observational techniques and develop observation instruments and to collect, organize, and display data. The next step in the process is to make sense of the data; that is, for you and the teacher to determine the implications of the data for what the teacher does in the classroom. There are, I believe, three major criteria to guide you and the teacher in the analysis and interpretation process. These criteria are presented below in the form of questions:

> Are there research findings that indicate the appropriateness or inappropriateness of certain behaviors revealed by the data?
>
> Do the data indicate congruency or discrepancy between what the teacher intended and what occurred in the lesson?
>
> Do the data reveal any patterns of behavior and, if so, can you hypothesize about possible student learnings that might accrue if these patterns repeated themselves often?

Let's explore each of these in a little more depth.

Criterion 1: Research Findings

In the last 15 or 20 years research on teaching and teacher effectiveness has taken giant steps forward. New paradigms and research methodologies have been developed and have produced findings that can guide supervisors and teachers to distinguish between more and less effective teaching behaviors.

Knowing these research findings will enable you and the teacher to interpret teaching behaviors with respect to their effectiveness in producing student learning. Although some of these research findings reinforce long-held beliefs about what constitutes effective teaching, other findings refute common practices. It is beyond the scope of this chapter to review pertinent findings, but Chapter 6 on Teacher Evaluation, particularly Objective 2, does mention some of the research having implications for supervisors and teachers.[1]

Criterion 2: Intention versus Action; Congruency or Discrepancy

Teaching should be goal-directed behavior; that is, the teacher should develop plans and strategies for what will happen in given lessons, and then implement those plans. The effective teacher intends that certain activities and/or learnings will occur. For example, a teacher who has been having problems getting lessons started on time may intend that within the first minute after the bell rings the lesson will begin. Or, a teacher who intends to have a lively and participative discussion will consciously attempt to involve as many students as possible in the lesson. One way teachers can make judgments about their effectiveness is to ask, "Did I accomplish what I intended?" Usually the answer to this question is a qualified one, a matter of degree, rather than an unequivocal yes or no. By examining observational data, you and the teacher can answer this question regarding the areas of interest or concern expressed by the teacher in the preobservation conference.

Thomas J. Sergiovanni discusses what he calls the *espoused platform* versus the *platform in use.*[2] The espoused platform consists of the teacher's values, beliefs, and intentions, which when asked about them, the teacher is willing to make public. The espoused platform is what the teacher says ought to be. The platform in use, on the other hand, consists of what the teacher actually does in the classroom and what activities and products the teacher seems to value by virtue of their presence or absence in the classroom. For example, a teacher might state that she values a classroom atmosphere where the students are free to disagree with her and to take independent positions on controversial issues. This would be part of her espoused platform. Observing her classroom discussions, however, might reveal that when students stated a position different from hers, the teacher took issue with their positions. When compared to her espoused platform, these data present an incongruency and the discrepancy provides food for thought and discussion. Social psychological research tells us that when people's behavior is inconsistent with their beliefs and values, then a dilemma or tension is created that needs resolution. This resolution can take place in several different ways: discounting the data as being inaccurate or atypical; ignoring the whole thing; changing the strength of the value or belief to make it conform more to the behavior; changing the behavior to bring it in line with the belief or value; or any of several other approaches.

The process of comparing espoused platforms with platforms in use is a powerful one for getting teachers to focus on their own teaching. When discrepancies do exist, they are often the motivation that propels teachers to seek changes in their teaching behaviors.

Criterion 3: Behavior Patterns and Their Effect on Students

Human behavior tends to be patterned, rather than random. When particular situations occur again and again we tend to respond in predictable, patterned ways. This phenomenon is true of teaching behavior as well as in our everyday out-of-class behavior. For example, many teachers have particular speech patterns, such as saying, "OK" or "You know." Other patterns may be mannerisms, ways of responding to certain students, procedures implemented in the classroom, or questioning techniques, to name just a few. Many patterns reflect habits; we may not even be conscious they are occurring. Other patterns are repeated consciously because we see some benefit resulting from them. In either case, examining teaching patterns and hypothesizing about their possible effects on students is a very powerful process for analyzing and interpreting observational data.

Supervisors are not usually interested in classroom events that occur only once or twice. After all, why should you and the teacher spend time on something that is not likely to happen again. Yours and the teacher's time is better spent examining behaviors that are likely to recur, in other words, patterns of behavior. Isolated teacher behaviors have little impact on the students and the atmosphere of the classroom, but patterns of behavior are like a series of waves breaking again and again on the shores of the classroom. Gradually, they begin to shape the way interaction in the classroom environment occurs.

Robert Goldhammer, in a provocative book about the supervision of teachers, proposes a thesis with significant implications for supervisors and teachers.[3] Goldhammer observes that a kind of learning entirely unrelated to the teacher's intended objectives takes place in the classroom. This learning, which he calls *incidental learning*, is not measured or evaluated by the teacher; in fact, the teacher is rarely even aware that it occurs. Incidental learning can facilitate, impede, or have very little effect on intended learning. Goldhammer's thesis is that if a teacher continually repeats certain behaviors, the students will grasp and digest the implications of these "teaching patterns." Isolated teaching behaviors will not have this effect, but behaviors repeated day after day for an entire school year will produce incidental learning that the teacher may not even recognize. Let's look at some examples of teaching patterns and make some inferences about what the students may be learning in response to them:

- All directions are given by the teacher.
- The teacher asserts that he or she will not call on people who answer, out of turn, but often does.
- The teacher assigns extra work, that is, more of the same thing, to children who finish their assignments quickly.
- When a pupil has finished reciting, the teacher generally responds, "Yes, but. . . ."
- The teacher corrects papers, figures attendance, and so on, while, at the teacher's direction, a pupil is reciting.

These practices are illustrations of negative teaching patterns; that is, they distract pupils from the intended object of study and teach children perceptions of themselves, of school, or of learning that can lead to distrust, self-deprecation, confusion, or insecurity. What about the teacher who assigns extra work to those who finish early? Perhaps the students learn to dawdle to avoid extra work. And how about the teacher who responds, "Yes, but . . ." to students' answers? Perhaps the students learn that the teacher has all the correct answers, or maybe they learn not to volunteer answers, since no matter what they say it is never right.

Needless to say, there are many positive teaching patterns as well. For example, teachers who listen intently to student comments and then build on them, without interjecting their own thoughts, may be teaching students that they value students' ideas and participation. Undoubtedly many teaching patterns have positive connotations for some students and negative meanings for other members of the class. The point to remember about teaching patterns and incidental learnings is that the teacher is usually unaware of them and of the power that they may possess. In many cases incidental learnings have a far greater impact on classroom environment and overall learning than do the intended learnings. Objective 3 of this chapter will provide you the opportunity to practice identifying teaching patterns from transcripts.

Analyzing Physical Movement Data

There are no accepted standards of behavior regarding where a teacher should be located in the classroom, or how often a teacher should move among the students. To appraise the appropriateness of a teacher's physical movement depends on numerous factors, including the teacher's objectives for the students, the type of lesson format, and the perceived needs of individual or groups of students. The teacher's plans may also change based on interactive feedback from the students. In other words, knowing what the teacher plans to have happen, and knowing why the teacher departs from the plan, if that in fact does occur, is all necessary to make judgments about the appropriateness of the teacher's movement in the classroom.

In addition, there are several questions that the teacher and supervisor can ask regarding physical movement data that might help to understand their significance. These include:

1. Did the teacher's physical movement relate to the instructional objectives of the lesson?
2. Were the data unique to today's lesson only, or were they representative of the teacher's usual behavior.
3. Were there any patterns to the teacher's physical movement? If so, were they likely to be beneficial and worth repeating, or detrimental and worth eliminating?
4. Was any area of the classroom or any specific student ignored?
5. Did any area of the classroom or specific students receive an unusual amount of attention and recognition?

Your Turn

Figure 4.4, which appeared in the last chapter on observation skills, is reproduced here. Examine the raw data and summarize them in terms of the number of conferences held with each student and the duration of the conferences. After summarizing the data, do you notice any pattern in terms of who does not receive the teacher's attention? Compare your analysis with the answer key.

NORMA	SAM	WILLA	JODY *(M)*	STEVEN
	① 1:30–1:31		⑧ 1:51–1:52	⑨ 1:52 (20 secs.)
DICK	**WALT**	**CHRIS *(F)***	**JEFF**	**CRAIG**
	⑪ 1:59 (30 secs.)		② 1:33 (30 secs.) ⑫ 2:00–2:02	③ 1:34–1:37 ⑥ 1:44–1:46 ⑩ 1:53–1:58

FIGURE 4.4 Observation of physical movement using seating chart.

FIGURE 4.4 *(Continued)*

LYN	MICKEY	CAROL	DELL *(F)*	MARTHA
1:40 Goes to bookshelf 1:55 Returns from bookshelf				
MARVIN	**CINDY**	**SUE**	**JANET**	**SHARON**
④ 1:40–1:41	1:48 Raises hand	Raises hand at 1:35 ⑤ 1:41–1:42		⑦ 1:48–1:50

Note: ① teacher-student conference at student's desk (number indicates sequential order); 1:30—1:31 time at which conference took place and its duration

Answer Key

Your Turn

You might have summarized the data in a frequency distribution such as the following:

STUDENT NAME	NUMBER OF CONFERENCES	DURATION OF CONFERENCES
Norma	0	0 sec.
Sam	1	60 sec.
Willa	0	0 sec.
Jody	1	60 sec.
Steven	1	20 sec.
Dick	0	0 sec.
Walt	1	30 sec.
Chris	0	0 sec.
Jeff	2	150 sec.
Craig	3	600 sec.
Lyn	0	0 sec.
Mickey	0	0 sec.
Carol	0	0 sec.
Dell	0	0 sec.
Martha	0	0 sec.
Marvin	1	60 sec.
Cindy	0	0 sec.
Sue	1	60 sec.
Janet	0	0 sec.
Sharon	1	120 sec.

A startling pattern in the data relates to the frequency and duration of conferences of boys compared to girls. Totaling the frequency distribution according to sex produces the following results:

	NUMBER OF CONFERENCES	DURATION OF CONFERENCES
Males	10	980 sec.
Females	2	180 sec.

Even though female students outnumber males in the classroom, 11 to 9, males had 5 times the number of conferences and almost 5.5 times the amount of time during the conferences as did females. Moreover, two of the males, Jeff and Craig, accounted for slightly more than three-fourths (750 sec.) of the boys' time with the teacher, and almost two-thirds of the total time of both males and females. Whether this is an unusual or normal occurrence is something that should be discussed with the teacher.

Other data worth noting include the fact that both Cindy and Sue raised their hands for a conference. Cindy was never recognized and Sue was recognized six minutes later. In addition, Lyn's 15-minute foray to the bookshelf might warrant discussion.

Pupil On-Task Behavior

Analyzing pupil on-task behavior is fairly simple and straightforward if you are familiar with appropriate instruments and the data collection process. The most useful units of analysis are: (a) the variety and frequency of behaviors exhibited by an individual; (b) the variety and frequency of behaviors exhibited by the group; and (c) the variety and frequency of behaviors exhibited at any one time. For individual students you can examine the data to see how many times they exhibited on- or off-task behaviors, what percentage of the time they were either on- or off-task, and how many different behaviors in which they engaged. For example, look at the data provided for John, an eighth-grade student, in Figure 5.8.

We can see that John was working on another subject (WS) five times, or 33 percent of the time; listening (L) six times, or 40 percent of the time; out of his seat (OS) two times or 13 percent of the time; and talking about nonclass-related topics (T−) two times or 13 percent of the time. Overall, he was off-task nine times or 60 percent of the time, and on-task six times or 40 percent of the time.

1	9:15	1	WS	6	T	11	L	9	9:34
2	9:17	2	WS	7	OS	12	L	10	9:37
3	9:20	3	L	8	OS	13	WS	11	9:40
4	9:22	4	L	9	T	14	WS	12	9:42
5	9:25	5	L	10	L	15	WS	13	9:44
6	9:27							14	9:47
7	9:29				JOHN			15	9:50
8	9:32								

Note:

On-Task		*Off-Task*	
L	Listening	R-	Reading (nonclass related)
TN	Taking notes	T-	Talking (nonclass related)
H	Hand raised	WS	Working on another subject
T+	Talking (discussion related)	OS	Out of seat
		O	Other

FIGURE 5.8 On-task behavior for one student.

He exhibited three different off-task behaviors (WS, T−, OS) and one on-task behavior (L).

The sequence of John's behaviors may also be of interest. He started off the observation period by working on another subject for the first five minutes, listening for the next seven minutes, being out of his seat for five minutes, talking about a nonclass-related item for three minutes, listening again for seven minutes, and finally, working on another subject for at least three minutes.[4]

Sometimes the sequence of behaviors may be indicative of a particular problem. For example, off-task behavior at the end of the period may mean that the student has completed the work assignment, or it might mean that the student was beginning to get bored. Although we cannot make this interpretation with certainty, hypotheses can be developed and discussed with the teacher.

By creating a matrix consisting of the time on one axis and the behaviors on the other axis, the individual cells provide data on the behaviors exhibited by the group. Table 5.1 illustrates such a matrix using the same legend as appears in Figure 5.8.

To interpret these data with some accuracy it is necessary to know what activities are supposed to be occurring throughout the lesson. For example, at 9:34 discussion-related talking suddenly appears on the matrix. This event is easily explained if you know that the teacher divided the class into discussion groups at that time. A warning, however—don't try to interpret too much from data unless you know what happened in the class.

There are several things worth noting about the data presented in Table 5.1. First, note the percentage of pupils on-task throughout the lesson. At the beginning of the lesson the figure is 70 percent and climbs to 87 percent after 12 minutes, varying only slightly during the next 15 minutes (9:27 to 9:42), before dropping off dramatically during the last 8 minutes of the observation. Is there some explanation for why it took 12 minutes to reach an 87 percent on-task rate? Similarly, why was there a sharp decline in the on-task percentage rate during the last 8 minutes of the lesson? The data do not provide us with answers to these questions, but they do provoke us to ask the questions. And this is the way data

TABLE 5.1 Matrix Summarizing Pupil On-Task Behavior

Tasks	*Time*														
On-Task	*9:15* *1*	*9:17* *2*	*9:20* *3*	*9:22* *4*	*9:25* *5*	*9:27* *6*	*9:29* *7*	*9:32* *8*	*9:34* *9*	*9:37* *10*	*9:40* *11*	*9:42* *12*	*9:44* *13*	*9:47* *14*	*9:50* *15*
Listening	19	21	21	21	23	24	24	22	17	17	18	14	14	13	12
Taking notes		2	1	1	1	1	1	3				1			
Hand raised	2			1	1	1	1		2		2		1		1
Talking (discussion related			1						6	8	7	4	3	2	2
Off-Task															
Reading (−)			1	1	1			1	1	1	1	2	2	6	7
Talking (−)	6	4	4	2	2	1	1	2	1	1	2	5	6	7	6
Working on another subject	2	2	2	2	1	2	1	1		1		2	2	2	1
Out of seat	1	1		2	1	1	1	1	2	2		2	1		1
Other							1		1				1		
Percentage of pupils on-task	70	77	77	77	83	87	87	83	83	83	90	63	60	50	50

analysis usually happens; rarely are there answers, but almost always questions are generated that can often be answered by the teacher and supervisor.

Second, during every observation period there were students who engaged in nonclass-related talking. The problem seems particularly acute at the beginning and at the end of the observation time period. Why? Again, this points toward another question to be discussed by the teacher and supervisor.

Third, the teacher and supervisor may also want to single out for discussion those students who were working on other subjects and/or were out of their seats. Are the numbers sufficiently large that the teacher is bothered, or does the teacher think that is a reasonable number to be engaged in those activities? Was the teacher aware during the lesson that there were students out of their seats or working on other subjects? If so, was there a reason why action wasn't taken to bring them back on-task? If the teacher wasn't aware of these off-task behaviors, what could he or she do to become more alert to these behaviors?

One of the major issues that always arises concerns what is an acceptable level of on-task behavior. Is 60 percent acceptable, or should it be closer to 80 percent? Or 90 percent? Determining the acceptable level is not easy. Classes differ from one another in terms of attention span, interest, and other variables that may affect on-task time. One way to help solve this problem is to discuss it with the teacher *in advance* of the lesson to be observed. Try to get the teacher to set a criterion level of acceptance with which the teacher is comfortable and that takes into account the characteristics of the students and the particular lesson to be taught. The first time this occurs the figure set will be somewhat arbitrary. If on-task data are collected several times, then you and the teacher begin to get a sense of the average on-task time for students in that class. Setting goals to reach higher levels of on-task time than achieved in previous lessons can encourage the teacher to improve in this important variable related to achievement. Results of the Beginning Teacher Evaluation Study, conducted with second and fifth grades in reading and mathematics, revealed that, on the average, students were engaged about 73 percent of the allocated time. Engagement was higher in teacher-led settings (about 84 percent) than in seatwork settings (about 70 percent).[5] These figures can serve as a starting point and a frame of reference, particularly for elementary school teachers.

Verbal Flow

As you remember, verbal flow data record who is talking to whom, the initiators and recipients of the verbal communication, and the kind of communication in which they are engaged. Typically, the technique is used to determine which students the teacher calls upon to answer questions, which students volunteer to answer questions, which students actually contribute to the discussion, which students the teacher praises or criticizes, or which students ask questions or make comments.

Analysis of verbal flow data consists of determining whether any patterns exist and, if so, hypothesizing about the possible effects of those patterns. The following types of questions may be useful as you analyze the data.

1. Which students talked and which ones did not?
2. Were there any identifiable differences between those who talked and those who didn't? (For example, such characteristics as sex, race, achievement level, or seating locations.)
3. Were there any differences among the students in terms of race, sex, and so forth, with respect to the various behavior categories which were coded, for example, students who volunteered, or students who received praise statements from the teacher?
4. Did any individual(s) or group(s) dominate?

As with pupil on-task data, analyses can be performed by examining data on individual students or by summarizing the data for the class as a whole. Consider, for example, the verbal flow data collected for the following five students.

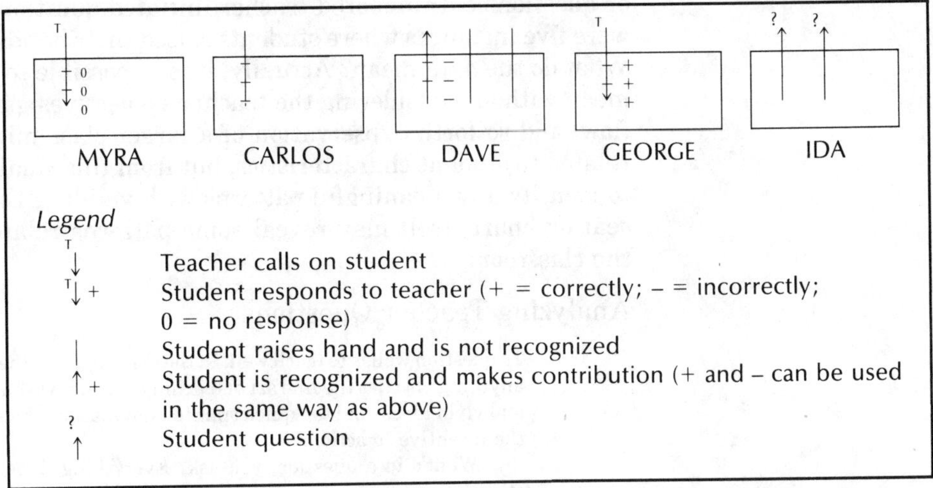

Looking at the data on an individual basis, we can see that the teacher called on Myra three times and each time she answered incorrectly. Carlos raised his hand four times but was never called on. Dave volunteered five times, was recognized three times and gave an incorrect answer each time. George was called on three times and responded correctly each time. Ida asked two questions.

A number of questions arise when looking at these data:

- Why was Carlos never recognized? Was the teacher aware of his volunteering?
- After Dave made three incorrect contributions, did the teacher purposely ignore him the next two times (assuming that left-to-right recording of data represents sequence)?
- Is Myra's lack of response typical? To what does the teacher attribute her lack of response?
- Why were George and Myra the only two students called on by the teacher?

Can you think of any other questions that occur to you as a data analyst?

If we want to examine these data on a group basis we could create a frequency distribution. Such a distribution would look like this:

LEGEND	FREQUENCY
Teacher calls on student	6
Student responds to teacher	6 {+ = 3, 0 = 3}
Student raises hand and is not recognized	5
Student is recognized and makes contribution	6 {+ = 3, – = 3}
Student question	2

When analyzing group data of this type you should note that the second behavior category, "Student responds to teacher," is dependent on the first category, "Teacher calls on student." The data reveal that student-initiated comments or questions outnumbered teacher-initiated questions, eight to six, and there were five instances where students raised their hands but were not recognized. What do the data mean? Actually, it is impossible to determine what the data mean without considering the teacher's objectives, previous patterns of verbal flow, and so forth. Observation of a larger class might reveal some patterns related to student characteristics, but from this small sample, it is impossible to identify any meaningful patterns with validity. Examining the data on the seating chart itself may reveal some patterns related to seating location in the classroom.

Analyzing Teacher Questions

> To question well is to teach well. In the skillful use of the question more than anything else lies the fine art of teaching; for in it we have the guide to clear and vivid ideas, and the quick spur to imagination, the stimulus to thought, the incentive to action.[6]
>
> What's in a question, you ask? Everything. It is the way of evoking stimulating response or stultifying inquiry. It is, in essence, the very core of teaching.[7]

Few educators argue the importance of effective questioning strategies, but there is little consensus regarding what constitutes effective questioning. This lack of agreement among educators makes the analysis and interpretation of questioning techniques a difficult task for supervisors and teachers. A number of different systems for categorizing questions have been developed, but there is little evidence that one system of questioning produces superior results to any other. Among the systems that have been developed are Bloom's *Taxonomy of Educational Objectives: Cognitive Domain*, Aschner's and Gallagher's classification system, Hilda Taba's system for cognitive development, and Ron Hyman's *Strategic Questioning*.[8] Familiarity with these systems will provide you with several different approaches to analyze questions as you work with teachers. It is beyond the scope of this chapter to review these comprehensive systems, but there are some less complicated approaches to analyzing questions that we can explore.

Selected Verbatim Data In chapter 4, we learned that one use of the selected verbatim technique is to write down all the teacher questions word for word (see Figure 4.1 for an illustration). These questions can be analyzed to determine cognitive complexity; that is, do they require simply memorization from the students in order to answer, or do they require the students to apply ideas or processes to new situations. Furthermore, the questions can be studied to determine which ones require the students to analyze, synthesize, or evaluate. Familiarity with Bloom's *Taxonomy of Educational Objectives: Cognitive Domain* will allow you to determine the cognitive level of the teacher's questions. The questions can also be analyzed to determine, among other things, patterns of word phrasing, multiple questions (questions in which the teacher asks two or more questions before giving the students a chance to respond), questions requiring one-word answers, or rhetorical questions.

Observation Instrument Figure 5.9 is a copy of Good and Brophy's observation instrument that can be used to analyze different items related to questioning techniques and strategies. The instrument can be used to record the questions directly as observed (which requires a high level of expertise with the instrument), or the questions can be recorded on audiotapes or by selected verbatim techniques and analyzed at a more leisurely pace at a later time. The instrument has five major behavior categories for coding, each having three possible choices. Looking at Figure 5.9 and the data that were recorded on it, we can see that the first question asked was coded as follows.

1 Academic: factual question

2 Student required to provide fact from memory

2 Teacher called on a volunteer after asking the question

1 Teacher paused a few seconds before asking question

2 Teacher presented the question in a matter-of-fact manner

USE: When teacher is asking class or group questions.
PURPOSE: To see if teacher is following principles for good questioning practices.
For each question, code the following categories:

BEHAVIOR CATEGORIES

A. TYPE OF QUESTION ASKED
1. Academic: Factual. Seeks specific correct response
2. Academic: Opinion. Seeks opinion on a complex issue where there is no clear-cut response
3. Nonacademic: Question deals with personal, procedural, or disciplinary matters rather than curriculum

B. TYPE OF RESPONSE REQUIRED
1. Thought question. Student must reason through to a conclusion or explain something at length
2. Fact question. Student must provide fact(s) from memory
3. Choice question. Requires only a yes-no or either-or response

C. SELECTION OF RESPONDENT
1. Names child before asking question
2. Calls on volunteer (after asking question)
3. Calls on nonvolunteer (after asking question)

D. PAUSE (AFTER ASKING QUESTION)
1. Paused a few seconds before calling on student
2. Failed to pause before calling on student
3. Not applicable; teacher named student before asking question

E. TONE AND MANNER IN PRESENTING QUESTION
1. Question presented as challenge or stimulation
2. Question presented matter-of-factly
3. Question presented as threat or test

Record any information relevant to the following:
Multiple Questions. Tally the number of times the teacher:
1. Repeats or rephrases question before calling on anyone _____
2. Asks two or more questions at the same time _____

Sequence. Were questions integrated into an orderly sequence, or did they seem to be random or unrelated?

Did students themselves pose questions?

Was there student-student interaction? How much?

When appropriate, did the teacher redirect questions to several students, or ask students to evaluate their own or other's responses?

CODES

	A	B	C	D	E
1.	1	2	2	1	2
2.	1	2	2	1	2
3.	1	3	2	1	2
4.	1	2	2	1	2
5.	1	3	2	1	2
6.	1	2	2	1	2
7.	2	1	2	1	1
8.	1	2	2	1	2
9.	1	2	2	1	2
10.	1	2	2	1	2
11.	1	2	2	1	2
12.					
13.					
14.					
15.					
16.					
17.					
18.					
19.					
20.					
21.					
22.					
23.					
24.					
25.					
26.					
27.					
28.					
29.					
30.					
31.					
32.					
33.					
34.					
35.					
36.					
37.					
38.					
39.					
40.					

FIGURE 5.9 Questioning techniques. (From T.L. Good and J.E. Brophy, *Looking in Classrooms*, 3rd ed., New York, Harper and Row, 1984.)

Subsequent questions were recorded in the same fashion. In addition, there is room at the bottom of the instrument to note other potentially relevant information.

Data collected in this manner can be analyzed in terms of the three major criteria discussed earlier in the chapter: relation to research evidence; congruency between teacher's intent and what the data reveal occurred; and patterns that might produce incidental or intended learnings. For example, behavior category D, pausing after asking a question, is strongly supported by research evidence as being a desirable teacher behavior. When teachers increase their "wait time" to three to five seconds after asking a question, (incidentally, most teachers wait only one second after questioning before speaking again), a number of significant changes occur in their classrooms:

1. Students ask more questions.
2. Students give longer answers.
3. Students volunteer more appropriate answers, and failures to respond are less frequent.
4. Student comments on the analysis and synthesis levels increase.
5. Students exhibit more confidence in their comments, and students whom teachers rate as relatively slow learners offer more questions and more responses.[9]

Failure on the part of the teacher to pause for three to five seconds after asking the question may interfere with the students' thinking processes. This illustration demonstrates how research findings can guide us in the analysis and interpretation of observational data.

One cautionary note: Although Figure 5.9 is presented as it was developed by Good and Brophy, behavior category E *tone and manner in presenting question* and a couple of the questions listed at the bottom of the instrument, are more judgmental than descriptive. Unless you can present evidence to support your judgment, for example, an audiotape recording that will be persuasive to the teacher, you are wiser to eliminate those items.

Mastery Test

OBJECTIVE 2 TO ANALYZE AND INTERPRET DATA GENERATED BY GIVEN OBSERVATION INSTRUMENTS

1. Identify three major criteria that are useful guidelines for analyzing and interpreting observational data.

2. Analyze the teacher physical movement data presented here (taken from Figure 4.5) and compare with the teacher's intention to spend approximately the same amount of time in each of the four quadrants of the room.

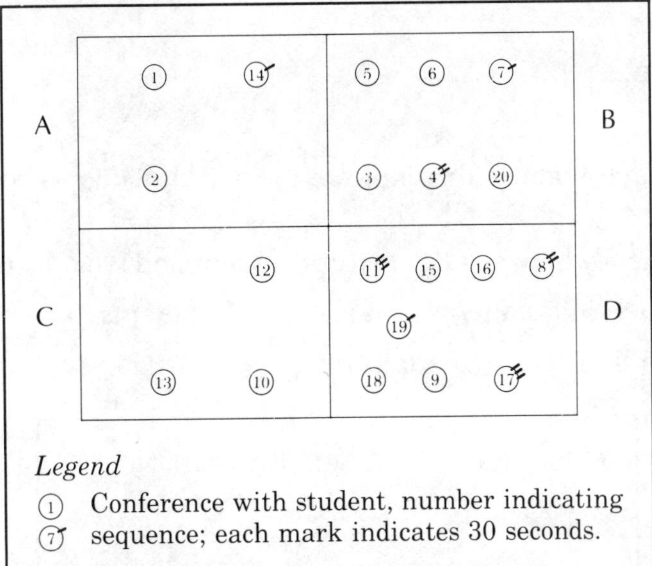

3. Figure 4.12 is an instrument designed to collect data on the on-task/off-task behavior of one student, as well as the physical location of the teacher, to see if any relationship between these two variables exists. The student's behavior is recorded every 20 seconds or whenever a change in the behavior occurs. Examine the data presented in Figure 4.12 and determine what relationship, if any, seems to exist between these two variables.

4. Figure 4.7 is a verbal flow instrument. Examine the data presented in Figure 4.7 and list any patterns or significant aspects about the data that you would want to discuss with the teacher.

5. Using Figure 5.9, the following data were collected. Identify any patterns that seem to exist.

	A	B	C	D	E*
1.	1	2	2	2	
2.	1	2	1	2	
3.	1	2	3	2	
4.	1	2	2	2	
5.	1	2	1	2	
6.	1	2	3	2	
7.	1	2	2	1	
8.	3	3	1	2	
9.	1	2	3	2	
10.	1	2	2	2	
11.	1	2	1	1	
12.	1	2	3	2	
13.	1	2	2	2	
14.	1	2	1	2	
15.	1	2	3	2	
16.	1	2	2	2	
17.	3	3	1	2	
18.	1	2	3	1	
19.	1	2	2	2	
20.	1	2	1	2	

*Not recorded.

Answer Key

Mastery Test, Objective 2

1. In any order:
   a. Are there research findings that indicate the appropriateness or inappropriateness of certain behaviors?
   b. Is there congruency between the teacher's intent and what actually happened?
   c. Are there any behavior patterns that may affect students in a helpful or harmful way?
2. A frequency distribution reveals the following:

QUADRANT	FREQUENCY (IN MINUTES)
A	2.0
B	4.5
C	1.5
D	8.5

   Approximately four minutes in each quadrant would represent an equal distribution. Obviously, the teacher spent considerably more time in quadrant D, and less than the average in quadrants A and C. Teacher and supervisor should explore reasons for the discrepancy between the teacher's intention and what actually occurred.
3. The data indicate that the following patterns are present:
   a. Whenever the teacher is at the desk, the student is talking.
   b. Whenever the teacher is close to the student, the student is on-task.
   c. Two-thirds of the time that the teacher is working with other students away from the student being observed, that student is off-task. Although the sample of behavior is small and no causation is ever implied by data, the teacher might want to locate physically closer to the student to see if his on-task behavior improves. In other words, the teacher may want to test the hypothesis that the student stays on-task more often if the teacher is physically near him.
4. A number of patterns exist, including the following:
   a. All verbal interaction occurred in the center and right sides of the classroom, none at all with the six students seated on the left side of the room.
   b. Only girls received praise from the teacher.
   c. Only boys received criticism from the teacher.
   d. Teacher praised only students who volunteered correct responses or who added to other student's comments.
   e. Teacher criticized only students who volunteered incorrect responses.
   f. Teacher used only girls' ideas, and only those girls who also received praise.
5. The teacher displayed the following patterns:
   a. Most of the questions asked were factual (18 out of 20).
   b. Most of the responses called for by the questions were factually oriented.
   c. Although the selection of respondents was fairly evenly divided among the three categories, there was a sequential pattern of 2–1–3.

d. In 18 of 20 questions, the teacher did not pause for a few seconds before calling on students to respond.

OBJECTIVE 3 TO IDENTIFY PATTERNS OF TEACHING BEHAVIOR FROM VERBATIM DATA, AND TO HYPOTHESIZE ABOUT THE POSSIBLE EFFECTS OF THESE PATTERNS ON PUPILS

One of the data-collecting techniques discussed in Chapter 4 was the use of verbatim transcripts, usually transcribed from audiotape recordings. One of the major advantages of verbatim transcripts is the ease of scanning the transcript for the existence of verbal patterns. Identifying verbal patterns from a transcript is much easier than trying to use an audiotape alone where the data appear and disappear so quickly that the identification of verbal patterns is very difficult. This section of the chapter will provide you with practice in identifying and displaying verbal patterns.

Identifying Patterns

As you read a verbatim transcript certain behaviors may become obvious to you very quickly. For instance, if the teacher uses pet words or expressions so often that it is difficult to miss them, then you have probably discovered a speech pattern. However, many instances of behavior are not so obvious, and you may find yourself wondering if those behaviors really constitute a pattern. A useful guideline in making this decision is: If a behavior repeats itself often enough that it becomes predictable under given circumstances, then a pattern probably exists. For example, you may notice that the teacher says *OK* after students respond to his questions. If this is a pattern then you would expect to find the teacher continuing to say OK after student responses. By checking the transcript of the lesson you can determine whether this is so. You can also identify whether this behavior is a pattern by observing other lessons. Several observations may be necessary to determine whether or not a pattern exists.

The patterns that we discover in a transcript are often the result of our own values, perceptions, and experiences. It is easier to look for patterns that are already familiar to us than to discover new patterns that we have not encountered previously. One of the potential dangers of pattern analysis is reading into the transcript patterns with which we are familiar, and ignoring or not recognizing other important patterns. We tend to identify patterns we have encountered before and to classify data into familiar categories.[10] There are two safeguards against this occurrence. First, when both the teacher and supervisor examine the transcript for patterns, there is less likelihood that one person's perceptions will unduly influence the interpretation of the data. Second, by always supporting the existence of patterns with actual data, the other party can examine the same data and reach a similar or different interpretation. This point is so important that neither the teacher nor the supervisor should ever assert the existence of specific patterns of behavior without providing evidence in the form of raw data. In the absence of data such an assertion becomes an unsubstantiated judgment with which the other person may disagree. As has been emphasized throughout the chapters on observation and analysis, effective supervision of instruction requires the collection of descriptive data.

At this point you may be concerned about your ability to identify teaching patterns. After some practice, however, the problem is not that of finding patterns in the data, but rather of determining which patterns mean something in terms of their effects on students. You will discover many teaching patterns whose effects on pupils will seem inconsequential to both you and the teacher. When this happens little or no time should be spent on them. Your time is more efficiently used concentrating on those patterns that you and the teacher believe may have positive or negative effects on students. But how do you know which patterns these are? The answer to this question is complicated by several factors. In the first place, you never know for certain the effects these patterns may have. At best, you are forming hypotheses about these patterns and their effects. You are really asking the question, "If this pattern is repeated over and over again, what are the students likely to learn?" Is the result likely to be positive in terms of contributing to student learning, self-concept, or whatever other learning outcomes are deemed important? Or is the result likely to interfere with the students' learning, creating poor self-concepts, or in some way adversely affecting what the teacher and school value?

A second complicating factor is that most teaching patterns cannot be clearly identified as being simply positive or negative. Although a few teaching patterns, such as teacher criticism and sarcasm, are clearly in one camp or another, many other patterns can be interpreted as being either positive and/or negative, or sometimes positive and sometimes negative. Also, a moderate teaching pattern may have positive effects, while an excess of the same pattern may produce negative results. Teacher praise, for example, may produce positive effects in moderation, but could produce negative results when used in excess.

A third factor to consider is that all students are not alike. A particular teaching pattern may produce positive outcomes for one student and negative outcomes for another. An instructional pattern of allowing independent work by students, for example, may foster learning in some students and hinder learning for students who require more direction.

Despite the fact that interpreting the effects of teaching patterns is never precise, the concept is powerful and makes sense to educators. As a supervisor it makes more sense to concentrate on repeating behaviors and their effects than on behaviors that occur seldom or erratically. Being able to hypothesize about the effects of these patterns also gives teachers the opportunity to reveal some of their *espoused platform* by expressing their values and beliefs in terms of what should be happening to their students.

Besides the effects of teaching patterns on students, two other criteria for selecting patterns should be considered: accessibility and fewness. Accessibility means that the patterns selected for examination are psychologically within the teacher's capability to deal with them. It will do no good for the supervisor to press the teacher to consider teaching patterns that the teacher is unable or unwilling to confront. Being able to read the teacher's feelings toward particular issues and patterns is an important skill for the supervisor to develop. The criterion of fewness is important because it is easy for the teacher to feel overwhelmed by data and not know what specific changes are called for. It is a much more effective supervisory practice to consider one or two important and accessible teaching patterns than to examine numerous patterns and their potential effects. The recommendation here is to keep the number of issues manageable.

Categories of Patterns

There are many types of behavior patterns that can be found in classrooms. It is sometimes helpful, particularly when you have had little experience in identifying teaching patterns, to think of possible categories in which teaching patterns might exist. One category, for instance, might be *questioning* procedures. All teachers ask questions. Do particular teachers manifest certain patterns of behavior in their questioning styles? To discover if this is true, the following questions might be asked:

1. Does the teacher ask questions at one particular conceptual level to the neglect of other levels?
2. Are the teacher's questions clearly stated?

3. Are there any patterns in terms of who the teacher directs the questions toward, for example, boys vs. girls, front of room vs. back?
4. Does the teacher answer his or her own questions?
5. Does the teacher use questions as a way of punishing or rewarding students?
6. Does teacher use multiple questions?
7. How does the teacher distribute questions in terms of inviting anyone to respond vs. calling on specific students?

Of course, this list of questions doesn't exhaust the possibilities. You can probably think of many other questions that might help you to discover if any patterns of questioning behavior exist.

Your Turn

Some of the most commonly occurring categories of teaching patterns and a few questions you might ask about each are listed below. As you examine these categories, see if you can think of any other questions you might ask which could reveal the existence of teaching patterns. Also, see if you can think of any other categories that you can add to the list.

1. Interaction patterns
   a. Is there any predominant interaction pattern, for example, teacher-student-teacher?
   b. Does student-student interaction occur?
   c.
   d.
2. Speech patterns
   a. Does the teacher use particular expressions, words, or phrases frequently?
   b. Does teacher use incomplete or run-on sentences?
   c.
   d.
3. Reactions to student responses
   a. How does teacher respond when students give unexpected answer?
   b. Does teacher use or accept student responses?
   c. Does teacher encourage students to respond to one another?
   d. When students give an incorrect response, how does teacher react?
   e.
   f.
4. Explanation patterns
   a. Does teacher use clear, precise language or vague, uncertain expressions? Examples of vague expressions might be *a bunch*, *sometimes*, or *all of this*, or any expressions signifying lack of clarity or assurance.

b. Does teacher give examples to illustrate new concepts and are the examples appropriate ones?

c. Does teacher permit and encourage questions from students?

d.

e.

5. Teacher-centered patterns

a. Does teacher draw unnecessary attention to himself?

b. Does teacher talk predominate? (The average amount of teacher talk, according to many studies, is about two-thirds of the total talk.)

c. Does teacher assume certain functions and tasks that could be performed by students, for example, summarizing major points, drawing conclusions?

d.

e.

6. Lesson organization patterns

a. During lesson presentations are major headings clearly presented?

b. Are there significant digressions from the topic, or does teacher stay with the topic?

c. Is there a logical order to the presentation of the topics?

d.

e.

7. Hidden agenda patterns (teacher has a message, often a value, to communicate to the pupils but does not inform them as to what is going on)

a. Does teacher keep asking same question until pupils change their viewpoints?

b. Does teacher interpret pupil comments to fit teacher's agenda?

c. Does teacher force a consensus when none really exists?

d.

e.

8. Reinforcement patterns

a. Are the teacher's verbal and nonverbal reinforcement patterns consistent?

b. Does teacher reinforce students for appropriate behavior, or does teacher only punish or reprimand students for inappropriate behavior?

c. Does teacher use a variety of praise statements or just a few over and over?

d.

e.

9. (Any other pattern)

10. (Any other pattern)

Pattern Analysis Display Charts

When you are examining data to identify teaching patterns, there are three elements that should come forth from the process: (1) identification of the pattern; (2) data or evidence to support the existence of the pattern; and (3) hypotheses about possible student learnings resulting from the patterns. These three elements can be easily displayed in a table form, such as the one shown in Table 5.2. Please note that in the middle column on the table the data that are provided are numerals representing the numbered utterances in the transcript. Instead of rewriting each utterance that would support the existence of a pattern, each utterance in the transcript is numbered sequentially and just the numerals are listed in the data column. This procedure saves considerable time and space by not having to copy each utterance in its entirety. The third column may include more than one hypothesis regarding possible student learnings, including hypotheses that may even be contradictory.

One issue that always arises at this point is the question of how much of the pattern analysis work is done by the supervisor alone and how much is done with the teacher. There is no single correct answer to this question, but I do have some biases on this matter. For several reasons, I think it is a mistake for the supervisor to complete the table working alone. If the supervisor completes all of the analysis, the teacher's sense of acceptance and ownership of the interpretations is likely to be lessened. The teacher may feel that the show belongs to the supervisor and that he or she is merely a spectator. Teachers are also more likely to develop defensive responses to negative interpretations and hypotheses that someone else has made and in which they have had no part. Still another reason for arguing that supervisors should not perform the complete analysis alone is that by doing so teachers receive no practice in analyzing their own teaching behavior; if they don't practice this skill they are not likely to develop it. If supervisors want teachers to become inquirers into their own teaching behavior then opportunities for teachers to do so must be provided.

One procedure that seems to work well is for the supervisor and teacher both to identify the patterns and supporting data independently of one another, and

TABLE 5.2 An Example of a Pattern Analysis Display Table

Teacher Behaviors that Are Patterned	*Support Data*	*Possible Student Learnings*
1. Teacher repeats student statements	7, 17, 37, 47	Students may not listen to other students if teacher repeats; what these students said may be right or important if teacher repeats their statements
2. Teacher accepts student opinions and statements	4, 6, 10, 11, 17, 23, 27, 29, 35, 37	It's OK to say what you think in this class
3. Teacher asks probing questions	21, 37, 39, 41, 43	Teacher wants us to think; teacher won't let us get away with simplistic answers
4. Teacher responds to student questions	23, 29, 33, 35, 37	Students can ask questions in free and open atmosphere; it's OK if we don't know everything
5. Teacher involves a variety of students	5, 9, 13, 15, 25, 39	Teacher wants everyone to participate
6. Teacher encourages students to respond to one another's comments	9, 11, 19, 27, 35, 43	We need to listen to one another; students have good ideas, too

then come together to compare their findings and to discuss possible learnings for the students. This process permits each person to analyze independently, but to work together to determine the meaning and implications of the data. Some supervisors and teachers prefer to work together right from the start, rather than identifying patterns separately and then coming together. What procedure you use should be decided jointly by you and each of the teachers with whom you work.

Mastery Test

OBJECTIVE 3 TO IDENTIFY PATTERNS OF TEACHING BEHAVIOR FROM VERBATIM DATA, AND TO HYPOTHESIZE ABOUT THE POSSIBLE EFFECTS OF THESE PATTERNS ON PUPILS

Analyze each of the following transcripts using a pattern analysis display table similar to Table 5.2. Each transcript represents about a five- or six-minute lesson. Be certain to use descriptive rather than judgmental or value-laden words when describing teaching patterns.

A. Lesson Transcript: Tenth-grade biology class (four students in a microteaching lesson). Teacher's major goal is to have students consider what criteria can be used to determine whether or not a person is dead.

1. TEACHER: These heart transplants raise a very interesting question; that is, "What is a definition of death?" Dave, could you start this out and give us some possible definition of death?
2. DAVE: I guess death would be, uh, when the body has no life whatsoever and can't have any more life.
3. TEACHER: All right, that's very good: when it has no life. But really you have just talked in a circle, haven't you? What's "have no life?"
4. DAVE: Not being able to think, I guess.
5. TEACHER: Not being able to think. All right, so you think that probably the brain is the most important organ, then?
6. DAVE: Un-huh.
7. TEACHER: Is that right? Okay. Then what would you say about a person who has had a massive hemorrhage in his brain—has had a stroke—and this person is not able to communicate, and nobody really knows how much this person is able to think, and yet this person's body is completely alive. Is this person living or dead?
8. DAVE: He's a vegetable.
9. TEACHER: He's a vegetable. But that evades the question—is he living or dead?
10. DAVE: He's living.
11. TEACHER: He's living. All right. So would you say then that we could use brain function as the definition of life?
12. DAVE: Um, human life, I guess.
13. TEACHER: Human life. Well now, let's back track a little bit. So, but do you think then that this person is dead?
14. DAVE: No.
15. TEACHER: No. So actually you've really got sort of a . . . ?
16. DAVE: Paradox.
17. TEACHER: Yeah, you do very definitely, so let's see if we can't find out something that's a little more clear-cut. Louie, do you have any ideas?
18. LOUIE: Uh, when something ceases to exist.
19. TEACHER: You mean when it evaporates?
20. LOUIE: No, when everything stops functioning.
21. TEACHER: All right; now what do you mean by "stops functioning."
22. LOUIE: Dies.
23. TEACHER: Dies. All right, but you really haven't told me anything. Are there any really vital organs that you think would probably define death if they were to stop working?

24. LOUIE: Um, well the major organs like the heart or the kidney or liver.
25. TEACHER: All right, very good. But then we come to the problem of what about machines—you know, kidney machines—that could keep somebody alive almost indefinitely. Would the person who is living only because he has this kidney machine be considered living or dead?
26. LOUIE: Living.
27. TEACHER: Living. So we can't really use that as a definition. Sandi, what do you think about breathing? Would it be possible to use breathing as a defining item?
28. SANDI: No, because I think, uh, that all organisms have to, you know, cease functioning, and then, and then you're dead.
29. TEACHER: You think all of your organs have to cease functioning? Now that's, that's very interesting. What about people whose fingernails keep growing after they're already in the grave; you know this is very common. Was the person buried too soon?
30. SANDI: Um, I don't think that they're functioning. I think it's the aftereffects of your death. I mean, what happened before. Except I'm not sure. I don't know, you know.
31. TEACHER: But it would appear, it would appear, though that there must be something alive then in order for this to happen, wouldn't it?
32. SANDI: I don't know.
33. TEACHER: Maureen, what do you think?
34. MAUREEN: I don't know. I kind of agree with Sandi—when everything stops, then you're dead.
35. TEACHER: When everything stops. Okay, that's, that's actually a very safe and conservative, you know, way to define it. But then we come to a very great problem, because in organ transplants one of the main objectives is to get the organ when it's fresh. There's a much better, you know, chance for success in this case. Therefore, they want to know the instant the person has died—the donor has died—so they can remove the heart or whatever it is. Do you see any moral problem here for the person who might be removing the organ?
36. MAUREEN: Well, if the person's not really dead. I mean, it's hard to tell the exact instant that somebody dies, and if he takes it out too soon then he's actually killing the person.
37. TEACHER: Yes, he really is, in a sense. In what sense would the doctor then be killing the person, do you think?
38. MAUREEN: Well, there might be some, you know, millionth of a chance that he would survive if he wasn't completely dead.
39. TEACHER: So do you think that the doctor has the right to—make this decision?
40. MAUREEN: Yeah, I do.
41. TEACHER: You do, but could you relate what you just said to what we have decided about a definition of death?
42. MAUREEN: Well, it's kind of hard, but he has sort of the experience of knowing that somebody is dead; he's, you know, done so much studying, seen so many people die, that he knows.
43. TEACHER: All right. That's very true—he has had experience with death; and yet even a doctor, even a scientist, can't define death precisely.

B. Lesson transcript: Fifth-grade microteaching lesson with four students. Teacher's major goal is to get students to draw a conclusion as to what kind of jobs and occupations might exist in a geographic area based on the natural geography of the land.

1. TEACHER: Boys and girls, tomorrow we're going to start studying a new state, which you haven't looked at before; and today I want to see if you can develop some good guesses about what kind of occupations we're going to find in this state. I've drawn a map for you; let me describe it briefly. We have the ocean on this side, coming into a bay. Most of the people—the majority of the people—live around this bay. We have rivers coming out; we have railroads leading down from the woods and from the mountains; and we have major highways going this way, and running along in this direction. Now, looking at the map, what kind of guesses do you have about what kind of jobs we're going to find in this state? Go ahead, Sandy.
2. SANDY: Fishermen.
3. TEACHER: Why do you say so? *(Teacher nods head and smiles.)*
4. SANDY: Because of the bay and the ocean.
5. TEACHER: All right, good, good. Cliff, go ahead. *(Teacher writes "fishing" on board.)*
6. CLIFF: Boating in the bay—there would be boating in the bay or sailing.
7. TEACHER: Uh, I think that's probably a good idea. Why do you say so?

8. CLIFF: Because of the bay.
9. TEACHER: The, the bay is, is, uh, protected enough? *(Teacher smiles at Cliff.)*
10. CLIFF: Uh-huh.
11. TEACHER: All right. Fine. *(Teacher writes "boating" on board.)* Go ahead. Darryl. *(Teacher smiles at Darryl.)*
12. DARRYL: Um, well, um, lumberjacks and because, um, 'cause they'll need wood to burn and to put . . . *(Teacher listens intently and steps closer to Darryl as he talks.)*
13. TEACHER: Okay, now hold on here a minute. You've got a good idea going. Now why do you say lumberjacks?
14. DARRYL: Because well, um, the trees and in the sort of forest and . . . *(Teacher nods his head.)*
15. TEACHER: Good, you're doing very well. Do you see anything else around the woods that would lead you to think that they do some lumbering up there? Or can someone else take Darryl's idea and build on that from there? Sandy. *(Teacher writes "lumberjacks" on board.)*
16. SANDY: The railways, they, they send the logs to the factories by railway.
17. TEACHER: All right, very good. You're building on Darryl's idea, and I think that's a, that's a very good point to make. Now let's keep going with Darryl's idea for just a minute. Where you have lumberjacks and where you have forest and logs going to a factory, what else might you expect to find? Darryl? *(Teacher smiles and steps closer to Darryl.)*
18. DARRYL: Um, well, um, they need the sawmill to sand the, um, the wood out so you won't get, you know, much scratches like usually when you first take a piece of wood, you scrub your hand on it, and you get a splinter . . .
19. TEACHER: Okay, you're doing fine. *(Teacher nods and writes "etc." after lumberjacks.)*
20. DARRYL: . . . in your finger.
21. TEACHER: We have other things, then, associated with the lumberjacks. Good, you're taking your own idea and doing something with it. Cliff?
22. CLIFF: Tourism in the city.
23. TEACHER: Very interesting.
24. CLIFF: Because of all the stores.
25. TEACHER: Because of all the stores in the city is why you have tourism?
26. CLIFF: Especially the ladies, because they like to go look through the stores. *(Teacher smiles and laughs.)*
27. TEACHER: All right. Uh, Cliff's got a good idea. Can you see other reasons why we might find tourism? Maybe some better ideas than Cliff had on it. Go ahead, Sandy.
28. SANDY: Well, there could be snow in the mountains, and they could ski . . .
29. TEACHER: All right, another reason . . .
30. SANDY: . . . and bobsled.
31. TEACHER: . . . for Cliff's idea. Melissa, you had another reason?
32. MELISSA: Well, maybe because of the bay, you know, some people like maybe to go boating or something. *(Teacher writes "tourism" on board.)*
33. TEACHER: That's excellent. We took Cliff's idea and we got at least two other reasons why that idea was a good one. I think we're doing fine. Darryl, go ahead.
34. DARRYL: Um, well, there is one other idea, um, I think, um, gold mining in the mountains. *(Teacher listens intently.)*
35. TEACHER: All right—keep going. Why? *(Teacher nods his head in agreement.)*
36. DARRYL: Um, because, um, well they'd be trying to find the mine, I mean, they'd go in the mines, and, um, they'd start hauling stuff like . . . *(Teacher writes "mining" on board.)*
37. TEACHER: Okay, but now, Darryl, hold on a minute. You got a good idea going here, but I'm not sure that you're giving the right reasons for it. What do you see on here that makes you think we're going to find gold mining, or mining in general?
38. DARRYL: Well there is a lot of coal in the mountains . . .
39. TEACHER: All right.
40. DARRYL: . . . and . . .
41. TEACHER: You're saying it right there, I think you see mountains.
42. DARRYL: Yeah.
43. TEACHER: Where you see mountains, you think you'll probably find some mining. Does anything else here suggest that you might find lots of things going on in the mountains? Go ahead, Sandy.
44. SANDY: The railways again, they send things. *(Teacher nods head.)*

45. TEACHER: Excellent, fine, and perhaps this as well. All right, other ideas? You're doing real well. You might want to take a look at some of the things you've said over here and forget about the map for just a minute. Build on your own ideas. Sandy has suggested we'd find fishermen; Cliff, you suggested that we'd find sailing going on here; here are some other things that have been suggested. Now, where we have these, what else might we find here? Melissa, go ahead.
46. MELISSA: I'm not sure this is right, but you know, people would be working on bridges, you know, to, uh, you know, at the end or something for people to pay their way.
47. TEACHER: Good, I think that's an interesting idea. Do you think, uh, it will be one of these? *(Teacher underlines the word "major" in "major occupations.")*
48. MELISSA: Well, uh, I . . .
49. TEACHER: Lots and lots of people doing it.
50. MELISSA: . . . guess so. I don't know.
51. TEACHER: All right. We'll put this down—bridge building, with a question mark, listed here. *(Teacher writes "bridge building?" on board.)* I know you have some other ideas—this is great—and you've taken, you've taken each others' ideas from what you've seen here and really built well with them. Tomorrow, when we get started, we'll have a chance to expand this some, and then you'll have a chance to go into the books and test how good your ideas really are. I think you're going to be surprised at how good your guesses are. Very good job. *(Teacher nods head and smiles at students.)*

Answer Key

Mastery Test, Objective 3

A. You may have identified patterns other than those presented here. If so, fine as long as you can support their existence with data.

Teacher Behaviors that are Patterned	*Support Data*	*Possible Student Learnings*
1. Teacher talks with each student in sequence	Dave (1–16) Louie (17–26) Sandi (27–32) Maureen (33–43)	Everyone will get his turn; once teacher has finished with you, you can relax because teacher won't come back again
2. Teacher repeats students' responses	5, 9, 11, 13, 15, 23, 27, 41	Students don't have to listen to other students because teacher will repeat the answers
3. Teacher asks probing or follow-up questions after student has answered to get students to expand on or extend answers	3, 5, 7, 9, 11, 13, 21, 23, 25, 29, 37, 41	Teacher wants us to think; teacher won't let us get away with simplistic answers
4. Teacher seems to accept students' answers, then questions their correctness	3, 11–16, 25, 35	Teacher sends contradictory messages
5. Teacher interprets students' answers to mean more than the actual words	5, 11, 19, 29, 39, 43	Teacher "steers" discussion in own direction
6. Teacher uses "all right"	3, 5, 11, 21, 23, 25, 43	If students are aware of a high-frequency occurrence, then it may be distracting; otherwise, it probably has no effect

B. You may have identified patterns other than those presented here. If so, fine as long as you can support their existence with data.

Teacher Behaviors that are Patterned	Support Data	Possible Student Learnings
1. Teacher praises students	5, 7, 11, 13, 15, 17, 19, 21, 23, 27, 33, 37, 45, 47, 51	Students feel good about themselves; students try hard
2. Teacher praises students for having good ideas and for using ideas already stated	13, 17, 21, 27, 33, 37, 45, 47, 51	Students learn to value thinking; students learn to listen to and appreciate others' ideas; students learn group problem-solving techniques
3. Teacher asks probing or follow-up questions after student has answered to get students to expand on or extend answers	3, 7, 13, 35, 37	Teacher wants us to think; teacher won't let us get away with simplistic answers
4. Teacher acknowledges and/or uses students' ideas	5, 11, 17, 19, 31, 32, 45, 51	Teacher thinks our ideas are important
5. Teacher uses nonverbal reinforcement (smiles and nods)	3, 9, 11, 14, 17, 19, 26, 35, 44, 51	Students feel good about themselves; teacher likes us

Acknowledgments

The author wishes to thank Howard L. Jones for his editorial comments on an earlier draft of this chapter.

NOTES

1. For a summary of some of these findings, see D.M. Medley, "Teacher Effectiveness," in *Encyclopedia of Educational Research*, 5th ed., edited by H. E. Mitzel (New York: Free Press, 1982), vol. 4, pp. 1894–1903.

2. T.J. Sergiovanni, "Toward A Theory Of Clinical Supervision," *Journal of Research and Development in Education*, vol. 9 (Winter 1976): pp. 21–29.

3. R. Goldhammer, *Clinical Supervision: Special Methods for the Supervision of Teachers* (New York: Holt, Rinehart and Winston, 1969), pp. 11–32.

4. Please note that we cannot say with certainty that John was engaged in each of these behaviors for the times given above since we only sampled his behavior during those time periods. However, since the whole process is built on the assumption that the sample represents the overall behaviors exhibited, we assume that if John were observed listening during the three to five observations, he was listening during all of that time.

5. B.V. Rosenshine, "How Time Is Spent In Elementary Classrooms," *The Journal of Classroom Interaction*, vol. 17 (Winter 1981), p. 24.

6. C. DeGarmo, *Interest and Education* (New York: Macmillan, 1902), p. 179.

7. J. Dewey, *How We Think*, rev. ed. (Boston: D.C. Heath, 1933), p. 266.

8. See *Additional Readings* for bibliographic references for these systems.

9. M.B. Rowe, "Wait-Time and Rewards as Instructional Variables: Their Influence on Language, Logic and Fate Control" (Paper presented at the National Association for Research in Science Teaching, Chicago, April 1972).

10. As a passage from the *Talmud* states: "We do not see things as they are. We see things as we are."

ADDITIONAL READINGS

Acheson, K.A., and M.D. Gall. *Techniques in the Clinical Supervision of Teachers*. New York: Longman, 1980.

Aschner, M.J. et al. *A System for Classifying Thought Processes in the Context of Classroom Verbal Interaction*. Urbana, Ill.: University of Illinois, 1965.

Bloom, B.S. et al. *Taxonomy of Educational Objectives: The Classification of Education Goals, Handbook I: Cognitive Domain*. New York: David McKay, 1956.

Boyan, N.J., and W.D. Copeland. *Instructional Supervision Training Program*. Columbus, Ohio: Charles E. Merrill, 1978.

Dunkin, M.J., and B.J. Biddle. *The Study of Teaching*. New York: Holt, Rinehart and Winston, 1974.

Goldhammer, R., R.H. Anderson, and R.J. Krajewski. *Clinical Supervision: Special Methods for the Supervision of Teachers, 2d ed.* New York: Holt, Rinehart and Winston, 1980.

Good, T.L., and J.E. Brophy. *Looking in Classrooms, 3rd ed.* New York: Harper and Row, 1984.

Hansen, J. "Observation Skills." In *Classroom Teaching Skills: A Handbook*, edited by J. M. Cooper. Lexington, Mass.: D.C. Heath, 1977.

Hyman, R.T. *Strategic Questioning*. Englewood Cliffs, N.J.: Prentice-Hall, 1979.

Taba, H., S. Levine, and F.F. Elzey. *Thinking in Elementary School Children*. USOE Cooperative Research Project No. 1574. San Francisco, Calif.: San Francisco State College, 1964.

Turney, C. et al. *Supervisor Development Programmes: Role Handbook*. Sydney, Australia: University of Sydney Press, 1982.

TEACHER EVALUATION

6

Robert F. McNergney

Donald M. Medley

Objective 1 To define the term *teacher evaluation*, to differentiate teacher evaluation designed to improve instruction from teacher evaluation designed to make judgments regarding teachers' effectiveness and fitness to remain in teaching, and to suggest how these seemingly contradictory functions might be combined

Objective 2 To establish a personal goal for becoming competent in methods of teacher evaluation, and to identify some of the knowledge from research on effective teaching that is relevant to teacher evaluation

Objective 3 To describe a model of teacher decision making that can be used to organize a supervisor's actions to collect and interpret information relevant to teaching

Objective 4 To specify the supervisory skills necessary to assess teachers' professional competencies

Objective 5 To describe how information about teachers' characteristics and competencies can serve as guidelines in designing interventions that will encourage the improvement of teaching performances

Objective 6 To identify factors beyond the immediate control of teachers that affect their teaching performances

Objective 7 To describe ways of improving existing methods of summative teacher evaluation

INTRODUCTION

This chapter concentrates on the supervisory knowledge and skills necessary for evaluating teachers. It does so by trying to accomplish a set of related objectives designed to enable a supervisor to set a plan of action for evaluating teachers, to follow that plan, making corrections when necessary, and to make a reasonable appraisal of his or her ability to reach the goal of a professional level of supervisory practice.

To say that teacher evaluation is one of the most important and troublesome tasks supervisors will ever undertake is a classic understatement. Given the recent spate of national reports critical of teachers and schools, it would be safe to say that it is *the most important task*. Whether supervisors are employed by colleges, universities, public or private elementary and secondary schools, state education departments, or private consulting firms, they are faced routinely with decisions about extending and withholding support for teachers. The job is tough not only because of the philosophical and methodological problems involved, but because these problems must be addressed in a superheated political environment—one where people are quick to blame teachers for our educational ills. Indeed, as Mackey (1976) noted, we are in danger of becoming a nation of teacherbeaters. Only reasonable teacher evaluation can keep this from happening.

But why should teacher evaluation be so difficult? Perhaps, as some writers have suggested, if people know more about the teaching profession than any other—by virtue of having passed so much of their lives with teachers—it may be that people know even more about teacher evaluation than they know about teaching. After all, students have "evaluated" teachers for years, alternatively praising and indicting them for real and imagined qualities. These practices and the attitudes they reflect, however, have had deleterious effects on teachers and teaching and devastating effects on practices of teacher evaluation. Too many people are ready to make judgments about teaching competence without being able to say any more about good teaching than: "I know it when I see it!" If folk wisdom suggests that most people can teach, then it screams that everyone can evaluate teachers.

Fortunately, the educational community and the general public are beginning to realize that a common-sense approach to assessing the quality of teaching is valuable, but not wholly adequate to the task. Problems of teaching and of teacher evaluation are too difficult and complex to be solved by folk wisdom alone. With this realization has come not only increased interest in supervision that tries to identify the weaknesses of teachers, but an increased interest in supervision that remediates such weaknesses while capitalizing on teachers' capabilities. It is this latter type of supervision that demands high levels of professional knowledge and skill on the part of those who evaluate teachers.

In order to select the supervisory knowledge and skills for inclusion in this chapter it was necessary to make several assumptions. The first assumption is that the best kind of information about teaching comes from direct observation of teachers' performances in classrooms and from conferencing with teachers before and after teaching. The second assumption is that teachers' possess certain preexisting characteristics and professional competencies that they bring to bear on their teaching. The third assumption is that possessing information about teachers' characteristics and competencies and their performances in classrooms can help supervisors make reasonable decisions about when and how to apply support to teachers. None of these assumptions may seem especially startling, but they all influence the direction of the chapter and potentially the course of teacher evaluation for those who use this material.

OBJECTIVE 1 TO DEFINE THE TERM *TEACHER EVALUATION*, TO DIFFERENTIATE TEACHER EVALUATION DESIGNED TO IMPROVE INSTRUCTION FROM TEACHER EVALUATION DESIGNED TO MAKE JUDGMENTS REGARDING TEACHERS' EFFECTIVENESS AND FITNESS TO REMAIN IN TEACHING, AND TO SUGGEST HOW THESE SEEMINGLY CONTRADICTORY FUNCTIONS MIGHT BE COMBINED

The term *evaluation* by definition connotes value. Accordingly, the term *teacher evaluation* can be described in terms of attaching value to various aspects of the performance of the role of teacher. Regardless of how formal or informal activities of teacher evaluation may be—from rigorous testing of teachers' skills, attitudes, and knowledge in a college program of teacher education to casual observation of teachers by students in classrooms—they involve collecting information about teachers and/or teaching that lead to judgments about the worth of those who play the role of teacher and the value of their performances.

Supervisors of preservice and inservice teachers, however, are usually concerned with two types of teacher evaluation: evaluation for the purpose of making decisions about entrance to and continuation in the profession, and evaluation for the purpose of improving teaching performance. The first type includes such things as evaluating teachers for admission to teacher preparation programs, evaluating progress in professional coursework and student teaching, evaluating overall progress for granting a college degree (and at the same time in many states, granting a teaching certificate), evaluating for the purpose of hiring, evaluating for continuing contracts or termination, and evaluating for merit. These evaluations are often referred to as *summative* because they represent summations of progress at various points in a teacher's professional life—points at which decisions are made to advance or end a teacher's career. The second type is directed to only one end: that of evaluating teachers in order to help them improve their teaching. This type of evaluation is typically referred to as *formative* because it is intended to form or shape the performance of teachers.

Traditionally, most supervisors have been expected to perform both types of evaluation; that is, they have been called upon to help teachers perform to the fullest of their abilities and to decide, or to help others decide, when teachers should be continued or terminated in training and on the job. Perhaps needless to say, this puts supervisors in a somewhat uncomfortable position. For example, the college or university supervisor of student teachers tries to help prospective teachers learn how to function effectively (or at least to survive) during student teaching. Often a close, even familial, relationship develops between the supervisor and student teacher. At the end of the experience, however, the supervisor is expected to give a grade for student teaching, or to make a judgment that could affect dramatically the future of the student—particularly if the grade is poor. The principal who tries to help the beginning teacher perform successfully and make a recommendation about whether to continue the teacher's contract is another example of a supervisor caught between the rock of supporting and the hard spot of passing judgment on teachers.

Can supervision be supportive and still be used to make decisions that might negatively affect a teacher's career? That is one of the most vexing questions college supervisors, school principals, and other supervisors of teachers face when considering purposes and methods of teacher evaluation. The answer, or more appropriately, answers, are anything but simple: a qualified "yes," a qualified "no," and a definite "it depends."

To the degree that teachers are personally comfortable with another adult in the classroom, supervision can be supportive or virtually free from the threat of negative reflections on their careers. The easiest and maybe the most effective way to make this happen is to separate the role of supervisor as helper from the role of supervisor as gatekeeper by having different people assume the roles. When a supervisor's responsibility is solely one of helping teachers understand how and why things happen as they do in classrooms so that teachers can make their own decisions about improving their performances, then it is likely that teachers will not be threatened by this supervisor. In this case, the primary restraints on supervision as support are the personal and professional confidence of teachers and the abilities of supervisors to offer the kind of guidance that teachers value.

These restraints, however, may be more powerful and pervasive than people realize or care to admit. Even the most capable, confident teachers—maybe especially these teachers—are well aware that good teaching can always be better. And maybe it is this awareness that causes excellent teachers to drive themselves toward higher levels of performance. In some cases, the last thing they may want is for a supervisor or another person to "get in their way" by trying to be helpful. Some beginning teachers who desperately need support and guidance, on the other hand, may be reluctant to take it for fear of appearing weak. The next to the last thing these beginners want is a crutch that appears to compensate for their inabilities to perform their jobs effectively and happily; the last thing they want is some massive and highly visible remedial effort to fix the things that are "wrong" with them. When these conditions exist, it matters little who plays the role of the supportive supervisor. What matters greatly is that the person has something substantive to offer teachers.

Can supervision be supportive and still be used to make decisions that might negatively affect a teacher's career with the same person fulfilling both responsibilities? This definitely depends on the person who serves as supervisor. In order to explore this possibility it is useful to consider briefly the metaphor of supervisor as teacher.

Most teachers are faced with problems of supporting student growth while having to make judgments that could adversely affect students' futures. The high school mathematics teacher, for example, can support students by giving positive corrective feedback on daily assignments, by spending extra time sponsoring the math or computer club in order to demonstrate that hard work can also be fun, and by tutoring individual students in their preparation for taking scholastic aptitude tests. All these activities may be undertaken with no motive other than to help students perform to the fullest of their abilities. Nonetheless, at the end of the term, this same teacher must give students grades in their classes—grades that can help or hinder students' chances for jobs or admission to college. People other than teachers rarely stop to consider the potential conflict in these teaching responsibilities; helping and grading are considered part of the territory of teaching. For the math teacher and his or her students, though, the conflict may be real and present. Even so, the talented teacher manages to balance both responsibilities and intelligent students seem to understand the necessity of doing so.

Supervisors, like teachers, are often expected both to support people and to make hard decisions about competence. It is unlikely that these expectations will change anytime in the near future, particularly if funding for educational programs continues its downward trend. School systems and colleges and universities appear unable to create new supervisory positions that would enable different people to assume responsibilities of supporting teachers and of making personnel decisions. What this means is that in most situations supervisors cannot trade away their responsibilities for making summative decisions in hopes of winning the trust of those with whom they work; they must learn instead to take on both sets of responsibilities. In short, supervisors must learn how to function like those good teachers they encounter—those who support people and, in the end, make reasonable and fair decisions about competence.

And how do supervisors learn to function like these good teachers? Through training? Through experience? By some mysterious reordering of their supervisory genes? The way to achieve an effective balance between supporting and judging is no easier or more clearly marked for supervisors than it is for teachers. But, no doubt, those teachers who have learned have done so, at least in part, by allowing themselves to be affected by their students—by viewing teaching and learning as reciprocal processes rather than by viewing teaching as something that is done only to students. When this view is taken, learner behavior is more than an indication of competence, it is information that instructs the teacher about his or her own performance. If the metaphor of supervision as teaching is to be any more than a vapid slogan, it would seem that supervisors must begin to teach and to be taught by teachers.

Your Turn

If possible, form a group of teachers, parents, and administrators for the purpose of discussing evaluation philosophies and practices. Use some of the following questions to stimulate the group discussion.

1. What should be the intent of teacher evaluation?
2. Who should conduct evaluations of teachers?
3. What role, if any, should members of the community play in the evaluation of teachers? What role, if any, should students play?
4. What should the relationship be between school philosophy and practices of teacher evaluation? If, for example, school philosophy seems to favor certain teaching practices, but there is little hard evidence to suggest that these practices have any positive effects on students, then what should change, philosophy or teaching practice?
5. How and by whom should evaluators be evaluated?

Mastery Test

OBJECTIVE 1 TO DEFINE THE TERM *TEACHER EVALUATION*, TO DIFFERENTIATE TEACHER EVALUATION DESIGNED TO IMPROVE INSTRUCTION FROM TEACHER EVALUATION DESIGNED TO MAKE JUDGMENTS REGARDING TEACHERS' EFFECTIVENESS AND FITNESS TO REMAIN IN TEACHING, AND TO SUGGEST HOW THESE SEEMINGLY CONTRADICTORY FUNCTIONS MIGHT BE COMBINED

1. Define the term *teacher evaluation.*
2. Differentiate formative from summative evaluation.
3. Although the distinctions between formative and summative evaluation are not always clear, note whether the following would typically be thought of as examples of formative or summative assessments.
   a. Interviewing a teacher for the purpose of hiring.
   b. Observing a teacher for the purpose of placing him or her in the appropriate staff development group.
   c. Observing a teacher in order to make a tenure decision.

d. Giving a prospective teacher an intelligence test to decide whether he or she is bright enough to be in the classroom.

e. Asking parents and students about a teacher's strengths and weaknesses so that a case can be made for termination.

f. Assessing a teacher's work habits and attitudes so that he or she may be placed with a team of teachers who will work together to help one another learn how to implement a new curriculum.

4. Do you think it is possible for the same person both to support and judge teachers? What things make these activities difficult? Do you know people who have managed to do both in reasonably effective ways? How have they succeeded?

Answer Key

Mastery Test, Objective 1

1. Teacher evaluation can be defined in terms of attaching value to various aspects of the performance of the role of teacher.
2. Formative evaluation of teachers is a process or set of processes designed to determine teachers' strengths and weaknesses for the purpose of improving their performances. Summative evaluation is also a process or set of processes designed to determine teachers' strengths and weaknesses, but it is undertaken for the purpose of making a personnel decision, i.e., a decision about admitting, failing, passing, hiring, granting tenure, and the like.
3. a. Summative
   b. Formative
   c. Summative
   d. Summative
   e. Summative
   f. Formative
4. There is, of course, no right or wrong answer here. We have tried to argue that it is possible for one person both to support and judge teachers, but there is little doubt in our minds that these tasks will never be accomplished by the faint of heart or the feeble of mind. Many things get in the way: the fear of teachers that information collected about their teaching will be used against them, teachers' general distrust of administrators, the number and level of skills necessary to support and judge effectively, and so forth. These difficulties notwithstanding, there are people who manage both to support and judge teachers. Indeed, it is difficult to imagine how one could offer genuine support without making some hard judgments.

OBJECTIVE 2 TO ESTABLISH A PERSONAL GOAL FOR BECOMING COMPETENT IN METHODS OF TEACHER EVALUATION, AND TO IDENTIFY SOME OF THE KNOWLEDGE FROM RESEARCH ON EFFECTIVE TEACHING THAT IS RELEVANT TO TEACHER EVALUATION

The supervisor who is competent in methods of teacher evaluation is the one who makes decisions about teachers and teaching based on the best information available. The decisions may in the long run turn out to be wrong, but as a professional he or she is responsible for gathering and interpreting such information, and it is on that basis that supervisors should be judged. Like other professionals, however, supervisors frequently have too much to do and not enough time to do it; thus their own methods of decision making tend to suffer. Limited by time and a shortage of resources, many supervisors are understandably anxious to find *the solution* to *the problem.*

H.L. Mencken was fond of pointing out that there are always simple solutions to complex problems, and they are usually wrong. He wasn't referring to teacher evaluation when he fired off this quip, at least he didn't think he was. But too often it seems, supervisors face the pressing, complex problems of evaluating teachers and grab for the first simple solution that comes along. They look for the best supervisory style, the best observation instrument, the best time to conference, the best way to present information and the like. These "best" solutions to supervisory problems usually mean "simplest" and "same in every situation." Unfortunately, these best solutions don't always work.

Competence in Evaluating Teachers

If the competent supervisor is the one who makes decisions about teachers and teaching based on the best information available, then in order to be competent, it would seem that supervisors must decide what information is best, plan and effect its collection, and be able to interpret it. Best information here, however, does not mean simplest information or same information in all situations; in this case best information means most appropriate information. Defining *best* as *most appropriate* is more than an exercise in semantics. In order for supervisors to make decisions about teachers and teaching based on the most appropriate information available, they must command a variety of strategies for collecting and interpreting information about many different teachers in many different teaching situations. Becoming a competent supervisor, then, is a matter of developing a wide array of evaluation skills that can be called up on demand.

This view of what constitutes competent supervision is, of course, similar to others' views of competent teaching. Teachers, it is argued, must accomplish a variety of objectives with many students who vary in needs and abilities. In order for teachers to be successful, then, they must possess a repertoire of skills that can be brought to bear on the problems they face (Joyce and Weil, 1972). No single way of teaching will work with all students and all objectives. The metaphor of competent supervision as competent teaching is more than a handy way of thinking about goals and objectives of supervision. As noted in Objective 1 in the discussion about the dilemma of supporting teacher improvement versus making decisions about continuing or terminating teachers, supervision *is* teaching—teaching teachers to help themselves learn more about how and why they perform as they do.

At the risk of running the metaphor into the ground, there is one more comparison of supervision and teaching that must be made. As the discussion in Objective 3 will point out, good teachers are good not only by virtue of their abilities to perform particular teaching skills, or because they hold a particular set of professional values. Good teachers are good because they can draw upon a base of professional knowledge to make reasonable decisions about teaching. They know their subject matter, they know about child growth and development, they know about the various cultures that shape and are shaped by their students, and the like. In order to be effective, teachers must be knowledgable about a variety of things.

Like teachers, supervisors, too, must build their professional knowledge if they expect to be effective. Supervisors must know their subject matter (for example, research on effective teaching), they must know about teacher growth and development, and they must know about the various cultures of teaching that shape and are shaped by teachers. Such knowledge is necessary if supervisors are to help teachers decide how to teach, structure feedback in ways that teachers will take it and act on it, and understand and appreciate the complexity of life in classrooms and in schools. It doesn't seem unreasonable to think that if supervisors are to reach a level of professional practice, they must know as much about the literature in their field as teachers are expected to know about teaching and learning.

So what, specifically, do supervisors need to know? Some supervisory knowledge is presented in various chapters of this book; for example, knowledge about methods available for collecting data and interpreting the results of observation, knowledge of formulating agreements for observation, knowledge of the methods of establishing plans and setting goals, and so on. But let's examine briefly one other important area of knowledge that supervisors must be able to command if they are to function professionally—that of research on effective teaching.

Research on Effective Teaching

The research literature on teaching effectiveness has grown remarkably in recent years. According to Mitzel (1960) and Dunkin and Biddle (1974) this has occurred largely as a result of researchers investigating interrelationships of the following four types of variables in their search for knowledge about effective teaching: (1) teacher characteristics; (2) contextual variables embedded in the classroom, school, and community; (3) process variables or measures of teachers' and students' transactions during the course of teaching; and (4) pupil products or learning outcomes. Studies that have examined relationships between and among these variables have begun to yield an impressive array of results.

Research on relationships between teaching processes and pupil products has been particularly fruitful. In the early 1970s when Rosenshine and Furst (1971) reviewed this general area of research they identified 11 teacher processes that related to student learning, the five strongest of which were: (1) clarity of presentation, (2) variability of teaching, (3) enthusiasm, (4) task orientation, (5) student opportunity to learn material about which they are later tested. Gage's (1978) later analysis of these types of studies suggested still other important teacher behaviors, or teaching processes that related to student learning. For example, teacher indirectness (willingness to accept students' ideas and feelings, ability to praise, and capacity to provide an accepting emotional climate) related positively to student learning. Teacher criticism and disapproval, on the other hand, related negatively to student learning.

The Beginning Teacher Evaluation Study (BTES), funded by the National Institute of Education and conducted in California from 1972 to 1978, represents the most massive study to date on teaching effectiveness. The various results of the BTES, drawn from research on second- and fifth-grade classes in reading and mathematics, are too numerous to list here. But the major contribution of the study appears to be its focus on academic learning time (ALT) as a measure of learning. Academic learning time is defined as the amount of time a student spends engaged in academic tasks of appropriate difficulty. To make a long story short (and consequently somewhat distorted) the ALT model suggests that the key to effective teaching, or to performing in ways that contribute to student learning, is to keep students engaged in academic tasks with which they can experience some success. This type of teaching, labeled *direct instruction* by Rosenshine (1979), involves maximizing student contact with an instructor (by either teaching the whole group at one time or by increasing the number of aides, volunteers, tutors, and so forth); monitoring student activity; providing corrective feedback; covering content extensively; selecting materials carefully for interest and level of difficulty; and using factual questions and controlled practice.

As Peterson (1979) noted, however, direct instruction may not be equally powerful with all learners and for all objectives. She argued that an "open" approach to teaching works better than a direct approach for increasing students' creativity, independence, curiosity, and favorable attitudes toward school and learning. Furthermore, different students function differently under the two general teaching approaches. "The implication is that, if educators want to achieve a wide range of educational objectives and if they want to meet the needs of all students, then neither direct instruction alone nor open-classroom teaching alone is sufficient" (Peterson, 1979, p. 67).

As any experienced teacher would tell you, there is more to teaching than selecting and implementing instructional strategies. A teacher has to get and hold students' attention before teaching can occur. Classroom management and discipline, then, are traditional concerns of teachers and consequently of education researchers. Kounin (1970), for example, found that effective classroom managers stopped problems in the classroom before they could escalate into serious disruptions. They were aware of what was happening, or "withit," and able to handle more than one thing at a time (that is, they had the ability to "overlap"). These same teachers kept the pace of lessons even and brisk by ignoring minor disruptions and not overdwelling on problems or insignificant details. Furthermore, they demonstrated abilities to keep students alert and accountable by varying their approaches—questioning students at random, creating suspense, looking at students' seatwork, and so forth. In short, research suggests that the effective classroom manager is one who has a fairly large repertoire of managerial tactics that can be brought to bear on whatever problems arise.

Research on effective teaching has taken a number of interesting turns in recent years. Researchers have adopted a variety of methodologies and theoretical perspectives to study problems of teachers, teacher education, and teaching. The result has been not only an increase in substantive knowledge, but a renewal of interest in the study of problems that affect the conduct of teaching and learning.

Your Turn

One of the most difficult aspects of evaluating teachers in terms of the results of research on teaching effectiveness is that of keeping oneself current with such results. In your efforts to do so, you may find the following activities helpful.

1. List the people in your work situation who might be both willing and able to serve as a committee on research on teaching—a study group that collects reports of research, meets periodically to discuss them, and provides information to interested school personnel.
2. Review the periodicals in your school library. Which carry regular features on educational research?
3. Make a list of people from outside your work situation who might be called upon to provide information or to conduct workshops on translating the results of teaching into practice. This might include people from nearby colleges or universities, state education departments, teachers' associations, administrators' groups, or private consulting groups. The use of outside consultants can be extremely helpful in dealing with issues of teacher evaluation and research on teaching, particularly when you define your needs and expectations fairly explicitly.

Mastery Test

OBJECTIVE 2 TO ESTABLISH A PERSONAL GOAL FOR BECOMING COMPETENT IN METHODS OF TEACHER EVALUATION, AND TO IDENTIFY SOME OF THE KNOWLEDGE FROM RESEARCH ON EFFECTIVE TEACHING THAT IS RELEVANT TO TEACHER EVALUATION

1. Describe your conception of an effective supervisor. How is this different from and similar to ours?

2. Research on teaching effectiveness has produced some solid and consistent findings. From the following list of teacher behaviors identify those that research has shown to relate fairly consistently with measures of pupil achievement.

   a. Using different media during class presentations
   b. Criticizing pupils
   c. Using inquiry approaches
   d. Giving task-oriented feedback to pupils
   e. Setting educational tasks that challenge but do not frustrate pupils
   f. Teaching the whole group
   g. Teaching with a philosophy of child-centeredness
   h. Letting pupils work independently
   i. Monitoring pupils' work
   j. Following the textbook closely

3. Argue for or against the following statement: The answer to the problem of poor student performance is to have teachers use a model of direct instruction.

Answer Key

Mastery Test, Objective 2

1. We think that practicing supervision effectively is a matter of making decisions about teachers and teaching based on the best information available. In order to do so, supervisors must be able to decide what kind of information is most useful, plan how to collect it, be able to collect it, and interpret it in a reasonable, understandable fashion. Being a competent supervisor is dependent on developing a wide array of skills that can be called up on demand.

2. b (negatively related), d, e, f, i

3. *For:* If *student performance* is defined as scores on standardized tests of reading and mathematics, then direct instruction may improve student performance.

   Against: If *student peformance* is defined in terms of creativity, independence, curiosity, and the like, using direct instruction may not result in the desired effects. In these cases, other teaching strategies may be more fruitful.

OBJECTIVE 3 TO DESCRIBE A MODEL OF TEACHER DECISION MAKING THAT CAN BE USED TO ORGANIZE A SUPERVISOR'S ACTIONS TO COLLECT AND INTERPRET INFORMATION RELEVANT TO TEACHING

One of the most challenging parts of teacher evaluation is to foresee what kinds of information will be useful in making personnel and staff development decisions. Given the limited time and resources that supervisors have to spend collecting and interpreting data, the efforts expended to identify important and usable information in advance of data collection are valuable investments in the process of teacher evaluation. When supervisors know what they want to find out and why, and communicate this to others who may depend on the results of observations, teacher evaluation can proceed reasonably efficiently, and the chances of a misunderstanding about the products yielded from evaluations can be minimized.

A Model of Teacher Decision Making

In this section we present a model of teacher decision making (see Figure 6.1) in order to help the supervisor think about the kinds of information relevant to teacher evaluation and to plan for its collection and interpretation. This model, like other physical representations of complex human phenomena, is an oversimplification of how people behave. But we think it provides a fairly useful representation of how a teacher's professional competencies are translated into action in teaching-learning situations; that is, what competencies are important in teaching and when they come into play.

As the flowchart in Figure 6.1 (p. 158) illustrates, when a teacher is faced with a particular situation or problem, he or she must first see or perceive the situation before any action can be taken. For example, several students in the teacher's class may be uninvolved in ongoing activities and chewing gum. A failure on the part of the teacher to perceive students' inattention and gum chewing could be an indication of poor eyesight, but more likely it means that the teacher's perceptual skills may not be fully developed. The result in this case, of course, is that no decision is made that requires further action on the part of the teacher—end of situation.

If, on the other hand, the teacher sees the situation, he or she then assesses it, or evaluates the importance of the students' behaviors in terms of some set of professional values. Are the inattention and gum chewing sufficiently serious breaches of classroom rules and etiquette that they merit some action on the part of the teacher? Is student inattention to the lesson an act of defiance or simply an indication of boredom? Is it better to let students have some fun than to risk squelching their spirits? And so forth. If the teacher holds no professional values, or is unaware of any, that suggest student inattention and gum chewing are inappropriate, then no decision is made to take further action. In reality, of course, this step of assessing a situation once it is seen, may not be a cool, calculated appraisal, particularly if the situation is one that offends (or even flatters) some strongly held professional value. But there is little doubt that teachers' professional values influence, either subtly or otherwise, their decisions about when, where, and how to direct their energies.

Assuming that student inattention and gum chewing at this particular time are considered inappropriate and disruptive, the teacher then must call up what professional knowledge he or she has that is relevant to the situation. Such knowledge, assuming it exists, is used to make a decision about how best to handle the situation. If the teacher's professional knowledge about dealing with inattentive, disruptive students is meager, the resulting decision will be amateurish, or devoid of serious attention to professional knowledge about controlling off-task, deviant behaviors in the classroom.

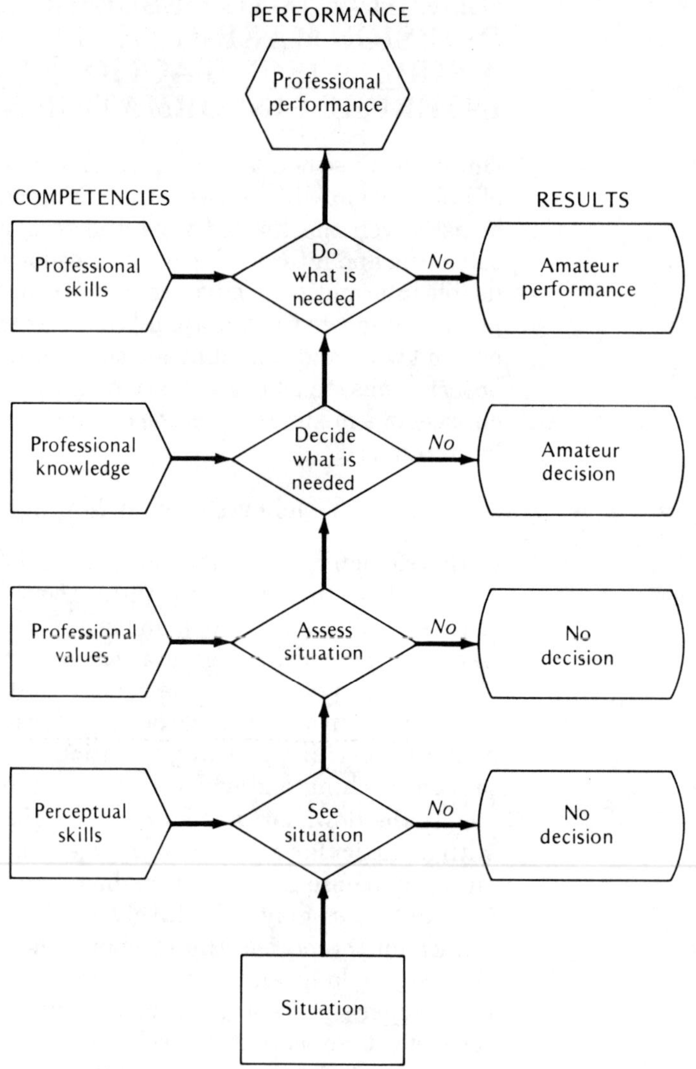

FIGURE 6.1 Teacher competency versus teacher performance.

Once a teacher decides what is needed in a situation, all that remains to be done is to act on that decision. It is at this point that a teacher's performance skills are brought to bear on the problem. If a teacher's skills are nonexistent or only rudimentary, then his or her resulting performance—like the decision that preceded the action—will probably be amateurish. To follow our example further, the teacher who gets involved in inattentive behavior and gum chewing to the extent that the rest of the class loses interest in the ongoing activity could create a set of problems that are worse than those that already exist. Or, if the teacher overreacts to the situation and is highly critical of the errant students in front of the whole class, other students may be alienated. As the flowchart indicates, it is possible that the teacher could make a sound diagnosis of the problem, but not have the professional skills to be able to handle it. If the teacher's performance skills are weak or nonexistent then he or she is likely to perform as an amateur.

If the teacher makes an amateurish decision, the resulting performance will probably reflect his or her lack of professional knowledge, but not necessarily. Teachers can misdiagnose a situation, make an amateurish decision that prescribes particular actions on their parts, and perform those actions competently. If this were to happen, a supervisor most likely would not recognize any professional knowledge deficiencies unless and until he or she questioned the teacher about the teaching episode after it was concluded.

The teacher may, of course, be able to call upon a set of performance skills that are well refined. He or she may reinvolve students in the ongoing activity and have them comply with the rule against chewing gum with little or no loss of momentum. If this happens, as the flowchart indicates, the result could be characterized as professional teaching performance, or the ultimate goal toward which teachers strive.

Each step in the decision-making process, then, provides opportunities for supervisors to collect information about teachers' decisions, and in turn, to infer relationships between those decisions and teachers' professional competencies. When situations are not seen or are misread, perceptual skills may be lacking. When situations are ignored or seized upon, professional values are involved. When decisions are made about handling particular situations, a teacher reveals something about his or her professional knowledge. When a teacher acts on a decision, he or she demonstrates particular performance skills.

Although the model does not prescribe how to collect information about teacher decision making, it implies that supervisors must be in situations where teaching decisions are made if they intend to examine relationships between teacher competence and performance. Barring the use of simulated teaching situations for assessing such relationships, this means that supervisors may usefully monitor teacher decision making in planning sessions before tasks of teaching are undertaken, in classrooms during the course of instruction, and in conference situations once teaching is concluded.

Your Turn

Making teaching decisions is largely a matter of anticipating problems that may arise in the course of teaching as well as perceiving such problems and responding to them when they do arise. Some of the following activities may be useful in helping you to help teachers deal with problem situations.

1. From your own experience as a teacher and/or observer of teaching, when during the course instruction would you say that problems most often occur? What sorts of problems did you have while teaching, for example, classroom management and discipline problems, problems of assessing student abilities, problems of presenting content in ways that students could understand, problems of motivating students, and so forth? Be specific.
2. If possible, form a group of teachers and ask them to respond to the questions above by writing short responses.
   a. Have the teachers share their responses with one another. Compare their responses with your responses. How are they alike? How are they different? What problems have they emphasized?
   b. Ask the group to rephrase their lists of problems to make them more specific. Pick one or two problems and have the group discuss how they would have handled them. Have the group speculate about how they might plan instruction to anticipate such problems in the future.
   c. Encourage the group to discuss what professional and personal values seem to drive their identification and response to particular problems.

Mastery Test

OBJECTIVE 3 TO DESCRIBE A MODEL OF TEACHER DECISION MAKING THAT CAN BE USED TO ORGANIZE A SUPERVISOR'S ACTIONS TO COLLECT AND INTERPRET INFORMATION RELEVANT TO TEACHING

1. Place the following decision-making activities in order (first to last) according to the model presented in this section.
   a. Drawing on professional knowledge
   b. Perceiving problems as they arise
   c. Performing in ways to alleviate problems
   d. Examining one's professional values

2. The model presented in this section is hierarchical, that is, each step in the model (or each competency) is subordinate to the one above it. Thus, it is possible—though not always certain—that difficulties teachers experience at a particular level may be a result of their inabilities to function at the preceding levels. For each of the situations that follow note what types of competencies (perception, values, knowledge, and/or performance) may be contributing to the teacher's difficulties.
   a. Ms. Nelson is part of a third-grade team that is trying to implement direct instruction in their classrooms. Everytime she tries to conduct whole-group lessons on mathematics concepts, the children seem to get lost and are generally disruptive.
   b. Mr. Keegan suspects that some of his students are sneaking cigarettes in the bathroom. Keegan is furious but he doesn't have the slightest idea how to handle the situation.
   c. Freida doesn't get along very well with the other children in her physical education class. They take advantage of every opportunity to abuse her, but the physical education teacher never seems to notice.
   d. Several parents have complained repeatedly about what they consider to be Mr. Johnson's insensitivity to the needs of the black students in his world history class. Students have been especially concerned during class discussions of apartheid in South Africa. In conversations with his colleagues Johnson has expressed his displeasure with parents who "butt in by trying to tell him how to teach history."
   e. Judy Mallan graduated magna cum laude with a degree in computer science from a prestigious university. Although she had no coursework in education or psychology, she got a temporary teaching certificate to teach computer courses at an urban high school. She spends every other night in tears because she doesn't seem to be able to get her students to do anything but play Space Invaders.

Answer Key

Mastery Test, Objective 3

1. c, a, d, b
2. a. Performance, and perhaps knowledge, values, and/or perception
   b. Knowledge, and perhaps values and/or perception
   c. Perception

d. Values and perhaps perception

e. Performance and perhaps knowledge, values, and/or perception

OBJECTIVE 4 TO SPECIFY THE SUPERVISORY SKILLS NECESSARY TO ASSESS TEACHERS' PROFESSIONAL COMPETENCIES

The supervisor who is competent in methods of teacher evaluation is the one who makes decisions about teachers and teaching based on the best information available, and that information is most likely to be gathered by conferencing with teachers and by observing them in classrooms. Although there have been many efforts through the years to describe and predict teaching abilities using various paper-and-pencil tests, as yet there appears to be no adequate substitute for observing teachers in action. This section concentrates on the conferencing and observation skills supervisors need in order to collect information relevant to teacher decision making and teaching performance.

The model of teacher decision making discussed in Objective 3 suggests four points at which teachers' competencies affect their behaviors in teaching situations. Each point represents not only teacher action to resolve a problem, but an opportunity for collecting information about the relationship of teacher competence to teacher behavior. In order to collect such information for purposes of either improving teaching performance or making summative judgments about competence, supervisors must command a variety of observation and conferencing skills.

Not all teacher competencies can be diagnosed equally well using both observation and conferencing techniques. As the discussion below will try to point out, teachers' perceptual and performance skills are most readily determined through direct classroom observation. These skills are not necessarily manifested in classrooms more often than teachers' values and knowledge competencies, but they are typically more amenable to direct observation. The professional values and knowledges of teachers—or what teachers believe and think—can be, and often are, inferred from their behaviors in classrooms. But the accuracy of these inferences need to be checked by conferencing with teachers.

Observing and Recording Classroom Indications of Teacher Competencies

Whether or not teachers see situations in classrooms as they arise is a function of their perceptual skills. To extend the example presented earlier in Objective 3, the teacher who sees students being inattentive and chewing gum might best be described as Kounin (1970) describes the teacher who is "withit." That teacher, according to Kounin, is the one who has eyes in the back of his or her head—the one who recognizes which students are off task and deviating from classroom norms, and when they are doing so. Demonstrating "withitness" is for Kounin a precondition to effective classroom management and discipline. But these perceptual skills might be considered a precondition for all professional teaching performances.

In order for a supervisor to determine if a teacher sees a situation, the first thing that must be done is to establish the existence of the situation, that is, to observe and make some record of it. Without the observation and record the supervisor risks having to wrestle later with the metaphysical equivalent of the now classic sophomore philosophy question: If a tree falls in the forest and no one is there, is there any sound? In other words, who is to say there was some situation to see, and that a teacher failed to see it, unless there is some record of the event?

Determining teachers' performance skills is also dependent on observing and documenting teachers' behaviors in classrooms. Whether a teacher's perceptual skills, values, and knowledge move a teacher toward amateur or professional performance in the classroom can only be determined if some record of that performance exists for later analysis.

Observing and recording teachers' perceptual and performance skills can be done several ways. Perhaps the most obvious way—but not necessarily the easiest—is to make audio and video recordings. As Gliessman (1981) points out, research on the effects of different types of feedback media (for example, video tape replay, audio tape replay, and verbal report) on teacher skill acquisition suggests that the medium frequently has made a difference in how teachers later perform. Generally, it appears that the more information a supervisor can provide the better, that is, video tape is preferred over audio tape, and audio tape is preferred over verbal report. The effectivness of the feedback medium, however, is dependent to some extent on the particular teaching skills involved.

The disadvantages involved in making and using taped recordings of classroom events for supervisory purposes, however, often outweigh the advantages. The presence of recording equipment in classrooms tends to alter the behaviors of students and of teachers. If efforts are made to conceal the equipment or to desensitize people to its presence, one must consider the ethical and potential legal issues involved in using surreptitiously collected information for the purpose of making judgments about teaching behavior. Another disadvantage of using audio and video recordings is the amount of time required to replay and analyze them. Supervisors do not often have the luxury of taping a lesson, reviewing it, and perhaps watching it and/or listening to it one more time in the presence of the teacher. But if teachers agree to their use, if a suitable setting can be arranged, and if time permits, audio and video recordings can be extremely helpful in processes of teacher evaluation. When done well, they offer unambiguous representations of the surface of life in classrooms, and can be used with teachers to demonstrate what happened and what might have happened if things had been done differently.

The alternative to taping classroom events is to observe them live and to record the actions of teachers and/or students as they occur.[1] This procedure is by far the more common approach to collecting information about teachers and teaching—but not because it is easy. Live observation of classrooms requires unusually high levels of skill on the part of the supervisor. He or she must be able: (1) to identify or create observation instruments that are fitted to the tasks of teaching, (2) to use these instruments validly and consistently to collect information, and (3) to interpret the data they yield in ways that are understandable to others (such as teachers) who may depend on the results of observation to make decisions.

Fitting observation methods to the tasks of teaching may be the most difficult part of live observation. There are essentially two problems. First, one must try to forecast what is likely to occur in the situation to be observed, Second, it is necessary to identify or construct an instrument or procedure that will be sensitive to the classroom behaviors of interest. Both problems can be simplified by conferencing with teachers before observation. But even when preobservation conferences are thorough and informative, the solutions are not always readily apparent or easily at hand. The complexity of teaching makes it highly unlikely that any instrument or even any set of instruments will be appropriate for all teaching situations. Supervisors can probably best prepare themselves for this eventuality by developing a repertoire of instruments that can be used in fairly common teaching situations and by learning how to construct instrumentation that is situation specific.

Collecting information about classroom behavior with some acceptable degree of validity and consistency is largely a matter of practice. When an instrument is made up of preestablished categories of teaching-learning behaviors that an observer is required to note at particular times during observation, then few inferences or judgments about classroom behavior are called for, and learning how to use the instrument appropriately is relatively easy. When higher-inference observation procedures are used—procedures that require the observer to make judgments about what to record and how to do so—learning proper observation techniques may require much more practice than learning how to use low-inference instruments. Higher-inference procedures, or various qualitative approaches to classroom observation, often require that an observer, in effect, be the instrument. Insuring validity and consistency of observation in this case are considerably more complex matters than they are when using low-inference systems.

Deciding when and how long to observe teachers is another important consideration for supervisors. Like just about every other issue related to teacher evaluation, there are several points of view on this subject. Teachers often express the concern that supervisors are not in the room when "the most important things happen." Many, it seems, would like to have supervisors observe for an entire class period at the very least. Some supervisors, too, think that they need to spend at least several hours on each observation in order "to be fair to teachers." Supervisors who use qualitative approaches to observation often need a considerable amount of time simply to collect data. If it were always feasible to observe for a class period, a morning, or a day, this could be time well spent. But it is not always feasible to spend this much time. The timing and duration of observations should be dependent, of course, on what the supervisor is trying to evaluate. If classroom management is a concern, it may be most useful to observe several transitions between activities—these are times when management problems often manifest themselves. If the supervisor is interested in the presentation of new content, observing the introduction of a unit would probably be wise. When the intent of observation is to develop a fairly complete representation of what normally occurs in a teacher's classes, the best strategy seems to be one of observing a teacher frequently in different kinds of settings for shorter periods of time.

Interpreting the results of observations, depending on the type of observational data collected, can require that a supervisor possess at least some low-level statistical skills. Low-inference observation systems typically yield data that are best summarized in quantitative terms (percentages, ratios, arithmetic means, standard deviations, and so forth). As the chapter on program evaluation indicates, there are times when it is advantageous to compare educational programs (with *programs* being defined as *teachers*). When this is done, still other statistical skills may be required to interpret observational results in a parsimonious, understandable way.

More important than the mechanical skills of applying statistical techniques in data analysis are the logical skills needed to unravel the meaning of observational results. These skills are important in interpreting information obtained from both high- and low-inference observation systems. Determining which patterns of teacher behavior are important, examining relationships between and among such patterns, speculating on the short- and long-term effects of particular teacher behaviors, and the like, are problems of interpretation that demand an abundance of logical skills. As the discussion in Objective 4 will argue, the results of observation must inform supervisors how best to structure interventions designed to improve teaching, should improvement be called for. Interpretation, then, must be done in ways that yield usable results, and this is heavily dependent on supervisors' logical skills.

Soliciting Information about Teachers' Competencies by Conferencing

There is little doubt that the effects of teachers' professional values and professional knowledge are felt in classrooms. What teachers value and know influence when and how they decide to take action in a variety of situations. A teacher's values can be expected to affect virtually every aspect of life in the classroom, from management and discipline through curriculum selection and emphasis to evaluation of students. A teacher's professional knowledge, too, pervades the many decisions a teacher makes about diagnosing children's needs, trying to meet those needs, and determining the success of such efforts.

The quality of these professional competencies, however, cannot always be gauged accurately by direct observation. As honest, open, and occasionally theatrical as teachers are, they should not be counted on to wear their values and knowledge on their sleeves, particularly in the presence of a supervisor. Classroom observation of teachers' actions may enable supervisors to infer professional values, knowledge, and skills, but listening to teachers' words may go a long way toward clarifying why teachers behave as they do. It is not until supervisors conference with teachers—allow them to talk about teaching and learning, ask questions about their beliefs and thinking, and listen to their responses—that inferences made from observational data can be checked.

Unfortunately, the supervisory skills involved in effective conferencing are not well understood. Some researchers have studied supervisor and teacher behavior in conferences much as others have studied teacher and student behaviors in classrooms (Blumberg, 1970; Weller, 1971). The results of such investigations have suggested that the interactions between teachers and supervisors in conferences can be quite complex, but sometimes not particularly useful when it comes to providing evaluative information. Using a low-inference observation system similar to Flanders's Interaction Analysis Categories, Blumberg and Cusick (1970) found that supervisors tended to dominate conferences. They gave information about five times as often as they solicited it from teachers, were typically direct (as opposed to indirect) in their statements, and spent more than two-thirds of their time controlling teachers, mostly through the use of criticism.

Despite this generally negative picture of conferencing practice, there are skills which supervisors can master that, when applied, yield useful evaluative information. These are: listening, observing, questioning, and providing information and feedback. These skills are important whether conferencing takes place before or after classroom observation. As noted above, in preobservation conferences, supervisors must try to anticipate what will occur in upcoming lessons so that observation instruments can be fitted to teaching. This involves asking teachers about what they will be trying to accomplish, how they plan to go about doing so, and probing for the reasons underlying teachers' decisions. While supervisors listen, question, and make suggestions, they can also observe teachers for indications or cues of characteristics that appear to influence teachers' professional competencies, and ultimately the course of teaching.

These skills are applied again in postobservation conferences by looking backward on teaching instead of ahead as in preobservation situations. Supervisors question and listen to teacher responses, probing to determine the reasons for teachers' actions. Was there some reason for concentrating on the pathos of Silas Marner rather than concentrating on the symbolism in the story, as you had planned? What approaches other than lecturing might have been useful in teaching students about verisimilitude? Have you tried them? What happened? And so on.

In post-observation conferences, supervisors must also be able to present the results of their observations in ways that teachers can understand. This involves summarizing either quantitative or qualitative data in clear, concise ways, that is, presenting conclusions so they are not lost in a morass of numbers and words. When talking with teachers about observation results, it can also be important to look ahead to future lessons or to project how lessons will occur as teachers change their behaviors.

Your Turn

Like all skills, those involved in observing teaching and conferencing with teachers are best developed by practice. The following activities are designed to help you practice these skills.

1. Define a hypothetical teaching situation that you might be expected to observe. For example, you might work with a secondary social studies teacher who is in the process of teaching concepts of political parties and pressure groups to high school seniors.
2. List the kinds of questions you might ask this teacher about a lesson to be observed—questions about what is to be taught, who is to be taught, how instruction is to proceed, and how the effects of instruction are to be assessed. For the hypothetical social studies you might ask questions such as: What do you want the students to learn from this lesson? How will you know if they have learned anything from this lesson? How much do they already know about political parties and pressure groups? What content do you plan to cover in this lesson? What learning activities will you use to get students involved? How much time will you spend on each activity? How will these activities be sequenced?
3. Watch an evening newscast with a pencil and a pad of paper on your lap. For a 10-minute period, write, as objectively and as fully and completely as possible, everything you see and hear. (Try not to crumple in frustration; this is a difficult task!) Review your notes, and look for any instances where you interjected your own opinion; mark these as inferences so as not to confuse them with statements of fact. If someone watched the newscast with you, have them listen as you reconstruct the broadcast from your notes. How accurate were you?

Mastery Test

OBJECTIVE 4 TO SPECIFY THE SUPERVISORY SKILLS NECESSARY TO ASSESS TEACHERS' PROFESSIONAL COMPETENCIES

1. Which of the following teacher competencies are most amenable to direct observation in the classroom: perception, values, knowledge, and performance?
2. Why is it important to record the behaviors of teachers in classrooms?
3. What does it mean if an observation instrument or procedure is characterized as high-inference or low-inference?
4. Why is conferencing with teachers such an important part of teacher evaluation?
5. What supervisory skills are involved in conferencing?

Answer Key

Mastery Test, Objective 4

1. Perception and performance.
2. Constructing a record of what occurs in classrooms is important because it serves as evidence of the degree to which the tasks of teaching were accomplished. Without a record it is impossible to verify what actually occurred and thus difficult to justify decisions about personnel and/or staff development.

3. A high-inference instrument or procedure requires the observer to make judgments about what he or she sees during the course of observation and to make judgments about what the observational data mean at the time of interpretation. A low-inference instrument is more behaviorally oriented than one that is high-inference. Fewer judgments are called for during observation and at the time of data interpretation.
4. Conferences with teachers serve both diagnostic and instructional purposes. When conferences are conducted before observation, they enable supervisors to forecast what is likely to occur during teaching, and thus help them fit instrumentation to the tasks of teaching. When conferences are held after observation, they provide opportunities for supervisors to check their perceptions about a lesson against teachers' perceptions and to provide feedback to teachers. Conferences also provide opportunities for understanding the values and knowledge which teachers possess and which influence the course of teaching and learning.
5. There are several skills involved in conferencing: listening, observing, questioning, and providing information and feedback.

OBJECTIVE 5 TO DESCRIBE HOW INFORMATION ABOUT TEACHERS' CHARACTERISTICS AND COMPETENCIES CAN SERVE AS GUIDELINES IN DESIGNING INTERVENTIONS THAT WILL ENCOURAGE THE IMPROVEMENT OF TEACHING PERFORMANCES

Observing and conferencing with teachers will provide information about teachers' professional competencies and, as noted below, information about their personal characteristics. But having such information is no guarantee that people can design and implement supervisory strategies that will complement or supplement teachers' capabilities. Supervisors who intend to translate the results of teacher assessments into action, or to cross the line from teacher evaluation to teacher development, must have information about teachers that suggests how best to apply support.

Supervisory Intervention

The flowchart presented in Objective 3 has been modified in this section to show that information obtained from conferencing with and observing teachers can be used to infer the teacher competencies involved in making instructional decisions and to guide supervisors in providing corrective feedback (see Figure 6.2). Each step in the flowchart, shown now as a series of communication loops, is an opportunity for the supervisor to collect diagnostic information about specific competencies in a teacher's professional repertoire and to structure suggestions intended to refine or further develop those competencies. In addition, the flowchart has been modified to suggest that teachers' personal characteristics influence their professional competencies. It will be argued that knowledge about certain kinds of characteristics can help supervisors organize support for teachers in ways that it is most likely to be accepted and helpful.

Supervisors obtain information about teachers' perceptual skills, professional values, professional knowledge and performance skills by observing and conferencing with teachers. Each step in the flowchart, then, represents an opportunity for a supervisor to collect information and, in turn, to organize that information for the purpose of intervening to enhance a teacher's competencies. Knowing what particular competencies affect particular types of performances, however, does not necessarily suggest what should be done to correct deficiencies—diagnosis does not automatically imply prescription. If, for example, a teacher fumbles 5 out of every 10 performance opportunities what does this tell a supervisor about how best to help the teacher improve his or her performance skills? Supervisors must be able to interpret the information they gather with

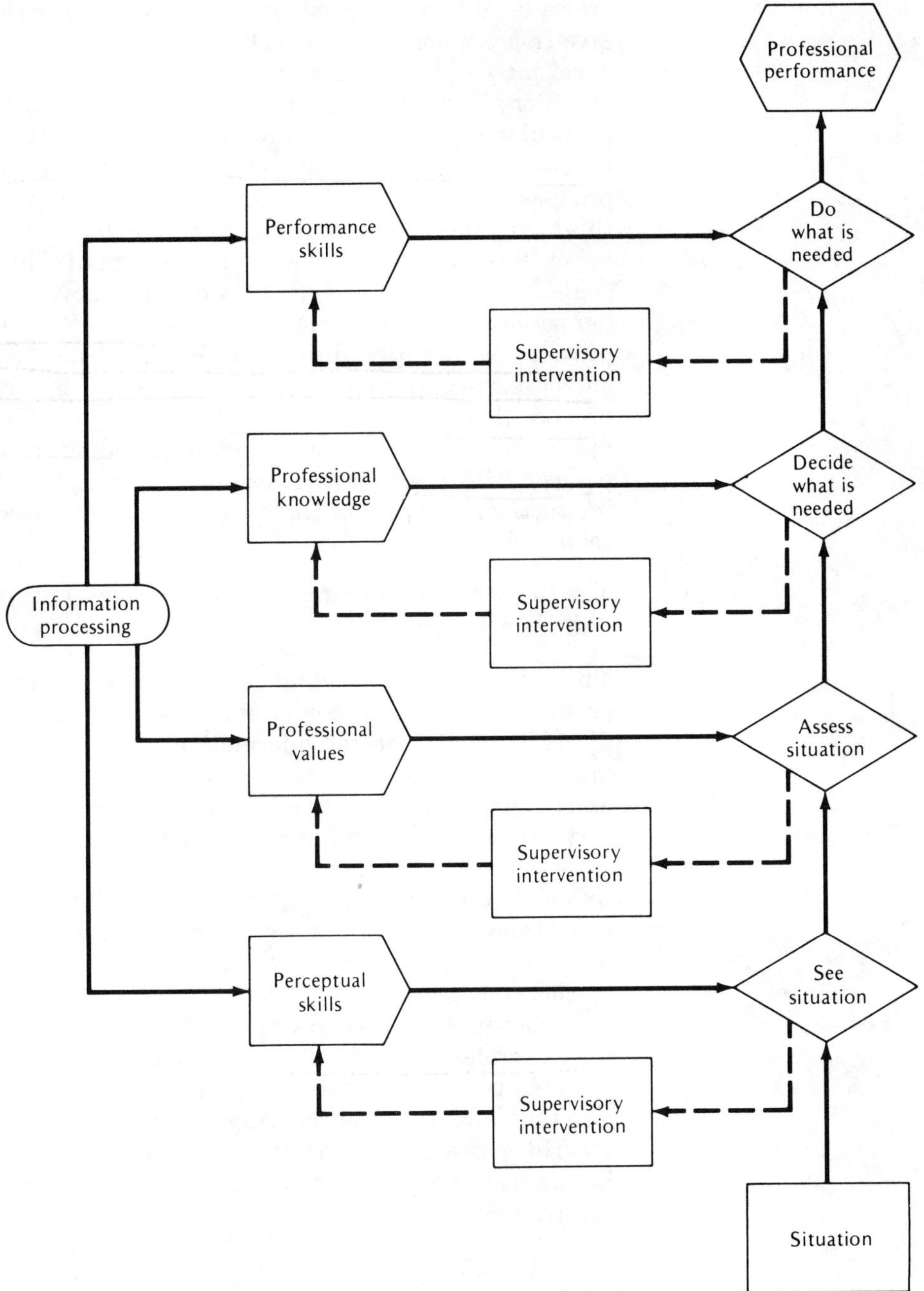

FIGURE 6.2 Supervisory intervention.

an eye toward structuring interventions that will be appropriate for particular teacher needs.

The following general hypothesis about a person's prior achievement—suggested by Tobias (1976) and tested in numerous instructional studies—may be especially useful in this regard: The higher the level of prior achievement the lower the level of instructional support required to accomplish instructional objectives. Conversely, as prior achievement decreases the level of instructional support required to accomplish instructional objectives increases. If one were applying this hypothesis to supervision, "instructional objectives to be accomplished" would be defined as increases or changes in teacher competencies, and "level of prior achievement" would be determined by observing teacher performances and by using conferences to probe the thinking underlying teachers' decisions. For example, if a supervisor diagnosed a teacher as adequate in professional knowledge but weak in performance skills, the teacher would be given more support to develop his or her performance skills and less support to develop his or her professional knowledge.

There is more to this stunningly obvious hypothesis than meets the eye, particularly when it comes to designing support. As Tobias notes, minimal instructional support implies simply supplying content. For the teacher with a professional knowledge base that is adequate (in need of slight improvement), this might mean suggesting a good book to read. For the teacher who fumbles 5 out of 10 performance challenges and is in need of higher instructional support, suggesting a dozen books to read would probably not do much to improve his or her performance skills. Instead, higher levels of instructional support would be provided by carefully editing and organizing instructional materials that bear on the particular competencies in question, by arranging opportunities for practice that are designed to develop and refine the subskills involved in the more inclusive competencies, and by providing corrective feedback at various points during these training or practice exercises.[2] Providing higher levels of instructional support, then, is not a simple matter of giving someone more of something.

The Influence of Personal Characteristics on Professional Competencies and Vice Versa

Up to this point, the chapter has been concerned mainly with teachers' competencies, their performances, and the supervisory knowledge and skills needed to obtain and interpret information about these competencies and performances. Very little has been said about influencing teacher competencies, except by way of the kinds of information that are useful in designing supervisory interventions, and even that was quite brief. Objective 6 will present some "contextual factors," or factors outside the control of teachers, that influence their behaviors in classrooms. But before turning the discussion away from teachers and toward factors outside their control, it seems appropriate to discuss those things that preface professional competency, that is, teachers' characteristics.

Teacher characteristics can be thought of as those formative experiences prior to professional training and various other properties such as age, sex, and personality. The flowchart in Figure 6.2 shows one particular type of characteristic that influences teacher competencies—that of information-processing ability. This particular characteristic is included only as an example, but one that has been shown to be particularly relevant to teaching (Hunt, 1971; Hunt and Sullivan, 1974).

Information-processing ability refers to how people think; not what they think or how smart they are, but how they handle information that confronts them. Information-processing abilities (also referred to as conceptual levels) vary in two ways: simple-complex thinking and self-other relationships. People who see the world in simple terms (black-white, right-wrong, good-bad) and are unable to see others' points of view would be described in terms of lower levels of cognitive development. In contrast, people who think in more complex terms (see grays, mixed blessings, relative benefits) and are able to entertain several points of view, without necessarily abandoning their own, would be described in terms of higher levels of cognitive development.

The relevance of information-processing abilities to teaching should be fairly obvious. Teachers who are cognitively prepared to integrate new information into their existing mental frameworks are more likely to develop professional competencies than those who are cognitively unprepared. Teachers who are unable to see multiple points of view, who are set on a linear course toward truth, are unlikely to develop a wide range of professional competencies, and thus are limited in the kinds of instructional competencies they can acquire.

This single teacher characteristic may influence the entire range of professional competencies. The earlier example of the teacher faced with inattentive, gum-chewing students may help to illustrate this point. If the teacher typically (1) sees only these types of incidents, (2) assesses them as bad, (3) knows they must be squelched, and (4) sends the students to the principal's office, then his or her information-processing abilities might well be described as having contributed to the ultimate result of amateurish performance.

A teacher's information-processing ability is not some kind of magic characteristic that tells a supervisor or teacher evaluator all there is to know about how a teacher thinks and why he or she behaves in certain ways. But supervisors who are aware of the indications of teachers' information-processing abilities will be prepared not only to interpret teachers' behaviors with some reasonable sense of what underlies them, but to organize supervisory feedback that has the potential of being accepted and acted on by teachers. In general, it can be said that people who are cognitively concrete might be expected to benefit most from, and even prefer, interventions that are structured to help them make decisions they cannot make for themselves. Cognitively complex people, on the other hand, might be expected to accept and act on information that is less structured or less prescriptive.

To be more accurate, the arrows in the flowchart in Figure 6.2 that are drawn from characteristics to competencies should probably be bidirectional. There is some evidence to suggest that when supervision is matched to teachers' information-processing abilities not only are teachers' professional competencies affected but their information-processing abilities are also affected (Sprinthall and Thies-Sprinthall, 1980). Changes in how teachers process information, if they come about at all, however, can only be expected to do so over fairly long periods of time.

During the last 80 years or so, researchers and evaluators have investigated the effects of a host of teacher characteristics on a variety of variables with mixed results. Typically, however, the intent has been to establish links between teachers' characteristics and the learning and attitudes of their pupils. When teachers are viewed as adult learners, and information about their characteristics is collected and interpreted with an eye toward helping them grow, the utility of concepts of teacher characteristics seems renewed. There are many characteristics of teachers, of course, that have little or nothing at all to do with how they engage themselves in training, how they learn, and how they ultimately perform in classrooms. Overlooking the potential importance of some, however, would seem to limit unwisely and unnecessarily the efforts of teacher evaluators.

Your Turn

1. Read about teachers' characteristics. There are literally thousands of references, so you must be careful not to get lost in the forest. The following two citations will get you started by providing demographic information about teachers and direction on characteristics that can guide the design of support that is fitted to teachers' needs.

   Bartholomew, B., and S. Gardner. *Status of the American public school teacher, 1980–1981.* Washington, D.C.: National Education Association, 1982.

   McNergney, R.F., and C.A. Carrier. *Teacher development.* New York: Macmillan, 1981, chapters 4 and 5.

2. Spend some time talking with teachers about their motivations for entering and staying in the profession. What sorts of things do they find rewarding about their work? What is most frustrating? What kind of support from others have they found most helpful? If possible, locate some former teachers, and find out why they left.

Mastery Test

OBJECTIVE 5 TO DESCRIBE HOW INFORMATION ABOUT TEACHERS' CHARACTERISTICS AND COMPETENCIES CAN SERVE AS GUIDELINES IN DESIGNING INTERVENTIONS THAT WILL ENCOURAGE THE IMPROVEMENT OF TEACHING PERFORMANCES

1. How might a teacher's information-processing ability affect the way he or she learns?
2. State Tobias's hypothesis about prior achievement and instructional support. What might "more instructional support" mean when working with teachers?

Answer Key

Mastery Test, Objective 5

1. The ways people process information about other people, ideas, and events influence how they behave. When teachers are able to decenter—to view teaching, learning, and children from different perspectives—they are more likely to be willing and able to learn a variety of ways of approaching their work than when they view their world in a linear fashion. Understanding teachers in terms of *how* they think can help supervisors decide how best to structure suggestions that will be most useful to teachers, that is, those accepted and acted upon.
2. Tobias's hypothesis can be stated as follows: The higher the level of prior achievement the lower the level of instructional support required to accomplish instructional objectives. Conversely, as prior achievement decreases, the level of instructional support required to accomplish instructional objectives increases. Higher levels of instructional support might be provided to teachers by carefully editing and organizing instructional materials that bear on the particular competencies in question, by arranging opportunities for practice that are designed to develop and refine the subskills involved in the more inclusive competencies, and by providing corrective feedback at various points during these training or practice exercises.

OBJECTIVE 6 TO IDENTIFY FACTORS BEYOND THE IMMEDIATE CONTROL OF TEACHERS THAT AFFECT THEIR TEACHING PERFORMANCES

It is short-sighted at best to evaluate teachers in isolation or with no regard for the conditions under which teaching takes place. The decisions teachers make and the ways they perform are dependent not only on their preexisting characteristics and competencies, but are influenced by a host of contextual factors as well. In recent years the context of teaching has become more complicated than ever before. Legislation has placed children with severe physical and mental problems in classrooms, technology has promised to revolutionize the ways teachers teach and children learn, parents have pressured schools and teachers to step up disciplinary measures, drugs and violence have intruded in one way or another on the lives of just about everybody involved with schools—all while public confidence in and financial support for public education have eroded.

Influences on Teacher Performance

Teachers do make a difference in the lives of their students—some teachers and some students more than others. But some factors, such as the abilities and interests of students, may be outside the control of even the most creative teachers. While educational researchers and evaluators have spent a great deal of time and energy investigating the effects of teachers' behaviors on children, they have rarely considered the effects of children's behaviors on teachers. Reason, and some research, however, suggest that transactions between adults and children are reciprocal, that is, not only do teachers affect children, but children affect teachers as well. Or to put it another way, teachers can be said to function in a context that is defined in part by their students.

One study that is often cited as an example of "student pull," or the influence of students on teachers, was conducted by Rathbone (1970). He found that students who thought in conceptually complex ways influenced the kinds of statements teachers made and the kinds of questions they asked. In his study, teachers encouraged students to theorize and to think for themselves nearly twice as much when they were matched with conceptually complex students.

As Emery (in press) and his colleagues note, there are other, equally subtle ways that students affect teachers' behaviors. In one set of studies, researchers (Graubard, Rosenberg, and Miller, 1971) taught special education students to change the behaviors of their teachers by using various reinforcement techniques. Children were taught to nod in agreement and to praise the teacher when the teacher paid attention to and helped them. They were also taught to break eye contact during scolding and otherwise ignore provocation. As a result, positive student-teacher contacts were increased and negative contacts were decreased. Other researchers have successfully taught children to raise their hands and to ask for feedback from teachers in order to increase the amount of praise teachers give (Stokes, Fowler, and Baer, 1978).

There are other contextual factors, of course, that influence teaching. Brophy and Evertson (1978) identified several of the more important ones that exist within classrooms. These include such things as the social class level of schools, the instructional setting, and the types of interactions that occur between teachers and students.

According to Brophy and Evertson, some aspects of teaching are effective regardless of the social status of schools, for example, skillful classroom management and emphasis on academic instruction. But teachers, whether consciously or otherwise, appear to modify their teaching methods to fit the social status of their schools. For example, effective teachers in high-socioeconomic status (SES) schools were found to concentrate on teaching the established curriculum, were critical and demanding, and moved students along quickly; while effective teachers in low-SES schools were supporting and encouraging, often substituted methods and materials for the established curriculum, and moved at a slower pace.

Instructional pace itself and group size may also affect how teaching proceeds. In the early grades, teachers typically work with small groups on skills and do so at a brisk pace. In the higher grades, however, more teaching is done with whole classes and involves discussion rather than skill work, thus the pace of instruction is slower. Teachers' behaviors in these two contexts differ considerably. Teachers in fast-paced lessons do not concentrate on improving student responses, instead they ask lower-level questions and look for right answers, moving around the group to insure that all students get opportunities to respond. Teachers in slow-paced whole-group discussions, on the other hand, rephrase questions, give clues, ask a variety of types of questions, give extended explanations, praise students for creative responses (and criticize them for poor responses), and identify students for input into the discussion in different ways. Pacing and group size, of course, may be controlled at least in part by teachers, but school curriculum and scheduling also dictate these contextual factors.

Researchers and evaluators of teaching usually concentrate on the behaviors of teachers and students that are visible or public. In the early grades, however, much of a student's day is spent alone in seatwork or in private conferences with the teacher. These private interactions may be initiated by either teachers or students, and can be concerned with a variety of matters.

Brophy and Evertson note that opportunities for public versus private contacts with students can affect the kinds of teaching that occurs.

Students often initiate private contacts with teachers to get help, to show off their work, or to seek permission to do something. In these instances teachers spend time giving directions or praising, but their praise appears to be less genuine than when they initiate the contact. When teachers initiate private interactions with students it is generally for purposes of monitoring work progress, requesting that an errand be performed, or handling a behavior problem. In these cases, teachers either succeed or fail in their efforts to build close relationships with students, they try to resolve problems of student misbehavior, and they provide (or fail to provide) corrective feedback to students. The time teachers spend in private vs. public interactions with students, then, might also be expected to affect teaching performances.

There are ways other than those noted above that grade level can affect teaching. In the lower grades teachers concentrate on the three R's and on socializing children into their roles as students. In the middle grades teaching is more a matter of helping students with their work. In junior high school grades, because of the special demands of dealing with adolescents, teachers tend to become classroom managers first and teachers second. From about tenth grade on, teachers focus more on teaching and learning as they did in the middle grades (Brophy and Evertson, 1978).

Not surprisingly, school class size is also an important factor in life in classrooms. Glass (1982) and his colleagues summarized the research on class size and concluded that the relationship between class size and pupil achievement is remarkably strong. In more than two-thirds of the studies they reviewed in which classes of approximately 18 and 28 pupils were compared, the performances of pupils in smaller classes were superior to those of pupils in larger classes. In 98 percent of the studies that compared class sizes of about 2 and 28 pupils, smaller classes achieved at higher levels than larger classes. When classes of 30 or more pupils were compared to classes of over 60 pupils, however, there was only about a 50 percent chance that the "smaller" classes showed superior achievement. As Glass et al. noted, "Small classes were very much better than large classes; large classes were hardly any better than very large classes" (1982, p. 47).

Class size also appears to affect the attitudes and feelings of both pupils and teachers. According to Glass and his colleagues, pupils are more interested in learning in smaller classes, and they seem to be less apathetic and frustrated than are students in larger classes. Teachers in smaller classes have higher morale, like their pupils better, have more time to plan, and are more satisfied with their performances than are their counterparts in larger classes.

The school and community contexts in which classrooms are embedded also affect teachers and teaching. The small rural school forces teachers to teach multiple grade levels and to play many supporting roles from custodian to counselor. This school may be free of highly politicized relations between labor-management, but it may also be largely free of human and material resources. In contrast, the comprehensive metropolitan school has a variety of specialists to handle teaching and learning problems and the physical capabilities to include a range of curricular options. Big does not necessarily mean rich, but large schools, by virtue of their size, present a unique set of problems for the teachers who populate them.

Although there are no easy formulas or directions for assessing the effects of contextual factors on teaching, there are several things that can be done to account for them when evaluating teachers. The first is simply to be aware of their existence. Teachers do not perform in a vacuum; it is a mistake to assume that they can control everything in a classroom. Second, evaluators should understand that what is competent teaching performance in one setting may be inappropriate in a different setting; there can be a variety of conditions, both overt and covert, that mediate the effects of teaching. Third, to the extent possible, contextual factors that appear and are perceived to affect teaching should be documented, that is, they should be described and taken into account during the course of evaluation. This is easy to say and hard to do, but necessary if one is to construct a round, full conception of teaching.

Your Turn

1. The concept of reciprocity is a powerful one in education. What it means for teachers is that they can expect not only to affect life in classrooms, but to be affected by it as well. One of the more useful ways of understanding how people, ideas, and events can affect others is to try to consider how they have affected you. In order to do so, think back to one of your more memorable years of teaching, perhaps your first year. Try to remember and describe the pressures and moments of exhilaration which you felt during those times. What things outside your control, that is, what factors in your environment, seemed to be especially strong influences on those feelings?
2. It might be well worth the effort to investigate the amount of time students in your school or organization spend away from their teachers, that is, time when they are not involved in face-to-face interaction with teachers. Studies have indicated that elementary school children spend as much as two-thirds or more of their time working alone or with other children at their seats. If teachers have little control over how this time is spent, they can hardly be held responsible for the results. If, on the other hand, teachers are unaware of how their own organization and management contribute to lost time, sharing the results of your investigations with them may help resolve potential problems.
3. How does class size seem to affect teaching and learning in your school or organization? Short of conducting your own statistical analyses of relationships between class size and student achievement, you might want to question teachers and program administrators about their perceptions of the effects of class size: Are there specific activities that cannot be done when a class reaches a particular size? What kinds of activities work better with larger groups? At what points do classes become so small or so large as to render certain activities useless? What effect, if any, does class size appear to have on the abilities of students to interact with one another?

Mastery Test

OBJECTIVE 6 TO IDENTIFY FACTORS BEYOND THE IMMEDIATE CONTROL OF TEACHERS THAT AFFECT THEIR TEACHING PERFORMANCES

1. Describe the concept of *student pull*. Give an example of how it works.
2. Does class size affect teaching? If so, how?
3. How does grade level affect teaching?

Answer Key

Mastery Test, Objective 6

1. Student pull refers to the influences that students exert on teachers. Research has shown, for example, that students can influence the amount of attention and praise they receive from teachers by using certain reinforcement techniques.

2. Yes, class size does affect teaching. It can be said, with certain caveats, that students in smaller classes achieve more, and feel better about themselves and about teachers than do students in larger classes. Teachers in smaller classes have higher morale, like their pupils better, have more time to plan, and are more satisfied with their performances than are their counterparts in larger classes.

3. In the lower grades teachers concentrate on the three R's and on socializing children into their roles as students. They work typically with small groups on skills and do so at a brisk pace. Much of a student's day is spent alone in seatwork or in private conferences with the teacher. These private interactions may be initiated by either teachers or students, and can be concerned with a variety of matters. In the middle grades teaching is more a matter of helping students with their work. In junior high school grades, because of the special demands of dealing with adolescents, teachers tend to become classroom managers first and teachers second. From about tenth grade on, teachers focus more on teaching and learning as they did in the middle grades. In the higher grades, however, more teaching is done with whole classes and involves discussion rather than skill work, thus the pace of instruction is slower.

   Teachers' behaviors in these grade-level contexts differ considerably. Teachers in fast-paced lessons (lower grades) do not typically concentrate on improving student responses, instead they ask lower-level questions and look for right answers, moving around the group to insure that all students get opportunities to respond. Teachers in slow-paced whole-group discussions (higher grades), on the other hand, rephrase questions, give clues, ask a variety of types of questions, give extended explanations, praise students for creative responses (and criticize them for poor responses), and identify students for input into the discussion in different ways.

OBJECTIVE 7 TO DESCRIBE WAYS OF IMPROVING EXISTING METHODS OF SUMMATIVE TEACHER EVALUATION

More often than not supervisors find themselves faced with existing teacher evaluation systems that are strictly summative, that is, unrelated to existing formative systems. These summative systems are not necessarily intended to be helpful to teachers; they are designed instead to yield information to be used in making decisions about retaining, releasing, assigning, and/or rewarding teachers.

In a revealing study of the teacher evaluation instruments used in one state, Wood and Pohland (1979) concluded that evaluating teachers for the purpose of improving instruction was a myth. Instead, they argued quite persuasively that teacher evaluation was more a reflection of how teachers measured up to what the school districts valued, rather than some measure of teacher effectiveness. The items on the instruments they reviewed focused on the characteristics of teachers and their entire world of work rather than on classroom instructional behaviors, and thus served an organizational maintenance rather than a teaching improvement function—maintenance of organizational stability, not organizational dynamism or change.

Unfortunately, even the vast majority of summative teacher evaluation systems are unable to furnish valid and reliable information upon which reasonable judgments about teachers' competence can be made. That many came into being by historical accident (somebody had to do something about teacher evaluation!) and remain in force through the power of inertia is of little consolation to a supervisor. Like the pyramids, once they are in place, they don't fade away over night.

It appears that the instrument of choice in existing teacher evaluation programs is the rating scale. A review of teacher evaluation systems in public schools across the nation found that 60 percent used rating scales of one type or another to quantify the characteristics and/or perceived behaviors of teachers (Kowalski, 1978). This is not surprising when one considers the convenience and abundance of such scales. Unfortunately, the ease with which rating scales can be constructed and applied tends to lull the unsuspecting user into a false sense of security. When used with care, rating scales can provide some worthwhile information about teachers and teaching; but they can be biased so easily that the results they yield are often worthless.

Such scales come in a variety of forms: category ratings (poor, fair, average, good, and excellent), numerical ratings (1,2,3,4, and 5), and various kinds of graphic ratings or segmented lines and accompanying phrases (poor . . . fair . . . average . . . good . . . excellent) that are intended to represent equal intervals between the points on a scale (Kerlinger, 1973). Sometimes numerical ratings are combined with expanded forms of category ratings to form a set of numerical ratings with "behavioral anchors," that is, a numerical scale that defines each point in terms of observable behaviors.

All rating scales share the same limitations, though not necessarily to the same degree. First, there is the problem of a halo effect or the tendency of the rater to mark each item or scale according to a general overall impression of the person he or she is evaluating. A teacher who is dull and pedantic during classroom presentations but happens to share the values of the evaluator may be highly rated simply because of the congruence in attitudes. Second, some raters are too generous, others are too niggardly, still others can't make up their minds about a rating and tend to mark the middle of the scales, thus limiting the variability of the judgments. Third, when ratings do not use fairly specific behavioral anchors with points on a scale, the scale itself can be ambiguous, and the result can be a highly subjective judgment. As Popham (1975) points out, however, when an evaluator's intent is to elicit opinion based on personal experience, the subjectivity of rating scales is not necessarily something to be avoided.

There are several things that can be done to improve rating scales and their place in summative evaluation systems. The ambiguity of rating scales can be reduced by specifying what the points on the scale mean in behavioral terms. People who use such scales can be trained by having opportunities to view the same events and to compare their impressions. Raters can be given multiple opportunities to view teaching and thus multiple chances to view phenomena upon which to base judgments. More than one rater at a time can observe a teacher, and the ratings of the observers can be averaged to yield what may well be a fuller, more representative picture of teaching than a single observer would obtain.

Regardless of the precautions that might be taken, it is important to rely on measures in addition to ratings when making summative decisions about teachers. Ratings can complement or supplement systematic observations of teachers' behaviors made for purposes of hiring, firing, promoting, and/or rewarding teachers. But by themselves, ratings cannot yield the quality of information needed to make such decisions.

Raths and Preskill (1982) suggest other ways of strengthening summative evaluations of teachers. One, first discussed by Torgerson (1958), is to make paired-comparisons of all the teachers in a department or school. This involves forming all the possible pairs in the group, and then, after studying relevant evidence about teaching and making observations one reviews the pairs for the purpose of identifying the better teachers. Once this is done, teachers can be ranked according to the number of times they were mentioned. This procedure enables the evaluator to make judgments by comparing all teachers (two at a time) rather than applying an abstract scale to an individual.

As Raths and Preskill point out, however, the major problem with summative evaluations of teachers is that evaluators use various criteria in the absence of standards. Evaluators can identify what aspects of teaching (criteria) they are interested in assessing; they cannot, however, determine how much of, or the degree to which, these variables are important. Thus, summative teacher evaluation is a highly impressionistic process—one that is necessary and useful, but one that must be conducted with care in order to safeguard teachers from capricious judgments.

Your Turn

There has been great deal of discussion recently about concepts of "master teachers." All concepts seem to be based on the assumption that it is possible, indeed desirable, to differentiate more effective teachers from less effective ones, and to reward them accordingly. Making such judgments, of course, is a matter of evaluating teachers using some particular process or processes.

If you have not yet studied one of the concepts of master teacher, you should do so. Regardless of whether or not programs of recognizing master teachers are established and survive, the issues such programs raise will be with us for years to come. Despite the logical appeal of these ideas, there are numerous methodological and political problems involved in implementing such evaluation systems. As you study one of the plans, you will want to seek answers to the following questions: What criteria would be used to differentiate among teachers? To what extent do these criteria reflect how teachers compare with district values rather than measures of teacher effectiveness? Who would evaluate teachers? How would the evaluators be evaluated? How would evaluations be conducted—by classroom observation, testing, testimonials, and so on? When and how often would evaluations be conducted? Where and under what conditions would evaluations be conducted? Answers to questions such as these will help you determine the feasibility and desirability of master teacher programs.

Mastery Test

OBJECTIVE 7 TO DESCRIBE WAYS OF IMPROVING EXISTING METHODS OF SUMMATIVE TEACHER EVALUATION

1. Most school districts rely on rating scales of one type or another to make summative judgments about teachers. List three weaknesses of rating scales.
2. List three ways that rating scales, or the use of such scales, can be improved.
3. What kind of summative evaluation does your school system/training program use? What are the strengths and weaknesses?

Answer Key

Mastery Test, Objective 7

1. Raters tend to mark each item or scale according to their overall impression of the teacher rather than making independent judgments. This tendency is often referred to as a halo

effect. Raters often mark the middle of scales when they are unsure about a particular characteristic or behavior; they are also frequently too lenient or too stringent in their judgments, marking the extremes of the scales. Rating scales, especially those which do not supply behavioral anchors or indicators for each point on the continuum, can be ambiguous.

2. Rating scales can be improved by specifying what the points on the scale mean in behavioral terms. The people who use such scales can be trained by having opportunities to view the same events and to compare their impressions. Raters can be given multiple opportunities to view teaching and thus multiple chances to view phenomena upon which to base judgments. More than one rater at a time can observe a teacher, and the ratings of the observers can be averaged to yield what may well be a fuller, more representative picture of teaching than a single observer would obtain.

3. How did your system get established? What do teachers, parents, supervisors think about it? Are there provisions for periodic assessments of the system? Does it work, that is, are children protected from incompetence and are outstanding teachers recognized?

NOTES

1. Observers in classrooms can also affect the behavior of students and teachers merely by their presences. This disadvantage can be minimized, however, by supervisors becoming familiar visitors to classrooms.

2. Practice and feedback have been shown to be especially effective in helping teachers improve their professional skills. See Gliessman, 1981.

REFERENCES

Bartholomew, B., and S. Gardner. *Status of the American Public School Teacher, 1980–81*. Washington, D.C.: National Education Association, 1982.

Blumberg, A. "A System for Analyzing Supervisor-Teacher Interaction." In *Mirror's for Behavior*, III, edited by A. Simon and E.G. Boyer. Philadelphia, Pa.: Research for Better Schools, 1970, 1–15.

Blumberg, A., and P. Cusick. "Supervisor-Teacher Interaction: An Analysis of Verbal Behavior." *Education* (November 1970): pp. 126–134.

Brophy, J.E., and C.M. Evertson. "Context Variables in Teaching." *Educational Psychologist*, vol. 12, no. 3, (1978): pp. 310–316.

Dunkin, M.J. and B.J. Biddle. *The Study of Teaching*. New York: Holt, Rinehart and Winston, 1974.

Emery, R.E. et al. "Children as Independent Variables: Some Clinical Implications of Child-Effects." *Behavior Therapy*. In press.

Gage, N.L. *The Scientific Basis of the Art of Teaching*. New York: Teachers College Press, 1978.

Glass, G.V. et al. *School Class Size: Research and Policy*. Beverly Hills, Calif.: Sage, 1982.

Gliessman, D.H. *Learning How to Teach: Processes, Effects, and Criteria*. Washington, D.C.: ERIC Clearinghouse on Teacher Education, 1981.

Graubard, J.S., H. Rosenberg, and M.B. Miller. "Student Applications of Behavior Modification to Teachers and Environments or Ecological Approaches to Social Deviance." In *New Directions in Education: Behavior Analysis 1971*, edited by E. Ramp and G. Semb. Lawrence, Kan.: University of Kansas Support and Development Center for Follow Through, Department of Human Development, 1971.

Hunt, D.E. *Matching Models in Education*. Monograph series no. 10. Toronto: Ontario Institute for Studies in Education, 1971.

Hunt, D.E. and E.V. Sullivan. *Between Psychology and Education*. New York: Holt, Rinehart and Winston, 1974.

Joyce, B. and M. Weil. *Models of Teaching*. Englewood Cliffs, N.J.: Prentice-Hall, 1972.

Kerlinger, F.N. *Foundations of Behavioral Research*, 2d ed. New York: Holt, Rinehart and Winston, 1973.

Kounin, J.S. *Discipline and Group Management in Classrooms*. New York: Holt, Rinehart and Winston, 1970.

Kowalski, J.P. *Evaluating Teacher Performance*. Arlington, Va.: Educational Research Service, 1978.

Mackey, James A. "How Can Teachers Be More Effective in the Classroom?" *Phi Delta Kappan*, vol. 57, no. 5 (1976):352.

McNergney, R.F. and C.A. Carrier. *Teacher Development*. New York: Macmillan, 1981.

Mitzel, H.E. "Teacher Effectiveness." In *Encyclopedia of Educational Research, 3rd edition*, edited by C.W. Harris. New York: Macmillan, 1960, 247–328.

Peterson, P.L. "Direct Instruction Reconsidered." In *Research on Teaching: Concepts, Findings, and Implications*, edited by P.L. Peterson and H.J. Walberg. Berkeley, Calif.: McCutchan, 1979, 57–69.

Popham, W.J. *Educational Evaluation*. Englewood Cliffs, N.J.: Prentice-Hall, 1975.

Rathbone, C. "Teachers' Information Handling Behavior When Grouped with Students by Conceptual Level." Ph.D. dissertation, Syracuse University, 1970.

Raths, J. and H. Preskill. "Research Synthesis on Summative Evaluation of Teaching." *Educational Leadership* (January 1982): 310–313.

Rosenshine, B.V. "Content, Time, and Direct Instruction." In *Research on Teaching: Concepts, Findings, and Implications*, edited by P.L. Peterson and H.J. Walberg. Berkeley, Calif.: McCutchan, 1979, 28–56.

Rosenshine, B. and N.F. Furst. "Research on Teacher Performance Criteria." In *Research in Teacher Education*, edited by B.O. Smith. Englewood Cliffs, N.J.: Prentice-Hall, 1971.

Sprinthall, N.A. and L. Thies-Sprinthall. "Educating for Teacher Growth: A Cognitive Developmental Perspective." *Theory into Practice*, vol. 19, no. 4 (Autumn 1980):278–286.

Stokes, T.F., S.A. Fowler, and D.M. Baer. "Training Preschool Children to Recruit Natural Communities of Reinforcement." *Journal of Applied Behavior Analysis*, vol. 11 (1978):285–303.

Tobias, S. "Achievement-Treatment Interactions." *Review of Educational Research*, vol. 46 (1976): 61–74.

Torgerson, W.S. *Theory and Methods of Scaling*. New York: Wiley, 1958.

Weller, R.H. *Verbal Communication Instructional Supervision: An Observational System for Research Study of Clinical Supervision in Groups*. New York: Teachers College Press, 1971.

Wood, C.J. and P.A. Pohland. "Teacher Evaluation: The Myth and Realities." In *Planning for the Evaluation of Teaching: National Symposium for Professionals in Evaluation and Research*, edited by W.R. Duckett. Bloomington, Ind.: Phi Delta Kappa, 1979, 73–82.

PROGRAM EVALUATION

7

Donald M. Medley
Robert F. McNergney

Objective 1 To define the term *educational program* and to identify and define the principal components of such a program relevant to program evaluation
Objective 2 To describe and choose among major alternative approaches to program evaluation
Objective 3 To state the uses of and be able to evaluate program inputs
Objective 4 To state a rationale for conducting process evaluation, and to describe and use the principal options for evaluating educational program processes
Objective 5 To evaluate the outcomes of an educational program

OBJECTIVE 1 TO DEFINE THE TERM *EDUCATIONAL PROGRAM* AND TO IDENTIFY AND DEFINE THE PRINCIPAL COMPONENTS OF SUCH A PROGRAM RELEVANT TO PROGRAM EVALUATION

After completing this section of the chapter you will be familiar enough with the basic elements of an educational program and related terminology to read about and discuss educational program evaluations of all kinds. But before you can acquire and use this knowledge you must be sure that you have a clear concept of what kind of an enterprise an educational program is, as well as of the nature of the process of evaluation itself.

Definitions

Educational evaluation refers to the process of judging the value of educational materials, methods, curricula, and so forth. Educational program evaluation is the process of evaluating an educational program, usually to provide a basis for a decision about the program. The process may be seen as having two phases: one in which relevant information about the program is obtained, and one in which the information is used to make the value judgment and the decision. This chapter will focus on the first phase, that of obtaining information about a program that is relevant to the value judgment.

Just what is an *educational program*? For our purposes we will define an educational program as follows: *An educational program is an enterprise or activity planned to provide those who take part in it with experiences that will produce specified learning outcomes*. A reading program is an example of a scheme designed to help pupils learn to read better and more quickly by providing them with a certain kind of experience that will result in a certain kind of learning.

Stufflebeam and some of his colleagues have identified four basic approaches to, or phases of, educational program evaluation, each of which focuses on one of four aspects of a program: *context, input, process, or product.*[1] In your own work you will usually be concerned with only three of these basic elements: inputs, processes, and products (which we will refer to in this chapter as outcomes). Context evaluation, the fourth, is important during the time in which goal definition, need assessment, and related activities take place. These activities normally precede the decision to implement a program; we will assume that this decision will have been made before you are asked to evaluate the program, as is usually the case. The aspects of program evaluation that will concern you (and us) are those that relate to programs that already exist, programs that have been or still are in operation. What you will learn in this chapter has to do with finding out what happened or is happening in a program, not whether or why a program should come into existence.

The variety of educational enterprises that can be thought of as educational programs is great; indeed, because almost everything done in schools or other educational institutions is intended to produce learning, almost anything the schools do is an educational program, one which you might conceivably be asked to evaluate. The entire program of a school system is one kind of educational program. So is what goes on in any one school building in the system, or, for that matter, in any one department, course, single class, or even in a single unit within a course. In spite of the many differences among them, each of these programs has inputs, processes, and outcomes, and can therefore be evaluated by the basic procedures you will learn to use in later sections of this chapter.

Your Turn

List 10 educational programs in which you have participated, including the widest variety you can, and state one outcome each was supposed to produce.

Inputs to Educational Programs

Inputs with which you will be particularly concerned in evaluating educational programs include:

1. The repertoire of instructional competencies of the teacher(s) or instructor(s) involved in the operation of a program. By this we mean the set of items of professional knowledge, the professional skills, and the professional values that instructors or teachers bring to the program.
2. The institutional support (material and other) provided for the program by the school system or other organization operating the program.
3. Participant group characteristics, such as average ability, ethnic composition, group cohesion and the like.

These inputs interact with one another to generate the events or activities referred to as *program processes*, which are the means by which the program achieves its outcomes. The processes in turn interact with the characteristics of individual participants to determine the effect the program has on each of them. And the sum total of these effects are called *program outcomes*. The three types of inputs affect program processes directly, but they affect program outcomes only indirectly, through the mediation of program processes.

When you evaluate a program, then, in order to understand it well enough to evaluate it you must ask questions about all five of these elements; you must ask about all three types of program inputs and about program processes, as well as about program outcomes.

The three major types of inputs include:

1. *Instructional Competencies* The repertoire or set of competencies possessed by the instructional personnel (teachers or instructors) in the program. As has been suggested, these include all the knowledge and skill the teacher possesses. Important also, and only too likely to be overlooked, are the professional attitudes or values the teacher holds.[2]

2. *Institutional Support* The support provided to the instructional personnel in the program by the sponsoring educational institution. Institutional support may take the form of access to facilities, textbooks and other teaching materials, equipment, supplies, and so forth. It may take the form of access to the services of auxiliary personnel, such as guidance counselors, consultants, and the like. It may take the form of psychological or moral support, encouragement, commendations, and the like. Any form of external support that may have a direct effect on program processes belongs in this category.

3. *Participant Group Characteristics* Those preexisting characteristics of the *group* of participants or students involved in the program which affect program processes. These include not only the mix of individual participant characteristics such as aptitudes, interests, and attitudes toward themselves and others, socioeconomic status and ethnic origin, and so on; but also characteristics of the group as a group, such as group cohesiveness and social structure as revealed in a sociogram.

We refer to these things as *program inputs* because they can be manipulated from without to affect the process which goes on in the program, and "mold it nearer to the heart's desire." Indeed, the only means by which program planners can act to increase the effectiveness of the program is by manipulating the inputs—by retraining teachers or replacing them (manipulating teacher competence); by providing different and better materials, facilities, or support personnel (manipulating program support); or by changing the complement of participants in the program (manipulating participant group characteristics).

Given a particular set of inputs, processes can be affected only by the teachers or other personnel actually working in the program, or by the participants themselves. And the outcomes are affected only through changes in these processes.

In order to illustrate some of the points we will be making by making them more real, we will use the three examples given below throughout this chapter. Study them carefully, and try to imagine each one as it would look if it were being implemented in some setting with which you are quite familiar, rather than in the imaginary one described.

Three Examples

Example 1: The Shadyvale workshop

The Shadyvale Public Schools are planning a week-long workshop for all of the administrators and teachers in the system, which will be held during the week before school starts. The theme of the workshop will be "Microprocessor Technology in the Schools of Today and Tomorrow."

The workshop will begin with welcoming speeches by the superintendent and the chairperson of the school board on Monday morning. The afternoon session will feature a keynote address delivered by a distinguished guest speaker and a film on microprocessors in the schools produced by a leading computer firm. Tuesday and Wednesday will be devoted to a mixture of didactic and hands-on instruction in programming with LOGO housed in the computer laboratory at the high school. Each staff member will spend Thursday in his or her own classroom or office getting things ready for the opening of school. Friday morning will be spent in districtwide meetings of teachers of the same subject or grade. Finally, there will be a general session on Friday afternoon that will feature an inspirational address and benediction delivered by a local clergyman.

This is an example of a rather elaborate educational program, not aimed at ordinary school pupils but at those responsible for educating them. Inputs include (1) the expertise and other qualifications of the various speakers and instructors, (2) the facilities in which the various sessions are held and the materials provided (particularly in the computer laboratory), and (3) the characteristics of the various groups that will be brought together for different purposes. A wide variety of program processes, including (4) lectures, film viewing, and laboratory exercises, are planned. The major intended outcomes include (5) changes in each participant's knowledge of microprocessors and their educational users, and (most likely) their attitudes toward them.

Example 2: The Fosdyke reading program

The Charles Brown elementary school has decided to try out a new reading program and compare the results with those they have been getting with the program they are now using. The Fosdyke program and the reader series that it uses have received considerable attention through a publicity campaign in the mass media aimed mainly at parents. Inputs into this program include (1) the competencies of the teachers who will try out the new program, (2) the new readers plus whatever supplementary materials the program provides, and (3) the classes in which they will be used. Program processes include mainly (4) the performances of the teachers and the responses of the pupils during reading instruction. The outcomes promised are (5) substantially greater gains in reading ability than have been achieved in the past.

Example 3: Mr. Softchalk's fourth-grade class

The instruction that a teacher named Softchalk delivers in his fourth-grade classroom may be regarded as an on-going educational program and evaluated as such. The inputs include (1) Mr. Softchalk's competence as a teacher, (2) the textbooks, instructional aids and devices, and other materials made available to the class, and (3) the kind of students who enroll in the class. Program processes (4) are defined by Mr. Softchalk's performance as he teaches the class. Program outcomes expected for each student (5) are (we shall assume) defined in some kind of a document such as a state or local curriculum guide.

What we are talking about doing is sometimes misconstrued as assessing how effective a teacher Mr. Softchalk is. But in reality we are assessing an instructional program in which Mr. Softchalk's competence is one input among several; a major input, but not the only one. We are less likely to misinterpret what we find if we think of it in this way.

Mastery Test

OBJECTIVE 1 TO DEFINE THE TERM *EDUCATIONAL PROGRAM* AND TO IDENTIFY AND DEFINE THE PRINCIPAL COMPONENTS OF SUCH A PROGRAM RELEVANT TO PROGRAM EVALUATION

1. How would you define an educational program?
2. What are the essential components of an educational program?
3. Think of a number of educational programs in your own institution—big ones, small ones, those directed at children, those directed at teachers and administrators, and so forth. In each case, think of the three types of inputs (instructor competence, support, and learner characteristics), the program processes, and the program outcomes. Which of these programs, in your opinion, would be most difficult to evaluate, that is, be most difficult to obtain information about their components?

Answer Key

Mastery Test, Objective 1

1. We define an educational program very generally as a scheme for providing learning experiences to students—experiences that are expected to result in certain learning outcomes.
2. There are three components or basic elements of an educational program: (1) *Inputs* include such things as the competencies of the teachers or instructors, the amount of material and human support provided, and the characteristics of the group of learners who participate in the program. (2) *Processes* are the actions and transactions of teachers and students that occur during the course of a program and that result in producing learning experiences for students or program participants. (3) *Outcomes* are indications of what program participants have learned.
3. This is an important activity for you to engage in; for it may be that any number of educational programs in your institution need to be evaluated, but that for one reason or another, information about these programs is either nonexistent or so difficult to get as to preclude a useful evaluation. The degree of difficulty of acquiring relevant information, however, must not govern decisions to select programs to evaluate. If this were the deciding factor, chances are that most programs that could truly benefit from a thorough evaluation would never be subjected to one!

OBJECTIVE 2 TO DESCRIBE AND CHOOSE AMONG MAJOR ALTERNATIVE APPROACHES TO PROGRAM EVALUATION

In this learning activity you will be introduced to some of the principal approaches to program evaluation that have been and are being used, to help you make intelligent choices when you are called upon to help evaluate a program. In order to keep this discussion reasonably brief, we will review just four of the many approaches to educational program evaluation that have been proposed, with the focus on their similarities and differences. As you gain experience you will probably want to learn about some of the others.

Each approach is based on a different set of assumptions, and each has different strengths (with the possible exception of the fourth, which does not seem to have any). If any single approach could be considered best or most appropriate for all purposes, you would only need to study that approach and become expert in its use. But this is not the case; sometimes one approach is best, sometimes another. And sometimes no method seems to fit very well.

The Objectives-Based Approach

The most familiar type of educational evaluation is one that tries to determine the degree to which certain instructional goals and objectives have been met. When Charles Brown Elementary School tested the Fosdyke Reading Program, the administrators wanted to determine the extent to which students have mastered the reading objectives of their school. When Mr. Softchalk plans and teaches a mathematics enrichment unit he wants to assess the degree to which it produces the learning gains he wishes to achieve. And so on.

When you use the objectives-based approach to program evaluation problems like these, the process of judging their worth can be expected to proceed systematically and in a fairly rational way. The degree to which program goals and objectives are achieved is probably most often determined by comparing them with measures of outcomes achieved by program participants.

Success with this approach, as advocates have noted through the years, depends on being able to define program goals specifically and clearly, and in terms of behaviorally stated objectives or in some other way that is specific and detailed enough to be measured objectively and reliably. The principal difficulty you will have if you use this approach arises from the fact that many important goals and objectives cannot always be defined and measured in this way. When you use this approach, you should avoid the mistake of limiting yourself to outcomes so narrowly defined that the degree to which they are achieved cannot shed much light on the overall worth of the program.

If, for example, you were to judge the worth of the Fosdyke reading program solely on the basis of changes in the childrens' scores on standardized achievement tests (goals which are easy to measure), without considering other kinds of outcomes, like changes in their attitudes toward books or the amount of reading they do (which are difficult to measure), the results would provide a doubtful basis for evaluating the program.

Your Turn

Define three potential objectives of a reading program that would be relatively easy to measure and three that would not, and discuss the difference between the two sets.

Discrepancy Evaluation A particularly useful form of objectives-based evaluation is one developed by Malcolm Provus.[3] Discrepancy evaluation requires you to compare *program standards*, that is, specifications of intended program processes and outcomes within *program performance*, the actual processes and outcomes observed, and to determine whether and to what extent there are discrepancies between the two. Information about such discrepancies may then be used as the basis for decisions about the program. What most evaluators like about Provus's model is that it presents a clearly definable set of steps or stages that you can use to guide your efforts to develop decision-relevant information about educational programs.

When you as an evaluator use the discrepancy model you must first document program standards and program performance; and then compare them to determine the degree to which they are discrepant (or congruent). Once you have accomplished this, you can support decisions to terminate a program or to alter the process standards, redefine the program objectives, or make changes in the actual processes implemented in the program that are calculated to bring program outcomes closer to program objectives. As Provus points out, you should weigh all of these alternatives in terms of their comparative costs and benefits.

The Goal-Free Approach

Sharply different from the objectives-based approach to evaluation is an approach known as *goal-free evaluation*, introduced by Michael Scriven.[4] When you use this approach to program evaluation you are equally concerned with intended and unintended outcomes of the program. This kind of evaluation has been described as a "consumer-oriented" approach, because as the program evaluator what you do is what any enlightened consumer would do. You try to judge the relative merits of an educational program in terms of what it can do for you, without specifying in any great detail what it should do. This requires that you assess the unintended effects of the program as well as the extent to which it accomplishes the objectives defined by those who set up the program in the first place (which may or may not be important to you).

According to Scriven you will function most effectively as a goal-free evaluator if you make your assessment of program effects without actually knowing what the program objectives are. Scriven argues that if the evaluator knows the objectives this knowledge can contaminate the evaluation by leading him or her to concentrate on the intended outcomes at the expense of unintended but potentially more important outcomes. Scriven recommends instead that the evaluator collect data on a wide variety of program effects of all kinds—psychological, social, and environmental as well as pedagogical—that the program may be having on participants.

You may find that a program like the Fosdyke reading program is achieving exactly what it was designed to do, that is, helping primary school children, acquire the mechanical skills necessary to get high scores on the reading test, as indicated by the number of learners who reach a desired level on that test. But the program's effects on the childrens' interest in and attitudes toward reading may be strongly negative.

In the case of the Shadyvale workshop, which was designed to develop participants' skills in microcomputer technology, it may be important to know whether these goals were reached. But in evaluating the program it would also be useful to know what happened to the morale of these teachers and administrators. Building strong group cohesion or esprit de corps may seem to be a much more important outcome than any gain in computer literacy. Goal-free evaluation is based on the premise that if you are not bound in your evaluation by the stated objectives of the program you are more likely to detect effects such as this one.

The case for this approach lies right here, in the claim that goal-free evaluation forces you to be more aware of outcomes other than those related directly to program objectives, to be more sensitive to the needs and feelings of the program participants—and those of the tax paying public. The case against goal-free evaluation is based on the danger that, when you focus mainly on what you perceive to be the concerns of participants, taxpayers, and the like, your evaluation may become so independent of the needs of those who administer and deliver the programs that the results of your investigation may not be relevant enough to the decision base to be taken seriously, and thus do very little to improve the programs.

It is important to note that at least some of the benefits of goal-free evaluation can be obtained in what is essentially an objectives-based evaluation, by paying careful attention to the unanticipated outcomes called *side effects.* If you use the discrepancy model, which is so closely concentrated on program standards, you may be well advised to document some other potentially important outcomes as well.

The standardized testing program which would probably be the mainstay of your evaluation of a program like the one being tried out at Charles Brown elementary school could well be supplemented with some measures of changes in the reading habits of the pupils and in their attitudes toward school, reading, and themselves. It is important, however, that you resist the ever-present temptation to do too much testing, to waste too many hours of pupil time collecting data that you will never use.

Your Turn

In response to the "back-to-basics" movement, a school system decides to put increased emphasis on the teaching of basic skills and to measure the effects with a standardized achievement battery. What side effects might you anticipate, and how might you measure them?

The "Watergate" Approach

The last approach we will discuss, as the title may suggest, is not a legitimate approach to evaluation at all, but it is something you may very well encounter. It is, instead, an unfortunate example of a way in which program evaluation is sometimes misused for political or propaganda purposes. It is discussed here only to alert you to some pitfalls you should watch out for in planning and conducting evaluation studies.

We call it the "Watergate" approach, and enterprises of this type are also known as *politically oriented studies*, *pseudo evaluations*, or *public relations–inspired studies*). What the instigator of such a project is trying to do is not to improve education in any way, but to gain some kind of personal advantage over another person or persons by distorting or hiding information if necessary, under the guise of performing a bona fide evaluation.

The methods involved in conducting this type of project may, and usually will, appear to be the same as those used to conduct a legitimate evaluation. Similar techniques of data collection and instrumentation such as surveys, interviews, and questionnaires; similar evaluation designs may be used; and reports very much like those you would prepare for a bona fide study may be issued. The critical difference is that any and all types of data collected, analyses made of the data, and reports based on them are subject to *intentional* bias. Results may be suppressed outright, they may be slanted by being presented only in part, or distorted during the analysis. The decision to gather and disseminate any information at all may be an act of desperation designed to forestall the damage likely to occur as a result of unfavorable publicity or a true evaluation.

If Mr. Softchalk happened to be unscrupulous enough, and caught up in a struggle for a merit raise or recognition as a master teacher, he might conceivably be tempted to "evaluate" his own instructional program in such a way as to secure a favorable decision. If he did a survey of parents, he might limit his sample to parents of students who had received good grades in his classes, and perhaps destroy any unfavorable responses he might receive.

What is most dangerous to you would be to fail to develop and maintain an alert and healthy sense of skepticism to accompany the strict honesty and high sense of ethics that are so necessary to any professional. Let us end this learning experience by recommending that your motto be les jeux sont faits, which we interpret as meaning, let them fall where they may—the chips, that is.

Your Turn

Two participants are required, one to play the role of the principal of a 600-student middle school, and the other a teacher and head of the mathematics program (who has had this course). The principal has strained the budget to acquire five Apple computers to be used in developing the students' computer literacy. This is to be accomplished by giving each child in the school a chance to use one of the computers. The principal calls the teacher in to plan an evaluation which will justify the purchase.

Mastery Test

OBJECTIVE 2 TO DESCRIBE AND CHOOSE AMONG MAJOR ALTERNATIVE APPROACHES TO PROGRAM EVALUATION

1. In objectives-based approaches to program evaluation the intent is to determine program success by comparing objectives and outcomes. The logic in these approaches is obvious and appealing, and often the results are quite useful. There can be difficulties, however. What might some of them be?
2. According to Provus, when program standards (objectives) are compared to program processes, and a discrepancy is found, there are two possible courses of action to take. What are they?
3. What are the advantages and disadvantages of using a goal-free approach to program evaluation?
4. On occasion, program evaluation processes and results have been manipulated for purposes of personal, political, and economic gain, purposes which are professionally unacceptable. What do you think are the appropriate purposes of program evaluation?

Answer Key

Mastery Test, Objective 2

1. a. Sometimes program objectives are so vaguely stated as to defy measurement, and a clear comparison of objectives and outcomes is difficult if not impossible to accomplish.

   b. Sometimes in trying to specify goals and objectives precisely and in measurable terms, the evaluator goes too far. When this happens the objectives may become trivial, and the results of the assessment may become so limited as to make the resulting judgment of program worth questionable.

   c. Using an objectives-based approach may lead one to ignore unintended program outcomes that may be important to program participants.

2. One is to terminate the program; the other is to alter either program standards or program processes.

3. The advantages to a goal-free approach to evaluation are that it offers opportunities for evaluators to explore educational programs without being constrained by the explicit program objectives and processes. An evaluator using such an approach can, for example, look for unintended outcomes or side effects of a program, speculate on reasons for their existence, and report his or her conclusions to those who have commissioned the study. The result may be a rounder, fuller conception of program operations and outcomes than one produced by an objectives-based approach.

   The disadvantages are that the results of the evaluation may simply reflect the biases of the evaluator, even when results are reasonably objective. Because the evaluator is "independent," the results may not be taken seriously by those responsible for conducting a program when trying to make program improvements.

4. According to Ralph W. Tyler, there are six.

   a. It is important for evaluation to make a periodic check on an educational institution's effectiveness so as to indicate the points at which program improvements are necessary.

   b. An evaluation is an opportunity to validate the hypotheses upon which an educational institution or program operates.

   c. An evaluation can provide information that will help guide individual students or program participants.

   d. Evaluation can offer psychological security to the staff of an institution or program, to students, and to parents and other members of the community.

   e. Careful and comprehensive evaluation can provide a sound basis for productive public relations.

   f. Evaluation can give both those who offer an educational program and those who receive it a chance to clarify their purposes and their progress.

OBJECTIVE 3 TO STATE THE USES OF AND BE ABLE TO EVALUATE PROGRAM INPUTS

You will have noted that the central focus of all three of the approaches to program evaluation described in the last section was on program outcomes. But there is an important role for the program evaluator to play long before the program produces any outcomes. The earliest point in the history of an educational program at which your services as a program evaluator are needed is when the idea of setting up a program to meet some specified goal has been adopted.

At this point it is very important to make a careful evaluation of inputs to the program. One main reason for doing this is to assess available resources. This is the time to ascertain whether qualified instructional personnel, adequate facilities, and usable equipment necessary to operate the program successfully are available locally; or whether you will need to procure additional personnel, facilities, or materials from outside. This, too, is the time to find out whether the potential number of participants capable of benefiting from the activities planned is large enough to justify the expenditures that implementing the program will entail, assuming that it will be effective.

In the next few pages we will discuss some ways in which you in your role as program evaluator can facilitate this process and help program planners design programs that use available resources more efficiently and effectively than would otherwise be the case.

The Importance of Input Evaluation

What you can learn about educational program input evaluation from studying this chapter and the readings cited in it will be rudimentary indeed; but the truth is that the present state of knowledge of the topic and its methodology is itself quite primitive. But you can still play a useful role, and make a contribution both visible and important to the success of any program by raising important questions at a time when something can be done about them, even though neither you nor anyone else has any definitive solutions. Timely answers that grow out of common sense are better than the wisest possible answers that come too late, or no answers at all.

Unfortunately, in too many cases no one even thinks of appointing an evaluator until some time after the program has been put into operation or, worse yet, after it is all over. In the first case a careful assessment of program inputs can still be useful in planning for process evaluation (which we will discuss in the next section). When the program to be evaluated is not a new one, but one that has been in place for some time, this may not be possible. But one of your main contributions as an evaluator may be to sensitize decision makers to the need to get an evaluator on board almost before doing anything else about a program.

Even though the concern that prompts such an evaluation will almost always center on the outcomes of the program, on how effective it is, it is equally important to program success to conduct a thoughtful assessment of program inputs and processes. Without reliable information about program inputs and processes, there is very little you can learn from any program, least of all from one that is ineffective.

Input Evaluation Strategy

Your purposes in evaluating program inputs are, first, to help planners decide how to make the most effective use of the resources that are available to them; and, second, to help them decide what additional resources, what new personnel, facilities, materials, and the like must be obtained if the program is to succeed. The full value of input evaluation can only be exploited when it is recognized as an integral part of program planning and can contribute to feasibility analyses of alternative program designs.

The ultimate goal of educational program input evaluation is to ensure that the best possible use is made of all available resources. As program evaluator you can achieve this goal only if you yourself attend the meetings and participate in the deliberations of the program planning committee. Your purpose in attending them is simply to ensure that all of the important questions about inputs are asked and discussed. Your overall strategy should be to be certain that inputs of all three types are considered; an inventory is made of the relevant organizational capabilities; all feasible alternative program designs are evaluated; and the best design for implementing the program in your situation is chosen.

Objectives Before you do any of this, however, you must press for clarification of program goals; you must raise and get the committee to deal with questions like these:

- Are program objectives clearly specified?
- Can they be measured accurately and economically?
- Are they consistent with the mission of the organization?
- Would they be acceptable to parents or other community groups?

Design Alternatives Next you should work with the committee to identify one or more alternative program designs and compare them with respect to benefits and costs. Some of the questions you will face here include:

- What program designs might be expected to achieve program goals?
- Is each alternative design feasible with the resources available?
- What are the relative costs and benefits associated with each possible design?

Instructor Competence Next you should try to identify any problems related to resources that must be resolved if each one of the designs is adopted, and consider alternate ways of solving them. Some of the questions you will have to answer will relate to personnel, such as:

- Are there teachers presently employed in the system who are qualified to provide the instruction required who can be used?
- If not, how and at what cost in time and money could some be trained?
- Would it be possible to hire someone with those qualifications?
- Should such a person be hired permanently or temporarily?

Physical and Material Support The next issue is whether and how the physical and material support needed can be provided; it involves, among others, the following questions:

- Are there existing physical facilities that are adequate for program needs?
- Are they readily available?
- If not, where, how, and at what cost could they be obtained?
- Are essential materials, media, equipment, and so forth at hand, or would they have to be procured elsewhere?
- Where, and at what cost could they be procured?

Participant Group Characteristics The final set of questions would have to do with the nature of the participant group. For example:

- What kind of clientele would the program serve?
- What criteria, if any, would be used to select participants?
- How many students or potential participants would qualify?

Your Turn

List at least three additional important questions that might be raised in each of these five areas.

The fact that we have listed these steps sequentially should not lead you to expect that you will be able to deal with them that way. On the contrary, you will find yourself going back and forth between them. For example, the kind of participants you will involve has a lot to do with the feasibility of proposed designs, the specific objectives you will adopt, and the exact competencies your instructional personnel will need.

An Example

Suppose that you were assigned as program evaluator on the committee appointed to plan the Shadyvale workshop. You would, of course, attend all of the meetings of the committee and be certain that questions like these were brought up and answered as well as possible. Considering for the moment only that part of the program concerned with the main topic, "Microprocessor Technology in the Schools of Today and Tomorrow," what are some of the concerns you might have about program inputs?

Perhaps the first question to be answered has to do with program objectives. Just what are the teachers supposed to know (and feel) about computers at the end of the workshop? How familiar with LOGO are they supposed to become? And how will you find out how much they have learned and what their attitudes are?

Perhaps you will plan to use a descriptive questionnaire to assess their attitudes at the beginning and end of the workshop. Or you might plan to administer an evaluative questionnaire at the end of the workshop, one that asked the teachers to estimate how much they think their attitudes changed during the workshop, and how much they thought they had learned. Although an achievement test would probably yield more accurate information about how much they learned, the teachers might object to having to take a test. Or you might plan to ask the instructors to judge the amount of progress made either by the group as a whole or by each teacher. But they could hardly be viewed as impartial judges. These are the kinds of questions you will want to discuss with the program planning committee, and answer as best you can.

Another group of questions would have to do with teacher competence as an input. How would you meet the need for instructors qualified to conduct the sessions in the computer laboratory at the high school? Could the high school teachers who run the laboratory during the school year handle the job? Would the firm that supplied the computers to the high school supply qualified instructors? Would their services be provided gratis? How about the people who teach computer courses in nearby colleges? Since the answers to these questions would depend on knowledge we do not have, we cannot suggest answers, but you would have to come up with some, one way or another.

Yet another set of questions would have to do with materials. Are there enough computers in the high school laboratory so that each program participant can spend the amount of time at the keyboard that the program design calls for? (Notice that the answer to this question depends on what objectives have been defined.) If more computers are needed than are available at the high school, where and how can they be obtained? If the cost of obtaining enough computers is large, should you redefine the objectives of the program at a more modest level?

It would be very useful to know more about the participants, that is, the teachers who will participate in the workshop. How much do they already know about microprocessors and LOGO, and what are their attitudes toward them? Do any of the teachers already own their own personal computers? Have some had experience with computers in their own school buildings? (The answers to these questions may have a bearing on the need for computers: perhaps those who have computers at home or in their schools could bring them along to the workshop.) There are almost certain to be some in the group who know nothing at all about these devices, and some, even, who feel they would rather not have anything to do with them. How many do you expect, and what will you do about them?

What kind of a strategy should be used in achieving the specified objectives? How will the allotted time be spent? How will the participants be grouped for instruction? What kinds of processes will you expect to take place, and what kind of evidence that these things were or were not happening could you obtain during program operation?

You can see that there are a great many questions to be answered, and that the answers to different questions are interrelated, with the answer to one question being dependent on the answer you get to others. In many cases, you will not have access to many of the facts you need to know before you can answer with any confidence.

Fortunately, the questions that come up in different programs tend to be very similar, although the answers vary so much that almost every evaluation problem seems unique. This illustrates the point that, however little expertise you are likely to be able to bring to bear on the input evaluation of the first educational program you encounter, you will acquire such expertise rather rapidly with experience.

Your Turn

Consider the questions you would raise in evaluating inputs to the program Mr. Softchalk is running in his fourth-grade class. Mr. Softchalk may be regarded as a one-man planning committee with whom you will work to define program inputs after the fact.

It may help you a little if we clarify the differences between three ideas about Mr. Softchalk; his competence, his performance, and his effectiveness. Mr. Softchalk's competence consists of the professional knowledge, skills, and values that he brings to the class; it is a program input. His performance refers to how he and the students behave while he is teaching; it is the same thing as what we have called program process. By his effectiveness is meant the pupil learning attributable to his classroom performance, which we have called program outcomes.

Mastery Test

OBJECTIVE 3 TO STATE THE USES OF AND BE ABLE TO EVALUATE PROGRAM INPUTS

1. When does input evaluation typically occur?
2. Name the five areas upon which input evaluation focuses.
3. If you were going to evaluate the inputs into the Fosdyke Reading Program at Charles Brown Elementary School what kinds of questions would you ask?

Answer Key

Mastery Test, Objective 3

1. Although input evaluation is often conducted during the course of a project, it is typically undertaken before a project begins. The reason for this, of course, is that if program objectives are to be achieved, it is obligatory to structure program designs and activities that promise to address these objectives in reasonably cost-effective ways.
2. Objectives, design alternatives, instructor competence, physical and material support, and participant group characteristics.
3. You might be interested in finding answers to the following questions: How much college course work and practical experience related to the teaching of reading have the teachers had? Will teachers' aides help with instruction in the Fosdyke program? How much time will be allocated to instruction in the program? How much, if any, homework will be assigned to pupils in the program? What sorts of supplementary materials accompany the reading textbooks—filmstrips, movies, workbooks, periodic tests of skills, children's literature, and

the like? Do these supplementary materials require the purchase of special types of hardware to use them? What are the prior reading experiences and interests of the children who will be using the new series? Are most of them reading on, above, or below grade level in their present series?

OBJECTIVE 4 TO STATE A RATIONALE FOR CONDUCTING PROCESS EVALUATION, AND TO DESCRIBE AND USE THE PRINCIPAL OPTIONS FOR EVALUATING EDUCATIONAL PROGRAM PROCESSES

As we noted in the last section of this chapter, all three of the approaches to educational program evaluation we have studied emphasize program outcomes rather heavily as the basis for judging the worth of an educational program; and you may also have concluded that (except in discrepancy evaluation) there is no meaningful role for process evaluation to play. Such a conclusion would be incorrect.

Functions of Process Evaluation

Program processes, the activities that go on during program operation, are critically important to program effectiveness because of the direct effect they have on program outcomes. Every educational program is based on the universal belief that *learning results from the activities of the learner*. What this means, among other things, is that different learner activities result in different learnings. Just as the focus of outcome evaluation is on the learning, so the focus of process evaluation is on the activities of the learner.

There are three major functions that process evaluation serves:

1. To monitor program processes, that is, to make sure that the program operating is the program that was planned. There is a particularly seductive booby trap here that you should avoid at all costs. It is easy to become so preoccupied with assessing outcomes that you fail to monitor the processes in a program, which then fails to achieve its goals. When this happens you will never know whether the program failed because of some defect in its design or whether the design was perfectly sound but was not implemented and therefore never tried out at all. The possibility that what was supposed to happen during the operation of the program never happened, that the participants never had any of the experiences that they were supposed to have, cannot be ruled out without evidence based on monitoring of program processes.
2. To provide a basis for operating decisions, decisions those operating the program must make on the basis of assessments of the experiences participants are having, how close they are to the experiences they are supposed to be having, and how the participants are reacting to the experiences. It is true that this function is not an evaluative function, strictly speaking, but it is one that process evaluation serves, and in a sense the most important of all because of its direct effect on program operation.
3. To provide a basis for program design revision, when needed. The kind of information used for program decisions, if supplied regularly to the designer of the program as well as to the teacher or instructor, can be used to correct weaknesses in the design (some of which might, if undetected, prove fatal to it) in time to save the program. And when a program fails to succeed as well as it should, such information can be used in a post mortem study to learn why.

All of this serves to emphasize how important it is to monitor program processes as closely and as constantly as possible throughout the period of operation of the program.

Some Techniques of Process Evaluation

The primary target of your efforts to monitor program processes will of course be the activities that go on in it. The methods and techniques you will use to a great extent will be determined by the program design, which will specify the experiences program participants are supposed to have, that is, the activities that should go on in the program. The nature of these activities will, in turn, determine the kinds of assessment techniques and devices you will need to employ.

The Fosdyke reading program design, for example, would probably specify how many and which selections the pupils in the program are to read, games they are to play, special activities with special materials like cards or charts, and so forth; as well as how pupils' time is to be distributed among the different activities recommended. Other program designs will usually be equally definite about program activities.

In addition, there are some aspects of program process you will want to monitor that are not unique to any one design, but are potentially important in any program. One example of this is the amount of time elementary school pupils spend engaged in academic tasks, which has been found to be strongly related to pupils' progress in learning to read.[5] Even in programs like the Shadyvale workshop, in which the participants are adults, you will probably want to monitor this aspect of process. The affective climate of the group and (in programs involving school children) the amount of order or disorder are others.

Process Observers

A competent process observer is the most generally satisfactory source of information about program processes. One who is well trained and experienced in observing and recording the behavior of program participants and instructional personnel is hard to find, however. So much so that you are likely to end up training your own, or playing this critical role yourself. But even a relatively unskilled and poorly trained process observer is better than no observer at all.

You may think of the information you will get from process observers as of two types: formal and informal. Formal data will usually be collected by the use of a *structured observation system* or some other systematic observation procedure in a series of scheduled observations.

Informal information will come from things noted during visits made for other purposes. Because data of this kind are less rigorously obtained they are, of course, less dependable than data formally collected, and often more difficult to interpret; as a matter of fact, they are not scientifically respectable at all. But you can learn a lot from them just the same, so much that you would be ill advised if you neglected this important source altogether. Informal data are particularly valuable as a sort of early warning system which may provide the first indication of a situation in urgent need of attention. For this reason, in recruiting process observers you should look for someone who is naturally observant and perceptive, someone with rather strong intuitions, as well as someone who can learn to collect the more formal data you will need.

Systematic Observation Techniques

Formal observational data may be obtained through the use of one or another of four systematic observation techniques: ethnographic, ecological, structured, or behavior ratings.

Ethnographic and Ecological Observations Ethnographic observers attempt to adapt techniques originally developed by anthropologists for studying intact cultures to the study of education. A program like the Shadyvale workshop might be viewed as something very like an intact culture that could be studied in this way, even though the length of time in which it exists is very brief—much briefer than the length of time it takes to do a proper ethnographic study. The ethnographic observer tries to make a complete record in a narrative-descriptive format of what happens during an observation, without any prejudgment as to what is important or unimportant.[6]

Although the idea of using this approach when evaluating a program that is large and complex may be appealing, there are problems that make it difficult to do so. Very few well-trained ethnographers exist; indeed, the number with even a minimum amount of training is not large. Even if you could find and hire one, the amount of time that it would take him or her to analyze the masses of data the method generates would be so great as to make them useless for anything but a post mortem.

Ecological observers also attempt to record everything that occurs during a period of observation without prejudging which events are relevant or important. In recent years, video tape recorders have sometimes been used to preserve the behaviors for the close scrutiny that the technique requires. Information is extracted from the written record by a posteriori examination and analysis. Because of the time that it takes to complete this process, the usefulness of ecological observations in process evaluation is, like that of ethnographic observations, almost entirely restricted to post mortem examination of the program.[7]

Structured observations are made with the aid of *observation schedules*, instruments that define the subset of events whose occurrence is to be recorded. The observer's task is to recognize and record occurrences of these, and only these, events. The events defined on the schedule are ones supposed to distinguish activities that characterize the program being evaluated from activities that do not. A record made on such a schedule can be scored quickly and objectively by what is essentially a clerical process.

The technique is particularly useful for monitoring day-to-day operation of the program for any purpose, since the data are highly objective, closely relevant, and become available almost at once. The chief obstacle to its use seems to be the need to construct a schedule tailored to the program to be evaluated.

Structured observation systems have already been developed to measure some of the process dimensions common to many educational programs mentioned earlier. Depending on how important a dimension like academic engaged time or affective climate may be in your program, it may be worth your while to use one of these existing instruments.[8] Also, Chapter 4 examines a number of instruments that are designed to collect process data in classrooms.

Behavior ratings are also made with the aid of instruments called *rating scales* which prespecify the aspects of behavior the observer is to record; but they do so in terms of dimensions of behavior rather than of specific events; and the observer's essential task is to describe what he or she sees by marking a point on a scale (usually from one to five). Behavior ratings are less objective than records made on structured observation schedules, but like them they provide information that is timely enough to be potentially useful.[9]

Self-Report Data

Instead of (or in addition to) nonparticipating process observers, you have access to two other important alternate sources of information about program processes: program participants, and program staff. Since staff members and participants are present when all of the processes take place, they have a better opportunity to observe them than any outside observer is likely to have, and there are so many of the latter that it is easy to check the consistency of what they report by comparing one participant's report with another's. There are two problems with using members of either of these groups as sources of information; one is that they lack the training that the process observer will have, and the other is that, since neither group is disinterested, there is some risk that what they tell you about the program will not be completely objective. Neither difficulty is insurmountable. You can design instruments that will elicit data from untrained observers that is usable if you interpret it with care. So much information can be obtained in these ways at so little cost compared to other ways that you can hardly afford not to use it.

The Instructor Log This is a particular kind of self-report instrument that constitutes perhaps the most useful and practical way available for obtaining certain types of process data from a teacher or other staff member. The teacher is asked to keep a simple log, that is, a daily record, of time utilization. The task should be made as simple as it can be and still provide the needed data.

You should first prepare a simple log form that consists of a two-way chart ruled horizontally and vertically. Program time divisions of convenient length (10 or 15 minutes is usually about right) should be marked on the left margin, and whatever categories of activities are appropriate to that program should be listed across the top. What you will ask the teacher to do is to check which category of activity predominated during each time period during the day in the appropriate box on the form, and to do so promptly. (If you are evaluating a program in which participants may be organized into more than one group, ask the teacher to mark the name or number of each group in the space instead of a check mark.)

Suppose, for example, that in each of the classes in which the Fosdyke reading program is being implemented there were three reading groups, each reading at a different level. The teacher in each class involved in the evaluation might be asked to mark 1, 2, and 3 instead of a check mark, to indicate what each group was doing during each period of time. The categories in this case might include silent reading, reading aloud, playing a game, using a workbook, and so on, depending on the nature of the program.

Your Turn

Design a log sheet of the type that you might ask the instructor in charge of the programming classes offered in the Shadyvale workshop to fill out.

Evaluative and Descriptive Questionnaires During the last session of an institute or workshop it is customary to ask each participant to fill out an *evaluative questionnaire*, a questionnaire that asks him or her to evaluate each of a number of elements or components of the program. A typical instrument will ask the participants to indicate how useful, important, or (perhaps) how relevant to their own purposes they judged each component to have been. The judgment is recorded (usually) on the ubiquitous five-point scale, which may run from "completely useless" to "very useful." Such a device is most often used for outcome evaluation, although it can also be of some use in process evaluation.[10]

This device also lends itself quite well to a different kind of process evaluation if a different kind of question is asked. If, instead of asking the participant to *evaluate* certain program elements you ask him or her to *describe* them, you have a *descriptive questionnaire* which has the potential of providing much useful information. You might, for example, ask each program participant to indicate how much time he or she spent in each of the different types of activities the program provides, or how often he or she used each device or learning aid provided.

If you prefer to make your own assessment of the program elements for yourself rather than asking the participants to evaluate them for you, you should use a descriptive questionnaire. If you are interested in participant satisfaction, you should use an evaluative questionnaire. You can administer similar questionnaires to program staff members as well. How good an idea this is depends on what you want to find out. A questionnaire filled out by an instructor at the end of a program is likely to be much less accurate than a log filled out daily by the same instructor. A questionnaire should be used with a teacher only to obtain evaluative judgments or descriptive information not easy to record in the kind of form used to keep a log.

Your Turn

Write 10 items for a descriptive questionnaire to be administered to participants at the end of the Shadyvale workshop.

Miscellaneous Techniques These are the most commonly used procedures for obtaining information about program processes from program staff and participants. There are others which you may find useful in special cases, including structured or unstructured interviews, sociometric devices, and "tests" of personality, interests, and the like; but we shall not discuss them here.

Triangulation One final point. When you interpret or otherwise make use of information gained by one of these methods (or any other) you should keep in mind the limitations of the particular source from which the information came. As always, it is a good idea to *triangulate* pieces of information that are particularly important, that is, to get information on the same point from two or more different sources (preferably of different types) and compare one with the other to check on the accuracy of both. You might, for example, get data on time allocations to different activities from an instructor log and from a descriptive questionnaire filled out by participants. If there are discrepancies, and you find out soon enough, you might tap a third source, perhaps by interviewing the instructor.

Mastery Test

OBJECTIVE 4 TO STATE A RATIONALE FOR CONDUCTING PROCESS EVALUATION, AND TO DESCRIBE AND USE THE PRINCIPAL OPTIONS FOR EVALUATING EDUCATIONAL PROGRAM PROCESSES

1. Why is it so important for evaluators to examine program processes?
2. There are various techniques that can be used to examine program processes. Those which involve the use of a process observer, yield either informal or structured types of information. Briefly describe each of the following techniques:
   a. Informal observation
   b. Ethnographic approach
   c. Ecological approach
   d. Observation schedules
   e. Behavior ratings

3. Other techniques that can be used to observe program processes involve collecting information directly from program participants. Briefly describe how each of the following might be used:

   a. Instructor logs

   b. Questionnaires

4. Briefly describe what is meant by *triangulation.*

Answer Key

Mastery Test, Objective 4

1. An evaluator must be able to monitor program processes in order to determine if a program is operating the way it was planned. If a program has failed, an evaluator who understands what happened during the course of that program may be able to suggest changes that will enhance the chances for success on a second attempt. It is important to collect information about program processes and to provide it to program decision makers so that they can make midcourse corrections in programs.

2. a. Informal observations are not purposefully scheduled, but rather made casually during visits to classrooms. Information acquired informally—through conversation and random observations of program processes—is less rigorously obtained than information obtained from formal observation and therefore is less dependable.

   b. Ethnographic observations try to adapt techniques originally developed by anthropologists for studying intact cultures to the study of education. The ethnographic observer tries to make a complete record in a narrative-descriptive format of what happens during an observation, without any prejudgment as to what is important or unimportant.

   c. Ecological observations are conducted for the purpose of recording everything that occurs during a particular time period. Observers who use an ecological approach try to construct richly detailed descriptions of experiences in classrooms so that they may determine why teachers and students behave as they do.

   d. Observation schedules are instruments that define the subset of events whose occurrence is to be recorded. The observer's task is to recognize and record occurrences of these, and only these, events. The events defined on the schedule are ones supposed to distinguish activities that characterize the program being evaluated from activities that do not.

   e. Behavior ratings are made with the aid of instruments called rating scales or high-inference observation instruments, which prespecify the aspects of behavior the observer is to record; they do so in terms of dimensions of behavior rather than of specific events. The observer's essential task is to describe what he or she sees by marking a point on a scale (usually from one to five).

3. a. A teacher's log is a daily record of time utilization. Logs are often constructed as two-way charts ruled horizontally and vertically, and used to note the program activities that occurred during particular blocks of time. They can be used to monitor time utilization from the point of view of the teacher.

   b. Questionnaires are of two types: evaluative and descriptive. Evaluative questionnaires ask participants to evaluate a number of elements or components of the program. A typical instrument will ask the participant to indicate how useful, important, or (perhaps) how relevant to his or own purposes he or she judged each component to have been. Descriptive questionnaires, as the term implies, ask program participants to describe particular aspects of programs, such as how much time they spent in each of the different types of activities the program provides, or how often they used each device or learning aid provided.

4. Triangulation is the act of obtaining and comparing two or more perspectives on the same event. In order to triangulate, you must gather pieces of information about important points from two or more different sources (preferably of different types), and compare one with the other to check on the accuracy of both.

OBJECTIVE 5 TO EVALUATE THE OUTCOMES OF AN EDUCATIONAL PROGRAM

There seems to be general agreement that the logical way to evaluate an educational program is the most obvious, and the simplest; that is, by assessing the effects it has on those who participate in it. While the advocates of the objectives-based approach and those who favor goal-free evaluation may disagree about which outcomes you should measure, they are in full agreement that you should measure some kind of outcomes. Even the "Watergate" types see the importance of outcomes. There is no question that the worth of an educational program ultimately depends on the learning it produces. In what is left of this chapter we will deal with the problem of deriving information about program quality—or worth—from measurements of program outcomes.

The Importance of Input Evaluation

We will assume that you will have performed an adequate input evaluation before you begin to evaluate outcomes. This means that you will have gotten substantial agreement on what outcomes of the program are to be measured, and that you have either found or developed valid, reliable, and practical measures of those outcomes. We realize that, in far too many cases, the decision to implement the program design you are supposed to evaluate will have been made long before anyone thought of asking you to help evaluate it, so that much of your input evaluation may have been done after the fact.

Among our examples, the Shadyvale workshop is especially likely to be like this, although it can happen to any program. The responsibility for planning the workshop, for deciding what the workshop will be like and what its objectives will be, will probably have been assigned to the committee in charge some time after someone else decided it would be a good idea to have such a workshop; and the committee's real job will be to dream up some meaningful objectives for such a program, and perhaps hire a charismatic speaker. When this has been done, someone may decide to bring in an evaluator; and you will learn first hand what we mean by input evaluation after the fact.

Somehow you must end up with a number of measurements of program outcomes on which you will base your evaluation; that is, after all, what you will have been recruited to do. What do you do with these data once they have been collected? That is what this learning experience should teach you. The emphasis will be on interpreting the results, not on doing the necessary computations. Since this is not a book on measurement or statistics, we will give as few details as possible about the statistical procedures that you will have to use.

Your Turn

Mr. Softchalk's program is another example of one likely to be well under way before the help of a program evaluator is sought. Choose another person to work with you, one of you to play the role of Mr. Softchalk and the other that of a program evaluator brought in in October or November to help plan an evaluation. Discuss the objectives and techniques to be used in the evaluation.

Triangulation

There is one point related to the choice of measurement techniques that we have made before but regard as important enough to reemphasize here. The point has to do with triangulating your measurements. As you may perhaps recall, triangulation requires you to have two (or more) measurements of the same thing obtained with different types of instruments. The term *triangulation* is used because of the practice surveyors follow of taking two (or more) sightings on an object they wish to locate, each from a different viewpoint. They do this to make sure they know exactly where the object is.

Whenever it is possible to triangulate an important measurement, that is, to measure it more than once, using a different instrument each time, you should do so, because any one measurement by itself will have such low validity. If you can supplement participants' own estimates of how much they have learned with their measured gains on a test of what they were supposed to learn, the composite will be much more accurate than either kind of information taken by itself.

Comparative and Noncomparative Program Evaluation

Many program evaluations are done to support policy decisions, to help decide whether the program is effective enough so that it should be installed instead of some other, competing one. The administration at Charles Brown elementary school, for example, will adopt the Fosdyke reading program if, and only if, an evaluation indicates that it is effective enough to justify the costs of adopting and operating it.

The critical question is, of course, *How effective is "effective enough"*? One way to answer this question is to find out whether participants in the program score higher on a specified test than participants in some other program called the *control*. Another way to answer the question is to set a standard or criterion, that is, to specify a score on some test or other instrument that must be equalled or exceeded by program participants, and then test participants to see whether they measure up to that standard. The first approach involves a *comparative evaluation*; the second a *noncomparative evaluation*.

Comparative Evaluation involves comparing program effects with effects of one or more other programs that have the same objectives, using the same outcome measures. It is essential, first, that all programs being compared have the same objectives, and second, that the same outcome measures be used in all of them. If it is possible, participants should be assigned to programs randomly, because if this is done any difference you find between program outcomes can be unequivocally attributed to differences in programs. Random assignment is rarely possible in practice; without it, you can never be sure whether the differences in outcomes of different programs reflect differences in the programs or in the participants in the programs.

Nevertheless, with care, you can learn a lot from comparative evaluations in which randomization is not possible. You should read Campbell and Stanley's classic treatment of the topic.[11]

If you decide to use the comparative approach, you should do as much process evaluation as you can in the control programs as well as the one being evaluated. These data can be used to get some clue as to why the outcomes differ (if they do) or why they do not differ (if they do not).

Noncomparative Evaluation compares the effects of a program with a standard or criterion rather than with the effects of an alternative program. Ideally, the standard or criterion should be specified in advance; but in practice it is sometimes decided upon after the results are in (especially, as we shall see, in the case of goal-free evaluation).

When the objectives of an instructional program in, say, reading or arithmetic are specified in terms of gains in scores on a standardized test or test battery, a criterion based on test norms is often used. Sometimes a mean gain of one year in age or grade scores is regarded as satisfactory; sometimes more is demanded. Sometimes allowance is made for the average academic ability of the class, sometimes not.

This is perfectly feasible when you are using an objectives-based approach, whether it is advisable or not; but if you are using a goal-free approach (or if you are looking at side effects) you will be unable or unwilling to set a criterion beforehand. Instead you must estimate the effect in question as accurately as you can, and then make your judgment. In the case of an undesirable effect, such as a lowering of students' self-esteem, you must decide whether the decrease is tolerable or not; in the case of a desirable effect, such as an interest in learning more about LOGO, you must decide whether the gain is worthwhile. About the only specific suggestion we have to offer is that you use an appropriate statistical test to protect yourself from the danger of over interpreting chance differences, ones that would not be found if the program were repeated.

Estimating Program Effects

There are two rather obvious points about estimating program effects that should be emphasized. One is that the status of program participants on any outcome measure at the end of the program is rarely a very good indicator of program effectiveness. Programs are intended to produce change, and change is what you should be measuring. The second point is that teaching is a group activity, but learning is an individual activity; that changes take place in participants as individuals, and differ in kind and amount for different individuals.

How much an individual learns, the effect the program has upon him or her, depends not only on the nature of the program but also on who the individual is—on things like how much aptitude and previous knowledge he or she possesses and his or her level of motivation to learn. The question *How effective is this program?* is, strictly speaking, unanswerable. The question *How effective is this program with this kind of person?* makes sense and can be answered. In most cases, the question we want answered is *How effective is this program with the average person for whom the program is intended?*

Estimating Change Measurement of change in an individual over a period of time, as during the operation of a program, requires measurements of his or her status at two points in time, one (called the pretest) obtained before the period begins, and one (called the posttest) obtained after it ends. There are a number of different statistical procedures that may be used to assess the amount of change; we recommend what is perhaps the simplest viable approach, based on within-group regressions. Because it is not widely used and involves only minimal knowledge of statistical methods, we shall present a brief description of how it works and how it is used.[12]

If you correlate the pretest scores of all program participants *within a single group or class* with their posttest scores, you can set up a simple linear regression equation for predicting posttest scores from pretest scores within that group or class.[13] This equation can then be used to estimate the expected posttest score of a participant with any pretest score you choose. In particular, you can use it to estimate the expected posttest score of a student whose pretest score equals the mean in the population served by the program. In other words, the posttest score of the *average person for whom the program is intended.*

There is no need to limit yourself to a single pretest score in defining this average person; a within-class regression equation can be set up for predicting posttest scores from two or more pretest scores as easily as from one. You could, for instance, estimate the expected posttest score of the average member of a minority group by using minority-group status as a second pretest. However, we will use only one pretest in all of our examples here, for the sake of simplicity.

Suppose that you get the following equation in the group enrolled in a certain program:

$$y = 8 + .64x$$

If x represents any pretest score, then y is the expected posttest score of any individual whose pretest score is equal to x. In simple terms, it is an estimate of the mean posttest score of a very large number of individuals with the same pretest score (x).

If x is the pretest score of the average person (as defined); and if the same test (or an equivalent test) is used for the pretest as for the posttest, then y estimates the posttest score the average person would get if he or she went through the program. If you have specified program objectives in terms of the posttest score the average person should achieve, this is precisely the information you need to decide whether or not the program was successful in achieving its objective.

Suppose, for instance, that x is 10; then, if we substitute 10 for x in the above equation we get:

$$y = 8 + (.64) \times (10) = 8 + 6.4 = 14.4$$

In other words, we estimate that the average person would score 14.4 points after participating in the program.

Your Turn

Estimate the posttest score that would be obtained in this program by participants whose pretest scores were 5, 13, and 20 points. Assuming that the program goal was to get each participant to achieve a score of at least 16 points, regardless of his or her pretest score, with which participants would the program succeed?

Estimating the Effects of Instruction Let us assume that you have obtained the pretest and posttest scores of all or most of the students in Mr. Softchalk's classroom during the school year, on equivalent forms of all of the subtests in a standardized achievement test battery; and that you have intercorrelated their pretest and posttest scores on each subtest and set up an equation like the one above for each subtest.

Next you consult the local test norms (or the national norms if you prefer) to ascertain what the pretest score of the average fourth-grade student in the local school system (or in the national norm sample) would be on each test. Using each of these values as x in each of your equations in turn, you can estimate how high the average child in the system (or the country!) would score in each subject measured by the test battery, after a year in Mr. Softchalk's class. By consulting the norms again you can estimate the gain in months the average child would make in that class in one year. If this gain is equal to or greater than one year, you would probably conclude that the instruction in that subject was satisfactory. If it was less, you might ask why.

Assessing the Effectiveness of a Reading Program You would use much the same procedure in estimating the effects of the Brown Elementary School's reading program, using scores on equivalent reading tests obtained at the beginning and the end of a school year of all the pupils in the program. If you are making a comparative evaluation, only some of the classes will be using the new program, but the same test will be given in all classes.

You would, of course, use a different equation for each class, and the value of x would be different for each grade, since the average fifth-grader does get a higher score on most tests than the average fourth-grader. Outcomes in months should be reported separately for each grade, and comparisons made between the Fosdyke program and the one already in place grade by grade, so that in each instance the programs would be compared on the basis of posttest scores of pupils with the same pretest scores.

Program effects could also be reported separately for each class within the same grade and school. Note, however, that differences found would reflect differences in the *programs* in different teachers' classes, not differences in the *competence* of the teachers. These measures could not and should not be used to evaluate teacher competence.

Effectiveness of a Workshop The procedure you would most likely follow in evaluating the Shadyvale workshop would be quite different from what we have been describing. Since there would be no other program with which to compare it, the evaluation would have to be noncomparative. And since none of the measuring instruments would have been standardized, you would have no basis on which you could specify what level of outcomes would be satisfactory. Nor could you specify the pretest score of the average person who might participate; all you could do is say what the average person who did participate was like.

If, as is likely, your evaluation was based on self-report data, there would be no pretest data. What you would be asking participants for would be their perceptions of the program effects, not of end-of-program status. Your analysis would be descriptive in nature, and much simpler than the one you would make of the reading program data.

Concluding Remarks One final note. It is important that you bear in mind the difference between the two activities of the program evaluator. In one mode you are concerned with collecting information about the program; in the other you are using the information to judge program worth. Try to keep the two activities separate, and know which one you are doing at any particular time.

It is, of course, impossible within the space of a single chapter to give as complex a topic as this one anything but a superficial treatment. If in your later career you do any amount of evaluation, we urge you to study the references cited throughout the chapter, or seek additional training.

Mastery Test

OBJECTIVE 5 TO EVALUATE THE OUTCOMES OF AN EDUCATIONAL PROGRAM

1. As you undertake a program evaluation, you may find that goals and objectives are vague or even nonexistent. What criteria should you use in helping people establish program goals and objectives?
2. If you were working on an evaluation of a secondary school English program, and the members of the evaluation team wanted to assess its effects by examining students' scores on a battery of four tests, all designed to assess verbal abilities, what might you suggest?

3. One important concept for the evaluator to understand is that of triangulation. If you were asked to assess the degree to which children learned to read after having participated in the Fosdyke Reading Program, how might you triangulate in order to provide your assessment?

4. Assume that you have three within-class regression equations—one each for Teachers A, B, and C—and you must help the principal decide which class would be the best for Student X. In other words, given Student X's pretest score, you must project the posttest score he or she would be likely to receive in each class, and determine where Student X would make the most gain. Given the following equations, which class would you recommend for Student X who has a pretest score of 22?

Teacher A's equation: $y = 18 + .36x$
Teacher B's equation: $y = 7 + .55x$
Teacher C's equation: $y = 4 + .79x$

Answer Key

Mastery Test, Objective 5

1. The first criterion that should govern the establishment of program goals and objectives is the appropriateness of the goal or objective, first, to the original intentions of whoever instituted the program and, second, to the mission of the school (or other agency) operating the program. The second criterion is the extent to which it is feasible to assess the degree to which the goal or objective is accomplished. One must be careful, however, to avoid the trap of favoring goals and objectives that are easily assessed over those that are important but difficult to measure. Unreliable information about important program effects is usually much more valuable than reliable information about trivial ones, and provides a much better basis for decision making.

2. You might suggest that using four tests to assess verbal abilities is a waste of time and money. These tests are likely to be highly correlated with one another, that is, they are all measuring essentially the same thing, and thus are likely to produce the same or very similar results. Instead, the team might select one or at most two of the tests by comparing the cost of administration and scoring and the ease with which results can be interpreted and used to improve the program.

3. In order to triangulate the children's reading abilities at the conclusion of the Fosdyke program, you might examine: (1) their scores on standardized reading tests, (2) the amount of time they spend reading, (3) their attitudes toward reading, (4) the number of books they check out from the library, and/or (5) teachers' judgments of children's abilities to read. The idea of triangulation is to acquire at least two fairly independent measures of the effect you are interested in assessing.

4. First you must substitute 22 for the value of *x* in each equation, and solve for *y*. Then subtract the value of *x* (or 22) from each *y*, and you get the following:

Teacher A: 25.92 = 18 + 7.92; 25.92 − 22.00 = 3.92
Teacher B: 19.1 = 7 + 12.1 ; 19.1 − 22.00 = −2.9
Teacher C: 21.38 − 4 + 17.38; 22 − 21.38 − 0.62

As you can see, Student X is projected to make the greatest gain (+3.92) in Teacher A's class. All other things equal, this would be the best class for Student X. It is interesting to note also that if Student X were placed in Teacher B's class, he or she would actually be expected to lose ground!

NOTES

1. D. S. Stufflebeam et al., *Educational Evaluation and Decision Making* (Itasca, Ill.: Peacock, 1971).

2. The value positions (expectations and standards) that characterize professionally prepared teachers affect the way the teacher behaves in the same way that knowledge or skill does.

3. M. Provus, *Discrepancy Evaluation* (Berkeley, Calif.: McCutchan, 1971).

4. "Pros and Cons about Goal-Free Evaluation," Evaluation Comment (Dec., 1972).

5. See C. Denham and A. Lieberman, eds. *Time to Learn* (Washington, D.C.: U. S. Office of Education, 1980).

6. See S. Wilson, "The Use of Ethnographic Techniques in Educational Research," *Review of Educational Research*, vol. 47 (1977).

7. See W. Doyle, "Classroom Tasks and Students' Abilities," in *Research on Teaching: Concepts, Findings, and Implications*, edited by P. L. Peterson and H. J. Walberg (Berkeley, Calif.: McCutchan, 1979).

8. See A. Simon and E. G. Boyer, *Mirrors for Behavior III: An Anthology of Observation Instruments* (Wyncote, Pa.: Communications Materials Center, 1974).

9. Much of what you will have learned from other chapters in this book about observing and evaluating teachers and teaching will be useful here.

10. See D. R. Berdie and J. F. Anderson, *Questionnaires: Design and Use* (Metuchen, N.J.: Scarecrow, 1974).

11. See N. L. Gage, ed., *Handbook of Research on Teaching* (Chicago: Rand McNally, 1963).

12. See L. Baldwin and D. M. Medley, "A Comparison of Analysis of Covariance to Within-Class Regression in the Analysis of Non-Equivalent Groups," *Journal of Experimental Education* (in press).

13. See, for example, K. D. Hopkins and G. V. Glass, *Basic Statistics for the Behavioral Sciences* (Englewood Cliffs, N. J.: Prentice-Hall, 1978), pp. 152ff.

CURRICULUM DEVELOPMENT AND SELECTION

8

Gerald R. Firth
John W. Newfield

OBJECTIVE 1 To recognize opportunities to exert leadership for curriculum development and identify components of curriculum viewed as a plan

OBJECTIVE 2 To identify goals and objectives, content, learning activities, evaluation procedures, resources, and statements of desired teacher-student interactions and factors related to including these specific components in the curriculum

OBJECTIVE 3 To classify statements of rationale for curriculum decisions according to criteria for selection, organization, or emphasis

OBJECTIVE 4 To recognize major beliefs associated with technical models of curriculum development and evaluate plans for curriculum activities for consistency with characteristics of these models

OBJECTIVE 5 To recognize major beliefs associated with interactive models of curriculum development and evaluate plans for curriculum activities for consistency with characteristics of these models

OBJECTIVE 6 To identify factors and forces influencing selection of instructional materials that require professional reviews and guidelines

OBJECTIVE 7 To associate descriptions of content with common reference sources of professional reviews of instructional programs and materials

OBJECTIVE 8 To identify four categories of criteria for selecting instructional materials, and identify questions to be asked to evaluate each category

OBJECTIVE 9 To describe two types of organizational structures for curriculum coordination and list the advantages and disadvantages of each

OBJECTIVE 10 To identify the nature of the participants who could be called on to accomplish the curriculum development or selection processes

OBJECTIVE 11 To prepare a budget to support management of the curriculum development or selection processes

INTRODUCTION

One thing that can be said about instructional supervisors is that they are called upon to serve many roles in local school districts and these roles vary considerably from district to district. Therefore, to be at all descriptive, lists of competencies for supervisors provide a formidable array of tasks. As indicated in Chapter 1, curriculum development, while not part of every supervisor's responsibilities, is common enough that it is included as one of the general tasks Harris has identified for supervisors.[1] In addition, curriculum is often influenced as much by selection decisions as by local development. Therefore, the supervisor needs to have competencies to handle both development and selection of curriculum. The goal of this chapter is to help instructional supervisors develop an awareness of four major tasks related to the development and selection of curriculum. These tasks are:

Task 1: Identifying the curricular issues in educational settings (Objectives 1–3).

Task 2: Establishing an approach to guide curriculum development (Objectives 4–5).

Task 3: Planning for the selection of materials (Objectives 6–8).

Task 4: Managing the curriculum development and selection processes (Objectives 9–11).

The first of these tasks refers to the development of a perspective. This includes becoming knowledgeable of concepts related to curriculum and of the terminology of this field. The second and third tasks refer to making choices concerning ways to structure and organize curriculum development and selection activities. The last task refers to the coordination and management of these activities. A set of more specific objectives has been identified for each of these major tasks. They are listed in each section.

OBJECTIVE 1 TO RECOGNIZE OPPORTUNITIES TO EXERT LEADERSHIP FOR CURRICULUM DEVELOPMENT AND IDENTIFY COMPONENTS OF CURRICULUM VIEWED AS A PLAN

If instructional supervisors find an item such as "assume leadership for providing a continuous program of curriculum development" on their job descriptions what does this imply? Many people have offered suggestions as to what constitutes an appropriate answer to this question. The curriculum field, perhaps more so than any other area in education, is characterized by a diversity of beliefs regarding its purposes in advancing programs for students. These beliefs are reflected by various groups who define curriculum in different ways that emphasize what they each believe should be done in education. For example, those who believe that learners should have a maximum amount of freedom to support natural growth and development tend to view curriculum as a general set of guidelines establishing conditions for teacher and student interactions. On the other hand, those who emphasize the importance of transmitting a body of knowledge that exists independent of the learner tend to view curriculum as a rather detailed prescriptive statement of learning outcomes. (For a description of some of these sets of beliefs see *Additional Readings*, Objective 1.) Thus the supervisor who searches for a single, well-accepted answer to fulfill the stated job description is bound to fail. Instead, supervisors need to be able to work with several views of curriculum and to seek to understand how others involved in curriculum development view this concept. Only then will supervisors be able to understand which educational issues fall within the scope of their job descriptions.

Curriculum Plan

As you might expect with a concept as complex as curriculum there are many ways to define it. Oliva lists 13 interpretations of the term *curriculum* which are: that which is taught in school; a set of subjects; content; a program of studies; a set of materials; a sequence of courses; a set of performance objectives; a course of study; everything that goes on within the school including extraclass activities, guidance, and interpersonal relationships; that which is taught both inside and outside of school directed by the school; everything that is planned by school personnel; a series of experiences undergone by learners in school; and that which an individual learner experiences as a result of schooling.[2]

To begin to answer the question about what supervisors' jobs require it is useful to look for common elements in these definitions of curriculum. One element that stands out in at least 10 of the definitions is the idea of a statement of intention, or a plan for the educational program of the schools. This element is evident in one definition that uses the term *planned*, and in other definitions that describe components of a plan, such as a course or program of study, content, subjects, and performance objectives. Intention is also suggested by the term *taught*, used in two definitions, which conveys the notion of some sort of proposed intervention.

The definitions that do not state or imply intent fail to provide much help in clarifying the nature of supervisors' responsibilities for curriculum development. For example, one definition refers to curriculum as "everything that goes on in the school." Such a view of curriculum does little to delimit the job responsibilities of supervisors. (However, we should mention that this statement is of value because it identifies extraclass activities as a central curricular concern. These activities are too often viewed as an incidental part of the school program.)

Other statements that do not convey the idea of curriculum as a plan are those that refer to curriculum as student experiences. At times it may seem appropriate for supervisors to think of curriculum as student experiences. For instance, when supervisors are involved in evaluating the curriculum, the concept of student experiences may direct attention to a broad range of actual as well as planned outcomes of the educational program. However, since development and selection precede actual student experiences, thinking of curriculum in terms of student experiences is not so useful as thinking of curriculum as plans.

Our discussion to this point shows that a key component in the concept of curriculum is planning for an intentional intervention. This concept of curriculum is well described by Resnick:

> Curriculum constitutes a planned intervention for the purpose of education. A curriculum can be thought of as a series of activities explicitly designed to change the knowledge and competence of those who engage in it. Whenever an educational experience is planned, whenever explicit efforts are made to optimize learning and development, a curriculum is being designed. The curriculum may be tight or fluid in style; it may specify activities in great detail or only in general outline; the instructor may control most moves, or much may be left to learners. Whatever the particular strategy or ideology of education employed, it is appropriate to speak of a curriculum whenever education is not simply left to chance.[3]

To understand more fully what viewing curriculum as a plan entails we need to expand the description of the plan by considering the nature of its components, the level of the school organization for which it is devised, and whether or not it exists as a formal written statement. Finally, we need to identify various representations of curriculum plans in order to help the supervisor identify curricular issues in educational settings.

Components of a Curriculum Plan

When supervisors work with curriculum development, they may use many types of curricular components. Supervisors may work with general or specific components and, in addition, with components that play major or supporting roles in determining the curriculum.

General Components The general components that might go into a curriculum development plan may be broad composites such as courses, subject areas, problems, or themes, as well as extracurricular activities or student activities. These usually relate to a placement in time, either a period during the school day or a grade-level assignment. For example, in an elementary school setting, general components of the curriculum would consist of: subject areas, such as language arts or science; problems or themes, such as consumption of goods and services, or westward expansion; and major school activities, such as assemblies. All of these are associated with time periods during the day, dates during the school year, or grade levels. At the secondary level, general components of curriculum plans would consist of courses, program requirements, intramural and interscholastic physical activities, student government meetings, and club meetings; all assigned to times during the school day, the school year, and grade levels. Viewed from this perspective, making decisions about what to include and how to allocate time during the preparation of schedules is a task related to curriculum development.

Specific Components When we break down the general components of the curriculum we see that they contain several specific components that might be used as part of a plan for an educational program. Most current literature centers curriculum development around *statements of goals and objectives*, certainly one of the key components of a curriculum plan. Another specific component is *content*, the outlining of which often represents a major curriculum development activity. *Descriptions of methods for evaluating objectives* comprise another component of curriculum viewed as a plan. These descriptions may be as general as suggestions of a format to use, such as an oral examination or an analysis of student projects, or as specific as to include individual test items. Another component frequently included in curriculum plans is *resources*, including various textbooks and workbooks, reference sources, films, television programs, community members, or any other materials that could be used to foster student learning related to the objectives. Whether or not to include *learning activities* as a curriculum component remains an undecided issue. Some insist that curriculum development should be separate from instructional planning while others want to incorporate instruction under the general heading of curriculum development. Although not emphasized so often as the other components, curriculum plans could also contain policy for or descriptions of *desired forms of student and teacher interactions*. For example, statements regarding student participation in determining learning activities could be useful, especially for people who primarily view the curriculum as experiences students have while at school.

Supporting Components Supporting components of curriculum viewed as a plan are the "finishing touches" that should be added to the document in which the curriculum plan is presented.[4] One of these is the statement of philosophy that guided the curriculum development activity, including basic beliefs about students, learning, and the roles of the school and the teachers. Another supporting component is a description of the processes by which the curriculum was developed, including information about who were involved and what their roles were. A third supporting component is a statement from the board of education in regard to the plan. This statement should clarify teacher responsibilities and community expectations. A fourth example is a set of instructions to users of the plan about how to put it into action and how to suggest improvements and revisions.

Levels of Planning

In addition to identifying the components of a plan another factor supervisors will need to consider when identifying curricular issues in educational settings is the levels within the school organization. For example, when supervisors help individual teachers to develop plans that include objectives, evaluation procedures, or any of the other components previously described, they have an opportunity for providing leadership for curriculum development and selection. When supervisors meet with the administration and faculty to establish a schedule for remedial classes, they have another opportunity for providing leadership for curriculum development. Supervisors involved with teachers in creating a sex education program to be used throughout the school district have still another opportunity to provide leadership for curriculum development. Supervisors should keep in mind that curriculum development and selection decisions occur at many levels—classroom, school, and district—of the school organization.

Written and Mental Plans

Another factor to consider when identifying occasions to provide leadership for curriculum development is that not all plans are written. In fact, if supervisors restrict their attempts to provide leadership to occasions when written plans are being developed, they will miss most of their opportunities. Far more mental than written planning occurs in schools; verbal interaction in faculty meetings, conversations, and individual conferences influence schooling much more than written documents. Educators are oriented to personal interactions, and these occasions provide the supervisor with significant opportunities to exert leadership for curriculum development. Supervisors need to remember that curriculum development means the development of the ideas people hold as well as the production of written documents.

Representations of Curriculum

The curriculum plan can take many forms. Some manifestations of the curriculum are formal documents such as curriculum guides, course catalogs, course outlines, syllabi, programs of studies, and lists of graduation requirements. Other manifestations are less obvious, such as schedules and school policy handbooks. Less formal but very useful for helping supervisors identify elements of the curriculum in a particular setting are textbooks, teacher guides to texts and other instructional materials, and test items. Supervisors should remember that discussions with teachers are a valuable source for identifying the curriculum. All of these sources can help supervisors exert knowledgeable leadership when planning action around one of the representations of the curriculum.

Awareness of Components

Not all of the components mentioned are involved in every curriculum development project. Some plans emphasize only goals and objectives. Others stress learning activities and resources. Few plans actually treat evaluation in any detail. However, directing attention to any of these components, whether part of a coordinated activity to produce a plan or an isolated issue, could be included under the general job responsibility of supervisors charged with providing leadership for curriculum development. Supervisors may be involved in a formal curriculum development project or in such piece meal tasks as determining what to order for the instructional materials center. In each of these cases supervisors can provide curriculum development leadership.

Your Turn

After reading the previous material you may wish to:

1. Have a class discussion in which members take turns presenting responses they would make to the state board of education which was considering changing supervisors' requirements for certification to include more formal courses in administration and fewer courses in curriculum.
2. Interview a practicing supervisor to determine the amount of time spent with classroom, school, and district-level curricular issues.
3. Visit a school and collect as many formal representations of the curriculum as can be identified.
4. Visit a school and conduct a mini "curriculum mapping" exercise in which teachers' ideas of the curriculum are compared with formal curriculum guides.
5. Examine some of the additional readings for Objective 1.

Mastery Test

OBJECTIVE 1 TO RECOGNIZE OPPORTUNITIES TO EXERT LEADERSHIP FOR CURRICULUM DEVELOPMENT AND IDENTIFY COMPONENTS OF CURRICULUM VIEWED AS A PLAN

1. Indicate (yes or no) whether the following instances offer a supervisor an opportunity to exert leadership for curriculum development.
   a. The superintendent asks the supervisor to meet with a group of physical education teachers who are preparing a new unit on movement education.
   b. The principal asks the supervisor to meet with department chairpersons to review the course schedule for the next school year.
   c. The superintendent asks the supervisor to coordinate a study of drug usage among students.
   d. The president of the PTA asks the supervisor to meet with parents to explain the basis for student assignment to reading groups in the elementary schools.
   e. A teacher asks the supervisor for help in getting ready to teach a new unit on career education.
2. Indicate whether each of the following is: a general component of curriculum, a specific component of curriculum, a supporting component of curriculum, or not a component of curriculum.
   a. List of topics in a textbook
   b. Teacher evaluation form
   c. Description of a spelling game
   d. List of subjects taught at the fifth grade
   e. Attendance report
   f. Statement of school philosophy

g. List of films related to career education

h. Set of practice exercises

Answer Key

Mastery Test, Objective 1

1. a. Yes

   b. Yes

   c. No. This activity does not directly relate to a planned intervention. While curriculum development may follow from this activity it does not produce curriculum.

   d. No. This function may be an important part of the job of the supervisor, but it is not curriculum development.

   e. Yes

2. a. Specific component—content

   b. Not a component of curriculum

   c. Specific component—learning activity

   d. General component

   e. Not a component of curriculum

   f. Supporting component

   g. Specific component—resources

   h. Specific component—learning activity

OBJECTIVE 2 TO IDENTIFY GOALS AND OBJECTIVES, CONTENT, LEARNING ACTIVITIES, EVALUATION PROCEDURES, RESOURCES, AND STATEMENTS OF DESIRED TEACHER-STUDENT INTERACTIONS, AND FACTORS RELATED TO INCLUDING THESE SPECIFIC COMPONENTS IN THE CURRICULUM

Goals and Objectives

A major component of curriculum viewed as a plan with which anyone involved in curriculum development will spend considerable time is statements of goals and objectives. Two factors instructional supervisors must consider in relation to this component are: what format should be used for their expression, and how specifically must they be stated?

Format for Goals and Objectives Determining a format for the expression of goals and objectives involves deciding whether to use descriptions of input conditions, such as things the schools will attempt to provide, or output conditions, such as statements of student learning. In addition, decisions have to be made about what to include in either type of statement.

The choice of format for goals and objectives, has significant implications in the curriculum development and selection processes and must be addressed early. It will reflect a set of beliefs about education and will shape the nature of the issues that are addressed in the total curriculum enterprise. For example, those who stress the importance of freedom in the classroom tend to support the use of input statements to express goals and objectives in the curriculum. Statements of this form, such as "students will be encouraged to learn to communicate in a least one of the world's major languages in addition to English"; "the teacher will attempt to present more than a single view of controversial issues or areas in which there are diverse opinions"; or "the schools will improve services to pupils identified as able, gifted, or talented throughout the district" provide a general sense of direction while leaving teachers free to work with students in defining their educational programs. They do this by describing conditions that schools will attempt to provide rather than specifying what the outcomes of these conditions will be. On the other hand, statements of goals and objectives written in an output format specify what students are to learn or even what behaviors they are to exhibit as a result of schooling. This format, which is most commonly legitimized in much of current professional literature, is expressed by statements such as: "students will develop an understanding of others"; "students will be aware of a wide variety of occupational fields"; or "students will describe ways that the bridge, the freeway system, and the subways have improved transportation in the cities." This format is most supportive of views of education's role in the transmission of knowledge of the culture, and of the school district's role in managing educational programs and establishing a program of accountability.

If goals and objectives are written as statements of student learning outcomes, additional factors need to be considered. For example, how will goals and objectives be differentiated? One possible answer to this question is that *goals* express outcomes that are somewhat visionary, are the results of situations existing in many parts of the school program, and are developed only over long periods of time. *Objectives* describe student learning outcomes that can be attributed to specific parts of the school program and are attainable. In general, objectives are written with two components, a description of content and a statement of desired student behavior. The statement of behavior is included to measure and standardize the intent of the objective. Because goals often are not directly measured the requirement to include statements of student behavior often is relaxed. Instead, general names for classes of behavior such as *understand, is committed to*, or *is able to perform* often are used in goal statements. However, for particular curriculum development or selection projects the supervisor needs to consider the appropriateness of the level of specificity of the student behavior statements. Many people advocate stating rather detailed objectives, often called *performance objectives*, which list conditions for assessing behavior. The behavior itself is described in a format that could easily be converted into a test item, and includes a standard of acceptable performance.

Specificity of Goals and Objectives Finally, another important factor with regard to goals and objectives in curriculum development that supervisors need to consider is the desired level of specificity of these statements. Perhaps the simplest method of describing a desired level is to indicate the number of statements required for a given portion of the school program. Thus, a charge to a committee to create some general goals may ask for 12–15 statements for the K–12 program while a charge to a committee working on the mathematics program for grades 6–8 may request 60–90 objectives, or several hundred objectives, depending on the degree of program control the district desires.

Content

Although emphasis on objectives recently has overshadowed concern for content in curriculum development, adequate description of objectives is impossible without reference to content. Moreover, decisions about content are at the center of curricular issues. Although often used, the term *content* eludes precise definition. In general, content refers to the knowledge and values included in the curriculum; for example, the topic outline with entries of government, religious beliefs, climate, customs, industry, and history. The themes, strands, or main ideas—such as self-understanding, opportunities and options, education and training, jobs and employment, and social responsibility—used to organize a career education course are other examples of content. Specific facts—Abraham Lincoln was the sixteenth president and a Phillips screw has two perpendicular grooves in its head—and general relationships—hot air rises, scarcity of products leads to high prices, and family income is related to medical attention family members receive—are examples of content. Content also includes beliefs about desired conditions, such as justice, respect for authorities, willingness to suspend judgments, and valuing individual dignity.

Perhaps the most fundamental factor related to content is how much and what should be required and how much and what should be elective. Providing an appropriate organization for the required content in the program, an area that has come to be called general education, has been a continual problem in American education. The following statement with regard to general education illustrates the basic tension between this area and specialized vocational and/or exploratory or special interest programs.

> The specific agenda—the preservation of democracy, the promoting of a common heritage, the development of citizen responsibility, a renewed commitment to ethical behavior, the enhancement of global perspectives, the integration of diverse groups into the larger society—has varied. But the underlying concern has remained remarkably constant. It reflects the never-ending tension between the individual and the group, between freedom and control, between independence and interdependence.[5]

Major structures that have been used in the curriculum to provide general education are the distribution requirements whereby hours in specific areas are mandated for students and, to a lesser extent, the core curriculum in which all students engage in common learning activities. Regardless of what structure is used supervisors as curriculum developers need to be aware of the necessity of providing for general education through decisions made with regard to content. These decisions may involve general curricular elements such as courses, themes, or problems, or they may involve specific elements such as concepts, relationships, and values.

Supervisors need to determine the emphasis given to both formal and informal content. Formal content refers to knowledge and values that are part of organized disciplines. Informal content refers to knowledge and values that are part of daily living. Information about the structure of a zip code directory, cooking times by weight for pork, prices of new cars, requirements on job application forms, and locations of public health services are all examples of informal content.

With regard to formal content supervisors need to consider what emphasis to give to each of the disciplines. There is a rich field from which to select formal content. The curriculum developer could draw upon the natural sciences (biology, chemistry, physics, geology, and astronomy); the social sciences (anthropology, sociology, geography, law, political science, economics, and psychology); mathematics (algebra, geometry, analysis, and statistics); history; religion; philosophy; language and literature (grammar, semantics, rhetoric, composition); and the arts (visual and performing). These disciplines can supply content for both the required and the elective portions of the curriculum.

For each of the disciplines in the curriculum, supervisors must decide what emphasis to give to the organized body of knowledge—the substantive structure of the discipline—and the method of investigation and rules of evidence—the syntactical structure of the discipline. During the period of discipline-centered curriculum reform from 1950 to 1970, much emphasis was given to the syntactical structure of the disciplines. The series of "new" programs in mathematics, physics, chemistry, biology, anthropology, and geography brought the concept of mode of inquiry to classrooms throughout the nation. Although this movement may never have attained the original developers' goals, it did raise the consciousness of supervisors to the need to look beyond the body of knowledge produced by a discipline.

Learning Activities

Learning activities are descriptions of tasks teachers and students are to perform in the classroom. Joyce and Weil have identified 22 models of teaching grouped into four families that are the sources of a variety of learning activities.[6] The *information-processing family*, which features learning activities designed to develop cognitive competencies of students, includes inductive thinking strategies, concept attainment strategies, use of advance organizers, a memorization system, strategies based on cognitive growth, and strategies based on the modes of inquiry of academic disciplines. The *personal family*, which includes nondirective teaching, synectics, awareness training, and the classroom meeting model, focuses on "processing by which individuals construct and organize their unique reality."[7] The third group of teaching models is the *social family* and includes group investigations, role playing, jurisprudential inquiry, laboratory training and the T-group model, interactive games and simulations, and social problem solving through academic inquiry and logical reasoning. This family features social interaction and democratic processes. The fourth family consists of *behavioral models*. The common thrust in this family "is an emphasis on changing the visible behavior of the learner rather than the underlying psychological structure and the unobserved behavior."[8] Models in this family are contingency management, self-control through operant methods, a direct training model, stress reduction strategies, desensitization techniques, and assertiveness training.

Some activities are considered superior to others for certain outcomes. Research results might suggest that certain models not be used for some outcomes, but even so, enough different kinds of curriculum outcomes exist to warrant the use of a variety of learning activity types. In addition, teachers differ greatly in their background in regard to experience with, and skills needed to implement, various teaching models and associated activities. Therefore, the major issue that supervisors as curriculum developers must face in regard to learning activities is how to design the curriculum and select materials so that a variety of models of teaching and associated learning activities can be supported. To meet the challenge of this issue, supervisors need constantly to review what is done during the development of a curriculum with regard to the support provided for multiple learning activities and insure that learning activities' listings in curriculum guides and other supporting documents reflect many models of teaching.

Evaluation Procedures

Another component frequently found in curriculum guides is a description for evaluating student learning. In some cases this may be a restatement of a specific behavioral objective that sets conditions for behavior and criteria of acceptable performance. In other cases suggestions might be included in the curriculum plan. Actual or sample test items might be used in the plan to help teachers develop tests. Commercial test developers or local test development teams might be referenced in this section of the plan. Also, instead of actual assessment devices, the curriculum plan might suggest other procedures to use to evaluate student learning. These might include a work-sample test where students are observed as they produce a product, an assignment containing criteria for evaluating the product, questions to use in an oral examination, or sample items for a checklist.

Because evaluation is a sensitive area, there are a number of factors of which the supervisor should be aware. The major concerns of reliability and validity are always considerations whenever measurement is involved because it is important that the procedures used to measure student learning yield dependable results. Also, there should be congruence between the objectives and outcomes being measured.

Another critical concern about evaluation is the appropriateness of the standards used. Standards, like objectives, are arbitrary, but one can insist on a formal procedure for establishing them which will stipulate who will be involved and how decisions will be made. One can also insist on an examination of the consequences of various decisions regarding standards. The supervisor can exercise an important leadership role in assuring that both of these things are done.

The accountability factor is becoming more important at all levels—classroom, school, and district—in determining standards. Traditionally, teachers have defined their own standards, or in some instances, grade-level or departmental examinations have been used. As new requirements for high school diplomas develop standards are being defined at the district or even state level. Supervisors as curriculum developers need to be aware of these trends and to address the issue when curriculum plans are being made about the level at which standards are set.

Resources

When developing curriculum supervisors should direct attention to attaining resources to implement and support the planned program. Printed materials such as textbooks constitute a significant portion of supporting resources. Associated materials, such as workbooks, worksheets, tests, and teacher's guides, often are developed in packages and reinforce textbooks. To further support the curriculum, supervisors need to identify, classify, and coordinate by specific topics other books, library holdings, magazines, articles, and newspapers that relate to selected content.

Audiovisual materials are another important resource. Films, television and radio programs, slides, photographs, posters, charts, maps, demonstrations, models, and transparancies are examples.

A third type of resources are the "realia" associated with a learning activity such as: office machines in a business education program; tools, equipment, and machines in a trade, agriculture, or industrial arts program; sports equipment in a physical education program; instruments in a music program; and laboratory equipment and supplies in a science program. Other areas for which these types of resources would be relevant are the graphic and visual arts, driver and safety education, and sites for field trips.

A resource that is becoming increasingly important is computer hardware and software. Developments in this field are so rapid that it is difficult to estimate the long-term impact of computers on education. However, in addition to providing management support for the schools, computers offer an increasingly viable form of support for classroom instruction.

Finally, supervisors need to consider human resources. These include people who can serve as qualified speakers or as aides in the classroom. Other roles would include tutoring, helping with field trips, providing "realia" for classroom demonstrations, serving as mentors for students, or providing special lectures or class activities.

The three important considerations that supervisors as curriculum developers need to remember are to represent a variety of resources in the curriculum, insure that they are relevant, and available. Variety of resources is important for the same reasons as variety in instructional activities. That is, different teachers with different students need different forms of support to advance educational programs. The relevance factor can be addressed by relating resources to the general educational goals of the district and the objectives of specific courses, as well as the age, emotional and social development, and abilities of students. Availability deserves special attention. Unless teachers can obtain the resources that have been identified as part of the curriculum when they need them without an unreasonable amount of lead time for requests, the resources are not going to have a significant impact on the curriculum. It is the supervisor's responsibility to attend to procedural matters regarding resource supply.

Statements of Desired Teacher-Student Interactions

We mentioned previously that some educators prefer to think of curriculum as the experiences that children have under the auspices of the schools. Associated with this view of curriculum are beliefs about the value of providing a maximum amount of freedom to support natural growth and development, and a desire to create relatively "fluid" curriculum. We also suggested that while the emphasis in these views is on experiences, it would be possible to develop plans to support desired experiences. However, to do so the plans will have to contain components that do not prescribe learning outcomes. One way of doing this is to develop policy plans or descriptions of desired forms of teacher-student interactions.

One example of policy statements that could be used as a component in a curriculum plan is the criteria for worthwhile activities suggested by Raths.[9] For example, he advances the propositions that: all other things being equal, one activity is more worthwhile than another if it permits children to make informal choices in carrying out the activity and to reflect on the consequences of their choices; if it assigns to students active rather than passive roles in the learning situation; or if it gives students a chance to share in planning, carrying out a plan, or using the results of an activity with others.[10]

Another example is provided by the statements of procedure that are used in *The Humanities Project*, a handbook for curriculum designed to develop understanding, discrimination, and judgment by discussion of controversial social issues.[11] For example, in this curriculum guide policy statements are used to indicate that the teacher should set a context favorable to discussion, encourage group identity and group loyality, or see that the accepted rules of discussion are observed.[12]

It is important that supervisors determine what emphasis to place on statements of desired teacher-student interactions. Because of the current emphasis on accountability it would be unwise to build a total curriculum around statements of interactions. On the other hand, there are areas of the curriculum that do not lend themselves to precise statements of behavioral outcomes and there may be a need to allow for freedom in outcome. In these cases statements of teacher-student interactions may be very useful. The significant problem for supervisors as curriculum developers is to recognize these situations and offer the appropriate view of curriculum components to support the creation of plans in all program areas.

Your Turn

After reading the previous section you may wish to:

1. Analyze some curriculum guides—an excellent source for sample guides is the Educational Resources Information Center (ERIC) system—to determine what components are most commonly used in these guides.
2. Have a class discussion in which pros and cons of using specific behavioral statements of outcomes in curriculum guides are debated.
3. Select a topic in the curriculum and review all of the nontextbook resources you can find related to this topic.

4. Interview practicing teachers to determine the extent of their support for classroom, school, and district level specification of standards for grading.
5. Examine some of the additional readings for Objective 2.

Mastery Test

OBJECTIVE 2 TO IDENTIFY GOALS AND OBJECTIVES, CONTENT, LEARNING ACTIVITIES, EVALUATION PROCEDURES, RESOURCES, AND STATEMENTS OF DESIRED TEACHER-STUDENT INTERACTIONS AND FACTORS RELATED TO INCLUDING THESE SPECIFIC COMPONENTS IN THE CURRICULUM

1. Which of the following are examples of goals and which are examples of objectives?
   a. Students will solve word problems that require construction of right triangles.
   b. Students will list three conditions for the germination of a seed.
   c. Students will develop an understanding of others.
   d. Students will describe ways in which the nineteenth-century novel reflected on the human condition.
   e. Students will value continuous learning.
2. Which of the following are examples of objectives written in an input format and which are examples of objectives written in an output format?
   a. Students will use dialogue to develop characterization.
   b. Students will identify the place value for each place of any integer.
   c. Students will be allowed to select the topic for any classroom writing exercise in which the topic is optional.
   d. Students will develop a plan to reduce the prejudices of a group of people.
3. Solar energy, latitude, barter, currency, auxiliary verbs, speaker's point of view, rectangle, and insurance are examples of:
   a. Learning activities
   b. Objectives
   c. Content
   d. Resources
4. Role playing, use of advance organizers, simulations, and classroom games are examples of:
   a. Learning activities
   b. Objectives
   c. Content
   d. Resources

5. Which of the following are examples of evaluation procedures and which are examples of resources?

   a. Using a sewing machine: plugs in the machine, threads the machine, checks needle, adjusts stitch length.

   b. Should governments maintain social welfare programs? Answer Yes or No and then defend your position in one to three pages.

   c. Books for the teacher—Harvey, M. *Lettering Design.* New York: Crown, 1976; A-V materials from the National Gallery of Art—Decoration and Design Motifs, Catalog #036; Journals—*Visual Merchandising.*

   d. Behaviors to be observed: Is sensitive to needs and problems of others, helps others meet needs, willingly shares ideas and materials, accepts suggestions and help, makes constructive suggestions.

6. Indicate which component of curriculum—goals and objectives, content, learning activities, evaluation procedures, resources, statements of desired teacher-student interactions—might be affected in each of the following situations.

   a. Teachers indicate a need for more freedom in developing the curriculum to meet student needs and allow for exploration.

   b. The board of education expresses concern with the large number of students on the honor roll.

   c. The superintendent wants to review the curriculum to insure that the emphasis suggested by the state department of education on life-coping skills is well represented.

   d. Critics of the school charge that the program is not meeting community needs.

   e. Teachers complain that the curriculum guide does not offer enough options and students become bored.

Answer Key

Mastery Test, Objective 2

1. a. Objective

   b. Objective

   c. Goal

   d. Objective

   e. Goal

2. a. Output format

   b. Output format

   c. Input format

   d. Output format

3. c. Content

4. a. Learning

5. a. Evaluation procedure—checklist
   b. Evaluation procedure—essay question
   c. Resources
   d. Evaluation procedure—checklist
6. a. Goals and objectives or statements of desired student-teacher interactions
   b. Evaluation procedures
   c. Content—informal
   d. Goals and objectives—validation
   e. Learning activities and resources

OBJECTIVE 3 TO CLASSIFY STATEMENTS OF RATIONALE FOR CURRICULUM DECISIONS ACCORDING TO CRITERIA FOR SELECTION, ORGANIZATION, OR EMPHASIS

In order to "assume leadership for providing a continuous program of curriculum development," instructional supervisors will need to identify criteria for selecting components of the curriculum, organizing the curriculum, and determining emphasis reflected in the curriculum.

Criteria for Selection

Criteria that have been advanced to justify content selection in the curriculum are *significance*, *utility*, *interest*, and *human development*.[13] While supervisors traditionally have used these criteria to justify content, they could also be used to justify behaviors that might be included in goals and objectives. Therefore, these criteria apply to components of both content and behaviors.

The first criterion, significance, is somewhat misleading since it doesn't mean "importance" in an unrestricted fashion. Significance refers to the value of content or behaviors in understanding the nature of formal organized disciplines. Content that illuminates a discipline's mode of inquiry, or content that constitutes a key component of the substantive structure of a discipline is significant and, as such, should be considered for inclusion in any curriculum in which the parent discipline is a part. For example, the concept of *sets* is fundamental to the discipline of mathematics and, therefore, it is often included in the curriculum on the basis of its significance.

The utility criterion refers to the value content or behaviors will have when the student becomes an adult. We could justify learning how to balance a checkbook in the curriculum on the basis of future value of this activity. We justify most of the informal content in the curriculum on the basis of the criterion of utility.

In contrast to the future value of the utility criterion, interest is a criterion selected for its focus on the present. Including readings featuring auto racing or a thematic unit in an English course based on science fiction are examples on content selection supervisors might justify because they appeal to student interests. Building a unit around frogs when a student brings a frog to class is another example. Perhaps this criterion ought to be called *personal relevance*, which seems to describe this criterion more accurately. A curriculum that fails to offer students something immediately relevant may not be effective in the long term if it fosters an attitude that separates school learnings from life concerns.

Zais uses the term human development in connection with justifying content and behaviors on the basis of their values as "instrument(s) for the intelligent direction of social change."[14] When we suggest content or behaviors for the curriculum we appeal to human development not because of what students need in order to survive in the present society but because of what they contribute to personal and social development. Using this criterion requires supervisors to analyze desired future conditions of society.

Criteria for Organization

In addition to selecting components for the curriculum, supervisors need to make decisions about putting these components together. One decision concerns assigning selected content and behaviors to grade levels in order to sequence them within grades. Usually arguments for sequence are related either to characteristics of the subject matter or characteristics of students. Sequences based on subject matter include organizations derived from logical relationships or prerequisites, chronology, or the order in which content will be used, as in some procedure or job-related task. Sequences based on student characteristics include organization derived from familiarity (focus on the home, then the neighborhood, then the community), interest, or stage of development. Occasionally sequencing decisions also are made on the basis of empirical studies of prerequisite relationships where different sequences are tried and optimal ones are identified, but this is not very common. Most sequencing is done on the basis of logical analysis of subject matter rather than empirical research on students. Also, although there are exceptions, decisions about sequencing at the general level, where the components being placed are courses, subject areas, themes, or large blocks of content, are often made on the basis of subject matter characteristics while decisions about sequencing at the specific level, in the classroom, are influenced by student characteristics.

Another major decision about organization that supervisors as curriculum developers will need to consider is how to structure the program so that students will gain understanding about content relationships among subjects. Programs that support this outcome have a high degree of integration. There are a number of ways programs can be designed to support integration. Examples are: putting content together in blocks of time for broad fields like language arts, social studies, or general science is one method; encouraging the use of thematic or problem-centered instruction; and helping teachers identify possibilities for common student assignments or coordination of schedules so that related content is presented in several classes is a third method. All of these are options for supervisors as curriculum developers to consider when using organizational criteria of integration to examine the curriculum.

Criteria for Emphasis

In addition to examining the selection and organization of content to offer leadership for curriculum development, supervisors need to consider the emphasis given various parts of the curriculum. Educators traditionally use the terms *scope* and *balance* to describe emphasis in the curriculum. Scope describes the extent of content coverage and can refer to the variety of behaviors emphasized in the curriculum. To examine the scope of the curriculum, supervisors would have to have committees review the breadth and depth of content or the variety of behaviors emphasized. Questions to be addressed include the following: Are we presenting sufficient major concepts and generalizations to help students develop accurate views of various disciplines? Are we providing students with the necessary foundation for later studies? Are we asking students to do more than memorize content?

To understand the factors that the concept of balance might suggest to supervisors an analogy may be useful. A playground seesaw provides a way to move the fulcrum from the center toward one end in order to compensate for different weights of children. Children can achieve balance, but the balance point may not be equidistant from both ends. So it is with balance in the curriculum. The general goals or statements of purpose underlying the curriculum and any priorities set for these goals determine the balance point for considering curriculum characteristics. For example, proper balance in the curriculum could exist in situations where art was not offered every day. However, it would be difficult to imagine a district's statement of purpose that could attest to a balanced curriculum where there was no art.

The criterion of appropriate emphasis—balance—can be applied to many aspects of the curriculum. For example we have mentioned the issues of appropriate representation among possible disciplines, balance between formal and informal content, balance of general and specialized education, and balance between the substantive and syntactical aspects of a discipline. Supervisors should examine other areas for balance, such as the emphasis given to behaviors that reflect cognitive outcomes and those that are associated with values and attitudes, or the emphasis given to knowledge and comprehension and that given to application or analysis, synthesis, and/or evaluation.

Your Turn

After reading the previous section you may wish to:

1. Have a class discussion in which members take turns presenting examples of specific content from a situation with which they are familiar that could be said to be included in the curriculum because of:

   a. Significance
   b. Utility
   c. Interest
   d. Human development

2. Prepare an outline of a presentation you would make to the board of education in response to their inquiry—Do we have a balanced curriculum? Select a specific school setting with which you are familiar in order to answer this question.

3. A common theme in suggestions for curriculum reforms is the need to integrate content among subject areas. Interview a subject area coordinator to determine the extent to which plans for this integration are addressed in curriculum development activities.

4. Examine some of the additional readings for Objective 3.

Mastery Test

OBJECTIVE 3 TO CLASSIFY STATEMENTS OF RATIONALE FOR CURRICULUM DECISIONS ACCORDING TO CRITERIA FOR SELECTION, ORGANIZATION, OR EMPHASIS

Indicate whether each of the following statements related to curriculum matters represents the use of criteria for selection, organization, or emphasis.

1. A science teacher suggests that students should be taught the concept of *hypothesis* since it is a fundamental aspect of the field of science.
2. The principal directs the social studies teachers to reexamine the treatment of economics in the program since he feels that students have superficial views of this field.
3. The music teacher requests more time for music in the elementary grades since the goals of the school support the development of all forms of the arts and music is not given as much time as the visual arts.
4. A teacher reorganizes a fourth-grade program around a theme approach since she felt that students were not using the language arts skills they have developed when doing assignments in other subject areas.
5. A group of parents present the board of education with a request to include a unit on insurance in the school program since they feel that their children should have sufficient knowledge in this area to make the decisions they will need to make as responsible adults.
6. At the beginning of the year a teacher decides to start with a unit on study skills since the material in this unit would be useful in all areas for the rest of the school year.

Answer Key

Mastery Test, Objective 3

1. Selection—significance
2. Emphasis—scope
3. Emphasis—balance
4. Organization—integration
5. Selection—utility
6. Organization—sequence

OBJECTIVE 4 TO RECOGNIZE MAJOR BELIEFS ASSOCIATED WITH TECHNICAL MODELS OF CURRICULUM DEVELOPMENT AND EVALUATE PLANS FOR CURRICULUM ACTIVITIES FOR CONSISTENCY WITH CHARACTERISTICS OF THESE MODELS

Two Styles of Curriculum Development

The manner in which curriculum development is approached is influenced by the general perspective of those who direct the process. Two general classes of curriculum development models that seem to reflect different views of education can be identified. They roughly correspond with the "tight" style—in which activities are described in great detail and the instructor controls most of the moves—and the "fluid" style—in which activities are specified only in general outlines and much is left to learners.

In presenting two types of models with their associated perspectives we are not suggesting that instructional supervisors should select one or the other as a role guide or find one or the other most consistent with personal beliefs. Both models have been meaningful in the field of education for a long time, and most likely this situation will continue. Supervisors may find that both models reflect some of their own beliefs for curriculum development and also that each model is useful in different situations. For example, a tight style may be appropriate when establishing those components of a mathematics program defined as required minimum competencies while a fluid style may be more appropriate when working on those parts of a mathematics curriculum designed to support creativity or exploration. Therefore, although the models are presented as distinct, supervisors will find it advantageous to become familiar with both.

Technical Models

One group of curriculum development models, *technical models*, are characterized by procedures based on a separation of ends and means. Those who support these models often view curriculum development as the production of plans, thought of as blueprints, that describe the outcome in terms of student learning. This outcome and the means to achieve it are specified in detail. The job of teachers, who may or may not have had a direct part in drafting the blueprint, is to follow the prescribed guide as closely as possible to produce the desired outcome. The job of supervisors in helping draft the blueprint is to insure that ends are clearly defined, preferably in measurable terms, and that means in the form of learning activities are selected to achieve those ends. As ends are separated from means so is development separated from use. Once the curriculum is produced, the job of supervisors shifts to insuring that teachers adopt the curriculum faithfully.

Supporting Assumptions Many educators believe that different views of education are best captured by the use of metaphors. Tom describes a metaphor for teaching that views teaching as an applied science.[15] The applied science metaphor presents teaching as a collection of "lawlike relationships" that support a "best solution" to a specific class of problems.[16] These lawlike relationships, or site independent regularities, are identified through empirical research that deemphasizes the uniqueness of specific settings. Also, to support the development of generalizable knowledge fundamental to a science, attempts are made to resist site specific solutions.

Another belief we associate with the view of teaching as an applied science is that we can determine ends independently from means and that ends have some sort of intrinsic value regardless of actions. These beliefs would support selecting ends before means and maintaining a clear distinction between them. People often give priority to ends and neglect to consider the means for achieving them. However, making the distinction between ends and means, it is often emphasized that education itself should be considered a means and not an end.

The present emphasis on accountability reflects a concern to separate ends and means. Ends are defined in terms of student survival in and contribution to society. School outputs are defined in terms of descriptions of student knowledge, skills, and attitudes that will contribute to these ends. Models for accountability can then be established that place emphasis on determining what proposed results have been achieved. To support these models of accountability a great deal of emphasis is placed on measurable student outcomes so that outcomes can be quantified. Thus, techniques and procedures of measurements are used to determine the form of curricular goals and objectives.

Other concepts that those who tend to view teaching as a science stress are standardization and control. If teaching is governed by lawlike relationships then the best response that the school district can make is to attempt to provide all students with those activities that are judged to be best. This does not necessarily mean that all students are provided with the same opportunities to learn and the same amount of instructional time. Some models place considerable emphasis on diagnosing student learning styles and/or prior learning and providing individualized opportunities for learning. However, these models attempt to link diagnosis with prescriptions in a fixed fashion and the definitions of success and the nature of the desired learnings are standardized. The emphasis on standardization and control is often linked with accountability. School personnel pressured for accountability seek curriculum and instructional validity as a response to critics when students fail to achieve desired outcomes. The concept of curriculum and instructional validity refers to the extent to which students are provided with the content and activities deemed instrumental in producing the measured outputs for which students and/or the schools are to be held accountable. To insure validity curriculum components are prespecified and records are kept to maintain standardization and control to the extent that all teachers provide the appropriate means for all students.

Procedures The procedures generally followed in technical models for curriculum development can be grouped under the four questions of Tyler's rationale for that process.[18]

1. "What educational purposes should the school seek to attain?"[19] These purposes are defined by a statement of educational philosophy and a derived set of goals and objectives. The philosophy—a statement of a good life and a good society; a view about the importance of material values and success; a view about the school's role in perpetuating and reconstructing society; a statement about the desirability of a different education for different classes of society; and a position with regard to general education and vocational education—serves as a screen to determine important objectives.[20] Sources for objectives are observations about society, students, and subject areas. The tasks for supervisors as curriculum developers at this stage of technical models is to aid in formulating a philosophy, analyzing sources, and developing objectives stated in terms of content and student behaviors that describe desired outcomes. (For related information review the section on Objective 2.)
2. "What educational experiences can be provided that are likely to attain these purposes?"[21] At this stage supervisors need to help insure that learning activities are selected primarily on the basis of the extent to which they will give students opportunities to practice the kind of behavior implied by the goals and objectives.
3. "How can these educational experiences be effectively organized?"[22] Once activities are selected supervisors need to help put them in some sort of order to insure a gradual progression leading to the development of complex outcomes. This involves assigning teachers, students, objectives, and learning activities into units organized with respect to time. Questions of scope, sequence, balance, and program design are addressed at this stage of the curriculum development process. (For related information review the section on Objective 3.)
4. "How can we determine whether these purposes are being attained?"[23] When working with technical models for curriculum development supervisors need to consider an evaluation plan. They must plan for measuring student outcomes to find out the extent to which the hypotheses about relationships between outcomes and learning activities are valid, and to determine the effectiveness of teachers and the organization in putting the curriculum into practice. (For related information review the section on Objective 2.)

Your Turn

After reading the previous section you may wish to:

1. Write the statement of "Charge to the Committee" that you would use for the steering committee for a curriculum development project that was to be guided by a technical model of curriculum development.
2. Have a class discussion in which the approach to curriculum development presented in R. Kaufman, and F.W. English, *Needs Assessment: Concept and Application* (Englewood, New Jersey: Educational Technology Publications, 1979) is examined for consistency with the beliefs and procedures associated with technical models for curriculum development.
3. Interview teachers who have recently been involved in a curriculum development project and write a report in which their experiences are compared with the procedures of technical models for curriculum development.
4. Examine some of the additional readings for Objective 4.

Mastery Test

Because of the similarity of Objectives 4 and 5 the Mastery Test for both objectives has been combined. This combined test is found after Objective 5.

OBJECTIVE 5 TO RECOGNIZE MAJOR BELIEFS ASSOCIATED WITH INTERACTIVE MODELS OF CURRICULUM DEVELOPMENT AND EVALUATE PLANS FOR CURRICULUM ACTIVITIES FOR CONSISTENCY WITH CHARACTERISTICS OF THESE MODELS

Interactive Models

Another group of curriculum development models, *interactive models*, rejects the separation of ends and means associated with technical models for development. Instead of attempting to present a detailed specification of objectives and then searching for learning activities for teachers to use to implement the curriculum, those who favor interactive models prefer to set out some general goals and let teachers create activities which then give shape and substance to a program. The view of a curriculum that best captures this approach is that of a game plan rather than a blueprint. As in a game plan a curriculum guide could be expected to present some procedural rules and a general strategy. However, specific details would not be included since these are expected to evolve as the activity unfolds.

Supporting Assumptions

A metaphor that captures the view of those who support interactive models for curriculum development is that of teaching as a craft. This view sees teaching as a collection of "bits and pieces of knowledge accumulated over the years by trial and error" that "elaborate sequences of skills that the master learns how to routinize."[24] Another aspect of a craft is the large number of alternative procedures that can be used for a particular purpose. Those who support interactive models recognize that since the list of alternate procedures is almost inexhaustive, "judging what should be done through a careful analysis of the immediate situation is of key importance," as is accepting the recognition that the procedure selected "may fail to bring about the desired result."[25] Because of this possibility of failure a craftsperson is also aware of the need to create a new procedure when the selected method does not seem to be working. With this view, emphasis is placed on making judgments about actions based on detailed analyses of specific situations. The particular features of specific situations and the uniqueness of individual problems become of paramount importance as does the willingness to modify procedures to meet unique demands.

The view of the relationship between ends and means often associated with interactive models of curriculum development is that expounded by Dewey. Dewey (1922) described the nature of the interaction of means and ends when he stated that "ends arise and function within action. They are not things lying beyond activity at which the latter is directed. They are not, strictly speaking, ends or termini of action at all. They are terminals of deliberation, and so turning points in the activity."[26] According to this view, ends are not ultimate, fixed, and unchanging "ideals" isolated from actions toward which we strive that have intrinsic value. Instead, ends are "foreseen consequences which arise in the course of activity and which are employed to give activity added meaning and to direct its further course."[27] Ends are hypothesized consequences of certain courses of actions; thus they are shaped and formed by actions. However, ends also direct the further course of actions. Therefore, ends and means are completely interactive and inextricably interrelated.

Procedures The procedures used in interactive models of curriculum development can be described in terms of overall component and three sequential stages of development.

1. *Overall component.* In order to work with an interactive model for curriculum deyelopment it is necessary to establish mechanisms for deliberation at all stages of the process in which problems may be clarified, redefined, and viewed from the perspective of all involved in the curriculum action under consideration, and through which movement toward consensus can be stimulated. Interactive models depend upon deliberation and negotiation at all stages since there is no detailed blueprint to follow. Instead supervisors must work to insure opportunities for deliberation are provided and that all parties affected by the curriculum are represented. In addition, during deliberation sessions the role of instructional supervisors is to guide group discussion. Providing opportunities for deliberation is not sufficient. Supervisors must help participants to take advantage of these situations.

2. *Stages.* The stages of an interactive model are:

   a. In the first stage, the *analysis of the present situation*, the supervisor must work with teachers to help them make an intensive study of students' interests and their past educational experiences. During the analysis stage teachers must also be aware of disciplinary content and structure and of general components of the culture. The teacher's task is to use this information and seek ways in which to link the experiences and interests of the child with the cultural heritage so that they can tentatively identify directions leading to growth. This cannot be done prior to interacting with students. For this reason thinking of curriculum as "student experiences" and using input objectives and statements of desired student and teacher interaction as a means for structuring curriculum plans supports an interactive model of curriculum development.

b. In the second stage, *formulation of a course of action*, the supervisor must help teachers select activities from the initial analysis that will help students expand their experiences, become conscious of their experiences and interests, and begin to reflect upon them. The activities selected should include subject matter that can be related to students' interest and experiences and that can support learning. Hypotheses about this learning can then be formed as "ends in view" to help direct the activities and to clarify their nature.

c. In the third stage, *implementation and revision*, the supervisor must work with teachers so that activities are implemented and the results are examined. When examining results the supervisor must help teachers reflect on their experiences in developing the curriculum in the same manner as teachers attempt to help students reflect upon experiences. In this way teachers are stimulated to become learners in their work which should aid them in creating similar situations for students. When these activities are completed the curriculum development cycle starts over at the first stage.

Your Turn

After reading the previous section you may wish to:

1. Write the statement of "Charge to the Committee" that you would use for the steering committee for a curriculum development project that was to be guided by an interactive model of curriculum development.
2. Interview teachers who have recently been involved in a curriculum development project and write a report in which their experiences are compared with the procedures of interactive models for curriculum development.
3. Examine some of the additional readings for Objective 5.

Mastery Test

OBJECTIVES 4 and 5 TO RECOGNIZE MAJOR BELIEFS ASSOCIATED WITH TECHNICAL MODELS OF CURRICULUM DEVELOPMENT AND EVALUATE PLANS FOR CURRICULUM ACTIVITIES FOR CONSISTENCY WITH CHARACTERISTICS OF THESE MODELS TO RECOGNIZE MAJOR BELIEFS ASSOCIATED WITH INTERACTIVE MODELS OF CURRICULUM DEVELOPMENT AND EVALUATE PLANS FOR CURRICULUM ACTIVITIES FOR CONSISTENCY WITH CHARACTERISTICS OF THESE MODELS

1. Indicate which of the following beliefs are most consistent with technical models for curriculum development and which are most consistent with interactive models for curriculum development.

   a. The development activity should produce a curriculum in which activities and outcomes are described in general terms.

   b. Specific statements of goals and objectives should be identified before activities are considered.

c. Teachers are expected to adopt the curriculum as specified.

d. Specific statements of goals and objectives can be derived from activities.

e. Teaching can best be viewed as a craft.

f. The development activity should produce a curriculum in which activities and outcomes are specified in considerable detail.

g. Teachers are expected to adapt the curriculum.

h. Curriculum guides should be thought of as "game plans."

i. Teaching can best be viewed as an applied science.

j. Curriculum guides should be thought of as "blueprints."

2. Is the following plan for curriculum development similar to technical models or interactive models?

Each staff member should serve on at least one subcommittee. Subcommittees are given basic responsibility for their topics which are: School and Community; Philosophy, Objectives, and Commitments; and Areas of Learning. The subcommittee's responsibility for School and Community should begin its work immediately. Their report should be made available to the faculty before work is done on other sections. Philosophy, Objectives, and Commitments is another basic section on which the project rests. It is important that the entire faculty review the results of this subcommittee so that the work of this subcommittee will guide the development of the total school program. The subcommittees for each of the major Areas of Learning should check to insure that teaching practices and procedures reflect the philosophy and objectives of the school.

Answer Key

Mastery Test, Objectives 4 and 5

1. a. Interactive models
   b. Technical models
   c. Technical models
   d. Interactive models
   e. Interactive models
   f. Technical models
   g. Interactive models
   h. Interactive models
   i. Technical models
   j. Technical models
2. Technical models

OBJECTIVE 6 TO IDENTIFY FACTORS AND FORCES INFLUENCING SELECTION OF INSTRUCTIONAL MATERIALS THAT REQUIRE PROFESSIONAL REVIEWS AND GUIDELINES

Selection of Instructional Materials

Instructional supervisors engaged in the processes of curriculum development and selection must recognize that it is the resource materials for instruction that operationalize the program. The interaction of student with materials in the classroom, or resources in other learning environments under the direction of teachers, constitutes the essence of schooling.

If instructional materials that will implement a planned curriculum design are not produced or purchased, the resources may inadvertently dictate the curriculum. Moreover, instructional supervisors must be able to predict with accuracy the likely consequences to the structure of the curriculum of various possible changes in instructional materials.

Unless instructional supervisors possess appropriate criteria for selecting or developing instructional materials, other factors will dictate their purchase. In effect, educational criteria are essential to the protection of curricula and students against the imposition of inappropriate economic, political, or social forces; philosophical or psychological factors; and special interests.

Cost is a fundamental problem in the support of public education. Because monies are derived from taxation, school officials constantly feel under pressure to buy at a competitive price. It is extremely difficult for superintendents and boards of education to resist the temptation to buy materials that to the layman appear quite similar although there is a substantial difference in price. While waste is intolerable in public service, supervisors should exercise caution so that appropriate education of children is not forfeited for a modest sum.

Materials widely used in special programs funded by federal grants, or textbooks appearing on the list approved by the state education department, enjoy a tremendous advantage over competitors. The burden is placed upon teachers and instructional supervisors to provide evidence that materials other than those in common use are indeed preferable. It is extremely difficult for superintendents and boards of education to ignore quasi-governmental endorsement especially when funds to purchase other materials must come from different sources. While such endorsements deserve careful consideration, school districts should retain their prerogatives regarding the selection of resource materials.

Some materials by their very nature, or due to the type of curricula they support, are subjected to intense social pressure. Textbooks containing profanity or unpopular positions, or authored by controversial individuals spark disagreement. Materials involving sex education, substance abuse, civil rights, and other social problems challenge communities. It is extremely difficult for superintendents to avoid potential conflict and adverse publicity by selecting more palatable materials. However, public schools must not indoctrinate indirectly by expressing a single point of view and fail to assist students in dealing with controversial issues.

Schools introduce some materials because they are presumed to influence students in desirable ways that will improve performance in school programs and activities. These involve materials based upon prevailing educational philosophies and applications of psychological determinants of learning. Such materials are based on views about measurement, human growth and development, attitudes and personality, interpersonal relationships, creativity, cognition, and new concepts of intelligence. They focus on behavioral objectives, mental health, classroom management, student discipline, and particular instructional strategies. It is important that superintendents and boards of education recognize the roots of such materials and examine them for consistency with the district's philosophy. School districts should provide an array of materials that are consistent and mutually supportive.

Included within the category of special interests are patriotic organizations, religious sects, civic clubs, textbook publishers, learned societies, parent-teacher associations, and a variety of vocational groups. Often these groups are viewed as philanthropic because they offer gifts and services to schools at nominal expense or no cost at all. It is extremely difficult for a superintendent or board of education to resist the offer of a library collection that may have a definite point of view or shop equipment that indirectly stress certain employment options. School districts must avoid being indentured to a local industry, business firm, or church that may reduce objectivity and flexibility in making curricular decisions.

Your Turn

After reading the previous section you may wish to:

1. Have a class discussion in which members take turns presenting the response they would make in the following situation:

   During a regular meeting of the board of education, a new member introduces a proposal that a particular type of science materials displayed at a recent conference should be introduced immediately into the schools of your district. The superintendent invites your reaction to the proposal at the meeting. Indicate the responses that you would provide in your role as instructional supervisor.

2. Arrange with a media coordinator to examine the promotional material received during a three-week period. Prepare a chart indicating the type of groups sponsoring this material.
3. Examine some of the additional readings for Objective 6.

Mastery Test

OBJECTIVE 6 TO IDENTIFY FACTORS AND FORCES INFLUENCING SELECTION OF INSTRUCTIONAL MATERIALS THAT REQUIRE PROFESSIONAL REVIEWS AND GUIDELINES

List four different examples of factors and forces influencing selection of instructional materials that require professional reviews and guidelines.

Answer Key

Mastery Test, Objective 6

The responses should be compared with the general categories: economic, political or social, philosophical or psychological, and special interests. A comprehensive response would include examples from each of these categories.

OBJECTIVE 7 TO ASSOCIATE DESCRIPTIONS OF CONTENT WITH COMMON REFERENCE SOURCES OF PROFESSIONAL REVIEWS OF INSTRUCTIONAL PROGRAMS AND MATERIALS

Sources of Instructional Programs and Materials

The selection of instructional materials is often more a function of political, economic, or social factors than educational factors. Teachers have greater confidence in the opinions of fellow teachers than in the judgments of curriculum specialists. Consequently publishers spend tremendous sums of money on workshops for teachers led by consultants, often employed by the company, and/or authors, often faculty members at institutions of higher education. While the workshops undoubtedly contribute to the in-service development of teachers, their major purpose is to acquaint teachers with particular textbooks or resource materials. It is assumed that such familiarity will lead teachers to recommend adopting a series indirectly through instructional supervisors or directly as members of selection committees.

As in public office, incumbent series tend to have an advantage over newcomers because of teacher familiarity. Moreover, it seems far easier to add textbooks and other resource materials to the existing set, even if a revision is involved, than to replace a long-standing adoption with a new one. Therefore, searches for new material tend not to be comprehensive and a definite bias exists in the reviewing process.

By extension, teachers often have greater confidence in materials created or generated by themselves or other teachers than in those commercially produced. There appears to be a feeling that publishers must of necessity be more interested in making a profit than in assisting student learning. School districts often exploit this belief by having teachers develop materials at considerable expenditure of time and energy that are far less appropriate than those available for purchase. Because the costs of materials preparation are hidden, people assume that they are less expensive than those on the market. In fact, a careful cost analysis would reveal that the costs were far higher because teachers were engaged in this project to the exclusion of other potential activities.

Instructional supervisors retain the tradition of trusting their colleagues in preference to professional reviews or publisher advertising. They are likely to call upon individuals serving neighboring school districts in similar capacities. It requires strong conviction in professional competence regarding materials selection to recommend textbooks or instructional resources that are not utilized in other school districts.

Because of the strong influences of political, economic, or social factors on the process of selecting instructional materials, a significant competency-qualification for supervisors engaged in curriculum leadership is knowledge of sources of formal professional reviews of instructional programs and materials. Three of these sources are the National Diffusion Network (NDN), the Educational Products Information Exchange (EPIE), and *Curriculum Review*.

National Diffusion Network (NDN) The NDN is a comprehensive system established by the United States Office of Education to promote the use of effective educational programs. The NDN has several components. One is *developers/demonstrators*, which consists of exemplary projects that are supported to provide training and assistance to those who adopt their projects. Another component of the network is *facilitators* who, at the state level, attempt to link potential adopters with developer/demonstrators. The basis for determination of whether programs are exemplary, the formal professional review, is accomplished by the Joint Dissemination Review Panel (JDRP), a group supported by the Department of Education. The source to which supervisors can turn to find the reviewed programs is a publication called *Educational Programs That Work* (available from the Far West Laboratory for Educational Research and Development, 1855 Folsom St., San Francisco, Calif. 94130). Each project is described with the following information:

Project name

Descriptors (index terms for the project)

Target audience (student characteristics for whom the project was developed)

Description (a statement of program components)

Evidence of effectiveness (brief statement of evidence submitted to JDRP)

Implementation requirements (training, visitation, or other needs)

Financial requirements (costs for materials and resources needed)

Services available (funding, visitation, training, and follow-up availability)

Contact person

Educational Projects Information Exchange (EPIE, Box 620, Stony Brook, New York 11790) The EPIE Institute collects and publishes descriptive and analytical information about instructional materials, equipment, and systems. The institute has two major publications, *EPIE Materials Report* and *EPIE Equipment Report.* Of the two, the report on materials is most directly related to the curricular choices although both may be of value to supervisors. The *EPIE Materials Report* is published quarterly. Issues are devoted to reviews of instructional materials or to other topics of interest to those charged with the selection of instructional resources. The reviews that are published in the *EPIE Materials Report* contain the following sections:

Identification and background

Intents (rationale, learner goals, and learner objectives)

Contents (scope, sequence, accuracy and fairness, values and valuing)

Methodology (presentation and description, learning environment, grouping, initiator, interactions, time and pacing)

Means of evaluation (purpose, reference, user, and description)

Congruence and summary (extent to which the constructs mesh)

Other considerations (physical characteristics, teacher training required, and fairness)

Curriculum Review (Curriculum Advisory Service, 515 S. Jefferson St., Chicago, Ill. 60607) The *Curriculum Review* publishes evaluations of textbooks, tradebooks, and supplementary materials in all areas of the curriculum at the elementary and secondary levels. The review is published five times a year. Each issue contains the following sections:

Articles (reports on trends in curriculum development)

Features (essays and reviews that focus on a theme such as life skills)

Subject area emphasis (essays and reviews that focus on curricula from specific subject areas including language arts, mathematics, science, and social studies; with bibliographic information and price, content emphasis, rationale, objectives, organizational methods, physical features, and recommendations)

Departments (special notes, columns, and letters)

An additional feature of the *Curriculum Review* is a postage-paid reply card with which readers can request further information from publishers.

Your Turn

After reading the previous section you may wish to:

1. Select a school district and interview the curriculum director to determine the areas of need in the program. Review the programs listed in *Educational Programs That Work* and write a report for the curriculum director in which relevant programs are identified and ranked according to the district's needs.
2. Select an article from *Curriculum Review* for which you can obtain the material being reviewed. Examine the article and the material and write a report in which you evaluate the accuracy of the review.

3. Examine copies of all three sources of curriculum reviews.
4. Examine some of the additional readings for Objective 7.

Mastery Test

OBJECTIVE 7 TO ASSOCIATE DESCRIPTIONS OF CONTENT WITH COMMON REFERENCE SOURCES OF PROFESSIONAL REVIEWS OF INSTRUCTIONAL PROGRAMS AND MATERIALS

1. Which of the following sources contain information about funding available to support the adoption of a program?
   a. *Educational Programs That Work*
   b. *EPIE Material Report*
   c. *Curriculum Review*
2. Which of the following sources contain information about a range of subject areas in each issue?
   a. *Educational Programs That Work*
   b. *EPIE Material Report*
   c. *Curriculum Review*
3. Which of the following sources contain articles and features about current trends in curriculum development in addition to specific reviews of curriculum products?
   a. *Educational Programs That Work*
   b. *EPIE Materials Report*
   c. *Curriculum Review*
4. Which of the following sources contains the least amount of descriptive information about the program or product reviewed?
   a. *Educational Programs That Work*
   b. *EPIE Materials Report*
   c. *Curriculum Review*

Answer Key

Mastery Test, Objective 7

1. a
2. a and c
3. c
4. a

OBJECTIVE 8 TO IDENTIFY FOUR CATEGORIES OF CRITERIA FOR SELECTING INSTRUCTIONAL MATERIALS, AND IDENTIFY QUESTIONS TO BE ASKED TO EVALUATE EACH CATEGORY

Evaluating Instructional Materials

Instructional supervisors must establish clear, concise, and useful criteria for evaluating textbooks and resource materials. Four criteria that could serve as the basis for developing evaluation forms for textbooks and resource materials are presented in the following section. Following the statement of each of the criteria is a list of questions that could be asked to further expand the intent of the original statements.

1. Instructional material should be consistent with the district curriculum.
   a. Are the objectives of the material consistent with the district philosophy?
   b. Does the material fit with the planned scope and sequence of the district curriculum? How much of the scope of the district curriculum will have to be met with supplementary materials?
   c. Will the transition of students using the material to present programs in the district create disfunctional problems?
2. Instructional material should be appropriate for the student population.
   a. Does the student population have the necessary background and/or academic preparation to profit from the instructional material?
   b. Does the material present examples that are meaningful to the local student population?
   c. Does the material read at an appropriate level?
3. Instructional material should be accurate.
   a. Has the material been reviewed by appropriate subject matter experts? If so, by whom? When has the material been judged accurate?
   b. Does the material present a balanced treatment of controversial issues?
   c. Are suggested learning activities clearly related to the goals and objectives?
   d. Has the material been tried? Has it been revised?
4. Instructional material should be usable.
   a. Do teachers require special training to use the material? Are training documents available to help teachers develop the skills to use the material?
   b. Can all necessary material be purchased given the district budget?
   c. Does the district process the library references, audiovisual equipment, and facilities called for in the instructional material?
   d. Can the consumable items used in the instructional material be replaced?

e. Are supplementary teachers' guides provided? Do these contain a variety of suggested instructional approaches? Are activities for remediation and enrichment provided?

f. Are tests available for the instructional material?

g. Is the organizational structure of the material clear?

Your Turn

After reading the previous section you may wish to:

1. Interview a teacher who has served on a textbook selection committee to determine the criteria that were used to evaluate the textbooks.
2. Select some instructional material and evaluate them with the criteria in the presentation section.
3. Have a class discussion in which members offer additional questions to examine the four criteria for instructional materials stated in the previous pages.
4. Examine some of the additional readings for Objective 8.

Mastery Test

OBJECTIVE 8 TO IDENTIFY FOUR CATEGORIES OF CRITERIA FOR SELECTING INSTRUCTIONAL MATERIALS, AND IDENTIFY QUESTIONS TO BE ASKED TO EVALUATE EACH CATEGORY

List four categories of criteria for the selection of instructional material. Identify two specific questions for each of those four categories that could be used in the selection process.

Answer Key

Mastery Test, Objective 8

Compare the responses with the listing of criteria and questions presented in this section.

OBJECTIVE 9 TO DESCRIBE TWO TYPES OF ORGANIZATIONAL STRUCTURES FOR CURRICULUM COORDINATION AND LIST ADVANTAGES AND DISADVANTAGES OF EACH

Organizing and Coordinating Curriculum Development

The instructional supervisor's responsibilities for curriculum development and selection often are extensive, varied, and complex. It is not unusual for an individual serving in this capacity to be providing leadership to several major projects in separate subject fields at different grade levels simultaneously. At the same time, he or she may be coordinating other activities and consulting on still others. Because this is typically an area in which supervisors possess limited formal preparation, the individual must generate a management system that allows him or her to maintain progress across a broad and broken front. Experience with the management system also should enable supervisors to address subsequent efforts at curriculum development and selection with increased effectiveness.

Two types of organizational structures that allow supervisors to exert influence over and maintain control of the process of curriculum development are the *curriculum council model* and *line-staff model.* The curriculum council model assumes that the instructional supervisor functions as a catalyst in a system of democratic decision making in which curriculum development percolates upward. The line-staff model assumes that the instructional supervisor functions as a delegate in a system of assigned decision making in which curriculum development permeates downward.

In the curriculum council model, representatives of schools, grades, subjects, and/or positions are selected to examine collectively the multiple aspects of the educational program. Supervisors may personally nominate the members of the council and/or serve as its chairperson. More consistent with the democratic principles on which such an organizational structure is predicated is a procedure that would provide for election of council members from designated constituencies and election of the chairperson by the council members. In this preferred form of the model, a supervisor would serve as continuing consultant to and executive secretary of the council.

The advantages of the curriculum council are considerable. In theory, the curriculum council utilizes the special interests of each member, provides for each to contribute to the program, and seeks to generate leadership among the members regardless of their positions within the school district. Its composition encourages teachers to submit proposals that might be reserved from superiors, allows consideration by a representative group, assures examination from a broad perspective and exploration of many viewpoints, and offers a broad base of support for those proposals recommended for approval.

Among the disadvantages of the curriculum council is the difficulty of scheduling meetings for a relatively large group whose members have other responsibilities in the school district from which they must be excused. This problem is intensified if the council includes a representative from each school. Other disadvantages are related to the diversity of the council and its independence from the power structure of the district. It is difficult to obtain consensus regarding a particular proposal when such divergent viewpoints are involved. Also, a single representative often is handicapped in establishing support for a project when the member returns to his school. Attempts to do so with teacher colleagues often invoke irritation by the principal who may feel bypassed in the process of curriculum development. Even the instructional supervisor may find role conflict if the curriculum council recommends a proposal that is unpopular with the superintendent, board of education, or influential citizens in the community. It is possible that the supervisor may be placed in the position of supporting a council recommendation about which he or she has substantive reservations.

In the line and staff organization model, leaders of the school district are assigned to positions that have either authority (line) or influences (staff). This organizational structure borrows mainly from the military forces where line officers are assisted by staff officers who do not command or participate in combat. The instructional supervisor, who occupies a staff position, is charged with the responsibility for determining appropriate proposals for curriculum change. However, the implementation of these projects—and often their approval as well—is achieved through the superintendent or principals who occupy line positions.

According to Douglass, Bent, and Boardman the staff officers are supplementary agencies that exist merely to offer advice and technical assistance and have no direct authority.[28] In this type of organization, authority is definitely centered in the line officers. While there may be committees of teachers or others involved at some stage of a project these committees are working groups assigned specific tasks and are not deliberating groups determining the nature of the project. The committees may be able to make decisions about the way to accomplish their task but not about the task itself. Control in this form of organization is centered in the administrative structure and teachers are expected to follow established policy guidelines.

The advantages of the line and staff organization model for curriculum coordination are numerous. It allows the selection of a specialist who is unencumbered by the administrative responsibilities of operating the schools or the district. The instructional supervisor has the obligation of presenting his professional opinion to his administrative superior who must reach the decision by weighing a number of factors. It also insures coordinated support from the power structure of the district. In addition, it permits a district to respond quickly to pressures for change. Finally, it helps establish specific responsibility for curriculum decisions.

Among the disadvantages of the line and staff organization model is the need to convince administrators of the worth of proposals for curriculum change. Because they operate from different perspectives—resulting in part from different preparation, experience, and/or philosophy—administrators often allot lower priorities to curriculum projects than to managerial duties. Consequently, adoption of an innovation often depends more on the success of the instructional supervisor in convincing administrators than the significance of the innovation itself. Because curriculum development is assigned to a staff position rather than to a line position, the impression is given that it is of less importance than certain aspects of management. Other disadvantages are related to the implementation of planned programs. The line and staff model may produce proposals that are difficult for teachers to implement since teachers' views often are not well represented when decisions are made.

Your Turn

After reading the previous section you may wish to:

1. Select a school district and interview a supervisor to determine the type of organization structure used for curriculum coordination. Present a report of your findings.
2. Have a class discussion in which two groups are assigned the responsibility of offering arguments that might be presented to the superintendent for the organizational structures for curriculum development described in the previous pages.
3. Examine some of the additional readings for Objective 9.

Mastery Test

OBJECTIVE 9 TO DESCRIBE TWO TYPES OF ORGANIZATIONAL STRUCTURES FOR CURRICULUM COORDINATION AND LIST ADVANTAGES AND DISADVANTAGES OF EACH

Which of the following are characteristics of a curriculum council model for curriculum coordination and which are characteristics of a line-staff organizational model?

1. Decision making is democratic.
2. Decision making is vested in the administrative structure.
3. Curriculum development permeates downward.
4. Curriculum decisions are made by elected representatives.

5. Exploration of proposals from many viewpoints is encouraged.
6. Coordinated support from the power structure of the district is insured.
7. Difficulty in scheduling meetings is created.
8. Principals may be alienated.
9. Leadership is generated regardless of formal position in the system.
10. Specific responsibility for curriculum decisions is established.
11. Teachers' views may not be well represented.
12. A broad base of support for approved proposals is offered.

Answer Key

Mastery Test, Objective 9

1. Curriculum council model
2. Line-staff organizational model
3. Line-staff organizational model
4. Curriculum council model
5. Curriculum council model
6. Line-staff organizational model
7. Curriculum council model
8. Curriculum council model
9. Curriculum council model
10. Line-staff organizational model
11. Line-staff organizational model
12. Curriculum council model

OBJECTIVE 10 TO IDENTIFY THE NATURE OF PARTICIPANTS WHO COULD BE CALLED ON TO ACCOMPLISH THE CURRICULUM DEVELOPMENT OR SELECTION PROCESSES

Who Should Participate?

A major task of instructional supervisors engaged in managing the curriculum development and selection processes is selecting participants and maintaining an appropriate balance among representatives from different groups.

The board of education is the legally constituted representative of the community. As a convened group, the board has the authority, responsibility, and obligation to approve curricula and instructional materials. That is, proposals for additions to, revisions in, and/or replacements of courses are presented to the board of education. In like manner, recommendations for approval of textbooks and other instructional materials must be approved by the school board directly or indirectly through authorization to purchase such materials. It is important to recognize that boards of education are vested with considerable power over curricula. The board is obligated to operate within the framework of provisions of the state constitution, statutes enacted by the legislature, and regulations of the state board of education and chief state school officer. Beyond these limitations, district school boards have exceedingly broad discretionary powers regarding the curriculum.

It is also important to remember that board members have no power whatsoever as individuals. Only the corporate board can exercise authority. However, deference given to board members by teachers, administrators, and instructional supervisors often takes on the appearance of an employer-employee relationship. When this occurs, individual board members may become lobbyists for particular curricula, advocates of programs for schools in a part of the district viewed as a constituency, and/or initiators of change in a particular direction based on personal opinion. For these and other reasons, in many school districts board members are elected in nonpartisan ballots to represent the district as a whole.

These considerations should restrict the inclusion of board members on curriculum councils. Even those who are willing to ignore the board affiliation are viewed by other council members with deference. Moreover, the board member finds difficulty in objectively considering a proposal for curriculum change generated by a curriculum council after participating in those deliberations. In effect he or she has forfeited the appropriate role as a board member because of unintentional advocacy. The appointment of a board member to a curriculum council with the intent of altering his or her opinion regarding curricula places the program at considerable risk.

It is of course important to tap community participation in curriculum development. This may be accomplished through the establishment of citizen advisory committees to the board or the inclusion of representatives of the community on curriculum councils. In either case, the charge, duration, and responsibilities of the citizens should be carefully delineated. It is difficult for the board to reject a proposal from an advisory committee appointed by the board of education. However, the board must retain all legal options or forfeit its authority to citizens who were not elected by the public. In many communities, the board of education is composed of the most favored classes—educationally, socioeconomically, and politically. Therefore, care must be taken to insure that the less privileged groups in the community are allowed and encouraged to express their opinions.

Also, proponents and opponents alike should be included among community representatives. Stacking an advisory council with partisans creates a false sense of support and exaggerated expectations of success. A fair examination of a proposal is more likely to result in a program that will be implemented and enduring.

It is difficult to separate parents from nonparents in representing the community on curriculum matters. Parents generally are more focused in their interests, viewing curriculum proposals in light of anticipated effects on their own children. While it is easier to enlist the participation of parents in a particular task, it is difficult to obtain objectivity in consideration. Also, the willingness of parents to serve on advisory councils or as members on curriculum councils declines as their children move from early elementary level through middle school and into senior high school. This pattern is reflected in lack of motivation to engage in parent-teacher associations, band parents groups, and sports booster clubs. Again, care must be taken to recruit parents who can consider objectively a proposal regarding implications for students other than their own children. The charge, duration, and responsibility of parents involved in curriculum development also must be delineated.

The role of educational professionals in the curriculum development and selection processes is as complex as it is important. Part of the difficulty stems from basic philosophy regarding the role of the teacher. If the curriculum council model is utilized, teacher representatives would be included among the members along with principals, counselors, and instructional supervisors. Because of their working relationships, it often is difficult for teachers to be accepted as peers on the council. Also, their views tend to be seen as more parochial—focused on subject, grade, or school—than other members of the council. The influence of administrators, while nullified to some extent, remains very real.

If the instructional supervisor possesses specialization in curriculum development, it is important to maintain this role on the curriculum council. In an attempt to insure democracy, qualifications of members may be subordinated and equity assumed when in fact great differences in expertise among members actually exist.

Professional roles in a line-staff model for managing curriculum development and selection are typically clearer than in the curriculum council model. The prerogatives of administrators to accept or reject proposals for curriculum change on the basis of other factors can be a serious deterrent to progress. While the mythology of the principal serving as the instructional leader persists, higher priority inevitably is given to more pressing concerns involved in school operation. By extension, specialists in particular subjects or school levels may be allowed discretion that is not appropriate when the school district is viewed as a whole. The segmentation of responsibility in a line-staff model may create an educational program where the whole is not well served by the sum of its parts.

The involvement of students in curriculum development and selection is more ceremonial than functional. While it is possible to include a student from the senior high school on the curriculum council, such participation at best is brief, sporadic, and limited. Moreover, such a student is typically selected by the principal from among the able and ambitious, thereby offering predictable support for a program in which the student has been academically successful. Those with less intelligence, initiative, and/or insight who might advocate curriculum change likely would be excluded. Even bright students would be intimidated by the presence of adult educational professionals.

Student input to the process consequently should be obtained directly from questionnaires or interviews, and indirectly from records or reports from guidance counselors. It is important to focus considerations upon particular student audiences. The preference of students already pursuing science for a particular course is quite a different matter than the investigation of particular courses intended to appeal to students not presently enrolled in any science program. Moreover, provision of ethnic studies to satisfy the desires of a particular group of minority students is quite a different matter than including study of different cultures in courses required of all students.

Data on aptitude and achievement of students obtained from a well-coordinated testing program throughout the grades is perhaps the most fundamental channel of student input into curriculum development. Follow-up studies of graduates, involving all programs rather than only those associated with vocational education, also are important sources of information regarding curriculum.

Your Turn

After reading the previous section you may wish to:

1. Interview a supervisor who has recently completed a curriculum development or selection project and determine the nature of the participants involved in the project. Determine the types of activities in which each group was involved.
2. Prepare a report to the board of education showing the nature of the participants and the roles to be assigned which you would recommend for each of the following:
   a. A goal identification project
   b. A textbook selection project
   c. A curriculum guide development project
3. Examine some of the additional readings for Objective 10.

Mastery Test

OBJECTIVE 10 TO IDENTIFY THE NATURE OF PARTICIPANTS WHO COULD BE CALLED ON TO ACCOMPLISH THE CURRICULUM DEVELOPMENT OR SELECTION PROCESSES

List four types of participants who could be called on to accomplish curriculum development or selection processes.

Answer Key

Mastery Test, Objective 10

The list should include community representatives, parents, professionals, and students.

OBJECTIVE 11 TO PREPARE A BUDGET TO SUPPORT MANAGEMENT OF THE CURRICULUM DEVELOPMENT OR SELECTION PROCESSES

Budgetary Considerations

Just as administrators are expected to possess competencies related to curriculum development and selection, so too are instructional supervisors expected to possess competencies related to managing that process. These competencies are most appropriately manifest in scheduling and budgeting time, personnel, and resource materials.

Training While supervisors are most often associated with staff development of teachers and implementation of curricula, they also must provide leadership to other programmatic activities. If teachers, administrators, and counselors, among the professional educators, are to participate in the analysis of existing curricula, planning and development of new curricula, and evaluation of curricula in operation, some training for these tasks is essential. The training becomes even more important when citizens, parents, and/or students also are involved in curriculum development and selection. Therefore, supervisors need to plan for training to support curriculum-related activities.

Despite the fact that professional educators deal daily with various aspects of the curriculum, few have extensive preparation in the field. Consequently, training for the instructional supervisor usually comes from curriculum specialists external to the school district. Staff from the state education department or faculty from colleges and universities usually provide this consultative service. Faculty also may be requested to serve as instructors for special problems classes in which teachers are enrolled for credit. The external consultant is assumed to possess the information needed to develop the curriculum on the basis of similar situations in other districts. In this pattern, curriculum is selected first and instruction evolves from the curriculum.

On those occasions where instructional supervisors believe sufficient competence exists within the school district to develop curriculum in a particular subject or programs at a particular grade level, considerable dependence is placed on assembling a "critical mass" of teachers. Collectively, the teachers are assumed to possess the information needed to develop the curriculum on the basis of their classroom experience. In this pattern, curriculum evolves from instructional practices used by teachers.

Whether generated with assistance from without or from within the district, opportunities for training sessions involving leadership personnel and participants are a basic feature of the management of the curriculum development and selection processes.

Time The work assignment of the teacher traditionally has been defined as classroom instruction plus such routine management activities construed as essential to the efficient operation of the schools. Although selected teachers are invited to participate in the processes of curriculum development and selection, time for such activities is unavailable during the normal work day.

The most common ways to provide time are through substitutes to release teachers from the classroom, extended school day for meetings after students are dismissed, extended week with meetings on Friday evenings or Saturdays, and extended school year with teachers employed during the summer months to develop or select curriculum. Teachers may, of course, be invited to prepare curricular materials during out-of-class time.

In some situations, the instructional supervisor must coordinate a combination of such time provisions depending upon the subject involved and/or teacher availability. Whatever procedures are utilized to obtain time for curriculum development and selection, financial considerations are essential. Although teachers in some parts of the country are still willing to look upon curriculum development or selection projects as a professional obligation, increased teacher militancy in contract negotiations and pressure from professional organizations reduce such opportunities.

Monies must be budgeted for substitute pay, teacher stipends, or overtime if adequate time is to be made available. Provision of time within the work day also would require expenses not presently covered in the school district budget.

Visitation Opportunities to visit other schools or districts with characteristics similar to those in which the instructional supervisors serve and/or potential curricular innovations already exist constitute an important factor in curriculum development and selection.

While it is helpful for principals and other administrators to discuss the implementation phase of curriculum change with counterparts in other schools and districts, it is imperative for classroom teachers to do so. Teachers believe strongly in viewing a program in action and discussing it with teachers and/or students actually engaged in the operation of the program. Acceptance of the program for adoption often depends upon the degree of congruence between the observed school's situation and the one to which the curriculum is to be transplanted.

Materials Production and Duplication In many instances, prototype materials for curriculum and instruction can be purchased from other school districts or commercial publishing companies. Even when this is possible, school personnel typically cannot resist the temptation to modify these materials for application in the particular situation. The general belief abroad among instructional supervisors engaged in curriculum development and selection appears to be that unique elements override common elements.

Whether purchased or produced, resource materials involve costs of paper, duplication, and distribution. It is unlikely that the substantial amounts of resources required in a curriculum development effort were anticipated in the budget for the respective schools or the district's central office.

Secretarial Aid Perhaps the greatest hidden cost in the processes of curriculum development and selection is secretarial aid. Teachers typically have no access to the time of school secretaries. Even instructional supervisors often share the time of secretaries in the central office pool. Consequently the preparation or modification of curriculum materials requires access to substantial secretarial time.

The format of materials often involve much mimeographing or photocopying. If such materials are to be printed, original documents must be carefully prepared and edited. Without adequate support personnel, instructional supervisors may become bogged down in routine reporting and editing.

Deadlines for curriculum development or selection will be missed unless production schedules take advantage of vacation periods during which secretaries in the school and central office have lighter work loads. Even so, it is imperative that supplemental secretarial assistance be provided to support the preparation of curriculum guides and instructional materials.

Your Turn

After reading the previous section you may wish to:

1. Interview a supervisor who has recently completed a curriculum development or selection project to determine the time required for various tasks and the money needed to support the project.
2. Have a class discussion in which the class is divided into three groups. Have one group assume the role of supervisor and prepare a budget to support a curriculum development or selection project. Have another group assume the role of the participants who will carry out the project. Have the third group assume the role of the board of education. Then have the supervisors present and defend their budget to each of the other groups.

Mastery Test

OBJECTIVE 11 TO PREPARE A BUDGET TO SUPPORT MANAGEMENT OF THE CURRICULUM DEVELOPMENT OR SELECTION PROCESSES

Assume that you are supervisor in a system with two high schools, three middle schools, and ten elementary schools. The faculty at one of the middle schools has submitted a proposal to the curriculum council to establish a program for the homeroom period. The faculty felt that academic advising was being handled well but that there was a need for a formal program to attempt to meet social and emotional needs of students. Topics suggested in the proposal included: school rules, orientation to student organizations, responsibility, dealing with feelings, peer groups, communication, and test-taking skills. The proposal recommended a program that would be implemented by every homeroom teacher two days per week for 30 minutes a day. The curriculum committee decided to support the proposal and asked you, as supervisor, to draw up a budget to present to the board of education to support the project. It was suggested that six teachers would constitute the basic project team and the budget would cover the initial development stage for one year. Prepare the budget that you would submit to the board.

Answer Key

Mastery Test, Objective 11

Your budget should contain funds for the general categories described in the previous pages. These are: training, time, visitation, materials production and duplication, and secretarial aid. To determine if the budget is appropriate complete the second activity in *Your Turn*.

NOTES

1. B.M. Harris, *Supervisory Behavior in Education*, 2d ed. (Englewood Cliffs, N.J.: Prentice-Hall, 1975), pp. 11–12; and Ben M. Harris, "Supervisory Competence and Strategies for Improving Instruction," Educational Leadership, vol. 33 (February 1976): pp. 332–335.
2. P.F. Oliva. *Developing the Curriculum*. (Boston: Little, Brown, 1982), pp. 5–6.
3. B. Resnick, "The Science and Art of Curriculum Design," in *Strategies for Curriculum Development*, edited by J. Schaffarizick and D.H. Hampson. (Berkeley, Calif.: McCutchan, 1975), pp. 35–36.
4. M. Winters, *Preparing Your Curriculum Guide* (Alexandria, Va: Association for Supervision and Curriculum Development, 1980), p. 13.
5. E.L. Boyer, and A. Levine, *A Quest For Common Learning* (Washington, D.C.: Carnegie Foundation for the Advancement of Teaching, 1980), p. 79.
6. B. Joyce, and M. Weil, *Models of Teaching*, 2d ed. (Englewood Cliffs, N.J.: Prentice-Hall, 1980).
7. Ibid., p. 9.
8. Ibid., p. 12.
9. J.D. Raths, "Teaching Without Specific Objectives," *Educational Leadership*, vol. 28 (April 1971): pp. 714–720.
10. Ibid., pp. 717–718.
11. *The Humanities Project: An Introduction*. (London: Heinemann, 1970).
12. Ibid., p. 20.
13. R.S. Zais, *Curriculum: Principles and Foundations*. (New York: Thomas Y. Crowell, 1976), pp. 342– 348.
14. Ibid., p. 346.
15. A.R. Tom, "Teaching as a Moral Craft: A Metaphor for Teaching and Teacher Education," *Curriculum Inquiry*, vol. 10 (Fall 1980): pp. 317–323.
16. Ibid., p. 316.
17. R.W. Tyler, *Basic Principles of Curriculum and Instruction*, Chicago: University of Chicago Press, 1950.
18. Ibid., p. 1.
19. Ibid., p. 22–24.
20. Ibid., p. 1.
21. Ibid.
22. Ibid.
23. Tom, "Teaching as a Moral Craft," p. 318.
24. Ibid.
25. J. Dewey, *Human Nature and Conduct* (New York: Henry Holt, 1920), p. 223.
26. P. Archambault, *John Dewey on Education: Selected Writings* (New York: Random House, 1964), p. 72.
27. H.R. Douglass, R.K. Bent, and C.W. Boardman, *Democratic Supervision in Secondary Schools*, 2d ed. (Boston: Houghton Mifflin, 1961), p. 23.

ADDITIONAL READINGS

Objective 1

Doll, W.E. "A structural view of curriculum," *Theory into Practice*, vol. 43 (1974): pp. 336–348.
Eisner, E.W., ed. *Conflicting Concepts of Curriculum*. Berkeley, Calif.: McCutchan, 1974.
Kliebard, H.A. "Education at the Turn of the Century: A Crucible for Curriculum Change," *Educational Researcher*, vol. 11, 1 (January 1982): pp. 16–24.
Shiro, M. *Curriculum for Better Schools*. Englewood Cliffs, N.J.: Educational Technology, 1978.

Objective 2

Brookover, W.B., chairman. *Measuring and Attaining the Goals of Education*. Alexandria, Va.: Association for Supervision and Curriculum Development, 1980.
Hambleton, R.K., and D.R. Eignor. "Competence Test Development Validation, and Standard Setting." In *Minimum Competency Achievement Testing*, edited by R.M. Jaeger and C.K. Tittle. Berkeley, Calif. McCutchan, 1980, pp. 367–398.
Joyce, B., and M. Weil. *Models of Teaching*, 2d ed. Englewood Cliffs, N.J.: Prentice-Hall, 1980.
Phi Delta Kappan Commission on Educational Planning. *Educational Goals and Objectives: A Model for Community and Professional Involvement*. Bloomington, Ind.: Phi Delta Kappa, 1972.

Objective 3

Zais, R.S. *Curriculum: Principles and Foundations*. New York: Thomas Y. Crowell, 1976, pp. 338–348.

Objective 4

McNeil, J.D. *Curriculum: A Comprehensive Introduction*, 2d ed. Boston: Little, Brown, 1981, pp. 77–104.

Oliva, P.F. *Developing the Curriculum.* Boston: Little, Brown, 1982, pp. 153–174.

Objective 5

Gay, G. "Conceptual Models of the Curriculum-Planning Process," In *Considered Action for Curriculum Improvement*, edited by A.W. Foshay. Alexandria, Va.: Association for Supervision and Curriculum Development, 1980, pp. 120–143.

Objective 6

Fitzgerald, F. *America Revised.* Boston: Atlantic-Little Brown, 1979.

Objective 7

Klein, M.F. *About Learning Materials.* Alexandria, Va.: Association for Supervision and Curriculum Development, 1978.

Woodbury, M. *Selecting Instructional Materials.* Bloomington, Ind.: Phi Delta Kappa, 1978.

Objective 8

Gall, M.D. *Handbook for Evaluating and Selecting Curriculum Materials.* Boston: Allyn and Bacon, 1981.

Klein, M.F., and L. Tyler. "On Analyzing Curricula." In *Curriculum: An Introduction to the Field*, edited by J.R. Gress and D.J. Purple. Berkeley, Calif.: McCutchan, 1978, pp. 438–449.

Objective 9

Saylor, J.G., W.M. Alexander, and A.J. Lewis. *Curriculum Planning for Better Teaching and Learning*, 4th ed. New York: Holt, Rinehart and Winston, 1981, pp. 80–89.

Objective 10

Doll, R.C. *Curriculum Improvement: Decision Making and Process*, 5th ed. Boston: Allyn and Bacon, 1982, pp. 321–356.

Saylor, J.G., W.M. Alexander, and A.J. Lewis. *Curriculum Planning for Better Teaching and Learning.* New York: Holt, Rinehart and Winston, 1981, pp. 98–109.

INTERPERSONAL COMMUNICATION

J. Bruce Burke

OBJECTIVE 1 To identify the characteristics of teachers as adult learners, specifically distinguishing between *andragogy* and *pedagogy*, recognizing the advantages of andragogical perspectives for supervising professional development

OBJECTIVE 2 To define interpersonal communication skills and to explain how attitudes and values influence the effectiveness of a communication

OBJECTIVE 3 To describe the communication gap that can exist between personal intentions and received behavior

OBJECTIVE 4 To describe a model of helping skills

OBJECTIVE 5 To define and recognize *attending behaviors* in a helping relationship

OBJECTIVE 6 To define and recognize *responding behaviors* in a helping relationship

OBJECTIVE 7 To define and recognize *facilitating behaviors* in a helping relationship

INTRODUCTION

This chapter presents information about what makes for effective communication in the helping relationship between supervisors and teachers. It reviews what has been learned about working with adult learners, as contrasted with teaching children. The focus of the chapter is on the rationale for and use of specific interaction skills that have been associated with effective interpersonal leadership. The chapter makes a major assumption throughout that the differences between supervisor and teacher are in the roles they play in educational organizations and not in status or value as human beings. Therefore, the skills described and the exercises offered are based on the assumption that the interactions presented are between equals. This assumption is crucial in that it is the foundation of the concept of leadership as influencing human interaction. Growth and change happens when adults take responsibility for themselves. Supervisors exercise leadership when they use their skills to help create a positive environment for personal responsibility. Effective supervisors neither distort nor minimize a teacher's personal resources for growth and change. As a result, the more effective supervisors are the ones who are usually involved in the professional lives of teachers as well as in their own professional development.

SELF-ASSESSMENT PRETEST

The following assessment items present you with an opportunity to check out your general knowledge of some characteristics of effective human interaction. (Upon completing these questions, turn to page 252 where you will find the answers for self-scoring.) Select the one best answer for each question.

1. Usually, people are most helpful as listeners when they:
   a. Offer concrete advice.
   b. Share their own similar experiences.
   c. Remain passive and uninvolved.
   d. Invite the other person to explore personal concerns.
   e. Seek to make the other person feel better.
2. According to research into the behavior of effective communicators, they:
   a. Always are reflective.
   b. Never share their judgments.
   c. Facilitate the other person's responses.
   d. Rarely get personally involved.
3. According to psychological research, most adults:
   a. Are unaware of the emotional states of others.
   b. Are ineffective in expressing emotional reactions.
   c. Are skilled in labeling emotional states in themselves and others.
   d. Feel uncomfortable dealing with the emotional states of others.
   e. Are usually insensitive to the emotional states of others.
4. The depth of a relationship is enhanced by:
   a. Maintaining social contact over a period of years.

b. Observing the rules of appropriate role behaviors.
c. Being a source of advice and problem solving.
d. Always being cheerful.
e. Exploring with another person his or her understanding of events.

5. In general, people who are identified as communicators tend to:
   a. Ignore rather than acknowledge highly emotional states.
   b. Recognize the harm that can be done by letting others vent their emotions.
   c. Try to "cool down" expressed emotional states rather than dealing with them.
   d. Are aware that highly emotional statements lead to resentment.
   e. Acknowledge highly emotional states as legitimate.

6. The supervision of teachers assumes that teachers are learners. There is a sense, then, in which supervisors are teachers of teachers. In this sense, it is best if supervisors:
   a. Maintain an authority-oriented environment.
   b. Treat teachers as dependent students.
   c. Acknowledge teachers' experiences as rich resources for learning.
   d. Focus on the subject matter content teachers need to master.
   e. Use social pressures to motivate teachers' learning.

Each of the following items will be a statement which could have been said directly to you. Regard each statement as an invitation for you to respond as a concerned listener. Choose *one* of the response options, which seems to you most appropriately facilitates the development of the communication. That is, make the choice which seems to you would most likely result in the other (the person who hypothetically made the statement to you) continuing to elaborate on their story.

7. "I don't know . . . What should I say? I mean, I want to talk about what's happened, but it's . . . Well, I just don't know where to start."
   a. You should start at the beginning.
   b. It's up to you.
   c. Where do you want to begin?
   d. I know; I have a hard time starting to explain things sometimes.
   e. If you don't know, who does know?

8. "I don't understand what's happened. Everything was going so well, and all of a sudden she just left . . . walked right out, you know? I must have done something . . . or said something . . . ?"
   a. What did you do? You must have done something.
   b. Where did she go? Why didn't you stop her?
   c. That's really tough; it makes you feel like you can't trust yourself.
   d. What do you think happened?
   e. Is it guilt that you're feeling, or just plain unhappiness?

9. "I've done everything they asked me to do. . . . I even tried to change my attitude, cause I know they wanted me to be more positive. But here I am again back where I started. Nothing seems to go right for me!"

   a. That may be just a phase you're going through.
   b. Maybe you're just trying too hard. . . . What do you think?
   c. Where does it say "you've got to please everybody?"
   d. What is it like for you to have things not go right?
   e. Do you think they're being too hard on you?

10. "All of my life I've wanted to take this trip . . . but now, all my money is gone."

   a. What is that doing to you?
   b. We all have disappointments from time to time.
   c. I know just how you feel.
   d. Is it the disappointment over the trip or the anger about the money?
   e. Why did you allow this to happen to yourself?

11. "This really great thing happened to me. . . . I finally got this letter I've been waiting for!"

   a. Oh, who is it from?
   b. It's amazing how just getting a letter made such a difference in you.
   c. That's great! Tell me about it.
   d. We all need a lift now and then.
   e. How come this letter is any different from other letters you receive?

(*Key to pretest:* 1 = d, 2 = c, 3 = d, 4 = e, 5 = e, 6 = c, 7 = c, 8 = d, 9 = d, 10 = a, 11 = c.)

OBJECTIVE 1 TO IDENTIFY THE CHARACTERISTICS OF TEACHERS AS ADULT LEARNERS, SPECIFICALLY DISTINGUISHING BETWEEN *ANDRAGOGY* AND *PEDAGOGY*, RECOGNIZING THE ADVANTAGES OF ANDRAGOGICAL PERSPECTIVES FOR SUPERVISING PROFESSIONAL DEVELOPMENT

This chapter reviews interpersonal communicational skills as they apply directly to the work of supervisors of instruction. Throughout the chapter a great deal of emphasis is placed on the attitudes and beliefs the supervisor (or any person) brings to a relationship. Positive and realistic attitudes toward those we seek to help, whether one is a teacher, counselor, or supervisor, are crucial to effective communication. This concept is so important that this chapter begins with a specific attitudinal problem that often plagues the supervision of professional teachers; namely, the tendency to treat all learners as if they were children. Supervisors are not alone in the misguided assumption that if a teacher is learning or growing, that activity is different in status from those activities specifically directed by teachers in their own classrooms. Teachers themselves often perpetuate the notion that learning is less powerful than teaching. I have watched teachers show professional competence and propensities in their classrooms by actively directing activities, monitoring complex behaviors, organizing various groups of learners, and so forth. Then on the same day, these same competent, self-assured teachers show up in an in-service, professional development course and take on the role of passive student. The shift is quite dramatic. In the morning a "master teacher," but by the afternoon a change to "dependent student," displaying the behavior of an inexperienced child. Such behavior easily "hooks" the supervisor or the in-service curriculum director into attitudes and behaviors of taking charge over a collection of less than competent persons.

Much of this problem can be understood in terms of how long it has taken educators to distinguish between adults and children as learners. In the past two decades the adult learner has begun to receive scholarly attention. Knowles (1973) and Cross (1981), are two scholars who have come to distinguish between what they call andragogy and pedagogy. *Pedagogy* literally means the art of teaching children. *Andragogy* refers to the teaching of adults. It is not sufficient simply to translate what is known about teaching children to the adult situation. The attitude of the pedagogue toward the student is often based on a set of assumptions about the learner that do *not* fit the adult. Knowles (1980) describes these contrasting assumptions about learners in the following manner:

ASSUMPTIONS ABOUT LEARNERS

	Pedagogy	*Andragogy*
Self-concept	Dependent	Increasingly self-directed
Experience	Small value	Learners possess rich resources for new learning.
Readiness	Biological/social development	Developmental tasks of social roles
Time reference	Delayed application	Immediacy of application
Learning focus	Subject centered	Problem centered

If adult learners have different educational needs than children, then it is not only inappropriate to bring the attitudes of the pedagogue to the supervisory relationship, but also destructive of genuine growth. Humans generally respond to others as they are expected to respond. So if a supervisor expects dependent, passive, and discounting behaviors from teachers, then such behaviors are usually given. Small wonder, then, that in-service education has such a poor reputation among teachers. To the degree that teachers are expected to set aside their own sense of personal value and power, discount their own expertise, and passively take others' advice, is the degree to which in-service education fails.

An entirely different orientation emerges if one begins with the assumption that teachers are adult learners. Tough studied adult learning; not only the what and why adults learn, but how they learn. He concluded that "most adult learning begins because of a problem or a responsibility or, at least, a question or puzzle, not because of a grand desire for a liberal education" (Cross, 1981, p. 188). Imagine the difference in design of learning/growth experiences for teachers, if supervisors approached the conceptualization of their tasks based on the assumption that teachers were adult learners. Such experiences would be problem focused. The teachers would accept a share of the responsibility for planning and executing the supervisory plan or project. They would feel a mutual commitment to these activities. The supervisor and the teachers would mutually define the goals of the activities and gain a sense of progress toward achieving these goals. In the process the teachers' past experiences would be used as a positive resource for new learning. In contrast, a child's experience is perceived as something which happens to him or her. For the adult, experience *defines who he or she is.* To devalue an adults' experiences, therefore, is to discount the person.

The supervisor who accepts an andragogical orientation toward his or her relationships with teachers has advantages on two fronts. First, the teachers themselves will respond responsibly to their role as adult learners, feeling positive about themselves. Their motivation for participation in in-service activities and learning projects is more likely to be intrinsic, internally defined. Second, the supervisor is "off the hook" in pretending to be the omnipotent, omniscient leader. It is much more pleasant to take on the more humble role of professional colleague, as well as more realistic. Supervisory leadership is exercised as a collaborative effort among peers, who are focused on immediate problems that call for creative resolution.

Mastery Test

OBJECTIVE 1 TO IDENTIFY THE CHARACTERISTICS OF TEACHERS AS ADULT LEARNERS, SPECIFICALLY DISTINGUISHING BETWEEN *ANDRAGOGY* AND *PEDAGOGY*, RECOGNIZING THE ADVANTAGES OF ANDRAGOGICAL PERSPECTIVES FOR SUPERVISING PROFESSIONAL DEVELOPMENT

1. List five characteristics of adult learners.
2. Label the following statements *pedagogy* or *andragogy* according to the implied assumptions in the statement.
   a. "I have studied the matter at some length and you must trust my judgment as to what is best in this situation."
   b. "What do you think is the central problem in this situation?"
   c. "If we get this material written up today, we can start using it tomorrow."
   d. "Here is an idea that you might find useful someday."
   e. "I really like your idea; let's give it a try."
   f. "As soon as you are ready to explore these strategies, let me know. I'll be glad to help."
   g. "I don't care what you learned at the university. Here we do it my way!"

Answer Key

Mastery Test, Objective 1

1. a. Self-directed
   b. Rich in experience
   c. Committed to self-development
   d. Here-and-now time orientation
   e. Problem centered
2. a. Pedagogy—implying that the "teacher knows best"
   b. Andragogy—assuming the learner can contribute

c. Andragogy—immediate application of learning
d. Pedagogy—delayed application of learning
e. Andragogy—respect for learner's knowledge
f. Andragogy—readiness to learn in learner's hands
g. Pedagogy—discounting others' experiences

OBJECTIVE 2 TO DEFINE INTERPERSONAL COMMUNICATION SKILLS AND TO EXPLAIN HOW ATTITUDES AND VALUES INFLUENCE THE EFFECTIVENESS OF A COMMUNICATION

Teaching is a people business. Therefore, teachers are professional communicators. There is no escaping interpersonal interaction between supervisor and teacher anymore than between teacher and pupil. The issue is the quality of these interactions. The basic perspective of this chapter is that *skill in communication is a function of facilitative interpersonal behaviors linked with positive attitudes toward self and others*. The point of this proposition is that there is no such thing as facilitation skill without the *intention* to facilitate. This means that it is impossible to listen to others, hear what they say, and respond with support without *wanting* to listen, to hear, and to support the other person. Knowing how to communicate effectively with others includes possessing the attitudes and values of positive support for others.

Carl Rogers argues that the effectiveness of a communication between a therapist and a client (or between any helper and helpee) rests upon the *quality* of the interpersonal encounter (Rogers, 1962). But what constitutes the content of quality in human interaction? According to Rogers, there are three core conditions that make for quality in the interpersonal encounter:

- Congruence
- Empathy
- Unconditional positive regard

Let's examine how these core conditions apply to the supervisory relationship and are essential to the quality of the interpersonal interaction between supervisor and supervisee. Congruence means a sense of genuine presence. The supervisor displays congruence by feeling comfortable with himself or herself. People know when someone is "putting them on," acting phony, or pretending concerns not really felt. It is more important to the success of a helping relationship to offer the other person a *real* interest, than to be right or perfect or admired. So Rogers' first advice to helpers is "don't pretend." People understand genuine human emotions; it is the pretense that they resist and resent. Empathy is sensing another person's "inner world of private personal meanings as if it were your own" (Rogers, 1962). Rogers emphasizes this "as if" quality of empathy to contrast it with sympathy. Empathy permits the listener to feel what another person feels while keeping an objective perspective of the experience. The supervisor demonstrates empathy for a teacher not by taking sides and agreeing with the teacher, but by communicating the intention to understand the teacher and his or her situation in all dimensions. Implied in genuineness and empathy is respect toward the other person, that what a person thinks or feels is worth understanding. Rogers calls the third core condition of a helping relationship "unconditional positive regard for the other person." This attitude is not a paternal feeling which can lead to discounting the other person's ability to take care of himself or herself. Nor is it sentimental or superficial social support. Rather, unconditional positive regard respects the other as a whole, separate person. The effective supervisor can distinguish between acceptance of the person and approval. We can accept another unconditionally as a person, without implying that we approve of all that person does.

Even though Rogers' view of the helping relationship was developed in the context of psychotherapy, there are many reasons for its appropriate application to the educational setting. First of all, people tend to act as they are expected to behave. They tend, also, to imitate the behavior of those around them, especially those in positions of authority. Flanders (1965) studied teacher-pupil interaction and observed that students of domineering teachers tended to display the same behavior, while students of more democratic teachers tended to be more spontaneous and personally responsible in their behavior. Likewise, among adults the quality of the relationship between manager and employee or between supervisor and teacher tends to be a function of positive expectations on the part of the person in authority.

There is another reason to take Rogers' core conditions seriously in developing the supervisor-teacher relationship. If people are to try new behaviors, learn new skills, or master new material content, then they need to be willing to risk. People who are afraid that they will be punished for failure are not likely to risk new behaviors. The supervisor can encourage risk taking by offering the teacher empathy for the challenge of learning. People should not be punished for being where they are in their development. The empathic supervisor communicates his or her support of the individual by accepting the person's here-and-now situation. Just as effective teachers do not blame the pupil for being developmentally behind the mean achievement of any particular stage, so too the effective supervisor does not blame the teacher for "not yet being perfect."

All this may seem like common sense. People of "good character" treat others with respect. And yet, there are many who have unblemished personal qualities and who intend the best for those with whom they work, who are not effective in their interpersonal interactions because they lack the skills. There is considerable evidence that training and practice in empathy and communication skills increases interpersonal effectiveness. Good character and good intentions are not enough. The next section of this chapter explains one of the major reasons why this is true.

Mastery Test

OBJECTIVE 2 TO DEFINE INTERPERSONAL COMMUNICATION SKILLS AND TO EXPLAIN HOW ATTITUDES AND VALUES INFLUENCE THE EFFECTIVENESS OF A COMMUNICATION

1. Define effective interpersonal communication.
2. List the three core conditions of a helping relationship according to Carl Rogers.
3. Give at least two reasons that support the relevance of Rogers' core conditions to supervisor-teacher interaction.

Answer Key

Mastery Test, Objective 2

1. Skill in communication is a function of facilitative interpersonal behavior linked with positive attitudes toward self and others.

2. a. Congruence (genuineness)
   b. Empathy
   c. Unconditional positive regard
3. a. People tend to act as they are expected to behave.
   b. People who fear they will be punished for failure are not likely to risk success.
   c. People should not be blamed for being where they are developmentally.

OBJECTIVE 3 TO DESCRIBE THE COMMUNICATION GAP THAT CAN EXIST BETWEEN PERSONAL INTENTIONS AND RECEIVED BEHAVIOR

A supervisor of instruction spends much of a morning at the district's curriculum office collecting materials for a high school history teacher to use in teaching reading in the content area. In the afternoon the supervisor brings the material to the teacher's classroom and gets the following reception: "How do you expect me to use all this stuff? I don't have time to do all I have to do now!"

This supervisor has just become a victim of the communication gap. This is the gap that often develops between what a person intends to communicate to another and what the other person understands or interprets from the behavior. The supervisor *intended* to be helpful, but the teacher *experienced* the action of collecting supplemental materials as a threat, one more burden to carry. Wallen (1973) calls this the interpersonal gap in communicating a message. Whenever we find ourselves puzzled by how our behavior has been misinterpreted, the chances are that we have experienced the communication gap.

The reason for this gap is that all of our intentions must be expressed by behaviors that others must interpret. Our intentions are private, internal states that require public action if they are to be communicated. Yet, we often assume that others have the power to "read our minds" and know we mean well. The problem is compounded by the fact that we often do not know ourselves what our "real" intentions are in a given situation. Therefore, it is not surprising that others have difficulty reading our behavior. But even when we know our own mind, know what we intend, the effect of our actions on others can be misconstrued.

There is a series of transformations of our message between intention and action, and between action and effect. Wallen (1973) describes the transformation of a message between intention and action as the *coding process*. The transformation that occurs between an action and an effect he calls the *decoding process*. For example, if a supervisor (Patrick) intends to help a teacher (Sue), he may choose to express this help by visiting her classroom. The choice to visit Sue's class is Patrick's coding of his intention to help. The actual visitation is the public action that conveys Patrick's coding. Sue's decoding of Patrick's action involves her own value system, which may judge Patrick's visit as a threat of evaluation of her teaching skills. The effect of this decoding may well be that Sue ends up angry or scared. Patrick, in his intention to be helpful, has just experienced the communication gap. The entire transaction can be diagrammed (following Wallen's model) as in Figure 9.1 (p. 258).

The gap between what Patrick intended and Sue's feeling of anger and fear is caused by the incongruity between Patrick's encoding and Sue's decoding. Neither one is to blame for this situation. However, if Patrick is to bridge the gap in communication between them, he must let Sue know more about his coding; that is, he must explain his choice of visiting Sue's classroom as an expression of

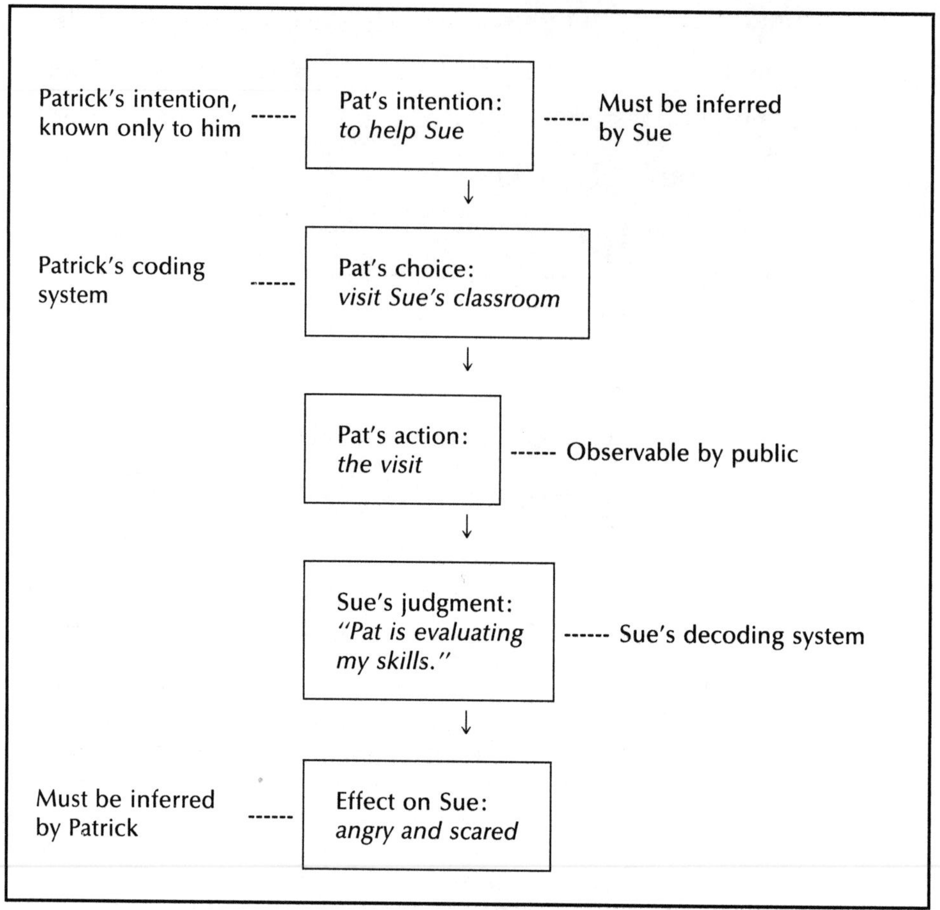

FIGURE 9.1 Supervisor's (Patrick) intention to help a teacher (Sue).

his intention to be helpful. Likewise, Sue needs to share her reaction to observation, so that her tendency to respond in anger and fear can be known to Patrick.

Because of the interpersonal nature of the supervisor's responsibilities, it is crucial for supervisors to become aware of their own coding and decoding systems. Another way to put this point is that supervisors especially need to know the impact they have on others and that others have on them in return. It is not a simple process to become aware of one's communication style. Wallen (1973, p. 221) suggests four factors which complicate the process:

1. The same intention may be expressed by different actions. For example, a supervisor's intention to show respect for teachers may be expressed by:

- Not interfering with teachers
- Asking for a teacher's help
- Praising a teacher for a job well done
- Responding to a teacher's question

2. Different intentions may be expressed by the same action. For example, a supervisor's request for a meeting with a teacher in the curriculum office may be an expression of an intention to:

- Get the teacher out of his or her classroom and on the supervisor's "turf"
- Build the teacher's self-confidence

- Have the teacher examine new materials
- Ask the teacher to chair a new committee

3. The same action may lead to different effects. For example, a supervisor stopping by a teacher's classroom may result in the teacher:

- Feeling scared and hostile
- Feeling "picked on" and resentful
- Feeling proud that the supervisor admires his/her work
- Feeling silly and ill-prepared for a visit

4. Different actions may lead to the same effect. For example, a teacher may feel proud and appreciated by a supervisor who:

- Singles out the teacher for special praise
- Visits the class to talk with the teacher
- Asks the teacher to stay for a beer after school
- Greets the teacher at the mall on a Saturday

Earlier we learned that there is no such thing as the communication of empathy (or any supportive behavior) without the intention to be empathic. Now we have learned that while intentions to be helpful are necessary to effective communication they are not enough. Because our intentions are private, internal acts, they must be described openly to others, if they are to understand our behavior. The other side of the coin is also important. Supervisors need to understand the meaning others make of their behavior. Even the best communicators will at times miss the meaning an event has for others. So it is necessary to learn how to listen to the mind at work in another person's communication. Specific skills in how this is done are described in the following sections.

Mastery Test

OBJECTIVE 3 TO DESCRIBE THE COMMUNICATION GAP THAT CAN EXIST BETWEEN PERSONAL INTENTIONS AND RECEIVED BEHAVIOR

1. Diagram and label the transaction (from intention to effect) in the following incident:

   Adele Newton, the principal at River Forks Elementary School, was concerned about the number of students Sarah Greenwood, a fourth-grade teacher, was sending to the office for disciplinary action. Adele was curious about the sudden rise in reported cases of disruption in Sarah's room and wanted to see if there was a way she could help. So Adele asked Sarah to stop in the office at the end of the school day. When Sarah showed up and was asked about the change in disruptive behavior, she burst into tears and said, "I knew you wouldn't support me!"

2. List the four factors Wallen says complicate the communication process.

Answer Key

Mastery Test, Objective 3

1. Your answer should include:

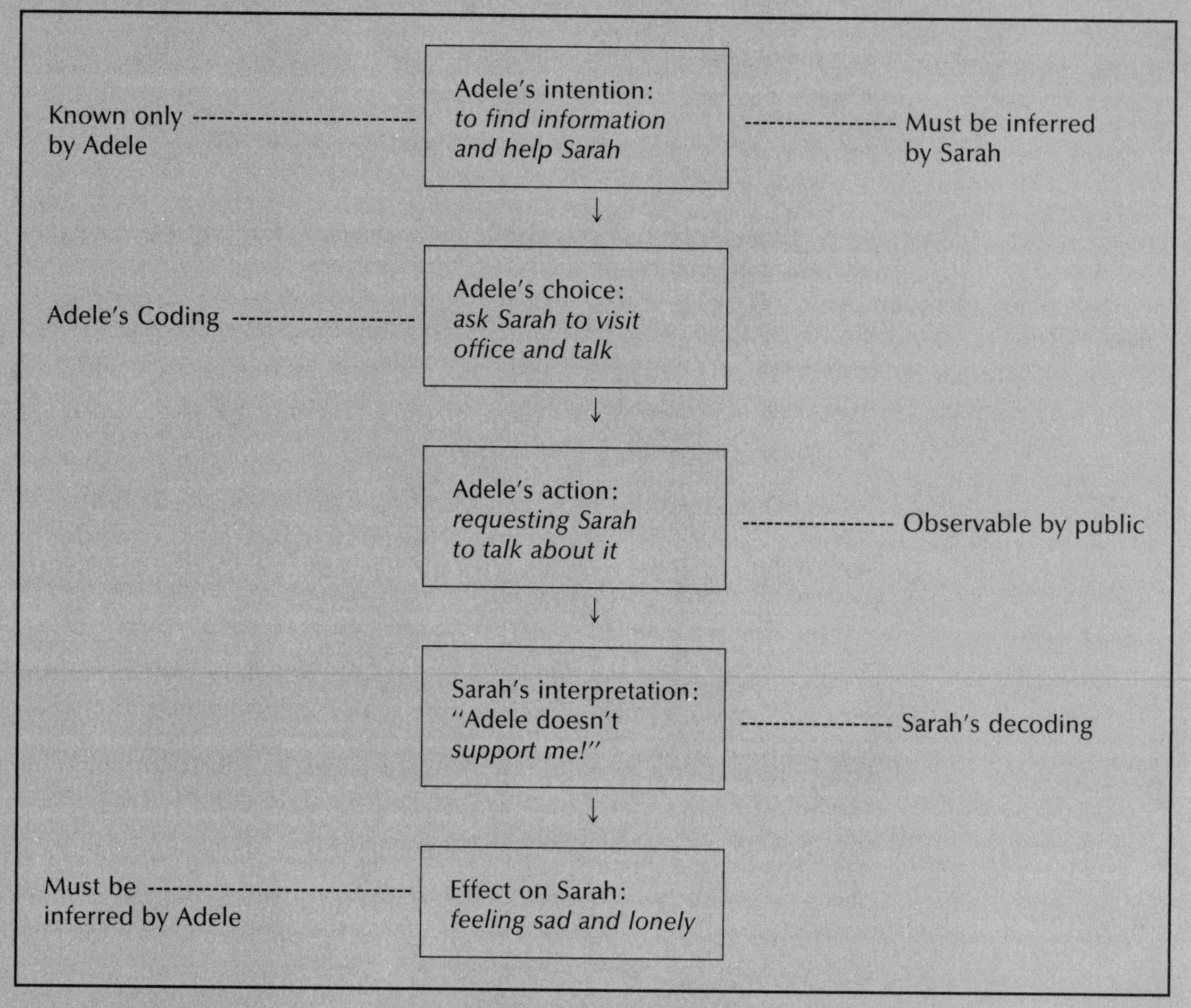

2. a. The same intention may be expressed by different actions.
   b. Different intentions may be expressed by the same action.
   c. The same action may lead to different effects.
   d. Different actions may lead to the same effect.

OBJECTIVE 4 TO DESCRIBE A MODEL OF HELPING SKILLS

Before presenting a model of skills that fosters the helping relationship, it is necessary to discuss a subjective yet crucial quality of effective human interaction: appropriateness. The issue of appropriateness is subjective because the appropriate use of communication skills often depends upon such factors as timing, context, and intentionality in each event. For this reason many experts in communication skills training disclaim the possibility of teaching appropriate judgment in their use. To some the judgment of appropriateness seems so private a quality that no guidelines are possible. Nevertheless, it is possible to suggest that in the case of the supervision of instruction two criteria for appropriate responding apply. When responding to others a supervisor's professional behavior should: (1) be goal directed and (2) not be a burden on the recipient.

Discriminating use of communication skills assumes a goal-directed meaning to the action. A supervisor has a responsibility to facilitate the learning and development of other educators. Supervisory behavior is judged by the learning outcomes of each action. So a supervisor must ask himself or herself if a specific behavior contributes to the learning environment of peers, administrators, and teachers. If not, the behavior is probably not appropriate to the supervisory relationship.

The second criterion is not burdening others with one's own trash. By trash I mean the unresolved "junk" we carry around inside us that blocks our own growth in some area. People in the helping professions need to be aware of their own struggles, road blocks, and hang-ups and refrain from passing them on to others. Often this burdening process is a very subtle action, outside of a person's awareness. The supervisor who casually mentions that she is getting divorced (perhaps offered with the intentions of seeming to be open and honest) can be passing the emotional burden of divorce on to the one who is seeking help. Or perhaps, the supervisor mentions to a teacher "in confidence" what a drinker a particular administrator is. Indiscriminant observations can be devastating to the one who receives them and can be understood as a kind of exhibitionism (even though unconscious). Such promiscuous asides say, in effect, "look at me!"

Another way supervisors can pass on burdens to those they intend to help is in the choice of anecdotes. Usually, it is quite appropriate in social contexts to swap stories as a sign of social interest and involvement. Yet, little personal asides can pass on burdens for teachers to carry. For example:

> "That reminds me of the year my father died, we were . . ."
>
> "I had that same operation five years ago and . . ."

No matter how innocent a supervisor's conscious intentions, such personal references can be a subtle bid for sympathy from others. It shifts the focus of attention away from the teacher and may be experienced by the teacher as a burden.

Finally, another temptation for supervisors is to talk about other school personnel: how badly they treat their students; or the affairs they are having; or how ineffective they are; or how sick or tired they are. Such confidences may be offered with the intention of creating an atmosphere of trust and intimacy between the supervisor and the teacher. However, they can be experienced as pressure from the supervisor for the teacher to agree. As such, these promiscuous confidences are burdens, extraneous baggage for teachers to carry around and, by the criteria offered here, inappropriate to the supervisor's professional role.

The communication skills presented in this chapter are all examples of *straight* communication. Straight communication assumes that both parties of a communicative exchange are responsible for themselves. The supervisor and teacher differ in professional roles but not in human status. Otherwise, straight communication would be impossible. Help that is demeaning, or perpetuates dependency, is not help at all. Rather, it is a way of rejecting another person as "not okay". The mode of communication skills discussed here is based on the assumption that people in a professionally helping relationship are okay, independent people worthy of our respect, and ultimately responsible for their own thoughts, feelings, and actions. This does not mean that basically okay people cannot have feelings of inadequacy, or that they need not learn new professional competencies. Effective teachers, as well as effective supervisors, have temporary feelings of inadequacy from time to time and the supervisor understands that these feelings are a normal part of adult functioning.

We have previously defined skill in communication as facilitative interpersonal behaviors linked with positive attitudes toward self and others. The helping attitudes are the "core conditions" of the helping relationship identified by Rogers. Because attitudes are intentions and because our intentions are private, internal states, they must be expressed in specific helping behavior. The core conditions of a helping relationship (genuineness, empathy, and positive regard) are expressed in helping behaviors. The behaviors will, in turn, strengthen the attitudes. This reciprocity between internal states and external actions is another way of representing the fact that the meaning of what we do is enhanced by this quality of our skills in action. The following table shows the relationship between helping behaviors and helping attitudes.

MODEL OF HELPING (SKILLS AND ATTITUDES)

Behaviors (Skill) ⇄ Strengthen ⇄	Attitudes
Attending (being with) self-disclosure "I-messages"	Congruence/genuineness
Responding (active listening) open-ended exploration paraphrasing/clarifying focusing on affect	Empathy
Facilitating (influencing) honest feedback encouragement	Unconditional positive regard

This chart may be read from right to left or in reverse. Behaviors strengthen attitudes and helping attitudes strengthen helping behaviors. In the sections that follow, each behavior—attending, responding and facilitating—is presented separately and sequentially linked with its corresponding helping attitude. In actual situations many of these helping skills and attitudes are combined and used in consort, given the appropriateness of the context. Here, for the purpose of clarity and analysis they are separated.

Mastery Test

OBJECTIVE 4 TO DESCRIBE A MODEL OF HELPING SKILLS

1. Name the two criteria for appropriateness in using helping skills suggested in this section.

2. Match the helping skill with the corresponding core condition or attitude in a helping relationship.

   Congruence and ______________________________.

   Empathy and ______________________________.

   Unconditioned positive regard and ____________________.

3. Explain what is the difficulty with the popular belief that learning helping skills is learning to manipulate people to do what you want them to do.

Answer Key

Mastery Test, Objective 4

1. a. Helping is a goal-directed activity.
   b. Helping should not be a burden on the helpee.
2. Congruence and attending
   Empathy and responding
   Unconditional positive regard and facilitating
3. First of all, people are not so docile that they are easily manipulated against their will to do what they don't want to do. But even more important is that fact that there is no such thing as a helping skill without a corresponding helping attitude. If the attitude is not there it shows. A person may fake active listening skills by using the words of clarification and exploration, but without the attitudes of empathy for the one listened to, the behavior is easily spotted as phony and, thus, does not work; and cannot fairly be called an example of active listening.

OBJECTIVE 5 TO DEFINE AND RECOGNIZE *ATTENDING BEHAVIOR* IN A HELPING RELATIONSHIP

To attend to the here-and-now dynamics of a relationship means genuinely to be present and available to the other person without front or facade. The best we have to offer another individual is our real selves, alert to what is occurring and open to the options of relational exploration. The supervisor may be tempted to feel the need of distancing himself or herself from those with whom he or she must deal. This is a natural feeling when one considers the role of supervisor carries with it many responsibilities. However, it is possible to distinguish between taking on a professional role in relation to one's colleagues and *role playing*. Role playing implies the pretense of different status, or knowledge and power not relevant to real helping of the other person. It may be safe to hide behind the mask of a supervisor's role, but it is a serious mistake if a genuine relationship is to grow.

There are many skills that make up attending behaviors, such as reading the nonverbal behavior of the other person; but for our purposes we will focus on one: self-disclosure (and a specific variation of self-disclosure, identified by Gordon, which he called "I-statements"). Egan (1976) suggests that self-disclosure skill is one of the distinguishing characteristics of effective communicators. They share a real self with the other person.

Self-Disclosure

Self-disclosure is the expression of a person's genuine reactions, both thoughts and feelings, to a current situation in which he or she is involved. Appropriate self-disclosure avoids overdisclosure and underdisclosure and communicates a real self available for participation in the here-and-now situation. Appropriate self-disclosure may be characterized by three criteria:

1. Statements in which we take responsibility for our thoughts, feelings, and actions. These are often referred to as *owning* statements, rather than ones which blame others.
2. Statements that are *concrete*, as opposed to ones that are highly abstract and vague.
3. Statements that are *immediate*, rather than distant.

Some positive examples of self-disclosure, all of which contain these three distinguishing criteria are listed here:

"I feel *(owning)* frustrated when we make an appointment to discuss this problem *(concrete)* and you are not prepared *(immediate)*."

"I get scared *(owning)* when you drive the car this fast *(concrete and immediate)*.

"I feel lost, even left out *(owning)* when this *(immediate)* discussion goes on about a person I don't know *(concrete)*."

"I'm impressed *(owning)* by the skill with which *(concrete)* you've just summarized both arguments *(immediate)*."

Some examples that do *not* contain self-disclosure are listed here:

"You made me mad by forgetting our appointment." *(blaming)*

"One should obey laws and drive within the speed limits." *(abstract)*

"You don't care about my feelings when you leave me out of the discussion." *(judging)*

"When some people are so clear and logical in their presentation, there's a lesson there for all of us." *(distancing)*

Owning statements puts the speaker making the statement right into the center of the conversation or interaction. In this sense the speaker takes on the responsibility of being here, now. The self-disclosing skill says in effect: "I am here"; "This is me, reacting and acting with you." The concrete quality of self-disclosure says in effect "I'm willing to deal with specifics," as opposed to staying at a level of abstraction and generality. The element of immediacy keeps the focus of the interaction in the present—what is happening now—as opposed to a past or future reference.

One way to understand the positive effect of self-disclosure on a relationship is to examine the negative example alternative behaviors that are often present when a person is not self-disclosing. Instead of owning his or her participation in a situation a person may take refuge in blaming others for problems. Even when others are substantially responsible for a particular crisis very little is gained by "convicting the guilty." Finding out who started a fire does not stop the fire from burning. More often people will take on a blamer role because it is easier, safer than owning one's own reactions. Notice the difference between the following:

Blaming: "*You* make me mad."

Owning: "*I* feel anger."

The blamer says, in effect, "You are responsible for how I feel."

Educators are especially prone to making abstract rather than concrete responses. Part of the reason is that teachers are trained to deal with abstraction and generalization. However, abstracting can be devastating to the quality of a message. Consider the difference in these two responses:

Abstract: "People should tell the truth, even when it hurts."

Concrete: "I suspect that I am not hearing the whole story of what happened."

Again, the abstract seems easier to deal with, but the concrete lets the other person know that you are taking what is happening very seriously; that you are involved. Likewise, distancing responses tend to put the problem or current situation "out there" somewhere, anywhere but in the immediacy of the current interaction. Notice the differences:

Distancing: "One doesn't know what one would do, if one were to meet such a problem."

Immediate: "I'm confused about which of these options is the best strategy."

Being in touch with the moment-to-moment transactions in an ongoing communication tells the other person(s) that you are here, and fully available for participation. It says you are willing to risk involvement now. The consequence on the quality of the relationship is positive. You are experienced as genuine.

The skill of self-disclosure neither overdiscloses nor underdiscloses. Overdisclosure is what has sometimes been called promiscuous honesty, the gushing of commentary of those who are oppressively open about themselves. Those who would tell you their life history on first meeting or who would advise you on the quality of your wardrobe at introduction, are hiding their real selves just as much as those who underdisclose. Neither are available for intimacy, nor for the tasks at hand in a problem-solving interaction.

I-Messages

I-messages are a special case of self-disclosure in which a person assumes responsibility to share assessment of self with another, while leaving the responsibility for the other person's behavior with that person. I-messages meet three criteria for effective communication: (1) they have high probability of promoting willingness to change; (2) they contain minimal negative evaluation of the other person; and (3) they do not injure the relationship. According to Thomas Gordon (1974) there are three components of I-messages:

1. The *what* of the behavior is described in nonjudgmental terms.
2. The *effect* of the behavior on the speaker is specified in concrete and tangible terms.
3. The *feelings* of the speaker in response to the other's behavior are specified.

The following examples are I-messages:

"When you interrupt me *(description of behavior)*, I get distracted and lose my train of thought *(tangible effect)* and I get frustrated *(feeling)*."

"When you leave the materials out on the art table *(nonjudgmental description)*, then I have to clean it up *(effect of behavior)* and I resent *(feeling)* doing your work."

"When you're late for an appointment *(behavior)*, I have to change my schedule around *(effect)* and I end up feeling taken advantage of *(feeling)*."

The following examples are *not* I-messages:

"When I'm annoyed, I can't see straight. If you know what's good for you, you'd better not make me angry."

"This is the messiest class I've ever had; what am I going to do with you?"

"One of these days you're going to push me too far and then you'd better watch out!"

I-messages are effective forms of self-disclosure because they describe what is happening from the speaker's point of view in a straight fashion. Straight communication assumes that both parties of communication exchange are responsible for themselves. The effect of I-messages on the other person is such that the speaker is being honest without blaming. Whether the content of the communication is positive or negative, each person gets a chance to see the impact they have had on another person.

In order to develop skill in self-disclosure and I-messages, a person needs to be in touch with his or her own reactions to events. This may seem obvious, that in order to describe what is happening one must be aware. However, many people find themselves reacting to events from habit and are unaware of the pattern of their reactivity or its meaning. Effective communicators are in touch with their thoughts, feelings, needs, and bodily reactions. Some students will say at the beginning of an interpersonal communications training program that they find it difficult to concentrate on what is happening outside themselves, while at the same time monitoring their own internal processes. They claim that they lose their sense of spontaneity and sincerity if they try. And yet, with practice it is possible to become aware of personal reactions, while maintaining the interaction with another. Many difficulties in communication occur when we simply react to others without awareness of the meaning of the reaction. Developing a descriptive mode of acting in interpersonal transactions prevents these difficulties.

In summary, the best we have to offer others is ourselves, our time, our being with them. Congruence in a helping relationship begins when we are really with another person, without pretense, preconceived ideas, advice, or judgments about the relationship. This does not mean that we have to deny our own values, perspectives, or commitments. Rather, it means that we bring to the helping relation our full attention, the full resources of our personality and experience, and make them available to genuine interaction with another. Self-disclosure is the interpersonal skill that makes this possible.

The instructional supervisor may find self-disclosure difficult to practice. The political structures of school systems often make it exceedingly difficult to be genuine in the presence of those for whom a supervisor has responsibility. It may be helpful to know that most of the fears that tempt one to disingenuous behavior are fantasies. We do not give up any of our own personal power when we describe for others how we are experiencing what is happening to us. In fact, we gain respect and acceptance from others when they experience the compliment we pay when our real selves engage them.

Mastery Test

OBJECTIVE 5 TO DEFINE AND RECOGNIZE *ATTENDING BEHAVIORS* IN A HELPING RELATIONSHIP

1. Define self-disclosure.
2. Name the three characteristics of appropriate self-disclosure.
3. Name the three components of I-messages.
4. Indicate "yes or no" to show which of the following statements are and which are not examples of self-disclosure and/or I-messages.
   a. "When people don't listen, your administrator gets mad."
   b. "When you read the newspaper during the meeting, I get distracted and then feel annoyed."
   c. "I like your suggestion that we call a brief recess and I appreciate your sharing the group's restlessness and need for a break."

   d. "If I were in your shoes, I'd feel ashamed even to show up at this meeting."

   e. "You're not paying attention and that makes me mad."

5. The following statements are all nondescriptive reactions. Write a hypothetical alternative that could be considered self-disclosing and descriptive. For example: "You always mess things up!" could be rewritten "I'm uncomfortable in this messy room."

   a. "So you have to show off all the big words you know."
   Alternative:

   b. "Be on time or else!"
   Alternative:

   c. "My, my, aren't we the sensitive ones!"
   Alternative:

   d. "I know just what you mean!"
   Alternative:

   e. "You administrators are all alike!"
   Alternative:

Answer Key

Mastery Test, Objective 5

1. Self-disclosure is the expression of a person's genuine reactions to the current situation, avoiding both overdisclosure and underdisclosure, and communicates a real self available for participation in the here-and-now situation.
2. a. Owning statements, rather than blaming.
   b. Concrete statements, rather than abstract.
   c. A specification of the speaker's feelings as a result of the behavior.
3. a. The *what* of the behavior.
   b. The *effect* of the behavior.
   c. The *feelings* of the speaker.
4. a. No
   b. Yes
   c. Yes
   d. No
   e. No
5. a. "I get scared when I hear you use big words."
   b. "I want to be able to count on your punctuality."
   c. "I feel like I've contributed to your negative reaction."
   d. "I have a hunch about what you experienced."
   e. "I feel like I've gone through this experience before."

OBJECTIVE 6 TO DEFINE AND RECOGNIZE *RESPONDING BEHAVIORS* IN A HELPING RELATIONSHIP

Responding behaviors are skilled expressions of the attitude of empathy for another person. We have already learned that Rogers describes empathy as sensing another's inner and personal meanings as if those meanings were one's own. But sensing another person's feelings is not a public behavior. The attitude of empathy needs to be expressed in skilled behavior. The effective communicator responds to another with "active listening" as the expression of empathy. It is called "active listening" in order to contrast the response skills from the "passive listening" of social interaction in which the listener passively receives another's message. Kagan (1976) and his associates investigated the differences between effective and ineffective interviewers. He found that there are some kinds of questions and statements which were consistently found to be in the repertoire of effective interviewers. Kagan called these kinds of statements "response modes." Although various experts label these responding behaviors of effective communicators differently, there are three kinds of responses that foster empathic understanding when listening to the concerns of another:

- Open-ended responses
- Paraphrasing/clarifying responses
- Focusing on feelings

Open-Ended Responses

Open-ended responses invite the other person to explore the nature of his or her experiences and describe the meaning of his or her concerns. Open-ended statements invite the other person to become an active participant in the interaction, rather than remaining a passive recipient of our advice and knowledge. There are five characteristics of open-ended statements:

1. They focus on the other person, inviting him or her to tell his or her own story.
2. They avoid problem solving and advice giving by seeking exploration.
3. They do not express judgments.
4. They ask for more information.
5. They are brief, avoiding long complicated sentences.

Open-ended responses are so labeled in contrast with those that are closed. That is, closed statements structure, confine the other person to a specific topic, offer specific advice, or ask for yes or no answers. There are, indeed, times in a relationship when closed responses are appropriate. The point, however, is that ineffective communicators tended to use closed responses almost exclusively. The effective communicator, interviewer, counselor is more interested in what the other person's concern is than in his or her own advice or problem-solving skills. Open-ended statements are exploratory because they invite the other person to explore concerns.

To notice the differences between what are and are not examples of these responses, imagine that the following statement was made to you.

COLLEAGUE: "I've been considering taking the buy-out plan for early retirement being offered by the board. But, I don't know if I should; I mean, what if I found out that I missed teaching?"

Closed Responses

"Well, first of all, you'll never know how it will be until you try it. It's probably better not to borrow problems in advance. After all, you may well like retirement. Most do!" *(problem solving)*

"Retirement time comes to all of us. Why not take it when you're still young to enjoy it?" *(advice giving)*

"I remember when I had the chance to retire early. I couldn't face it. I stayed at the job, continued teaching and I couldn't be happier." *(story-swapping)*

"What's wrong with you? Why are you doubting yourself? Have you talked it over with your wife?" *(interrogation)*

Open-Ended Responses

"What do you think will happen?"

"What are your fears?"

"Is there more?"

"Tell me more about this."

Notice these responses are short, avoid making judgments or giving advice, ask for more information, and in general, invite the other person to tell his or her own story. Ineffective closed responses tend to be long, highly abstract commentaries. Inevitably, they tell another person what to do, or in some way take charge of the conversation as if the listener knew best what was good for the other person. Whatever else may be true about closed responses, there is one danger that makes them suspect for use in a helping relationship, and that is that they can imply a discount of the person seeking help or understanding. If you can solve the other person's problem so easily, perhaps after hearing only a few of the facts, then you imply there must be something wrong with the other person to have a concern or problem in the first place.

Another mistake often made by those trying to be helpful is to interrogate the one seeking help. This is what Gazda (1971) calls "playing detective." "Why do you feel that way?" can be read as a challenge, as though there is some need to defend oneself. Interrogations and specifically "why-questions" are not very helpful to someone trying to sort out self-understandings. The fact is that with many things in life we may not know the reason why we feel as we do. Further, even if we knew why we have a problem, knowing the cause may not lead to a solution. Especially, early in an interaction, why-questions are more apt to provoke a person to assume a defensive posture, often resulting in a retreat or an attack. So, avoiding the use of why-questions gives the listener the option of inviting the other person to explore the meanings in an event or experience that may be troubling them.

Finally, it is important for people to explore their own minds, come to their own conclusions. Therefore, open-ended responses avoid labeling or judging the other person. It is not necessary that an active listener approve of the behavior, thoughts, or feelings of the other person. Rather, it is important to accept where the individual is for the moment. When a person comes to us with a concern he or she is often confused, maybe even frightened and needing understanding. What is helpful is if the person can find his or her own words to express the concern. Borrowing our words, using our labels, is not only unhelpful, but can restrict a person's self-exploration. Even when our labels are accurate inferences from observed behavior, they remain our words. If our objective is to help the other person clarify his or her own thinking and feeling it is far more effective to encourage self-exploration. Open-ended responses, in effect, invite the other person to write his or her own essays on the subject of his or her concern, as opposed to answering a series of multiple-choice questions. Empathy for another is expressed in active listening, letting the other person discover or learn, rather than insisting on our "expert" advice.

Your Turn

In this practice exercise you are asked to read the printed statement as though it were spoken to you, and then to write an exploratory response, one you think would *encourage the speaker to explore more deeply her or his concern(s).*

After you have completed your responses to these statements, look at the responses in the answer key. How do they compare with yours? Would your response encourage the speaker to explore more deeply, to elaborate, and to want to continue talking with you?

1. "I don't know. . . . What should I say? I mean, I want to talk to my supervisor about what's happened, but it's. . . . Well, I just don't know where to start; how to tell her."
2. "I don't understand what's happened. Everything was going so well, and all of a sudden she just left . . . walked right out, you know? I must have done something . . . or said something. . . ."
3. "I've done everything they asked me to do. . . . I even tried to change my attitude, 'cause I know they wanted me to be more positive. But here I am again back where I started. To hell with them—I'm not gonna try to please them anymore. From now on I'm strictly out for me, number one!"
4. "I really wanted to take this trip . . . but now, I guess I'll have to put it off."
5. "This really great thing happened to me. . . . I finally got this letter I've been waiting for!"

Answer Key

Your Turn

1. *One response:* "What have you considered saying to her?"

   Rationale: Encouraging the other person to go and tell more about the concern allows that person to disclose whatever he or she wants to and gives the listener a good chance to understand the person's perspective. Also, there is an implied recognition that the other person is responsible and a partner in the conversation, rather than a student at a lecture.

2. *One response:* "What has it done to you."

   Rationale: Instead of problem-solving or giving advice, it is often appropriate for the one who is listening to keep the focus on the other person's concern. When someone is dealing with genuine concerns they usually have many thoughts and feelings, most of which they have never been encouraged to verbalize. Helping one explore may enable a person to hear himself or herself say things he or she have never said before.

3. *One response:* "What's it like to have things go badly for you?"

   Rationale: Asking someone to identify the emotional state accompanying a statement can be a practical way to help the person explore another facet of the experience. In this case the person is invited to look at and describe what happens when "nothing seems to go right," rather than trying to persuade or problem solve.

4. *One response:* "Is that a familiar experience for you?"

   Rationale: This helps the person look for patterns in his or her life. Is the present situation one which occurs repeatedly for the person?

5. *One response:* "Tell me about it."

Rationale: We often assume we know what something means for a person. It is preferable to ask, rather than to assume that we "know what it's like."

Paraphrasing/Clarifying Responses

A paraphrase is the restatement of another's concern in your own words and is usually accompanied by a clarifying tag, as in: "Is that it?" or "Have I got it?" Instead of assuming an understanding of another person, the effective communicator periodically checks this out by requesting clarification in the form of a restatement or verbal summary of what has been heard.

There are three reasons why paraphrase/clarifying responses are helpful to active listening:

1. They help the other person to listen to his or her own words and ideas being expressed. This can help to clear up confusion.
2. They help the listener to understand precisely what the other's concern really is.
3. They advance the quality of the interaction between the listener and the other person by communicating respect. In essence, when you paraphrase you tell the other person that you have listened very carefully to what he or she has been saying, so much so that you can offer his or her ideas and words back for clarification.

Paraphrasing can be overused. It is not a way of responding to everything a person says, but rather an effective tool for *periodic* checks on where the conversation is going. A paraphrase restates what the other person says, and needs to be offered in a tentative tone of voice, accompanied with a clarifying tag on the end, such as: "Have I got it?" or "Is that it?" Without the tentativeness, a paraphrase can sound accusatory. Its periodic use in active listening lets the other person know how seriously you are trying to understand him or her.

The following are examples of paraphrasing/clarifying responses:

"If I've heard you correctly, you're concerned with . . . , is that it?"

"As I listen to you, I hear you say . . . , have I got it?"

"Are you saying that. . . . ?"

The following are *not* examples of paraphrasing/clarifying responses:

"How do you know that? I mean, what gives you the right to criticize anyone?" *(defensive)*

"Stop right there, I don't want to hear any more from you on that subject!" *(interrupting)*

"Surely, you don't believe that. When you think about it, you'll feel differently!" *(judgmental)*

"What do you *really* mean? You can be honest with me!" *(doubting)*

As we listen to others we may be tempted to pick up the strands of the cognitive reasoning in these remarks and debate the logic or common sense of the words themselves. There may be situations in which challenging the other person's logic is precisely appropriate. Nevertheless, in active listening the objective is to keep the focus on the one to whom we are listening. It is easy to argue with the assumptions of most people who raise a personal concern, often out of a state of emotional intensity and cognitive confusion. That is the reason they will seek to talk to those who are willing to listen. So it is a cheap response to attack the person with a concern from the vantage of uninvolved objectivity. The use of paraphrases and clarifying responses helps us to avoid this temptation. They also do something else that is helpful to others. By repeating another's words and offering them back, he or she has an opportunity to hear again what they are saying. This helps because people are often unaware of what they have said; so that hearing their own words again helps them to decide whether this is, indeed, what they mean to say.

Your Turn

Again, in this practice exercise you are asked to read the printed statement as though it were spoken to you, and then to write a response that would show the person that you intend to understand his or her concern. Although, no written exercise is a substitute for here-and-now oral conversation, nevertheless, you may improve your skill in listening to others by practicing and then discussing your choice of responses.

After you have completed your responses to these statements, look at the responses offered as examples. How do they compare with yours? How could these responses be improved?

1. "I can't figure him out; I just don't know what is going to happen next. First, he wants to marry me; then, he wants to wait; now, he says he doesn't know what he wants. I get confused, then angry and then scared; so I kind of force a smile, you know?"

2. "Hey, you know what he (the administrator) said to me? He said that if I don't do what he tells me in my class, then he'll kick me out! How'd you like that . . . like I'm some kind of animal he's going to break!"

3. "I've never been so embarrassed in my life. My boss called me and told me to get down to this meeting right away. When I got there everybody wanted to know where my report was, and you know what? Nobody believed me!"

4. "I just don't want to make trouble for anyone, that's all. If I can get by without bothering anyone, do my own thing, you know, then I'd be happy. But I keep getting involved; it's very upsetting!"

Answer Key

Your Turn

1. *One response:* "I hear that you are confused and angry about his behavior, but I'm not sure I understand what's involved in your smiling. Tell me more about that?"

   Rationale: Asking for clarification is a way of letting the other person know that you are actively listening to what is being said. This response begins with a paraphrase and then asks for further elaboration.

2. *One response:* "Forcing his will on you was like his trying to break you? Is that what it was like for you?"

   Rationale: Here we have repeated most elements of what was said and asked for confirmation or correction. This communicates that what the person is saying is important enough for us to check out the exact meaning. Paraphrasing and asking for clarification are ways of accepting what someone says without implying approval or agreement.

3. *One response:* "Your boss called you into a meeting and you were asked for a report? Help me understand the business about your not being believed."

   Rationale: When asking for clarification or information rather than accusing the other person of not making sense, simply saying "help me understand" enlists that person's aid in explaining what was meant.

4. *One response:* "You don't want to make trouble for others and you want to do your own thing. But I'm not sure what you mean about getting involved."

   Rationale: By restating the message that we've heard the person give, we invite the person to correct the message, if necessary, or even to change the message, if he or she wants. By asking for specific clarification, we are focusing the person's attention on what is unclear to us and perhaps to the speaker as well. In typical social communication we often do not ask for such clarification, but as part of helping another know and solve problems active listening responses are useful and appropriate.

Focusing on Feelings

The third skill to active listening is focusing on feelings. It may be surprising but many people are unaware of their own feelings. They may be experiencing anger (for example) and they may express their anger nonverbally, but they are often unaware that what they are feeling is anger. So the effective communicator learns to focus on feelings.

A focus on feelings is a response that indicates willingness to deal with the affective component in a person's communication: the moods, sensations, attitudes, and values expressed in an interaction. Usually, the affective or feeling component of a message is central to what concerns an individual. Willingness to focus on those feelings communicates an acceptance of the other person and a respect for what that person is experiencing, whether positive or negative.

It should be noted that it may not always be appropriate to focus on a person's feelings. When the content and concern of a message is mainly cognitive, it is not useful to go digging for some unacknowledgeable emotion behind the person's words. For example, if someone asks for directions on how to find the superintendent's office, it is inappropriate to respond: "I know, but first—you must be really upset if you have to go see the super. . . ."

Most of the time the mistake communicators make is in the direction of avoiding emotional content, even when it's staring them in the face. Kagan (1976) found that there were consistent preferences by the ineffective communicators for the cognitive issues in an expressed concern. What Kagan and his associates discovered is that ineffective interviewers tended to prefer ideas, facts, and data rather than explore a person's feelings. In contrast, effective communicators tended to focus on feelings, moods, and sensations. This turns out to be helpful to those with concerns in two ways. First, it helps the person recognize his or her own emotional reactions; and second, it helps by letting the person know that you are willing to deal with their emotions, which implies an acceptance of them as persons.

The public has a difficult time accepting human emotionality as normal. There remains a cultural suspicion that our feelings are somehow not nice, or at least not as nice and clean as thoughts. This is not to suggest that what we think is not important. Rather, it is to affirm that what we feel is equally important. Most of what motivates human action has an emotional or affective origin. So the effective communicator will be available for focusing on the feelings of an interaction.

The following are examples of an affective focus:

"Tell me, what are you feeling right now?"

"I have a hunch you're feeling sad about this, am I right?"

"How does that affect you?"

"What does that do to you?"

"Are there feelings associated with that thought?"

The following are *not* examples of an affective focus:

"Some people are really cry-babies, aren't they?" *(ridicule)*

"I appreciate your modesty, John; but, of course you have lots to be modest about." *(sarcasm)*

"You don't have to publish your ignorance, John; the news has preceded you." *(sardonic)*

"I would never presume to question your authority on any subject, John." *(irony)*

Sometimes people are so uncomfortable with their emotions they make fun of themselves or others. Think of how rare it is to have a person accept your own emotional responses when you are occasionally sad or depressed. Rather, we are apt to receive either ridicule or attempts to cheer us up. How refreshing it is then for a person to accept our emotional side as a normal part of a healthy person's dealings with the world. Even more so it is the case in the helping relationship that focusing on feelings is a skilled expression of the empathy we have for another person. Consider the following vignette:

> Mark Taylor is not well accepted by his fellow teachers. He comes to you, his supervisor, after the following incident. He had come up with the idea for a faculty play as a fund-raiser for the scholarship fund. After selling the idea to his colleagues, they get excited, take over his idea, select a play, cast the parts, and so forth. In essence, they leave Mark out of the activities. Mark gives up and comes to you feeling rejected once again.

What do you do? What do you say? The temptation is to cheer Mark up—"Don't worry about it, Mark, things will turn out OK!" Or there is the possibility of belittling the whole incident: "Why take it so hard, Mark? What's so important about a play?" But it takes both courage and skill to stay with Mark's feelings: "How is this affecting you, Mark?" If you ask such a question (or another with the same genuine interest), it may be a turning point in Mark's own self-assessment and growth.

Your Turn

In oral communications the feeling tone or "affect" is one of the important elements in a message. A written exercise is no substitute for practice in here-and-now conversations in which one listens for the affective quality of a message. Still, you are again asked to respond to these written statements as though they were spoken to you directly. Write out a response which you think would help the other person to focus on the affective element in the statement. This will require that you imagine the voice tone implied in the following written statements.

After you have completed your responses to these statements, look at the suggested responses. How do they compare with yours? How would you improve these responses so that the other person would more likely feel free to focus on her or his feelings?

1. "He used to make over $200 a week and we got along fine, but now . . . well, he makes much less and it's not easy."
2. "Boy, I had to learn a thing or two when I first came to this school. My principal always said how he wanted to be a regular guy and for me to tell him things I'd tell friends; so I did. He said he wanted my honest feelings; so I told him. Did he get mad!"
3. "This morning when my kids went to school, I realized they're gonna be 18 soon. You know, soon all I'll have to get up for is work. I mean, except for the job, what will I have to get up for in the morning?"
4. "I just got a letter from home. My mother's operation was successful, there's no trace of cancer!"

Answer Key

Your Turn

1. *One response:* "It's really discouraging to have to scrape along—it sounds like it's really getting you down."

   Rationale: This response reflects the emotional content of the message we believed we heard. This is likely to encourage the person to talk about feelings connected with not having enough money. When the response used is said with a tentative but supportive emotional tone, the other person has the opportunity to focus on her own feelings, but also to correct our statement if it is not quite on target.

2. *One response:* "You feel like he double-crossed you—like you were 'had'?"

   Rationale: The intention here is to make it easier for the person to talk about his feelings, if he chooses to. Because sometimes people are unaware of what they are feeling, it can be very useful to them to mirror the emotional tone of their message. Caution should be taken not to make an affective response sound like an accusation.

3. *One response:* "You get really down when you anticipate the kids not needing you anymore, that you don't feel needed as you used to be?"

   Rationale: Focusing on the person's feelings gives him or her permission to talk more about them, if he or she wants to. Avoid the temptation to give advice or easy assurances which the person could experience as minimizing or ignoring his or her emotions.

4. *One response:* "You must feel great. I'd feel really relieved."
   Rationale: Affective responses are offered for "good" feelings as well as "bad" ones. Here we have reflected the person's emotional content and shared our own feelings.

Mastery Test

OBJECTIVE 6 TO DEFINE AND RECOGNIZE *RESPONDING BEHAVIORS* IN A HELPING RELATIONSHIP

1. Define open-ended responses.
2. Define paraphrasing/clarifying responses.
3. Define focusing on feelings responses.

For questions 4–8 choose the one active listening response that seems most appropriate to you.

4. "I don't know what I could have done. . . . I mean, we used to get along so well . . . but now. . . ."

   a. "I'm sure it isn't your fault."

   b. "Now she doesn't like you anymore?"

   c. "Go on, tell me more. . . ."

   d. "Everybody gets upset now and then."

   e. "Now, you have doubts about how well you really did get along?"

5. "What am I going to do? If I can't be the way she wants me to, then I just don't know what to do."

   a. "Here's what I'd do, I'd. . . ."

   b. "Who do they think they are, telling you how to be!"

   c. "What do you want to do?"

   d. "What should you have done for her?"

   e. "I don't know what I'd do either."

6. "I mean, just what is his problem? I wish he would just get off my back and leave me alone!"

   a. "Why did you get yourself in this position?"

   b. "I know . . . I hate it when people get on me about something."

   c. "What effect is he having on you?"

   d. "Maybe he'll get the message and go away."

   e. "Is he on your back all of the time, or just some of the time?"

7. "I expected the conversation to be the same as all the other ones . . . and all of a sudden, it just didn't turn out that way. . . ."

   a. "What happened?"

   b. "You had no warning? How could it happen just like that?"

   c. "That's really a strange feeling when something like that happens, isn't it?"

   d. "What other conversations? Who were you talking to?"

   e. "It is better to check out our expectations before acting."

8. "I used to feel like it would be good just to know . . . Now I feel like I don't want to plan at all. I just kinda wait to see what happens."

   a. "Effective people, usually are ones who plan their lives carefully."

   b. "That is a good idea! Just let it happen."

   c. "I know just what you mean . . . I always get messed up when I try to plan things out."

   d. "What are you afraid would happen if you were to plan it out?"

   e. "How is just waiting to see what happens working for you?"

For questions 9–13 write in an appropriate active listening response.

9. "I don't know, I feel really upset because I don't understand her."

10. "Yeah . . . I remember what it was like when we bought our first house."

11. "I wish he would just listen to me once in awhile instead of just going off and . . . well, you know what I mean."

12. ". . . in the high school that I went to . . . these guys . . . from when they were little kids, they were told they were going to go to college, so they automatically enrolled . . . but not me. . . ."

13. "Yes, that's because if I can get far enough away from myself to laugh at myself, then it won't hurt."

Answer Key

Mastery Test, Objective 6

1. Open-ended responses invite the other person to explore the nature of his or her experiences and describe the meaning of his or her concerns. Open-ended responses invite the other person to become an active participant in the interaction, rather than remaining a passive recipient of our advice and knowledge. Open-ended responses are brief, nonjudgmental, avoid advising or problem solving, seek more information, and generally keep the focus on the other person.
2. A paraphrase is the restatement of another person's concern in your own words, accompanied by a clarifying tag, as in: "Is that it?" Not to be overused, the paraphrase/clarifying response is offered in a tentative, exploratory tone, letting the other person know you are really trying to understand his or her concern.
3. A focus on feelings response indicates willingness to deal with the affective component in a person's communication: the moods, sensations, attitudes and values expressed in the interaction. Focusing on the feelings expresses the listener's acceptance of the person as is without implying approval or agreement with the content of the statement.

The preferred responses for 4–8 are:

4. c
5. c
6. c
7. a
8. e
9. You don't feel you understand her and that upsets you.
10. You can remember how you felt when you bought your first house.
11. You wish he'd listen to you and not just go off.
12. Your friends were told they were going to college but no one ever told you that. You felt bad about that.
13. You feel hurt now.

OBJECTIVE 7 TO DEFINE AND RECOGNIZE *FACILITATIVE BEHAVIORS* IN A HELPING RELATIONSHIP

In the first two modes of helping responses to others—attending behaviors and responding behaviors—we have skills that are used with relatively little risk. It is true that they will involve the listener more deeply in the interaction with another person, but the risk to the listener is minimal in terms of personal commitment. With facilitative behaviors the personal risk level increases dramatically. This is, perhaps, why facilitative skill is so rare; because it is risky in helping the other person. Kagan (1976) showed that there are significant differences between effective and ineffective interviewers in how they dealt with emotionally difficult situations. The less effective counselors tended to back away from areas of differences, emotional subjects, and matters of depth that might lead to greater interpersonal intimacy. That is, the less effective tended to stay "on the surface" in the relationship or communication; and as a result, they tended to lack commitment to the ongoing explorations of a helping relationship. There are two facilitative behaviors that influence the other person and communicate a listener's personal regard and respect for the other. These facilitative behaviors are *honest feedback* and *encouragement*.

Honest Feedback

Honest feedback responds to another person in an ongoing relationship with descriptive statements dealing with the here-and-now reality, neither overstating nor understating the reality situation, *and* matching the emotional level of intensity that the other person seems to be experiencing.

This skill is called "honest" feedback as opposed to dishonest or inaccurate descriptions of the reality situation. This is not an advocacy of promiscuous honesty upon first meeting. Rather, what we are seeking to avoid here is the temptation to respond to others in ways that distort the reality situation by: (1) lessening the intensity, (2) cleaning up the message, or (3) offering false optimism. The impact of less-than-honest feedback on others is usually the opposite of what the speaker intends. Instead of communicating support for the person less-than-honest feedback usually conveys the message: "He's being easy on me or nice to me." This can be understood as a discount of the person, as in, "He thinks I'm too weak, or too stupid, or too inexperienced to deal with things as they really are." In contrast, honest feedback matches the emotional level of the individual and says in effect, "You can take it." "You're competent to cope with what's happening now."

The person offering the facilitative response of honest feedback can comment on the true dynamics that normally occur in any here-and-now interaction. The facilitator can comment on:

1. How the other person seems.
2. How the facilitator feels.
3. What seems to be the nature of the transactions between the two of them.

Honest feedback communicates the respect for the other person by honestly describing what is happening to the best of the communicator's abilities. Kagan (1976) says that the effective communicator has the capacity of being brutally frank . . . without being brutal. Most people respond to such honesty positively, almost with relief, as in, "At last, someone who will deal straight with me, as I am!"

Following are examples of honest feedback from supervisor to teacher:

"As I listen to you, I have the feeling that we've been through this before, that a pattern may be forming in our relationship in which you goof up and then apologize. What do you think?"

"You seem sad today, as if you had just lost your last friend on earth."

"As I listen to you, I feel left out; as if you were keeping something from me or as if there is something I am not supposed to know."

Following are examples that are *not* honest feedback:

"Well, everybody goofs up sometimes. You can't make an omelet without breaking eggs, you know!"

"Where did my cheerful friend go today?"

"Whatever you want to tell me, you can; trust in my professional confidence."

Your Turn

You are asked to respond to the written statements below as though they were spoken to you directly. Respond in such a way that you honestly describe what you hear the other person saying. The impact of honest feedback on the other person is that you are taking what he or she is saying very seriously, enough so to describe what it is that you are hearing in the person's statement. Your response should be as frank and honest as possible, yet it should not be brutal or punitive. After you have written out your response, check them with a colleague or friend. Then compare the responses with the ones on the feedback given in the answer key.

1. "Administrators, who do they think they are? Gods?"
2. "I know people like me, especially boys. But, you know, sometimes I wish I weren't so popular. It's such a burden."
3. "I hit him! I just hauled off and slapped him good. Wow! Was he surprised! And, frankly, so was I."
4. "He says things to me like, 'Be polite,' or 'What's wrong with loving your country?' or worse, 'When are you going to grow up?' Can you imagine what that's like? How I feel?"
5. "Damn it! There are idiots everywhere messing up this world. Even at school nobody seems to know what they're doing or even care what happens. It makes me sick!"

Answer Key

Your Turn

1. *One response:* "You're furious at them for their godlike attitude toward you."

   Rationale: This response labels the emotion in the person's statement as it was heard. The tone of this response is not accusatory nor judgmental, but a description of the emotion. The other person is likely to know that you heard the emotion and didn't avoid dealing with it.

2. *One response:* "I can hear that your popularity is a burden at times, but I also hear your pride in being popular at the same time?"

   Rationale: We hear the complaint, but the way it's stated suggests that she is proud of her popularity. We describe what we hear. If our description is off target and our statement was offered with some gentleness, the person can correct our impression, while at the same time getting feedback on how her communication was heard by us.

3. *One response:* "This time you behaved differently than you usually do and it felt good?"

   Rationale: The response names the messages we heard in the person's statement, that is, the undertone of satisfaction in having hit him. It lets the person know we have heard both the cognitive content and the affective message. Again, if we are wrong, the person can correct us. Such a response lets the person know that we are directly participating in this interaction.

4. *One response:* "You feel discounted; and you want to be sure that I understand how hard that is on you."

   Rationale: The response stays with the person's feelings by describing the emotions heard and the expectations laid on the listener. It avoids the temptation to ignore or minimize the person's depth of feeling about the situation described or the feelings between the listener and the person.

5. *One response:* "You're livid with anger."

   Rationale: Confronted with real anger or fury, the honest feedback response tells the person you have heard the full intensity of the message. The response does not imply that we approve or agree, only that we are not going to avoid the emotion or "cool" the person.

Encouragement

Encouragement is a convincing demonstration that the other person has resources and options that can be applied to the solution of problems and the achievement of goals. Encouragement as a skill fosters a person's self-esteem, which includes feelings of belonging, competence, and worth. The specific action most often associated with encouragement is *descriptive praise*, an open describing of the others' action coupled with how the speaker feels about it.

What people get most of the time is discouragement. Think for a moment: when was the last time someone told you how competent you are, or what a worthwhile, valuable member of the staff you are? All of us want, and need the sense of belonging, competence, and worth (Felker, 1974). Yet, how rare it is that we get such feedback! The reason for this may be that helping others is mostly cast in the mold of pointing out others' deficiencies. "Professionals ought to be able to take the bitter truth!" Right? Wrong! Professional educators are like everyone else and need to feel that they are valued by others. Adults need to know that they are involved, making a contribution to the group, and making progress toward a specific goal. Out of such awareness springs real commitment and personal motivation.

This is not an argument for easy reassurances that everything is all right. Adler (1956) saw encouragement as a demonstration that the other person possessed strengths, resources, and choices that make a difference to other people. Teachers' commitment to their craft cannot be expressed in financial terms. They simply do not earn enough money to match the quality of dedication, effort, and creativity many bring to their work with students. What keeps most high-quality, productive teachers going is their own sense of self-worth, accompanied by their knowledge that they make a real difference in the development of their students. Healthy adult development depends upon a person extending himself or herself through interest in the welfare of others (Adler, 1956). This is what Adler called "social interest." Given this fact of human nature, it is amazing that so few administrators or supervisors of instruction are adequately skilled in the facilitative behavior of encouragement.

The skill of encouragement is not a matter of using a set of "stock" phrases, but an ongoing process of discovering the strengths of others. One aspect of encouragement is the use of *descriptive praise*. Descriptive praise, in contrast to evaluative praise, describes an observed performance and how the observer feels about it. For example: "When you ended the meeting with a reminder of the agenda for next time, I felt terrific that no one could leave without realizing how much work we have to do before we meet again." Notice that in evaluative praise, by contrast, there is no description of the valued behavior: "Great meeting, George!" The problem with evaluative praise is that the one receiving the praise does not know what he or she did that merited the specific praise and, even more costly, it hooks the person on the praiser. If we are dependent on others for our strokes, we do not become self-stroking, confident individuals. The difference is between helping someone develop an internal locus of control (for example, "I can trust my skills") versus fostering a dependent relationship, hooked on external sources of control over one's life. Those who receive encouragement in the form of descriptive praise are more likely to "own" their own behavior as praise-worthy.

Facilitating the growth and development of adults calls for exceptional skill on the part of a supervisor. If we take seriously our responsibility to be a positive influence on others, then much of what needs doing is focusing on the developing strengths of others. When there are specific problems which need attending, most adults are helped by encouragement to use their own resources and those of their colleagues to solve them. Honest feedback attends to the need for straight commentary on the ongoing interaction, while encouragement calls on the individual to put forth the mind's best work. There are particular strategies that are useful in encouraging others to use and extend their own strengths. These strategies are not always appropriate, but, depending on the context, may stimulate positive actions by others.

Elaborate on the Reality Situation It is easy for educators to get discouraged. We often do not see the direct results of our labors. The more we know, the more we get in touch with our ignorance. For example, public education is under heavy attack in the popular press recently, focusing on what is being called a national crisis. Without minimizing the very real problems (public support being a major one) that education faces, it is possible to elaborate on the reality situation. That is, we need to be reminded of the great goals of universal education and equal access to opportunity we have set for public education in the United States. We can elaborate on how teachers are expected to be the babysitters, moral developers, tutors, mentors, and coaches of a whole generation, while mother and father are both working and unable to give much time to support the teachers' expanded role. Teachers tend to get hooked by criticism and become defensive. It is much more helpful for supervisors to elaborate the reality situation each teacher faces. If teachers feel the supervisor knows what risks they are taking in using new materials, experimenting with new strategies, and inventing new behaviors, they are more likely to respond positively to the challenges of their profession.

Specify Others' Strengths Likewise, when you have a choice, always go for the gold. If you are going to work with teachers, stressing the teacher's strengths will get you farther. You will get even farther if you can encourage teachers to pool their strengths and collaborate. Supporting collaboration multiplies the effect.

Express Respect for Efforts Since we know there is little an adult can do about his or her previous history, achievement, and opportunities, it makes little sense for a supervisor to focus on such things that teachers cannot change. Better to have the teachers know of your respect for their here-and-now efforts. Efforts to change do make a difference. The supervisor who expresses his or her respect for teachers' efforts is encouraging the best teachers can do.

Show Interest in What's Happening Now Finally, the supervisor can show interest in what's happening now. No matter how great the past or how promising the future, it is the present in which we live and work. The ultimate personal regard we can offer another person is to spend time with him or her. The best encouragement, therefore, is involvement in the here-and-now concerns of teachers. This is easier to say than to do. In interactions between two adults there are no guarantees of success, no protection of previous achievement, and no certainty of choices. That is why Robert Frost's poem about the "road not taken" seems so compelling. We constantly make choices that shape our future. The supervisor exerts his or her best influences in the encouragement of here-and-now participation in what is happening.

Mastery Test

OBJECTIVE 7 TO DEFINE AND RECOGNIZE *FACILITATING BEHAVIORS* IN A HELPING RELATIONSHIP

1. Define honest feedback.
2. Define encouragement.

For questions 3–10 indicate "yes or no" to show which of the statements are and which are not examples of encouragement.

3. "You can do it, Burt! If I can do it certainly you can do it."
4. "As they say, 'A stitch in time, saves nine.' So keep up the good work!"
5. "I know you don't like to do this task, but trust me, you'll learn a lot by the time you are finished."
6. "If you will finish the evaluation reports by Tuesday, I'll see that you get your new materials for next term on time."
7. "When you asked that question at the meeting, it showed a lot of guts. I admire that."
8. "Having to change classes in the middle of the school year is hard to do. I'm amazed that the transition went as smoothly as it did."
9. "That's not a very big job; it's just an important job. So I'm sure you will get it done."
10. "I want to learn more about how you motivate your students to work independently on their math problems. Can I sit in this week to watch?"

Answer Key

Mastery Test, Objective 7

1. Honest feedback responds to another person in an ongoing relationship with descriptive statements dealing with the here-and-now reality, neither overstating nor understating the reality situation, *and* matching the emotional level of intensity that the other person seems to be experiencing.
2. Encouragement is a convincing demonstration that the other person has resources and options which can be applied to the solution of problems and the achievement of goals. As a skill, encouragement fosters a person's self-esteem, which include feelings of belonging,

competence, and worth. The specific action most often associated with encouragement is descriptive praise, an open describing of the other's action, coupled with how the speaker feels about it.

Statements 3, 4, 5, 6, and 9 are not examples of encouragement.
Statements 7, 8, and 10 are examples of encouragement.

Your Turn

Role play and practice of school-context vignette

In groups of three, participants are invited to choose among the following three roles:

The teacher

The supervisor

The process observer

After reading the situational vignette, the teacher will maintain the perspective of one seeking help from the supervisor. The person role playing the supervisor will call on his or her repertoire of interpersonal skills, including attending, responding, and facilitating, to offer help. Dialogue continues until the teacher and the supervisor reach the problem-solving stage. The observer makes actual or mental notes to review the interaction at the end of the simulation, giving feedback to the supervisor. After one simulation is complete, the group can switch roles and read the second vignette, and so forth, until all participants have taken each role.

Vignette 1: Josephine is a capable teacher, yet her self-esteem is so low that she constantly discounts her own competence. In meetings and in the faculty lounge, Josephine often makes fun of herself as being stupid, or a klutz. When offered opportunities to have time off for in-service activities, Josephine refuses saying that she has all that she can handle just keeping up. As the supervisor, you have asked Josephine about what is going on. Josephine isn't sure that there is a problem. What does the supervisor say and how will the "helping" conversation go?

Vignette 2: This morning several students told Bill, a fifth-grade teacher under your supervision, that on the way to school they had their lunch money taken from them by force. Bill comes to the supervisor and says that this has happened before and nothing has been done about it. He is upset and says, "How can anyone teach in an environment of violence and disregard for personal morality?" As the supervisor, what do you say and how does the "helping" conversation go?

Vignette 3: Jenifer is a new high school English teacher. She has the "low" classes for basic English courses. She is overwhelmed by the fact that the majority of her students are reading below grade level. She comes to you for help. At this point, halfway through the school year, she does not see any chance to finish the required material in her classes. She says to you, "How can I teach if the students are not capable of doing the assignments?" As Jenifer's supervisor, what do you say and how does the "helping" conversation go?

REFERENCES

Adler, A. *The Individual Psychology of Alfred Adler* (edited by H. L. Ansbacher and R. R. Ansbacher). New York: Basic books, 1956.

Bartky, J.A. *Supervision as Human Relations*. Boston: D. C. Heath, 1953.

Berman, L.M., and M.L. Usery. *Personalized Supervision: Sources and Insights*. Washington, D.C.: Association for Supervision and Curriculum Development, NEA, 1966.

Burton, W.H., and L.J. Brueckner. *Supervision, A Social Process*, 3d ed. New York: Appleton-Century-Crofts, 1955.

Cross, K.P. *Adults as Learners*. San Francisco: Jossey-Bass, 1981.

DeCharms, Richard. *Enhancing Motivation: Change in the Classroom*. N.Y.: Irvington, Publishers 1976.

Egan, G. *Interpersonal Living. A Skills/Contract Approach to Human Relations Training in Groups.* Monterey, Calif.: Brooks/Cole, 1976.

Flanders, N.A. "Teacher Influences, Pupil Attitudes, and Achievement." *Cooperative Research Monograph,* No. 12. Washington, D.C.: U.S. Government Printing Office, 1965.

Felker, D.W. *Building Positive Self-concepts.* Minneapolis: Burgess Publishing, 1974.

Gazda, G.M. "Systematic Human Relations Training in Teacher Preparation and Inservice Education." Journal of Research and Development in Education, vol. 4, no. 2 (1971):45–51.

Gist, A.S. *Elementary School Supervision.* New York: Scribner's, 1926.

Goldhammer, R. *Clinical Supervision: Special Methods for the Supervision of Teachers.* New York: Holt, Rinehart and Winston, 1969.

Gordon, S. *Psychology for You.* New York: Oxford, 1974.

Gordon, T. *T. E. T.: Teacher Effectiveness Training.* New York: Peter H. Wyden, 1974.

Kagan, N.I. *Interpersonal Process Recall: A Method of Influencing Human Interaction.* Mason, Mich.: Mason Media, 1976.

Knowles, M. *The Adult Learner: A Neglected Species,* 2d ed. Houston: Gulf, 1973.

———. *The Modern Practice of Adult Education: From Pedagogy to Andragogy,* revised and updated. Chicago: Follett, 1980.

Kyte, G.C. *Problems in School Supervision.* Boston: Houghton Mifflin, 1931.

McClelland, D.C., "Toward a Theory of Motive Acquisition," *American Psychologist,* vol. 20, no. 2 (1965):321–333.

McNeil, L.M., "Negotiating Classroom Knowledge: Beyond Achievement and Socialization." Occasional papers. Madison, Wisc.: Wisconsin Center for Public Policy, 1980.

Noller, R.B., S.J. Parnes, and A.M. Biondi, *Creative Actionbook.* New York: Scribner, 1976.

Rogers, C.R. "The Interpersonal Relationship: The Core of Guidance." *Harvard Educational Review,* vol. 32, no. 4 (Fall 1962):416–29.

Schwab, J.J. "The Concept of the Structure of a Discipline." In *Conflicting Conceptions of Curriculum,* edited by Elliot W. Eisner and Elizabeth Vallance. Berkeley, Calif.: McCutchan, 1974, pp. 162–175.

Sergiovanni, T.J., and Robert J. Starratt. *Emerging Patterns of Supervision: Human Perspectives.* New York: McGraw-Hill, 1971.

———. *Supervision Human Perspectives,* 2d ed. New York: McGraw-Hill, 1979.

Shafer, H.T., chairman, ASCD Commission on Problems of Supervisors and Curriculum Workers. *The Supervisor: New Demands New Dimensions.* Washington, D.C.: Association for Supervision and Curriculum Development, NEA, 1969.

Unruh, A., and Harold E. Turner. *Supervision for Change and Innovation.* Boston: Houghton Mifflin, 1970.

Wallen, J.L. "Developing Effective Interpersonal Communication." In *Communicating Interpersonally,* edited by R.W. Pace, B.D. Peterson, and T.R. Radcliff. Columbus, Ohio: Charles E. Merrill, 1973.

Weiner, B. "A Theory of Motivation for Some Classroom Experiences," *Journal of Educational Psychology,* vol. 71 (1979):3–25.

ADDITIONAL READING LIST

Burke, J.B., and Kagan, N.I. *Influencing Human Interaction in Public Schools, Studies of IPR Effectiveness as an Inservice Teacher Training Program* (NIMH Final Report). East Lansing, Mich.: College of Education, Michigan State University, 1976.

Burke, J.B. "Communicating with Students," In D. Orlosky (ed.), *Introduction to Education.* Columbus, Ohio: Charles Merrill & Co., 1982.

Carkhuff, R. *Helping and Human Relations: A Primer for Lay and Professional Helpers* (vol. I). New York: Holt, Rinehart, and Winston, 1962.

Hamachek, D.E., *Encounters with Others, Interpersonal Relationships and You.* New York: Holt, Rinehart and Winston, 1982.

Luft, J. *Of Human Interaction.* Palo Alto, Calif.: National Books, 1969.

LEADERSHIP AND MOTIVATION 10

Joyce Putnam

OBJECTIVE 1 To describe the key elements of the cooperative professional development model for supervisory leadership including the focusing question and desired outcome of each

OBJECTIVE 2 To describe the supervisor's human relations resources and the steps and rationale for Stage I of the cooperative professional development model

OBJECTIVE 3 To describe the task of assessment, its needed resources, and its consequences in Stage II of the cooperative professional development model

OBJECTIVE 4 To describe the steps and rationale of Stage III of the cooperative professional development model and to identify the supervisory human relations skills necessary to implement the stage

OBJECTIVE 5 To specify the necessary knowledge about motivation theory to implement the cooperative professional development model

OBJECTIVE 6 To specify supervisory leadership knowledge and skills necessary to implement the cooperative professional development model

OBJECTIVE 7 To apply the cooperative professional development model to a case study of individual teacher problems

OBJECTIVE 8 To apply the cooperative professional development model to a case study of a group of teachers and their needs

INTRODUCTION

This chapter incorporates and extends the knowledge about human relations skills presented in Chapter 9 as it applies specifically to supervisory leadership. As concluded in Chapter 9, exercising supervisory leadership solves problems of educational practice and gives the teaching staff positive self-esteem.

Leadership is described in a variety of ways. For example, Hersey, Blanchard, and Natemeyer (1979) define leadership "as the process of influencing the activities of an individual or a group in efforts toward goal accomplishment." In *Management of Organization Behavior: Utilizing Human Resources*, Hersey and Blanchard (1977) define two concepts that are related to the definition of leadership. These two concepts, which are related to the leader's role, are *task behavior* and *relationship behavior*. Task behavior is described as the amount of one-way telling communication from the leader to the follower. This telling behavior includes explaining what each follower is to do, when it is to be done, and how the task is to be accomplished. The second concept, relationship behavior, is described as the extent a leader engages in two-way communication and includes providing socioemotional support, psychological strokes, and facilitating behaviors. How do these two concepts relate to the role of the instructional supervisor? To help understand this, first we will review the perspectives of many teachers today.

The instructional supervisor and, in most cases, in-service education experiences are viewed as someone (or something) that does something to someone else. The conceptual problem this poses rests upon the discrepancy between the instructional supervisor's perception of what another needs to know or do and the teacher's notion of what he or she needs. As one teacher put it, "Help is opinionated." Many teachers want help. In fact, they are encouraged to ask for help. Helping becomes problematic by hiding the political power implied in being a helper. Teachers are presumed to need help because they are seen as somehow being deficient, lacking some skill or competency, like a disease needing a cure. To define leadership as it is currently viewed by most people is to establish superior and subordinate roles, to make it clear who gives orders and who takes them, and to justify in advance the inhibitions placed upon the subordinate class. Schwab (1974) has explained that people do not want to be helped for their own sake because of the implication that the one who is helped is somehow not okay. An analysis of where requests for in-services originate and where requests to the instructional supervisor originate indicates that the supervisor role is frequently viewed as the expert who has the answers for others.

Teachers are under tremendous pressures as they are expected to carry out the burden of adaptation and educational change. Policy makers have assumed that, given a noble cause, or the right new program, or the text that will make life easier, teachers will adjust readily and willingly. Yet, the economic stringencies of these times and the changing pattern of school staffing are taking their toll. The mean age of teachers in schools is steadily rising, which results in a loss of youthful replacement on faculties, along with their energy, idealism, and excitement. Nevertheless, teachers are not without interest in their own professional development. Nor are teachers without commitment to their students' achievement and growth. Teachers do need the time for authentic reflection and the room to be creative. As Paulo Freire (1980) has commented, "Authentic reflection cannot exist apart from action." Teachers themselves must act to transform the concrete reality of schools and, thereby, create the future of their profession. Given the perspective described above, the major function of the supervisor's role as a leader as presented in this chapter is one of influence and support rather than of power.

The definition of leadership and the concepts of task and relationship behavior presented earlier are helpful in understanding the role of the instructional supervisor as illustrated in this chapter. First, the instructional supervisor must understand the goals or missions of the district and the goals of the individual and/or group with whom he or she is working. The supervisor must then be able to communicate the relationship of the individual or group goals to the goals of a given district. It is the supervisor's responsibility to communicate his or her perceptions of conflicts between sets of goals and to facilitate resolution in those conflicts. The supervisor can work quickly to establish or support already existing individual internal motivation and ownership of the problems needing resolution.

A supervisor of instruction must possess the leadership knowledge and skills necessary to participate successfully and provide leadership to others in solving problems of practice. In addition, problem solving and motivational skills that facilitate personal development and promote a sense or feeling of belonging, competence, and personal worth are necessary . This chapter shows how these important supervisory tasks may be accomplished by the use of a model of leadership called the Cooperative Professional Development Model for Supervisory Leadership.

The model for cooperative professional development is based on data collected from actual professional development experiences that were carried out during 10 years of Teacher Corps–sponsored projects (Barnes and Putnam, 1981; Wanous, 1981). Data from the studies indicate that the teachers and administrators who participated in these projects felt as though something significant had happened in their professional experiences. They reported changes in their perceptions about, and ability to discuss, problems of professional practice. They expressed positive feeling about themselves as particpants in the process. They felt that something was accomplished and that they had a direct hand in the achievements, and were willing to share with nonparticipating colleagues what they had learned.

OBJECTIVE 1 TO DESCRIBE THE KEY ELEMENTS OF THE COOPERATIVE PROFESSIONAL DEVELOPMENT MODEL OF SUPERVISORY LEADERSHIP, INCLUDING THE FOCUSING QUESTION AND DESIRED OUTCOME OF EACH

The supervisor of instruction has the same problem everyone has who seeks to be of help to another person or group of people. That problem is to identify correctly what is going on. This is often difficult because of the assumptions we make about what we are experiencing. Instead of seeing that our statements about a given event are actually interpretations of that event, we generally assume that we are describing what is *really* happening. For example, a teacher may forget to say hello when passing us in the hallway, and we may assume that he is angry at us for some reason when actually he is very busy or didn't see us. To avoid making *unwarranted assumptions* it is crucial to test publicly our inferences about events. The Cooperative Professional Develpment Model turns out to be a practical variation of theoretical problem solving (see for example, Parnes, 1975) or inquiry (see for example, Argyris, 1982) models. This model incorporates previous supervisor theory development, as in the work on clinical supervision (Sergiovanni and Starratt, 1971) and human relations theory in supervision (Berman and Usery, 1966; Bartky, 1953; Goldhammer, 1969). Also see: Noler, Parnes, and Biondi (1976) who describe a five-step plan similiar to the model presented here. Its problem is that it fails to take as seriously the interaction with the social context that this model of supervisory leadership does. Their model goes: (1) Fact finding, (2) Problem finding, (3) Idea finding, (4) Solution finding, and (5) Acceptance finding. All of these theories of supervision support a leadership strategy that responds to genuine human needs. The

Cooperative Professional Development Model is constructed out of three simple actions:

- Identification
- Assessment
- Intervention

These actions are sequential stages for exercising leadership and each has a specific developmental purpose. Each action is considered a task and has its corresponding question and set of steps for accomplishing it. In the following sections of this chapter, we will examine each step in each action stage in detail, giving examples of its rationale and application. Here, the goal is to specify and describe the stage sequence. When the actions are sequenced in stages they look like this:

Stage I: *Task:* Identification
Question: What is the problem/phenomenon with which we are dealing?

Stage II: *Task:* Assessment
Question: What do we know about this problem/phenomenon?

Stage III: *Task:* Intervention
Question: What can we do to change the conditions for the better?

Stage I of this supervisory leadership model is the process used to identify the problem/phenomenon that the supervisor, teachers, and others want to resolve. As with our example of the supervisor and teacher passing in the school hall, people often fail to identify what is actually going on in a given situation. In schools the difficulty can be compounded by the fact that supervisors are directly involved and affected by the context in which they work. Others do have an impact on them and it is difficult to separate the personal desire to be rid of a problem from the need to solve a problem in such a way that people and the system are helped. Effective leadership begins with the task of identifying the real problem or phenomenon confronting individuals or groups. At times we approach problems by blaming others for the difficulties or by stating the predicaments in impossible terms. It is easy to point to others and say, "If they would only be more dedicated to their job we wouldn't have this problem." The person with a problem might say, "If we had the support we deserve, then our job would be easier." The difficulty with looking for someone to blame is that it does not help. The first principle of a helping relationship is to begin where we are, not where we are "supposed to be." Thus, by asking the following questions the supervisor and other participants can determine the phenomenon with which they are dealing.

- What perceptions does each member have of this situation?
- What are the current difficulties?
- What concerns, interests, and problems are expressed?
- Which concerns have the highest priority to the group or system?

These questions require that the supervisor interact directly and openly with all the teachers and administrators involved in the situation.

Knowing what is happening requires careful exploration of the full range of concerns. Again, the difficulty of describing what people really want to happen comes from the often obscure relation between wants and needs. People may say they want one thing, yet they have not identified the need to which they are responding. The supervisor exercises leadership in sorting through the descriptive statements made about wants and needs. Premature identification of a problem statement can leave participants feeling alienated from the activity or problem resolution because they do not own the problem as theirs. One of the most famous examples of such a process of alienation was the creation of the new science materials in the 1960s. National commissions decided that teachers needed a new science curriculum to bring their teaching up to date with what was happening in various scientific fields. The American Association for the Advancement of Science (AAAS) materials were developed by university professors, and distributed by national outlets, and training workshops were offered on this "last word" on the teaching of science in schools. The teachers in many districts were given their materials and training to implement them. What happened? The teachers did not use them. With a few isolated exceptions, most of the expense and effort involved in creating the AAAS materials were wasted.

The Rand Corporation study of the years of federal funding of Title III innovation projects tells the same story. Those projects judged most successful, by the standards of permanent change and utility of results, were those that had a strong local leadership and involvement. From the beginning of those successful projects teachers in the particular school districts were involved in the definition, development, and implementation of the changed practice. Those projects that did not involve local personnel at every level and through all phases were the ones that disappeared after the funding period was over. The lesson is a powerful one for those seeking to exercise supervisory leadership; namely, the first stage of identification of problems involves *all participants and their several perspectives in the formulation of the focal problem.*

Stage II of supervisory leadership is the assessment of what is known about this problem. Given an initial problem definition, it is necessary for the success of any action that evolves to be based on the best knowledge available. The first step of the assessment involves the documentation of what is currently known about the problem at the local level. Second, a period of study of the problem ensues. Information is gathered from a variety of sources by the participants themselves.

As the supervisor and other participants gain information about their problem, the effective leaders structure a forum for sharing the knowledge. The sharing process itself involves participants with each other. As a result, they begin to see their fellow professionals as resources for their own growth and understanding. Thus, the third step of assessment is sharing new knowledge.

As people gain knowledge about the problem, those affected begin to use this new knowledge to refine the problem definition further. For this reason it is necessary that the initial problem statement identified in Stage I be treated as a tentative statement of the problem or phenomenon under study. New knowledge can change the perception of reality, so the supervisory leader must be prepared to facilitate refining the problem definition continuously based on new data.

After, and only after, sufficient study of the problem's knowledge base is accomplished, does the supervisor lead the group or individual to Stage III by asking, "What can be done to change the conditions for the better?" The task of intervention by now becomes a consequence of definition and study of the problem. From this perspective, whatever action is chosen to intervene into the system is chosen in context. The value of the intervention arising out of a specific context and knowledge base is that we avoid choosing actions that are simply available, but do not really fit. Sometimes people choose courses of action that are familiar, whether or not they are relevant or effective. For example, "Let's change the textbook for this course" is suggested simply because students are having reading problems. This does not mean that people intentionally choose counterproductive actions. Rather, a best-intention choice may be an inappropriate course of action when it is not anchored in a knowledge base related to the context.

What stops people from choosing actions relevant to contexts is often imbedded in personal value systems, habits, and even the conventional local system for "doing things certain ways." Without Stages I and II, intervention choices are almost guaranteed to fail. We cannot choose new actions if (1) we do not know the problem, (2) we do not know that we do not know, and (3) we have not confronted considerable data that ensure we will choose an appropriate course of action. Adults, in particular, do not learn new behaviors without the intention to change. Effective leadership involves helping to create the context in which people will develop the intentionality to choose appropriate behaviors. In the cooperative model the supervisor helps people to participate in the identification of problems (Stage I), creates a climate of assessment and study of the knowledge base of a problem (Stage II), and facilitates the generation of appropriate responses for problem resolutions (Stage III).

Mastery Test

OBJECTIVE 1 TO DESCRIBE THE KEY ELEMENTS OF THE COOPERATIVE PROFESSIONAL DEVELOPMENT MODEL FOR SUPERVISORY LEADERSHIP INCLUDING THE FOCUSING QUESTION AND DESIRED OUTCOMES

1. List the three stages/tasks of the leadership model discussed in this section in their proper sequence.
2. State a question that provides the focus for each stage and the related desired outcome.

Answer Key

Mastery Test, Objective 1

1. The key elements of the Cooperative Professional Development Model are:

   Stage I: Identification
   Stage II: Assessment
   Stage III: Intervention

(These stages are sequential in the development of professional response to problems.)

2. The three focusing questions and the desired related outcomes are:

   A. Stage I: Identification
      The question: What is the problem or phenomenon with which we are dealing?
      The outcome: Responses to the questions provide a means for people to communicate and clarify for themselves and others.

   B. Stage II: Assessment
      The question: What do we know about this problem or phenomenon?
      The outcome: Responses to the question provide a means to open the door for explanation of information within the context of problem definition.

   C. Stage III: Intervention
      The question: What can we do to change the conditions for the better?
      The outcome: Responses to the question provide a means for identifying worthwhile alternatives and developing an ownership commitment for the changes.

OBJECTIVE 2 TO DESCRIBE THE SUPERVISOR'S HUMAN RELATIONS RESOURCES AND THE STEPS AND RATIONALE FOR STAGE I OF THE COOPERATIVE PROFESSIONAL DEVELOPMENT MODEL

The major task in Stage I involves the identification of a problem statement that all participants agree represents their own as well as the group's statement of concern. This stage incorporates two steps:

Step 1: Identify concerns

Step 2: Develop an acceptable, tentative problem statement

The identification process of Stage I is similar to a teacher's explorations with a student who has some kind of problem. The teacher does not assume that he can read the student's mind. Following Gordon's process of open-ended explorations through the use of active listening and I-statements, the teacher seeks a mutual understanding with the student. They work together to bring a concern into focus. Active listening and verbalizations of inferences about a person's concern eventually brings clarity to what may have been a jumble of concerns, or perhaps a premature commitment to a single theory about one's own or another's problem. An example of the workings of the first stage/task of the Cooperative Professional Development Model is the best way to illustrate the process.

A school district decided that they had a problem with students' reading development. Both teachers and administrators wanted to do something about the problem, which was illustrated by low assessment scores and not confined to any particular levels. It seemed to many that the problem in this district was obvious. However, by taking Stage I of the model seriously, it was possible to explore the nature of the problem adequately. The supervisor assigned to handle this problem began with the desire of the educators and the community to "do something about reading." By actively listening to all parties, the supervisor discovered that various parties had different impressions and assumptions about the nature of the problem and its solution.

Secondary teachers and administrators felt frustrated because their students couldn't read textbook assignments. They blamed the elementary teachers and wanted them to do a better job teaching reading. The secondary teachers' assumption could be summarized by this simple diagnosis and prescription: If elementary teachers were doing the job they were supposed to do—teaching children to read—then secondary teachers wouldn't have a problem with students not being able to keep up with their secondary reading assignments. In essence, the secondary teachers accused the elementary teachers of being the cause of the problem. The feelings the secondary teachers expressed included frustration in being held accountable for things their students were not prepared to learn.

The elementary teachers, on the other hand, had been struggling with their own assumptions about the nature of the reading problems. They felt that they had invested years of time and effort in developing a reading management system that was ignored by secondary level teachers. They said it was their observation that once students reached the secondary level their needs were not treated individually. They said they felt defensive and were tired of being blamed rather than supported. Thus, the elementary teachers placed a good deal of the blame for the problems on the secondary teachers who did not use the individualized data on student reading performance developed by the elementary teachers.

Parents in the group tended to express the same point of view that the elementary teachers communicated. The parents communicated the feeling that they felt they were left out of involvement and uninformed once their children reached junior or senior high school.

The students said the problem was uninteresting teaching and/or content. They said students who really needed special help received it. Students who needed help at special times could only get the help if teachers would help at noon or before or after school. The feelings the students shared were related to their perception that on a regular basis no one listened to them.

Parents, students, and teachers in the district held firmly to their inferences about the causes of the problem. What was needed was for each role group to test their inferences in the context of cooperative explorations. The supervisor met with individuals and groups until a statement was developed in as objective a perspective as possible. The final discussion took the form of reaching consensus on a statement of the problem. The supervisor was firm about not allowing statements of solution to take the place of statements about the problem. During these discussions the participants became aware of unstated assumptions, beliefs, and knowledge upon which the various role groups made their statements. The problem statement that the total group finally agreed upon was: Some of the secondary-level students are having problems reading their textbook assignments. There seems to be little communication between elementary and secondary educators about specific students' needs and abilities.

The supervisor had started with everyone's desire to "do something about the reading problem," but quickly discovered that there were many different assumptions about the nature of the problem. Only after the range of assumptions were tested publicly in a cooperative context was an adequate or workable statement of the actual problem possible.

Exercising leadership in this cooperative model requires the supervisor to draw on various human relation skills discussed in Chapter 9. Specifically, the supervisor organizes the group of participants in a context of safety and openness. Participants need to feel that they belong to the group and are being heard without threat of personal or professional jeopardy. The supervisor enhances the process by modeling self-disclosure skills, including I-statements. Actively listening to each participant's views includes paraphrasing and clarifying individual statements. The supervisor questions the participants in a nonevaluative manner, seeking to synthesize the range of views into a tentative hypothesis about the nature of the problem upon which all participants can agree.

The consequences of using these human relations skills on the participants is that they sense they have contributed to the formation of the problem statement. The individuals develop a group sense of participation and *can focus on talk about the problem rather than debate about solutions*. Premature focus on solutions often involves defending idiosyncratic solutions previously tried in other contexts. Such "canned" solutions can rarely be applied directly to new problems. In fact, the very act of holding out for one's pet solution can hinder one from seeing clearly the current phenomenon with which the group must deal. This is a difficult task for the supervisor because people sometimes tie up their personal credibiltiy with past performances in solving problems. If the supervisor is interested in helping the group learn new actions in solving new problems, then he or she must focus on creating conditions that enable individuals and systems to continue to learn (see Argyris, 1982, p. 160). Group processing of a tentative problem statement suspends the impulse to rely on previous strategies or actions.

In the case of the school district illustration, Stage I: Identification Process moved people away from a narrow focus on "what needed to be done." Secondary teachers stopped insisting that elementary teachers were at fault, and vice versa. The group accepted a preliminary definition of the problem as student difficulty in reading textbook material and lack of K–12 teacher communication.

Table 10.1 illustrates the relationship of the stage, task, focusing question, and steps in the supervisor's role in Stage 1.

TABLE 10.1 Stage I Sequence

Stage	*Task*	*Focusing Question*	*Steps*	*Supervisor Role*
I	Identification	What is the problem/ phenomenon with which we are dealing?	1. Identify interest, concerns and/or dissonance occurring in participants experience	a. Call groups together b. Reflect observations c. Elicit information from all participants d. Actively listen/paraphrase speakers' contributions; communicate both feelings and cognitive information you have heard e. Ask clarifying questions f. Make statements that link commonalities among the speakers (synthesize) g. Make statements that illustrate key differences among participants
			2. Identify the problem embedded in participants concerns by public testing of the inferences of all participants and develop a tentative problem statement	a. Use structured strategy or group discussion for reaching a consensus agreement on a statement b. Use language of participants when writing down the statement c. Facilitate keeping discussion open until everyone really agrees on statement

Mastery Test

OBJECTIVE 2 TO DESCRIBE THE SUPERVISOR'S HUMAN RELATIONS RESOURCES AND THE STEPS AND RATIONALE OF STAGE I OF THE COOPERATIVE PROFESSIONAL DEVELOPMENT MODEL

1. What are the task and the step sequence for Stage I?
2. What knowledge, attitudes, and skills are required in order for the supervisor to implement the steps in Stage I?
3. What are the human relations consequences of the steps of Stage I on the participating teachers?

Answer Key

Mastery Test, Objective 2

1. *Task:* Identification

   Step 1: Identify participants interests, and/or dissonance

   Step 2: Identify problem and develop a problem statement

2. Group organizing skills

   Self-disclosure skill (congruence)

   Active listening skill: open-ended explanation, paraphrasing/clarifying focus on effect

   Questioning/probing skills linked to organization and synthesis skills, including hypothesis formation (tentative)

3. All participants feel they are heard and belong to the group. In fact, supervisor understands all participants perspectives. Participants sense their contribution to formulating a problem statement. Participants talk about the problem instead of arguing about solutions without a clear understanding of the nature of the problem.

OBJECTIVE 3 TO DESCRIBE THE TASK OF ASSESSMENT, ITS NEEDED RESOURCES, AND ITS CONSEQUENCES IN STAGE II OF THE COOPERATIVE PROFESSIONAL DEVELOPMENT MODEL

After a group has a working, tentative problem statement, they can turn to the Stage II task: assessment of the problem. In the second task the supervisor helps the group examine the question, What do we know about this problem? Problems exist in contexts and there are often reasons embedded in the organizational system for the counterproductive behaviors that nourish the problem. This task opens up for inspection the organizational and contextual factors that contribute to the problem. For example, teachers are isolated from each other within schools and, especially, between schools. In our example of the districtwide reading problem it is not surprising that the teachers found a communication problem between the elementary and secondary school teachers. An example of an organizational structure problem can be found in teacher evaluation practices. Highly individualistic evaluations perpetuate the frustration teachers feel for being held accountable for consequences they did not wholly create. Again, it is not a surprise to find that the teachers in our example were frustrated with student reading levels.

This phenomenon has been described by Argyris (1982, p. 459) as "programmed incompetence," by which he means the ways we are informed by contextual influences both to maintain counterproductive practices and to be blinded to the dysfunctionalities of these practices. This does not mean that people intend to err in their professional behavior. Rather, the best of intentions are thwarted by errors about which we are unaware. What the supervisor must deal with are the designs in teachers' heads that produce counterproductive practices. Once a problem has been identified, leadership is exercised in the task of assessment: What do the participants know about the problem? The question implies that the participants know a lot, but possibly are not aware of everything. Raising awareness is a subtle and demanding task that requires the supervisor to respect group participants as adult learners.

As Chapter 9 pointed out, adult learners are characterized as needing to participate in the process of assessing their own learning goals. The supervisor leads, but does not program the assessment process with preconceived content. The exploration of current and needed knowledge must be real, or the teachers will experience it as another set of "lay ons" or "ought tos," of which they already have too many. The last thing a group of in-service teachers needs is to perceive another "innovative practice" about which they should feel guilty for not doing. Real knowledge, however, is always useful. In Stage II of the Cooperative Professional Development Model the supervisor creates an environment for the task of assessment in three steps:

Step 1: Assess current knowledge

Step 2: Study and share findings

Step 3: Restate the problem

Let's return to the example of the school district's reading problem. By Stage II the supervisor created an atmosphere of mutuality so that participants could investigate what types of programs and resources for reading instruction were already available in the district. Many resources were identified. Many individuals and groups of teachers were found to have made heavy investments in improving the reading ability of pupils. The participants shared their explorations with each other and, as a group, organized their new credible data into three areas for further study. The first area emphasized those teaching strategies that seemed most successful in helping students who were missing critical elementary reading objectives. The second area focused on seeking an understanding of reading from a systematic perspective. For the teachers this area seemed so confusing that there was room to doubt whether anyone knew what to do about anything in organizing reading instruction in a systematic manner. The third area was the major concern of the secondary level teachers, namely, how to teach reading in the content areas.

In order to help the group in the first step of assessing the current knowledge of the problem, the supervisor brought to the process of assessment certain knowledge, attitudes, and skills. In context the supervisor had to know the human and commercial resources available in the building and district. Respect for the participants as adult learners was expressed in open-ended–exploration skills and a willingness to give honest feedback to participants in the process of assessing what they know and do not know. The use of such human relations skills reduces the frustration of teachers at being "in the dark" about resources available to help them. This use of human relations skills also can increase dramatically the potential range of responses to problems, an essential feature, as we shall see, in Stage III intervention strategy. Knowledge of what is already occurring also reduces the temptation "to reinvent the wheel," that is, to duplicate the effort and expense of existing efforts.

The second step of the Stage II was to study and identify needed information about reading instruction and to share findings. Each role group participated in data collection as was realistic, given their other responsibilities. Reading experts at a nearby university helped in the review of literature (research findings, evaluation studies, and theoretical and practical suggestions). Resource personnel in the district were drawn into the process through greater involvement with the participants as they struggled to understand the scope and definition of their task. New information is acquired during this step of the process, which makes it possible to accept varying views. To the uninformed, the conflict among reading experts appeared as though nobody knew the "right" answer to a given problem about reading instruction. So without increased understanding of the data about reading and theoretical discussions of this particular educational issue, teachers could assume a relativist position: "Everyone has a right to his or her own opinion." New information gained in this step helped participants to account for the multiple perspectives of the theoretical and research literature. It further helped to eliminate simplistic inferences as the data were shared. For example, the assumption "secondary teachers don't care about students as individuals" could not be maintained by the end of the study. Nor did secondary teachers continue to believe elementary teachers were not doing their jobs.

The supervisor needs to have sufficient time available for himself or herself and for others in the group to study the problem thoroughly. Also, the skill to find and analyze appropriate resources must be available to the group. The supervisor may not personally possess the required skills, but the resources must be available. Part of the study process in this model is sharing relevant information as it develops. There are not many models of cooperation and openness in our society. Controlling information is the usual pattern of behavior (see McNeil, 1980). What is personally known is used typically by some people as private power maneuvers. The effective supervisor, therefore, must have the group leadership skills to motivate the sharing of information as a positive and rewarding activity.

The consequences of such leadership on the group participants are that they see the supervisor as a valuable colleague who is willing to do his or her job while others do theirs. Gradually, a group will develop a sense of participating in a common endeavor and gain personal satisfaction from a new source of identify and self-worth. When people see others as resources for personal growth, rather than as competitors for scarce recognition, powerful forces for productivity are released.

The third step in the assessment stage is the restatement of the problem. In this step consensus is reached on a new wording of the problem statement. As a result of the study and discussions in the previous step participants will generally agree that they no longer find the first problem statement as helpful as it could be. When each role group shared a new perspective they were eager to restate the nature of the problem, which they felt looked different from what the original phrasing of the concerns reflected. The group agreed that the new problem statement should be made in the form of a question: How do we address the issue of reading problems at all levels of schooling?

In restating the problem, the supervisor exercises his or her feedback skills and works with the group to achieve a parsimonious rewording. The result is a new problem statement characterized by group ownership in which a shared reality has been formed. On the basis of this new understanding of reality, the group is ready for Stage III: Intervention. Table 10.2 illustrates the relationship of the stage, task, focusing question, and steps of the supervisor's role in Stage II.

TABLE 10.2 Stage II Sequence

Stage	*Task*	*Focusing Question*	*Steps*	*Supervisor Role*
II	Assessment	What do we know about this problem/phenomenon?	1. Assess current knowledge	a. Organize with participants their knowledge into 3 categories: (1) what is known, (2) what is known and needs clarifying and (3) what is it we need to learn b. Volunteer to collect part of the needed information c. Facilitate each participant's agreement to do a specific task. Encourage give-and-take exchanges among members so that all feel they have something to do d. Give everyone materials they ask for
			2. Study and share findings	a. Complete your tasks b. Volunteer to take a teacher's class for an hour or two c. Check with other participants to see if you can assist them d. Organize a group meeting to share information

(Continued)

TABLE 10.2 *(Continued)*

Stage	*Task*	*Focusing Question*	*Steps*	*Supervisor Role*
				e. Link new information with previous knowledge, individual comments, and or problem statement
			3. Restate problem	a. Use structured strategy or group discussion b. Use language of participants in writing up the statement c. Facilitate keeping discussion open until everyone really agrees on a statement

Mastery Test

OBJECTIVE 3 TO DESCRIBE THE TASK OF ASSESSMENT, ITS NEEDED RESOURCES, AND ITS CONSEQUENCES IN STAGE II OF THE COOPERATIVE PROFESSIONAL DEVELOPMENT MODEL

1. What are the task and the step sequence for Stage II?
2. What knowledge, attitudes, and skills are required in order for the supervisor to implement the steps in Stage II?
3. What are the human relations consequences of the Stage II steps on the participating teachers?

Answer Key

Mastery Test, Objective 2

1. *Task:* Assessment

   Step 1: Assess current knowledge participants have about the problem/phenomenon

   Step 2: Study to gain needed information and share findings among participants

   Step 3: Restate the problem based on new data

2. Knowledge of building, district, human, and commercial resources

   Open-ended exploration skills

   Honest feedback skills

   Skill and time available to find, review, and synthesize research and other relevant materials

   Skill and time available for using permanent institutional support systems

   Group leadership skills for motivation of study and sharing of findings

   Honest feedback with analysis and synthesis skills

   Parsimony of expression

3. Reduces frustration, increases potential range of responses to problems (also reduces duplication of effort and expense)

Supervisor is seen as worthwhile, willing to do his job while others do theirs

Facilitates quick response and reduces frustration associated with institutional use of support systems

Increased sense of participating in common group endeavors

Results in a problem statement owned by the group, clearly understood: a shared reality

OBJECTIVE 4 TO DESCRIBE THE STEPS AND RATIONALE OF STAGE III OF THE COOPERATIVE PROFESSIONAL DEVELOPMENT MODEL AND TO IDENTIFY THE SUPERVISORY/HUMAN RELATIONS SKILLS NECESSARY TO IMPLEMENT THE STAGE

Once a problem has been defined and researched, it is then possible to ask: What can we do to change conditions for the better? Stage III of the Cooperative Professional Development Model is characterized by the task of intervention, which is a form of invention. Given the information created in Stages I and II, participants are ready to invent solutions to defined problems. We have identified four steps in the task of intervention.

Step 1: Generate potential responses and specify knowledge/skills necessary to carry out responses

Step 2: Choose, develop, and implement responses

Step 3: Evaluate outcomes

Step 4: Disseminate results to others

The role of the supervisor in Step 1 is to create an environment in which invention of a range of responses to problems is possible. People tend to link their own credibility with their competence (Argyris, 1982, see p. 161), so teachers may have a predilection to identify their personal esteem with previous solutions to problems. The supervisor helps by creating conditions of interaction in which a single solution can be set aside in favor of generating multiple solutions without challenging teachers' sense of competence. With each potential response to a problem the supervisor challenges the teachers to specify the needed knowledge and skills to implement a response. "If we were to choose to do that, what would we need to know in order to carry out this response?" Generating multiple solutions and testing the resources necessary to choose any one of them is what Argyris (1982) calls "double-loop" thinking. Single-loop thinking operates within the confines of established patterns of practice. "This is how things are done," or "In my experience, this is what should be done." There is a self-fulfilling prophecy to single-loop thinking that "seals" a person to the confines of his or her own perceptions of practice. Double-loop thinking challenges the validity of these perceptions by generating a variety of potential responses and the associated conditions and consequences of such actions.

Generating and assessing multiple options for problem resolution requires the supervisor's tolerance for dealing with a wide set of variables. Such tolerance can be developed within a context of commitment to the process of resolving problems. Openness and flexibility are often misunderstood as a lack of commitment, as in, "I'm still open on the subject (so I can afford to be flexible)." The popular notion seems to be that flexibility comes from distancing oneself from an issue. If one does not care which way an issue is resolved, so the thought goes, then one can be flexible. However, not caring creates a self-defeating cycle that communicates an activity is not important. We can distinguish between flexibility and openness, on the one hand, and commitment to the process of problem resolution, on the other. Both are necessary if a supervisor is to involve others who may very well possess a narrower range of tolerance for ambiguity. The consequence on the participants of supervision is their own commitment to problem resolution. When such commitment is generated, participants learn to manage dissonance in creative ways.

Step 2 of the intervention is the choice, development, and implementation of responses to problems. The supervisor must possess the skills to grapple within the context in which problems have been identified. As choices are made for responding to problems, the supervisor has to be close enough to the context to "muck around," or "get one's hands dirty" in the schools and classrooms of the participants. How this works is best illustrated by returning to our example of the district reading problem. The group had concluded that different levels required different strategies. The teachers at the elementary level chose to study the "critical objectives" that students most consistently missed and to develop teaching strategies to respond to pupils who had trouble with these objectives. A second strategy the elementary teachers chose was to seek parental cooperation in working with pupils who were below grade level. If they were to have a parental tutoring program in reading, what needed to be done? The supervisor and teachers had to grapple with the question, which turned out to be many questions. How do you contact parents? How are they to be organized? How do you communicate the pupil assessment data to parents who are nonprofessionals? How do you train the parents to do the tutoring? How do you evaluate the program?

At the secondary level a different approach was generated. First, the participants decided to stop sending students with reading problems to specialists and to start doing something about it themselves. This meant that secondary teachers had to learn about teaching reading in content areas. In order to acquire the necessary knowledge and skills, university and district-level experts in reading in the content areas were asked to help. The secondary group decided to use two models. One group of department chairs learned about teaching reading in their content area and used their new knowledge in their own classrooms. A second group of department chairs decided that they would learn the new knowledge and skills about teaching reading in the content areas and then teach other teachers how to apply these skills. (In terms of encouraging change in teaching strategies, the second method proved to be a superior design.)

The supervisor demonstrated the ability to grapple with the context by (1) accommodating to the environmental demands of the different schools and levels of instruction, and (2) encouraging participants' efforts as a positive tool for motivation. In this content, accommodation and encouragement meant refusing either to rescue or to blame the participating teachers. As discussed in Chapter 9, rescuing is doing for others what they can do for themselves. Blaming is finding a culprit or scapegoat to fault, thereby avoiding dealing directly with a problem.

As a result, the participants feel that they are competent, worthy, and belong to a problem-solving group. They experience satisfaction in accomplishment and possession of new resources.

Step 3 of the intervention task is the evaluation of outcomes. The supervisor helps participants to organize their data-collection and documentation procedures. Activities have consequences. If planned activities are to be evaluated, the consequences have to be carefully documented. Without the step-by-step collection of the action's outcomes, actions can appear, at best, serendipitous. In educational practice this is especially troublesome. Without data teachers cannot make connections between actions and outcomes, and thus cannot explain either success or failure. Without data analysis, teachers and administrators often feel powerless to change and, accordingly, discount their own importance in the scheme of things.

However, the effective supervisor helps teachers to collect and analyze the outcomes of their actions. This means a supervisor must be able to give and receive honest feedback. Honest feedback was discussed in Chapter 9; and here the application is a case in point. The supervisor neither "cleans up his/her message" to make it acceptable, nor exaggerates the content by "blowing it out of proportion." As a result, the teachers experience the implied respect for their competence to deal with reality. They feel they are making real contributions to improving the educational system when the consequences of actions are traced objectively.

The fourth and final step in the intervention task is dissemination. In Step 4, the supervisor's task is to help participants tell their story to other teachers and administrators. As a consequence, teachers will become teachers of teachers and fully functioning colleagues. Replications will occur and the study of problems of practice will be valued as opportunities for growth.

Communicating one's experiences to others has several benefits. First, other professionals can learn from their colleagues' experiences. Second, the process of preparing to communicate to other professionals helps clarify and structure one's own thinking about the personal experiences. And third, the preparation for a presentation helps teachers to organize their thoughts for future implementations of their practices.

Table 10.3 illustrates the relationship of the stage, task, focusing questions, steps in the supervisor's role in Stage III.

TABLE 10.3 Stage III Sequence

Stage	*Task*	*Focusing Question*	*Steps*	*Supervisor Role*
III	Intervention	What can we do to change the conditions for the better?	1. Generate potential responses and specify knowledge and skills necessary to carry out responses	a. Facilitate brainstorming session eliciting potential responses b. Ask questions to elicit what knowledge and skills would be necessary to carry out each potential response c. Link needed knowledge with assessment of what is known as completed in previous stage
			2. Choose, develop, and implement responses	a. Review each potential response; facilitate group interaction about the pros and cons of each response; encourage everyone to speak b. Identify a response(s) everyone can agree on. More than one strategy may be appropriate c. Write out steps and individual responsibilities for implementing plan and collecting evaluation data; include your tasks d. Do your tasks e. Ask others if you can do something to help them; do not do all of someone else's tasks; provide support by doing other things for them or doing parts of a task (get books from library, copy something, take classes)

(Continued)

TABLE 10.3 *(Continued)*

Stage	*Task*	*Focusing Question*	*Steps*	*Supervisor Role*
				f. Respond to any request for materials, information, or support g. Facilitate finding solutions to implementation problems
			3. Evaluate outcomes	a. Facilitate discussion-group sessions b. Elicit information from each participant; include planned-for information that was collected, observations, and feelings c. Share your information as other members do d. Facilitate reaching agreement on a statement concerning the experience e. Meet with group to discuss written statement until all points of view are included and the group agrees that statement reflects the experience f. Report is the product of the group. Have it copied and give to members within a week of last meeting
			4. Disseminate results to others	a. Facilitate a group discussion to identify and implement a plan to tell others about the experience Focus on keeping the options open b. Support a diverse response from participants c. Arrange for subsets or individuals to work with you and/or each other to write up a plan for telling others about the experience (see format for a plan) d. Communicate in formal setting your experience; invite members of your working group to attend if they like

Mastery Test

OBJECTIVE 4 TO DESCRIBE THE STEPS AND RATIONALE OF STAGE III OF THE COOPERATIVE PROFESSIONAL DEVELOPMENT MODEL AND TO IDENTIFY THE SUPERVISORY HUMAN RELATIONS SKILLS NECESSARY TO IMPLEMENT THE STAGE

1. What are the task and the step sequence for Stage III?
2. What human relation's resources does the supervisor bring to Stage III?
3. What are the human relations consequences of Stage III on in-service teachers?

Answer Key

Mastery Test, Objective 4

1. *Task:* Intervention

   Step 1: Generate potential responses and specify knowledge/skills necessary to carry out responses

   Step 2: Choose, develop, and implement responses

   Step 3: Evaluate response outcomes

   Step 4: Disseminate results to others

2. Ability to assess multiple variables: double-loop thinking; tolerance for dealing with a wide set of variables, linked with ability to work with others who may possess a narrower range of tolerance for ambiguity.

   Grappling with the context for development and implementation: accommodating to environmental demands (developing new schemes); refraining from rescuing and blaming, using encouragement.

   Organize data collection and documentation.

   Help teachers tell their story.

3. Participants commitment to problem resolution; managing dissonance in creative ways.

   Participants feel they are competent, worthy, and belong to problem-solving groups; experience satisfaction in accomplishment and feel they possess new resources.

   Participants sense having made a real change/impact; teachers who teach others follow through in classrooms and value this approach to problems of practice.

OBJECTIVE 5 TO SPECIFY THE NECESSARY KNOWLEDGE ABOUT MOTIVATION THEORY TO IMPLEMENT THE COOPERATIVE PROFESSIONAL DEVELOPMENT MODEL

Change can be an uncomfortable, even painful process. Leadership can be understood as helping people confront the need for change and then overcoming the pain of changing. Much has been learned about what motivates people to change, to grow, and to achieve. The effective supervisor needs to understand and use knowledge about motivation. The human drive for homeostasis (psychic balance) can keep people from facing difficulties, or it can be used as the force to overcome imbalance. Much depends upon the quality of leadership a supervisor offers.

The quality of leadership depends upon attention to motivation, about which there are three basic theories:

- Needs Theory
- Achievement Theory
- Attribution Theory

Abraham Maslow (1970) is most often connected with the creation of a theory of human needs. An unfulfilled need is a motivator calling up behaviors to satisfy the need. If a person is hungry, for example, behavior becomes increasingly focused on acquiring food until the need is satisfied. Maslow posited a hierarchy of needs, from low-level survival needs to high-level personal fulfillment needs. His hierarchy of needs is:

1. Physiological needs
2. Safety needs
3. Belonging or affiliation needs
4. Esteem needs
5. Self-actualization needs

At the lower levels of this list an individual strives for survival. The physiological and safety needs are the most powerful motivators, in that if they are not met, they will inhibit any other activity. This rule applies to the adult learner as well as to children. The supervisor must attend to such matters as breaks in long meetings and providing a safe and pleasant environment, if only to avoid resistance to tasks at hand that result from neglect of such fundamentals.

All humans have needs to belong to a group and to be recognized by others as a significant being. The supervisor who develops a strong sense of belonging to a professional group among participants in in-service activities taps one of the basic human drives and increases the motivation of participants to value the in-service activities. Directly related to belonging are esteem needs, or a sense of self-worth. People with low self-evaluations, need more external praise and support to risk participation in group activities. The supervisor can strengthen participants' commitment to in-service activities, if their self-worth is tied to those activities. This is one of the reasons why a supervisor must attend to the principles of group leadership discussed in Chapter 9. Each member of the group needs to feel he or she is affiliated with others and is an important contribution to the group's success.

The need for self-actualization is the highest level of Maslow's hierarchy. Self-actualization is the sense of achievement and competence that comes from fulfilling one's potential for growth and development in a given area of activity. The motivation associated with self-actualization is powerful, Maslow tells us, because it deals with deeply personal identity or "being needs." The self-actualizing drive can be understood as a propensity for "personal causation," as Richard de Charms (1968) calls it. This is the desire to have a sense of control over one's behavior, to be self-controlled rather than controlled by circumstances or by others. It is, therefore, crucial for the supervisor to involve participants in real activities in which they have direct contributions to make. Adult learners, especially, need to feel they are making real decisions that affect their own professional activities.

Achievement motivation theory was developed by David McClelland and others and distinguishes between the motives for success and the motives to avoid failure. If a person's motives for success are stronger than the need to avoid failure then the likelihood of risky new behavior is high. Since the need or motive to avoid failure is strong, the motivation for successful achievement often must be developed to overcome the tendency to avoid failure. McClelland (1965) suggests that there are four factors to attend to in developing motivation for achievement.

1. Clear definition of goals
2. Perception of self-improvement
3. Increasing responsibility taken for performance
4. Supportive social environment

These factors may be taken as guidelines for supervisory leadership. In implementing the three stage Model for Cooperative Professional Development, the supervisor has these four factors built into the steps. A clear definition of the problem statement makes the in-service a goal-directed activity. The study of needed knowledge and skills about the identified problem provides the experience of self-improvement. As teams tackle problem resolution strategies, they take on increasing responsibility for their performance. For example, the teachers in the example given stopped sending their problem students to experts to solve reading difficulties and started taking responsibility for remedial activities. Finally, the entire enterprise is conducted in an atmosphere of mutual support: "We are in this together." The support of social environment provided strong incentives for achievement.

Another dimension of motivation supervisors must consider are the attributions people give to explain success or failure. Weiner (1979) and others have developed attribution theory as a way to describe causal explanations of achievement. Weiner suggests that people explain their success or lack of success by using causal categories, such as ability, luck, or the degree of task difficulty. The point is that how someone thinks about the causes of success or failure affects his or her motivation to achieve. Locus of control is one variable to consider in attribution theory. Is the explanation of success/failure an internal cause (lack of effort) or external (difficulty of task)? People can control how much effort they put in an activity, but they cannot control the difficulty of the task. "I could have done it if I had worked as hard as you." Other times a person may consistently take on impossible tasks, in order to have built-in explanations for inevitable failures. "Nobody can change the system."

The supervisor of instruction needs to be sensitive to the ways teachers talk about their activities as clues to their motivational strategies. By and large, people tend to respond to rewarding activities. It is necessary to support effort at moderately difficult tasks so that the attribution for success can be for the individual's efforts. The belief that goals are accomplished through effort puts the responsibility and credit for achievement on the individual. Persistent effort that succeeds tends to increase an individual's motivation. The supervisor supports this perception by modeling the behavior and providing group support for individual effort.

Mastery Test

OBJECTIVE 5 TO SPECIFY THE NECESSARY KNOWLEDGE ABOUT MOTIVATION THEORY TO IMPLEMENT THE COOPERATIVE PROFESSIONAL DEVELOPMENT MODEL

1. Name the three theories of motivation discussed in this section.
2. List the five levels of Maslow's hierarchy of human needs.
3. Explain why self-actualization is labeled a "being need."
4. List four factors in enhancing achievement motivation.
5. What is the significance of causal explanations of achievement, according to Weiner?

Answer Key

Mastery Test, Objective 5

1. Maslow's Hierarchy of Human Needs

   Achievement Theory (McClelland)

   Attribution Theory (Weiner)

2. Physiological needs
   Safety needs
   Belonging or affiliation needs
   Esteem needs
   Self-actualization needs
3. Self-actualization is the sense of achievement and personal competence that comes from fulfilling one's potential and, thus, is associated with a sense of personal causation, being in control of oneself.
4. Clear definition of terms
   Perception of self-improvement
   Increasing responsibility taken for one's performance
   Supportive social environment
5. How someone thinks about the causes of success or failure affects his or her motivation to achieve.

OBJECTIVE 6 TO SPECIFY SUPERVISORY LEADERSHIP KNOWLEDGE AND SKILLS NECESSARY TO IMPLEMENT THE COOPERATIVE PROFESSIONAL DEVELOPMENT MODEL

The role of the supervisor as a leader is integrated into objectives two, three, and four. The knowledge and skills for the leadership role are presented in Table 10.4. Knowledge about effective leadership is crucial to the success of the supervisor. As stated in the introduction to this chapter, exercising supervisory leadership results in solving problems of educational practice and in the teaching staff possessing positive self-esteem. To be an effective leader the supervisor must view himself or herself as a member of the educational team of a given school building, grade level, or whatever the grouping for the given situation.

TABLE 10.4 Leadership Role Components

Personal Skills	*Knowledge*	*Skills*
The supervisor sees self as a member of a given faculty group trying to resolve some problem of practice	Knowledge of interpersonal communication and their effects	Interpersonal skills: active listening, exploration, and clarifying questions, including ability to empathize
	Knowledge of group dynamics	Ability to organize people and information, synthesize information and encourage others to participate
	Knowledge of problems of practice	Ability to provide information as a resource and response to need, not as an additional problem
	Knowledge of resources available to faculty	Ability to offer support and have it accepted
	Knowledge of problem-solving process	

The supervisor who views himself or herself as outside the group and its problems will have difficulty gaining acceptance from the group.

As a leader, the supervisor manages all of the organizational work of the group. This permits the other members to spend their group time on the heart of the problems and the tasks to be done. As the leader, the supervisor acts as a facilitator for the group's work, encouraging members to participate when they haven't been taking an active part, synthesizing information as it is presented by participants, pointing out similarities and differences among the various perspectives and suggestions, and keeping the group on-task and goal oriented. The supervisor as leader also provides information to the group relative to research findings, material, availability, personal expertise, and other kinds of available resources.

Table 10.4 is a synthesized version of the information presented in Chapters 9 and 10. It reflects the essential leadership qualities of the supervisor who implements the Cooperative Professional Development Model and thus solves problems of practice.

Mastery Test

OBJECTIVE 6 TO SPECIFY SUPERVISORY LEADERSHIP KNOWLEDGE AND SKILLS NECESSARY TO IMPLEMENT THE COOPERATIVE PROFESSIONAL DEVELOPMENT MODEL

1. List the five sets of knowledge necessary for supervisory leadership.
2. List four sets of skills necessary to providing successful supervisory leadership.

Answer Key

Mastery Test, Objective 6

1. The five sets of knowledge are:
   - Knowledge of interpersonal communicators and their effects
   - Knowledge of group dynamics
   - Knowledge of problems of practice
   - Knowledge of available resources
   - Knowledge of a problem-solving sequence
2. The four sets of skills necessary to successful supervisory leadership include:
   - Interpersonal skills, including ability to empathize
   - Ability to organize people and information, synthesize information, and encourage others to actively participate
   - Provide support and have it accepted
   - Provide materials and other resources

OBJECTIVE 7 TO APPLY THE COOPERATIVE PROFESSIONAL DEVELOPMENT MODEL TO A CASE STUDY OF INDIVIDUAL TEACHER PROBLEMS

You are asked to imagine that you are the supervisor in the following case. After reading the case of Ms. Green, you are to suggest how you would adapt the Cooperative Professional Development Model to this situation.

THE CASE OF MS. GREEN'S DISRUPTIVE CLASSROOM

Ms. Green is in the second year of her teaching career. She teaches junior high school social studies to five different classes and has one homeroom period at the beginning of the day. The school is racially mixed, in a low-socioeconomic status neighborhood. By the end of the first marking period it has become clear that there is a problem in Ms. Green's classes. She has taken up the policy of sending children to the principal's office for misbehavior. By November she is sending one to two students each class period for disciplinary action. The principal is annoyed. The parents in the community have called in complaints. Students are upset. And Ms. Green is apparently increasingly obsessed about "her situation." You are assigned from the school district office to supervise the instruction in this school as part of your duties as a curriculum consultant. You decide on the following procedure. First, you will visit Ms. Green's class. Second, you talk to all the parties in the case. You collect the following information:

Class observations Ms. Green threatens her students a lot, but rarely follows through with punishment until the noise level is high, and then she orders a student out of the room for disrupting the class. When Ms. Green does react to students she tends to overact, belittling them. Ms. Green seems to have little personal authority with the students. Most of her interaction with students is in giving orders and asking for answers to simple memory recall level of questions. Transitions are not handled well, with what seem to be conceptual gaps in the directions Ms. Green gives to her students. When these incidents occur, the students tend to take the opportunity to visit with one another socially.

Interviews

TEACHER (MS. GREEN): The students don't listen to me. They don't follow instructions. They won't behave in class and I blame the parents. I've sent messages home with students but it doesn't do anything. The kids still act up. There's a lot of racial tension in the building. But still the kids don't do their homework, they don't come prepared to learn. How can I teach, if they are not going to work at it?

PRINCIPAL: Ms. Green upsets my routine by flooding my office with her problem students. She has aroused the community. I get calls from parents every week about her. I don't think she knows how to teach. I do know that she can't manage the kids and something has to be done.

STUDENTS: Ms. Green is mean. She's supposed to be the teacher, but she doesn't teach. Everytime something happens she makes it worse.

COMMUNITY: The problem is not that Ms. Green has disruptive students, but that our children have a disruptive teacher.

Question: Given the above information what would you do to initiate Stage I?

Answer: Step 1 is to identify the participants' interests and/or dissonance. This the supervisor seems to have done. Step 2 is to develop a preliminary problem statement. In this case, it seems as though the key personnel were working against each other so that students were suffering. It would be easy to blame the teacher for incompetence in classroom management skills, but that does not solve anything. The fact that Ms. Green has completed a full year of teaching and that this problem shows up in the second year argues for some caution in simply blaming her as "incompetent."

Question: Stage II asks: What do we know about this problem. With a preliminary problem statement, "Key personnel are working against each other so that student learning suffers," what are the steps you would take in assessing the problem using this model?

Answer: The steps of Stage II are:

- Assess
- Study and share
- Restate the problem

The effective supervisor in this case is likely to work with all parties: teacher, principal, and community. What can be done to help students in this situation? With this question in mind the supervisor actively listens to each party so that each feels that he or she has been heard. The supervisor may invite the teacher, principal, and community representatives to study what others know about classroom management, group dynamics, and the common elements (students, teachers, environment, and subject matter) of educational systems that need to be coordinated to accomplish a successful school mission. If this is to be accomplished the supervisor might ask the parties to the problem: "What do we want to study in order to understand better what is going on here? What are some of the areas that might help?" Some suggestions might be:

- Teacher effectiveness research
- Information about socioeconomic status (SES)
- Community goals for education
- The stated mission of the school

As the participants share, it should be possible for each party to move away from emotional assessments of the problem to a statement about school mission. For example, "Students are not progressing in achieving school missions." This is a more realistic appraisal. It also has the possibility of fitting the teacher into the center of the change process through direct involvement. Restating the problem would include the expression that all parties have had unrealistic expectations of each other. By avoiding blaming and scapegoating, what can the parties now do to intervene in this case?

Question: Given the above information what would the supervisor do next to implement Stage III of the Cooperative Professional Development Model?

Answer: The supervisor asks, "What can we do to change conditions for the better?" With each party there needs to be a focus. "What one thing can you do to make things better for these students that you are willing to work on?"

The teacher may discover with the help of the supervisor that there is a discrepancy between espoused theory and her theory-in-use. For example, in social studies teaching Ms. Green may express a belief in the value of cooperative learning strategies, such as TGT (Teams-Games-Tournaments), but she has never tried them. The supervisor may suggest giving it a try. In one area of study with one class, the teacher may put together cooperative teams. They do trials of the strategy, expanding to other classes as they get data back showing interest and change. They document what happened and share results. For example, the number of students sent to the principal's office decreases as the teacher focuses on the TGT strategy.

At the same time, the principal has been asked what one thing he can do to make things better in this situation. Perhaps he agrees to take the problem of ethnic tensions to the parent-teacher advisory committee. Out of these discussions the school may decide to do more to emphasize ethnic awareness weeks, for example, Black Culture Week, Mexican-American Heritage Week.

Meantime, the supervisor may get the parents in the community group to agree to support one night per week for social studies homework as a way of supporting changes in the class and helping to raise pupil achievement. Students may be approached to participate in a pilot experiment of giving written feedback and self-evaluations for each week's work.

The supervisor agrees to work with each of these parties once a week, with student achievement as the goal. Given such extensive grappling with the context and focusing on the real issue of student learning, all parties will feel a part of the accomplishment when it occurs.

Finally, at the end of the semester (or year) the supervisor and participants organize a panel presentation. Preparation for the presentation allows for the review of progress and problems and a chance to identify "where to go from here."

OBJECTIVE 8 TO APPLY THE COOPERATIVE PROFESSIONAL DEVELOPMENT MODEL TO A CASE STUDY OF A GROUP OF TEACHERS AND THEIR NEEDS

You are asked to imagine that you are the supervisor in the following case. After reading the case of the mathematics teachers, you are to suggest how you would adapt the Cooperative Professional Development Model to this situation.

THE CASE OF THE MATHEMATICS TEACHERS

The mathematics teachers had met for several years, deciding on such things as the textbooks they would order, objectives for grade levels, and particular courses for the junior and senior high school. The teachers have been aware that while their students do fairly well on standardized tests, they have not improved their test scores over the last several years. The school system is located in an average-socioeconomic status area, all buildings have a racially-mixed population of students and teachers. No new teachers have been laid off. Several teachers have been transferred across grade levels or are now teaching in their minor areas. At the last meeting of the mathematics teachers several of them said that they were dissatisfied with their current teaching strategies. They felt that they needed to do something to liven up their teaching, their interest, and their students. The chairperson of the mathematics group agreed to contact the curriculum supervisor to have the supervisor attend the group's next meeting.

When the chairperson calls, you are assigned from the school district office to go to the meeting and see if you can work with the mathematics teachers. You decide on the following procedure. First, you will call the mathematics chairperson. Second, you will go to the meeting with the mathematics teachers. You collect the following information:

Conversation with the chairperson The chairperson tells you that the mathematics group has been meeting for several years. There was a pattern to what the group did over the years. They talked about problems with students and instructional ideas among themselves. However, they did not discuss these things formally. Their responsibilities had been to review curriculum, write objectives, develop districtwide tests and select textbooks for the district.

The chairperson says that the group has changed during the last few years due to the shifts in teacher assignments and the decline in student enrollments. Thus the traditions and solidarity of the group have been threatened. Members of the group at this time may not even be mathematics majors. The disruption of the group membership may even be partly to blame for some of the experienced teachers' feelings that there are problems with their instruction and their feelings of worthwhileness.

Conversations at a mathematics teachers meeting While you are at the meeting you hear teachers make the following comments:

"Who knows what I'll be teaching next year."

"I've taught these same classes since I got my job 15 years ago."

"Nothing ever changes, we buy books, use them, they get old and we buy new books."

"My students don't work like they used to."

"The general mathematics classes are getting harder to handle."

"I haven't taught a mathematics class since I did my student teaching."

"We don't talk about anything that is important in these meetings."

Question: Given the above information, what would you do to initiate Stage I?

Answer: Step 1 in Stage I requires that you identify the participants' interests and/or dissonance. You've been able to identify the general dissonance that exists among almost everyone. That is, that people are dissatisfied in general with what they are doing and how they are doing it.

The second step is to develop a preliminary problem statement. In this case, it seems as though the staff have identified that they are dissatisfied and that they want to do something about it (they called you to work with them). The major problem seems to focus on the teachers' affect and attitudes about what they are doing. However, student outcomes are mentioned. This final point is one that needs to be clarified as to whether it is within or outside the initial problem statement.

Question: The next stage (Stage II) asks: What do we know about this problem statement "We want to do something to improve our affect about our teaching." What are the ways you would go about assessing the problem using this model?

Answer: The steps of Stage II are:

- Assess
- Study and share
- Restate the problem

The effective supervisor in this case is likely to work with all parties: teachers, principals, students, department chairs, and the committee chair. The supervisor would talk with representatives of each group or, if in a small enough district, with everyone. The supervisor would formulate a question that could be asked to elicit information about the mathematics classes. The question could be, "What can be done to improve instruction in the mathematics classes?" (Please note: While pupil outcomes are of interest, the original problem statement focused on the teachers' needs.) In other words, the supervisor is beginning to assess what is already known.

The supervisor would then call a meeting of the committee and ask the committee members to share their information, and the supervisor would share the information he or she had collected. Having shared the information, the supervisor would then ask the committee the following questions: What do we want to study in order to better understand what is going on here? What are some of the areas that might help us understand? Some suggestions that the supervisor might offer are:

- Teacher stress
- Development of effective groups

- Cooperative learning strategies
- Thinking strategies for problem solving for elementary, junior high, and high school students

As the participants share, it should be possible for each party to move away from emotional assessments of the problem to a statement about a school mission, a curriculum goal, an instructional goal, or a student outcome goal. For example, "New instructional strategies are needed for both improved teacher affect and student performance."

Question: Given the above information, what would the supervisor do next to implement Stage III of the Cooperative Professional Development Model?

Answer: The supervisor and teachers ask, "What can we do to change conditions for the better?" Each party needs to have a focus: "What one thing can I do to make things better?"

The supervisor and the committee members therefore meet and brainstorm ideas for improving their instructional situation. The supervisor and the participants identify for each idea what additional information or skills the committee members would need in order to carry out the suggestion. Next, the supervisor and the participants review the ideas and identify those that they will try to implement. (In a problem of this type, the mathematics teachers in one building may try one thing, and those in another building something else. Or a department may decide that it will divide into two teams and try two different things. Still another alternative is for each teacher to choose to implement something different.) Next a plan for implementation would be developed. The plan would include an evaluation proposal. The plan would then be implemented and the evaluation data would be collected.

Having implemented the plan and collected the evaluation data, the supervisor would call a meeting of the participating teachers to share the evaluation data they collected, their personal experiences, and feelings about the project. The supervisor would report his or her findings as a member of the group. Then the supervisor would work collaboratively with the committee to write a report that presents their experiences and the evaluation data. The report is a responsibility of the group but the supervisor takes the responsibility for getting it typed and back to the committee for their review and approval. When the group agrees that the report reflects the experience, the supervisor then has it copied and returned to the group members within a week.

Finally, the supervisor meets with the team members to discuss how they will communicate their experiences to others. The supervisor may suggest that a teacher give verbal reports to faculty at regularly scheduled meetings, that a teacher report to the union curriculum committee, report at a grade level meeting, submit an article to one of the professional magazines, or submit an article to the district newsletter. The supervisor will also report what mode he or she will use for the formal sharing experience. The supervisor suggests that since the final evaluation report is a group product the group should submit a synthesized report as an article to a journal.

CONCLUSION

The leadership role of instructional supervisor in staff development is critical. Knowledge about adult development, learning, subject matter, instructional methods, classroom management and organization, child development, and the workings of institutions are among the types of knowledge an instructional supervisor needs to possess. Even more crucial to supervisory success is knowledge of process that facilitates not only change, but also ownership of *the need for* that change by all participants.

The Cooperative Development Model presented in this chapter provides a way that instructional supervisors can bring together many principles from a variety of perspectives and see how they fit and support one another. The development and implementation of this model occurred over several years providing a K−12 grade range of implementation experience. A variety of building staffs (groups) and numerous opportunities to work with individuals were a part of this experience. Thus, this model is not only theory based, but a concrete example of translating theory into practice. The instructional supervisors were responsive to the problems of practice faced by teachers in the real world.

The instructional supervisor assumes leadership responsibilities so that schools can better achieve their goals. In order that schools can be more effective, instructional supervisors must provide leadership for the people involved in the school's goals. The instructional supervisor does this not as an outsider, but as one who holds membership in the group. The supervisor, thus, can speak of our problems of practice, our needs to change, our goals, our responses, and our successes. The supervisor is not compelled to communicate that they need to change, or that they should choose a particular strategy. The Cooperative Development Model focuses on problems of practice and facilitates the dynamic difference that can be seen when their perspective is changed to *our* perspective. The resulting instructional improvements are embedded in the self-initiated actions of professional teachers who see themselves as life long learners.

REFERENCES

Adler, A. *Superiority and Social Interests.* Edited by H.L. Ansbacher and R.R. Ansbacher. Evanston, Ill.: Northwestern University Press, 1964.

Argyris, C. *Reasoning, Learning, and Action: Individual and Organizational.* Series in Social and Behavioral Science and in Management Training and Development. San Francisco: Jossey-Bass, 1982.

Barnes, H., J. Putnam, and D. Wanous. *Multiple Delivery Systems.* East Lansing, Mich.: Lansing School District/Michigan State University Teacher Corps Project, 1981.

Bartky, J.A. *Supervision as Human Relations.* Boston: D.C. Heath, 1953.

Berman, L.M., and M.L. Usery. *Personalized Supervision Sources and Insights.* Washington, D.C.: Association for Supervision and Curriculum Development, NEA, 1966.

Burton, W.H., and L.J. Brueckner. *Supervision, A Social Process,* 3d ed. New York: Appleton-Century-Crofts, 1955.

Cross, K.P. *Adults as Learners.* San Francisco: Jossey-Bass, 1981.

Cusick, P. *Egalitarian Ideal in the American High School.* New York: Longman, 1983.

DeCharms, R. *Personal Causation: The Internal Affective Determinants of Behavior.* New York: Academic, 1968.

Egan, G. *Interpersonal Living. A Skills/Contract Approach to Human Relations Training in Groups.* Monterey, Calif.: Brooks/Cole, 1976.

Felker, D.W. *Building Positive Self-Concepts.* Minneapolis: Burgess, 1974.

Flanders, N.A. "Teacher Influence, Pupil Attitudes and Achievement." Research monograph no. 12. Washington, D.C.: U.S. Government Printing Office, 1965.

Freire, P. *Education for Critical Consciousness.* Continuum, 1980.

Gazda, G.M. "Systematic Human Relations Training in Teacher Preparation and Inservice Education." *Journal of Research and Development in Education,* vol. 4, no. 2 (1971): 45−51.

Gist, A.S. *Elementary School Supervision.* New York: Scribner's, 1926.

Goldhammer, R. *Clinical Supervision: Special Methods for the Supervision of Teachers.* New York: Holt, Rinehart and Winston, 1969.

Gordon, S. *Psychology for You.* New York: Oxford, 1974.

Gordon, T. *T.E.T.: Teacher Effectiveness Training.* New York: Peter H. Wyden, 1974.

Hersey and Blanchard. *Management of Organizational Behavior: Utilizing Human Resources,* 3d ed. Englewood Cliffs, N.J.: Prentice-Hall, 1977.

Hersey, Blanchard, and Natemeyer. *Situational Leadership, Perception, and the Impact of Power.* Center for Leadership Studies, 1979.

Kagan, N.I. *Interpersonal Process Recall: A Method of Influencing Human Interaction.* Mason, Mich.: Mason Media, 1976.

Knowles, M. *The Adult Learner: A Neglected Species,* 2d ed. Houston: Gulf, 1973.

———. *The Modern Practice of Adult Education: For Pedagogy to Andragogy,* revised and updated. Chicago: Follett, 1980.

Kyte, G.C. *Problems in School Supervision.* Boston: Houghton Mifflin, 1931.

Maslow, A. *Motivation and Personality*, 2d ed. New York: Harper and Row, 1970.

McClelland, D.C. "Toward a Theory of Motive Acquisition," *American Psychologist*, vol. 20, no. 2 (1965): 321–333.

McNeil, L.M., "Negotiating Classroom Knowledge: Beyond Achievement and Socialization." Occasional papers. Madison, Wisc.: Wisconsin Center for Public Policy, 1980.

Noller, R.B., S.J. Parnes, and A.M. Biondi. *Creative Actionbook*. New York: Scribners, 1976.

Parnes, S. "Effects of Extended Effort on Creative Problem Solving." *Journal of Educational Psychology* (1961): 117–122.

Rogers, C.R. "The Interpersonal Relationship: The Core of Guidance." *Harvard Educational Review*, vol. 32, no. 4 (Fall 1962): 416–429.

Schwab, J.J. "The Concept of the Structure of a Discipline." In E.W. Eisner and E. Vallance (eds.), *Conflicting Conceptions of Curriculum*. Berkeley, Calif.: McCutchan, 1974.

Sergiovanni, T.J., and R.J. Starratt. *Emerging Patterns of Supervision: Human Perspectives*. New York: McGraw-Hill, 1971.

———. *Supervision Human Perspectives*, 2d ed. New York: McGraw-Hill, 1979.

Unruh, A., and H.E. Turner. *Supervision for Change and Innovation*. Boston: Houghton Mifflin, 1970.

Wallen, J.L. Developing Effective Interpersonal Communication. In *Communicating Interpersonally*, edited by R.W. Pace, B.D. Peterson, and T.R. Radcliff. Columbus, Ohio: Charles E. Merrill, 1973.

Weiner, B. "A Theory of Motivation for Some Classroom Experiences," *Journal of Educational Psychology*, vol. 71 (1979): 3–25.

ADDITIONAL READING LIST

Gist, A.S. *The Administration of Supervision*. New York: Scribners, 1934.

Schmuck, R.A., and P.A. Schmuck. *A Humanistic Psychology of Education: Making the School Everybody's House*. Palo Alto, Calif.: National Press Books, 1974.

Shafer, H.T. (Chairman—ASCD Commission on Problems of Supervisors and Curriculum Workers). *The Supervisor: New Demands New Dimensions*. Washington, D.C.: Association for Supervision and Curriculum Development (NEA), 1969.

Stanford, G., and A.E. Roark. *Human Interaction in Education*. Boston: Allyn and Bacon, 1974.

Index

Notes and Calculations Notes and Calculations Notes and Calculations

Notes and Calculations Notes and Calculations Notes and Calculations

Notes and Calculations Notes and Calculations Notes and Calculations

Notes and Calculations Notes and Calculations Notes and Calculations